Sharia and the Making of the Modern Egyptian

Sharia and the Making of the Modern Egyptian

Islamic Law and Custom
in the Courts of Ottoman Cairo

Reem A. Meshal

The American University in Cairo Press
Cairo New York

First published in 2014 by
The American University in Cairo Press
113 Sharia Kasr el Aini, Cairo, Egypt
420 Fifth Avenue, New York, NY 10018
www.aucpress.com

Copyright © 2014 by Reem A. Meshal

All rights reserved. No part of this publication may be reproduced, stored in a retrieval system, or transmitted in any form or by any means, electronic, mechanical, photocopying, recording, or otherwise, without the prior written permission of the publisher.

Exclusive distribution outside Egypt and North America by I.B.Tauris & Co Ltd., 6 Salem Road, London, W2 4BU

Dar el Kutub No. 1840/13
ISBN 978 977 416 617 4

Dar el Kutub Cataloging-in-Publication Data

Meshal, Reem A.
    Sharia and the Making of the Modern Egyptian / Reem A. Meshal.—Cairo: The American University in Cairo Press, 2014.
      p.   cm.
    ISBN 978 977 416 617 4
    1. Customary Law—Egypt
    2. History—1517–1882
    340.596203

1 2 3 4 5   18 17 16 15 14

Designed by Jon W. Stoy
Printed in Egypt

For my father, Amin Hamed Meshal

Contents

Preface and Acknowledgments ix

Introduction 1
  A Very Modern Crisis 1
  Mapping the Terrain 5
  Structure of the Book 9
  The Sources 12
  Conclusion 16

1. The Empire in Theory 17
  Introduction 17
  The Empire in Historiography 20
  The Empire in Theory 27
  Conclusion 40

2. Custom in Sharia and in the *Siyasat-i ilahi* (Divine *Siyasa*) 41
  Introduction 41
  The 'Good' and the 'Detestable' in Islamic Legal Theory 43
  Custom in Islamic Legal Theory 46
  The *Siyasat-i ilahi* and *Namus* Laws 55
  Conclusion 66

3. The Construction of Orthodoxy: Renewal *(Tajdid)* and Renunciation *(Takfir)* 69
  Introduction 69
  Inter-empire Trade and the Rise of Local Capital 71
  Takfir: The Intra-Muslim Jihad 79
  Tajdid: The Social Conquest 83
  Conclusion 100

4. "This *Sijill* is a *Hujja*!" Mass-producing
    Legal Documents in Ottoman Cairo ... 103
    Introduction ... 103
    The Document Triumphant ... 105
    The Document in Theory ... 107
    The *Sijill* as Text and Testament ... 114
    The Fusion of Speaking and Writing ... 121
    Conclusion ... 124
5. The Documented Life ... 125
    Introduction ... 125
    The Document in Stasis: Territorializing Sharia ... 127
    Archival Violence and Memory ... 128
    The Document in Motion ... 133
    Conclusion ... 138
6. The Rights of God (*Huquq Allah*): "A Moral Transgression
    but Not a Crime" ... 141
    Introduction ... 141
    The *Hudud* ... 143
    The Threshold of Morality ... 148
    Civil Marriage ... 155
    Divorce *(Talaq)* and Annulment *(Faskh)* ... 166
    Waqf ... 169
    Conclusion ... 174
7. The Rights of Humans *(Huquq al-Adamiyyin)* ... 177
    Introduction ... 177
    The Empire in the City: Multiplicity and Conformity ... 180
    Private *Mu'amala*: The Empire in the City ... 184
    Public *Mu'amalat*: The Community in the Empire ... 189
    Conclusion ... 207

Conclusions ... 211

Notes ... 221

Abbreviations ... 267

Bibliography ... 269

Index ... 287

Preface and Acknowledgments

It was not my intention to write a book wading into the sticky quagmire that constitutes the academic discourse on Muslim political modernity. My subject, the sharia courts of sixteenth- and seventeenth-century Cairo, seemed as remote from the current struggle over the role of religion and the political state (or *din wa dawla*) as it was possible to get. Moreover, nothing in my training, whether as an undergraduate student of political science or as a graduate student of Islamic Studies, had prepared me to see in the reforms of the sixteenth century the indelible seeds of a Muslim political modernity. The overarching clichés used to frame the discussion on Muslims and political modernity have been used and reused to lock us—academics, popular audiences, and activists—into a cycle of analysis that begins with the birth of European political modernity and ends with its impact on Muslims and others. And so, whether we perceive the calls for the implementation of sharia as a fundamentalist backlash against modernity, or as an expression of 'alternative modernities' born of the synthesis between modernism and local exigencies, we are left to toil within the confines of a singular idiom: political modernity as a uniquely European phenomenon. Citizenship, mass culture, constitutionalism, secularism, and even the state itself, we continue to be told, are the emblems of a European enlightenment bearing slim resemblance to anything that had come before.

Yet the markings of a uniquely Muslim political modernity continued to foist themselves, with greater insistence over the years, on my reluctant psyche. This was no carbon copy of Europe's political modernity; it never produced the 'nation' in its narrow racial sense but pushed in a more expansive direction toward multinational statehood. Most noticeably, it did so by transforming its subjects into citizens. Generating many of the models of state and religion which lie at the root of Islam's political modernity, this forgotten 'reformation' also stands at the base of Islam's current crisis of authority.

As always, there are teams of people whose support made the writing of this book possible. Because I am a rather solitary scholar, there are not many people I can thank for reading and commenting on parts of this book directly. But there are scores of scholars, cited throughout this work, on whom I have piggybacked to make my arguments and to whom I am indebted. On a personal level, special thanks are due to my son Ilyas for showing a maturity far beyond his years in understanding my deep preoccupation and long absences during the endless hours of writing. No less my spouse, M. Reza Pirbhai, for filling those hours and for his invaluable collegial contributions to this work. His careful reading of multiple raw drafts and his always astute critiques were instrumental in its development. My mother, Samira Sanad Meshal, for the emotional and financial support she so readily lent over the years, and my younger brother, Ashraf, for his unwavering faith in my ability to finish this book. No less, of course, the man to whom this work is dedicated, Amin Hamed Meshal, my father and first teacher.

Away from family, long conversations with my dear friends and colleagues Gail and Peter Sutherland have helped shape this work in ways they can scarcely imagine. I am also indebted to the staff at the American University in Cairo Press, in particular Randi Danforth and Johanna Baboukis, for bringing this work to the light of day. As well, the helpful staff at Dar al-Kutub and Dar al-Watha'iq Cairo deserve special mention for making my sojourn into the archives as painless as possible. And finally, to the anonymous readers of this manuscript, who were both generous and exacting in their comments, and who contributed much to the refinement and streamlining of my major arguments.

In conclusion, a word on the spelling of Arabic and Turkish names is in order. For the sake of consistency, all Turkish names referenced in Arabic texts have been rendered into Arabic spelling. The only exceptions are the names of Turkish authors of Turkish texts. The reader will also note that there is no transliteration, and while I wish I could claim that this was the result of a considered choice, in truth the word-processing program by which I was transliterating when I began the writing of this book was already antiquated by the time it went to production. Faced with the prospect of re-transliterating the entire manuscript, I have chosen to forego transliteration altogether.

Whatever merit or fault the reader may find with this work, I hope that my plea for pushing back the timeline of the 'Muslim political modern' is heard.

Introduction

A Very Modern Crisis

On 22 March 2011, just over a month after a popular revolt swept Egyptian President Hosni Mubarak from power, the Grand Shaykh of al-Azhar, Ahmad al-Tayyib, made an unexpected announcement: depending on the source you read, he was "giving back" or "donating" his salary to the state.[1] Various news outlets reported that al-Tayyib asked the minister of finance to stop issuing paychecks to him, expressing the desire to serve al-Azhar and the call to Islam, without the reward of a state salary. This was no gesture of personal piety, but rather a well-considered political salvo into a torrid climate of political upheaval from which the venerable institution was not immune. Since the mid-sixteenth century, when the Ottoman state first allocated salaries to scholars of al-Azhar, the issue of the 'paycheck' has been symbolic of the state's cooptation of private religious institutions and of their transformation into bureaucratic, public entities. It has frequently resurfaced as a point of contention in debates between the state and ulama (scholars) over the separation of political and religious authority in Islam. Thus there are layers of historical and political meaning to al-Tayyib's gesture, all of which underscore the importance of the sixteenth century to the modern discussion on the limits of religious and political authority. A few weeks previously, on 17 February, al-Tayyib had convened a press conference in which he made demands echoing those of his sixteenth-century predecessors, notably that the Grand Shaykh of al-Azhar should be an elected representative of his peers, insisting: "Al-Azhar is a thousand-year-old institution that is responsible to Muslims all over the world and isn't a tool in anyone's hands, but decides its stances based on what it sees right and will remain above governments and revolutions."[2]

The irony that these demands should come from al-Tayyib, who is himself a state appointee, was lost on no one. Indeed, to his many critics, the Grand Shaykh was a latecomer to the cause of Azhari independence. In the throng of the Tahrir uprising of January and February 2011, where history unfolded before a global online and mainstream-media audience, it was lower-ranking Azharis, prominent in their distinctive institutional regalia, rather than the Azhari elite, who pried open an old debate by brandishing signs calling for transparency, accountability, and the restitution of al-Azhar's independence from the state.

While religious institutions in Egypt today are undoubtedly weak in comparison with the Ottoman past, when they were vibrant, prestigious, and at least semi-autonomous centers of learning, this book regards the contemporary struggle between the state and ulama as the latest installment in a protracted, historical struggle over the limits of religious and political authority in Islam. It is not incidental that the current struggle between al-Azhar and the state has its origins in the sixteenth century, for that is when the seeds of Islamic political modernity were sown. Then, as now, the sharia (Islamic law in its broadest religious and secular scope) was the fulcrum of debate, a host to alternative imaginings of the 'perfected moral cosmos' and to an always tense, but lively, debate on its limits in temporal life. The contest of ideas over the scope and defintion of the sharia is inherently political. The institutional developments of *fiqh* (jurisprudence) and *siyasa* (political philosophy/governance), for example, undergird the legitimation and limitations of political authority in Islam and cannot be understood in its absence.

In the past two hundred years, new groups have arisen to lay claim to this authority, namely revivalist fundamentalists such as the Wahhabi and Salafi movements, who dismiss the authority of tradition (or the authority of scholarship in Islam) and the authority of scholarly credentials to reimagine the sharia. They seek, in their discourse, to uphold it, often in its most essentialized form, by 'restoring' a direct engagement between the believer and the written word. Another popular discourse is the western mainstream one, which holds the Arabic language (specifically its technical legal terms) hostage to popular neo-Orientalist tropes, lending its vocabulary to the War on Terror. Fatwas, non-binding juristic opinions, morph into "death sentences," while jihad, the theory of just war in Islamic international law, is defined exclusively as 'holy war' against infidels *qua* infidels.

The apparent convergence of views from the two outwardly antagonistic discourses of 'Islamism' and 'western modernity' presents us with a glaring irony: the discourse of revivalist Islamists and of their critics in the west is informed by a strikingly similar definition of the sharia as a spartan, codified list of Qur'anic fixed penalties *(hudud)* where all sins are de facto crimes. Both perspectives imagine the same sharia, defining it almost exclusively in opposition to the concept of 'secularism,' which itself has had an uneven and often confounding history in the west. The result is a discourse which blights not only the contemporary discourse on law in Islam, but the historical record as well.

To refute the Orientalist/revivalist discourse is not to suggest that there ever existed an ideal sharia, practiced by ideal Muslims in some hermetically sealed past. To the contrary, this is the ahistorical romanticism of the revivalist schools. For Islamic jurists, the sharia existed in the realm of ideas as an 'absolute truth' and a worldly abstraction of the perfected moral cosmos. Like the 'ideal tree' in Plato's doctrine of ideas/theory of forms, it constituted the infinite and *unattainable* standard by which worldly trees were to be measured. But as distinct as the revivalist's conceptions of sharia may be from those of traditional Islamic jurists, the two are not unrelated. Both are inheritors of sixteenth-century bureaucratization and legal codification, or what Foucault called the 'governmentalization' of society.[3]

The rise of the centralized state, and the transformation of Islamic law into a public, corporative enterprise, laid the basis for a modern political economy that portended the rise of the individual, mass culture, and citizenship. Historians of the modern Middle East tend to trace the roots of the modern state to the nineteenth-century 'westernizing' reforms (Tanzimat) of the Ottoman Empire, and attribute these developments to the impact of European modernity. Yet they overlook the ways in which these reforms also represent the intensification of sixteenth-century Islamic institutional and political trends. While it is true that Muslim political modernity was indelibly shaped and transformed by the encounter with European modernity, its roots extend well beyond the Tanzimat, reaching back to an earlier, sixteenth-century movement of reform and renewal *(tajdid)*; ignoring this period obsfuscates an important chapter in Muslim political history and neglects its critical role in staging Islam's modern secular crisis. Without the binding historicist assumption that the origins of political modernity are exclusively European, it becomes possible to rotate perspectives and to posit the Ottoman state as an early template of its modern successors, rife with all the configurations of a religious and political crisis of authority in the making.

The Ottoman state haunts the political modernity of its successor states. From the public archive to the state judiciary and the bureaucratic civil court, the Muslim judicial landscape was forever altered by its administrative hand. Under its auspices, the law was transformed into a public, governmental entity and the state made a partner in the firm.[4] Wedged in a judicial hierarchy with the Grand Mufti of Istanbul at its top, the jurists of the sixteenth century were public servants, appointed, dismissed, and financially reimbursed for their services by the state. This structural transformation implied a downgrading in the authority of Islamic scholars, whose task had hitherto been to apply a set of exegetical and judicial principles to an infinite variety of situations. Over the course of the nineteenth and twentieth centuries, further downgrading occurred as the empire's successor states accelerated its policies of 'governmentalization' through the 'nationalization' of religious institutions. And as the religious establishment continued to retreat, a revivalist, lay vanguard advanced in its wake, laying claim to the authority to define the sources and limits of Muslim moral behavior. As the differences between sins and crimes, between the rights of God and the rights of humans, were reconstituted and consciously conflated in their discourse, Islam's crisis of secularism deepened.

The creeping hegemony of the sixteenth-century state over the most critical social-ordering mechanism, the law, allowed for the promotion of a political and moral economy grounded in a peculiarly Ottoman orthodoxy, or Ottoman sharia, to be distinguished from that of rival Muslim states, past or present. But it was precisely this hegemony which allowed the state to transform its ties to the individual, and in turn, to transform the latter's status from 'subject' to 'proto-citizen.' As the law became a public entity, a new social covenant emerged, cleaving essential 'personhood' from local custom and freeing individuals to adopt the new translocal orthodoxy. For this to happen, the sharp distinction between sins and crimes, between the 'rights of God' and the 'rights of humans,' would have to be blurred.

The phrase 'a moral transgression, not a crime,' used in the Islamic legal literature to describe a variety of activities (such as abortion), stems from a conceptual distinction in jurisprudential theory between the 'rights of God' *(huquq Allah)* and the 'rights of humans' *(huquq al-adamiyyin)*.[5] More often than not in the span of Ottoman history, notable religious sins, including prostitution and the sale and consumption of alcohol, carried no criminal penalty, and were regulated and taxed by the state. But for rights and obligations to be standardized in the early modern state, broader categories of moral misconduct, such as public indecency, intoxication, or rape, would have to fall under the discretionary authority *(ta'zir)* of the state.

None of this is meant to suggest that the Ottoman Empire was a morally authoritarian state—quite the opposite. As Khaled Abou El Fadl reminds us, there is a marked difference between an 'authoritative' law and an 'authoritarian' one.[6] Anyone remotely familiar with Ottoman history can attest to the state's wide moral compass, by today's Muslim standards. Nonetheless, insofar as it impinged on what Leslie Peirce has called "a new sober, social orthodoxy,"[7] it took the business of public morality very seriously, banning for short intervals the drinking of coffee and alcohol and the smoking of tobacco, on pain of death. The synthesis of moral revivalism with social reform in this agenda purported to promote the moral edification of society by unifying the administration of justice and the laws produced, but it also justifies a lower barrier between sins and crimes.

Mapping the Terrain

In the sixteenth century, the Ottoman Empire embarked on a project to harmonize Islamic law (sharia) with state law *(qanun)*. According to the secondary literature, state law was 'Islamized' in the process, transforming imperial institutions into bastions of Sunni orthodoxy. The Ottomans, an amalgam of loosely Muslim Turkic tribesmen who emerged from obscurity in the thirteenth century to vanquish the remnants of Byzantium and their great Sunni rival in the Islamic heartlands, the Mamluk state, had 'discovered' orthodoxy. That, at any rate, is the dominant narrative.

If by 'Islamization' scholars mean more rigor in the dispensation of law, both *fiqh*-based and *qanun*, then the narrative stands. But if by 'Islamization' we are positioning the Ottomans on the passive, receiving end of a prepackaged Arab–Persian politico-judicial orthodoxy, then the narrative is somewhat overburdened. There is no doubt that the formidable Islamic intellectual and institutional heritage against which the Ottoman caliphate measured itself in the sixteenth century produced a more consciously Islamic discourse. But it did so through a discursive process of appropriation and engagement that did more than reproduce received wisdom. The Ottomans were not merely 'discovering' orthodoxy, they were inventing it.

The new orthodoxy set the tone for center–periphery relations in the Ottoman Empire, subduing the "colourful cultural palette" of a multiconfessional, multiethnic state, and bringing its myriad communities and their subregional customs under a unifying cultural, economic, and political rubric.[8] Rooted in the practical need to unify an empire, which at its height exceeded the size of Rome, the new legal hegemony was cast by structural and substantive means that were enormously innovative, at least by comparison with the Mamluk state which preceded it.

Catapulted from a frontier state on the peripheries of Islam to the central orbit of Sunni imperial grandeur, the Ottoman state expanded in unprecedented geographic and demographic directions in the sixteenth century. The conquest of two great empires—and with them the symbolical weight of Constantinople (1453), Mecca, Medina, and Jerusalem (all in 1517), as well as the great Arab urban centers of Islamic learning, such as Damascus (1516), Cairo (1517), and Baghdad (1534)—gave Ottoman sultans an enormous geographic cache. Rendered the de facto holders of two of the most important titles in imperial religious history, Holy Roman Emperor and Keeper of the Two Holy Shrines—the latter title worth its weight in gold in Islamic imperial currency—Ottoman sultans pressed their claims to the classical caliphate, replete with its temporal and spiritual authority.

There had, of course, been numerous Ottoman and non-Ottoman claimants to the title of caliph prior to the sixteenth century. But the weight of Mecca, Medina, Jerusalem, and Constantinople meant that Ottoman sultans could pursue these claims with an audacity scarcely witnessed since the classical Abbasid state's tenth-century Mihna (inquisition), which attempted to establish the caliph's authority over the ulama (religious scholars).[9] In particular, Sulayman Qanuni's (r. 1520–66) appropriation of the symbolism of the classical caliphate signaled real and radical change in the cultural and political economy of Cairo.

By broad, though by no means unanimous, consensus, however, the secondary literature holds that the strength and lineage of the Egyptian judicial establishment served as a formidable and effective bulwark against Ottoman reform and as a catalyst for its eventual 'Islamization.' Helping recast the sixteenth century as one of 'crises and readjustment' rather than decline, the thesis of Islamization proposes the harmonization of *qanun* with sharia as a mid-sixteenth-century phenomenon. Generating new paradigms in the secondary literature, the 'crises and readjustment' thesis argued that the Ottoman Empire was transformed in three ways: growth, decentralization, and 'Islamization.' In this analysis, economic growth serves as a forerunner to the rise of provincial, capitalist elites who contribute to the political decentralization of the empire. At the same time, the Islamization thesis posits local jurists as a bulwark against the state, able to withstand and reshape Ottoman ideas about the law. Together, provincial elites and local jurists generated the conditions necessary for a legal system heavily informed by local custom.[10] At best, however, this is a speculative conclusion, as it is drawn not from a quantitative survey of the *sijill* (complete record of a judge's or court's records), but rather from a qualitative assessment of the nature of society and state in this century.

Curiously, while the theory of political decentralization has undergone considerable revision, no comparable revisions to the narrative of Islamization, or to its central claim that the sharia orthodoxy of the 'heartland states' made Islamization an imperative for the empire, have been forthcoming. The thesis of Islamization thus continues to feed the qualitative dictum that Ottoman legal reforms were procedural rather than substantive, which is to say that the administration of justice changed, but not the laws produced. The argument I propose links the administration of justice to the laws produced by interrogating the conceptual totems erected by the thesis of Islamization, principally its dichotomy of 'orthodoxy' vis-à-vis 'heresy.' Ignoring the structural and rational organization of law in Islam, these totems overlook the basic proposition that the law in Islam lends itself to the concept of orthopraxy (emphasis on models of correct conduct) more so than orthodoxy (correct opinion).[11] The sources of Islamic law *(usul al-fiqh)* may be limited to the Qur'an, Hadith, *qiyas* (analogical reasoning), and *ijma'* (consensus of the scholars), but the deductions made there from them are not limited to a single, authoritative legal opinion. Islamic law is, therefore, structurally incompatible with any kind of 'orthodoxy' (correct opinion), as it ensured the circulation of competing opinions on a host of gray issues, preventing the coalescence of the sharia into a codified law. So long as a consensus had been achieved, the positions adopted within the limits of the *madhhab* (particular school of law) were equal in weight and authority. This, at least, was the scholarly ideal enunciated in legal theory. But the policies of the state, especially in the period under study, suggest the emergence of another ideal: a new social orthodoxy fundamentally at odds with the pluralism of Islamic law, its multiple schools *(madhahib)*, and their standing conventions on local custom.

Broadly speaking, the topic of custom has generated meager research in the field of Islamic studies, mostly focused on the so-called Islamic 'periphery.' The omission is troubling, not only because it stunts our understanding of one of the more important processes by which societies appropriate and reproduce Islam, but also because it obscures this process in one of the great urban centers of Islamic law at a time of exponential growth. Indeed, the most basic questions about this process are yet to be posed. How do the customs of local communities intersect with Islamic legal theory and its attendant institutions to produce, expunge, or modify Muslim culture in a universalizing state? Where are the lines drawn between what is inside and what is outside the limits of the sharia, and how do they (re)define the boundaries of Muslim 'orthodoxy'? What role does the state, and its bureaucratic judiciary, play in this history?

Standing at the nexus of ties binding the community, the state, and the individual, customary laws are an important marker of communal identity. They give the community a legislative voice and reflect the degree of political autonomy it enjoys in the arbitration of internal disputes. By definition, a system that is less welcoming of customary arbitration is one that seeks to subordinate the community to the state by muting ethnic and regional differences. In this context, the antidote to communalism is individualism, with its dim promise of citizenship encased in a new, translocal political hegemony. The benefits to a centralizing, multiethnic, multisectarian state are obvious, as are some of the factors motivating fierce communal opposition, both in Europe and in the Ottoman Empire, to the new political covenant.

Insofar as it is already riven with the quarrels of later centuries, the century of 'crises and readjustment,' as the sixteenth century is often called by Ottoman historians, is of critical importance to the Muslim transition to modernity. It represents a last chapter before the challenge of the west and the entanglement with European modernity. But it also represents a new chapter, embodying some of the more regenerative cycles to overtake Islamic society since the Mongol conquests and foreshadowing that peculiar configuration of elements that would come to comprise Islamic political modernity.

Structure of the Book

Testing the limits of modernization theory and its dominant cognitive paradigms, historicism and secular criticism, chapter one situates the empire and the law in modern historiography. Examining the ways in which the European secular lens distorts the dialectic between law and society in Islam by projecting a Christian binary of things 'religious' and things 'secular' onto the Muslim past, it pleads for a more tailored approach, less inclined to artificial dichotomizations. Rather than adequately explaining the moral limits of *'ibadat* (matters of ritual piety in fulfillment of the 'rights of God') and *mu'amalat* (matters relating to the legal conduct of men and women among themselves), for example, the European secular lens ignores, obscures, or misunderstands them, to overlook one of the most vital, and indigenous, moral dichotomies in Islamic law—the separation of 'sins' and 'crimes.' The moral boundaries inherent in this legal dichotomy cannot be explained, nor adequately classified, by the secular/religious binary. Utilizing internally generated ideas about moral limits ('rights of God' = sins; 'rights of humans' = crimes), this chapter explains the rational and procedural confusion of these historically separable categories in modern historiography.

Deepening the discussion, chapter two explores conceptions of self and moral sovereignty through the discursive philosophical, Sufi, and juridical theory of custom. In Islamic law, the basis of local customary law is frequently treated as custom rather than judicial precedent, even though acceptance of the rule of custom actually stems from local judgments rather than from antecedent local behavior. To become law, custom must conform to the criteria established by the Islamic jurists and, increasingly in the Ottoman period, by the sovereign before it can attain the status of *qanun*. The presumed universalism of the latter provoked the condemnation of Ibn Nujaym, a prominent Egyptian jurist whose theory of custom was unique in emphasizing and condemning "innovation" *(bid'a)* in the rights of humans. Unlike his predecessors, who were more generally concerned with innovation in the rights of God, Ibn Nujaym speaks of a perceived Ottoman disregard for local custom and for its role in regulating the rights of humans. To the alarm of jurists like him, the *qanun* had done what only the prophets were permitted to do: it had breached custom, thereby severing the link between a people's past and present. In so doing, argued Ibn Nujaym and other Egyptian and Syrian nonstate jurists, the *qanun* had breached the sharia itself. State jurists, on the other hand, held a very different perspective.

Giving state jurists the floor, chapter three highlights the contribution of Islamic thought and institutions in the construction of late modernity by drawing attention to Islamic political philosophy under the aegis of the early modern Ottoman sultans. A variety of juristic, philosophical, and Sufi works, thoroughly couched in contemporary historiography, reveal the sixteenth-century origins of a shared new theory of caliphate, both responsive to early modern conditions and influential in the construction of late modern institutions. The intellectual basis for caliphal claims—the Ottoman *siyasat-i ilahi* (loosely translated as 'divine governance')—universalized by state jurists and bureaucrats upon the foundations of Jalal al-Din al-Dawani's concept of 'imamate' erected a highly bureaucratized as well as ethnically and religiously inclusive political community. Projecting these antagonistic discourses from law, philosophy, and Sufism, in vivid political theater, is the sixteenth-century biography of Ottoman chief judges by the Egyptian chronicler al-Damiri.

Based largely on al-Damiri's biography of Cairo's sixteenth- and early seventeenth-century Ottoman chief judges, chapter three brings the history of state centrism and popular dissent into sharp relief. A black comedy of subterfuge and resistance, Damiri's history is saturated with the rhetoric of *takfir* (accusations of unbelief) and *tajdid* (renewal). Freely wielded by Ottoman state jurists against even the most prominent of Cairo's scholars, charges and countercharges of *kufr* (unbelief) were the order of the day. And while the sustained and combined opposition of the local judiciary could at times win a concession from the Sublime Porte, it was able neither to stem nor to reverse the tide of *tajdid*.

Three institutions—the archive, the *sijill*, and the court—none invented by Ottomans, were administered so innovatively as to render the sixteenth-century reforms irreversible. As argued in chapter four, the Ottoman Empire was neither the first nor the only Muslim state to produce and archive important legal documents, but it was the only one to *mass*-produce them, generating millions of documents pertaining to the lives of ordinary men and women. Moreover, its court system was the first to reverse the authority of written documents vis-à-vis oral testimony and the first to assign to the documents, en masse, the status of a *hujja musattara*—written proof. The archive, for which they were ultimately destined, was both the source of this authority and of a uniquely early-modern phenomenon: the 'documented life.'

But how are we to explain the ambiguous status of the written document in Islamic legal theory and its overwhelming preponderance in the life of Ottoman subjects?[12] Scholars can be forgiven for seeing this as Islam's longest-standing legal fiction, but this hardly resolves our basic paradox; in fact, it compounds it. The assertion that theory and practice are hopelessly bifurcated makes an integrated reading of the *sijill*, one that treats the document as a legal institution *and* as a social narrative, well-nigh impossible. While the secondary literature concedes that more and more people were using the courts in the Ottoman centuries, and that more and more documents were being generated, it fails to correlate this phenomenon with the histories produced. This is the gap that chapter five seeks to fill.

As a repository of institutional memory, the archive is as adept at forgetting as remembering, the documents it holds reshaping political identity through a dexterous process of textual manipulation that privileges geography (the earliest vestige of Ottomanism) and territorializes the Islamic court into an integrated venue for all Ottoman subjects, Muslim or non-Muslim, Arab or non-Arab, rich or poor, military or civilian. In so doing, it transforms Islamic law into a civil law for all Ottoman subjects. But the document, or more precisely the *hujja*, also mediates between its holder and the world, renegotiating the bonds between individuals and society at large. Cleaving one's essential personhood from locale, community, and custom, the *hujja*, *sijill*, and archive were the progenitors and custodians of proto-citizenship.

Chapters six and seven demonstrate the new concepts of personhood as filtered through the new Ottoman categories of the 'rights of God' (*huquq Allah*) and 'rights of humans' (*huquq al-adamiyyin*), and their intersection in *fiqh*, *qanun*, and custom in the *sijill*s of Ottoman Cairo. Here, the demise of local custom is seen in cases ranging from personal status laws (marriage, divorce, child custody) to municipal and market law (*ihtisab*) and the management of *awqaf* (endowments). Rights and obligations within all of these institutions were increasingly standardized, such that legal variation based on non-Hanafi *fiqh*, or on local custom, was considerably circumscribed. By way of conclusion, both chapters find that even rulings which appeared to vindicate or employ local practice did so provisionally, were reviewed annually, and were issued only on a case-by-case basis. In other words, insofar as the courts endorsed local practice, this was often exceptional in nature and cannot be viewed as a generalized endorsement of local custom or of the autonomy of provincial communities.

By definition, law is the engine of social conformity. But, as these last two chapters will show, the particular set of norms to which the communities and individuals of Ottoman Cairo were asked to conform in the sixteenth century were precisely tailored to Ottoman specifications. The new orthodoxy held out the sharia of the state jurist as an alternative to that of the nonstate jurists, with its promise of a new political covenant standardizing rights and obligations and releasing individuals from the authority of the community, even as it instituted a new hegemony—that of the state.

The Sources

The *sijill*s have proven to be an invaluable source of social and economic history. With few exceptions, however, they have yielded surprisingly little insight on legal practice. Writing on the significance of the Haram documents, D.P. Little identified Islamic law as

> one of three areas for which the documents hold promise . . . the study of which has been bedeviled by what scholars suspect to be the discrepancy between Muslim legist theory recorded in the manuals of Islamic jurisprudence and that which Muslim judges administered in practice . . . and the insistence of eminent Western scholars that there is little, if any correspondence between the two, in spite of the fact that there has heretofore been hardly any evidence of legal practice with which to compare the allegedly theoretical manuals.[13]

The daunting requirements of such a project—mastery of Arabic, "chancery and notarial scripts, the sharia as embodied in the works of *fiqh*,"[14] and history—explain, no doubt, why few have endeavored to meet the challenge. Additionally, as many scholars have complained, the *sijill*s reveal little about the legal reasoning behind a judgment, providing only a summary of the events and the ruling with little embellishment. That said, they do shed some light on this seemingly opaque process. For one, they always indicate the *madhhab* of the judge and on occasion even include the fatwa (legal opinion) that informed his ruling. They are also a little more forthcoming on the subject of custom, often indicating when a ruling has been issued in conformity with, or in contravention of, a given custom. Aside from the judicial ruling itself, marital and commercial property contracts, in which people of varied religious, ethnic, or regional backgrounds modulate their rights and obligations within the parameters of Islamic law and *qanun*, can be very revealing of the degree to which individuals define themselves in conformity with, or in contradistinction to, their local ethnic, religious, or professional community.

The *sijill*s used in this research span the dates AH 965/1558 CE to 1056/1646 and include the courts of Mahkamat Tulun (the Tulun Islamic court), *Sijill* 165: 1–5, 284–87, AH 965–66; Mahkamat al-Qisma al-'Arabiya (the Islamic Court of Arab Affairs), *Sijill* 5: 1–45, AH 985; Mahkamat al-Qisma al-'Askeriya (the Islamic Court of Military Personnel), *Sijill* 5: 1–15, 275–85, AH 970; Mahkamat al-Bab al-'Ali (the Islamic Court of the Bab al-'Ali), *Sijill* 96: 10–22, 445–46, AH 1023–24; *Sijill* 66: 1–5, 51–65, AH 1005–1006; *Sijill* 124, 1–2, 160–78, 405–408, AH 1055–56.

Documents in general, particularly legal formularies (model contracts), were part and parcel of the Near Eastern pre-Islamic tradition.[15] Describing the contents of the Haram documents which survive from the Mamluk era, Little lists deeds (*'uqud*) of purchase and lease, bills of sale, marriage, and divorce; testamentary bequests (*wasiya*s); written legal depositions made before legal witnesses (*ishhad*s); written, witnessed, and binding legal acknowledgments (*iqrar*s);[16] estate inventories; decrees; petitions (*qisas* in Mamluk usage, *ma'rud/ma'ruz* in Ottoman registers);[17] vouchers; receipts (*qabd*); reports (*mutala'at*); death inventories; the solicitation of a legal opinion and the reply (*istifta'* and *futya*); and finally, court records containing a summary of the case and the decision of the judge.[18]

S.A.I. Milad provides an appendix of the types of documents found in Cairo in the court of the Salihiya al-Najmiya, which include all of the above, as well as documents pertaining to reconciliation between spouses, adoption, appointments of wet nurses, embezzlement of public foundations, embezzlement more generally, imprisonment, and release from prison.¹⁹ Most of these documents are found in the collection under study, although the cases highlighted pertain to marriage, divorce, *sulh* (customary arbitration), *iqrar*s, and *awqaf*, as well as municipal disputes, *iltizam* (binding peasants to the land), morality, and metrology. And finally, of course, there is that supremely important document, the *hujja musattara*, which has barely evoked any mention or study.

A few words on the merits and demerits of the microanalytic and macroanalytic approaches to the *sijill*, both of which are employed by scholars, are also necessary. While Peirce, for example, examines a single *sijill* from one year in the life of an Aintab court, Sonbol employs a more sweeping macroanalytic approach to the text, seeking recurrent patterns over several decades or centuries.²⁰ One provides a holistic picture of social life at a given moment in time, the other a survey across time. The research presented in this book takes a broadly macroanalytical approach, using some sixty documents spanning a hundred-year period. Representing a random sample of documents from various courts, at different points in time across the sixteenth and early seventeenth centuries, these records allow for an approach that is cognizant of change over time and across communal lines. This enables a quantitative as well as a qualitative understanding of the role of custom in the Islamic court.

On a final note, it is prudent to recall one of the more prescient criticisms of histories based on the *sijill*—the circularity of the sources. Anchored to one body of documents, *sijill*-based histories are often devoid of the historical detail and movement found in the historical chronicles. To avoid this circularity, the works of two chroniclers are used as counterweights to the *sijill*. The first is Ibn Iyas (d. 1524), a historian well known to scholars of Ottoman Egypt, while the second is a lesser-known biographer, al-Damiri (d. 1621/25?). Ibn Iyas' chronicle of the Mamluk state's demise in 1517 and of Egypt's transition to Ottoman rule has earned an important place in the secondary literature. While it is generally considered a reliable first-person account, scholars regard it as pertaining only to the early years of Ottoman rule, capturing the vagaries of conquest, embodied in chaos, harsh retributive justice, and institutional disorder, and have been understandably reticent to treat it as a long-term harbinger of the Egyptian condition under Ottoman rule. Furthermore, legitimate questions about the objectivity of the narrative have been raised. Although Ibn Iyas's narrative conflates his personal interests and fate with those of all of Egypt, it remains the perspective of an aristocrat. As a member of the civilian, Mamluk-descended nobility *(awlad al-nas)*, Ibn Iyas delivers a predictably partisan, anti-Ottoman narrative. These important cautionary notes notwithstanding, some of the longstanding assumptions that have pervaded the secondary literature, particularly regarding Ottoman legal reforms, would benefit from a more serious reading of Ibn Iyas. A dearth of published sixteenth-century sources has made a comparative analysis of Ibn Iyas's work rather difficult, however. Al-Damiri's manuscript, *Qudat Misr fi-l-qarn al-'ashir wa-awa'il al-qarn al-hadi 'ashar* (Egypt's Judges in the Tenth and Early Eleventh Centuries),[21] is, therefore, an important addition to this genre.

Not unlike Ibn Iyas, al-Damiri was born of privilege, a descendant of the prominent Maliki jurist al-Damiri ibn Musa ibn 'Isa Kamal al-Din (1341–1405).[22] Given that more than two hundred years elapsed between Kamal al-Din's death and that of his descendant, we must dismiss the editorial preface of *Qudat Misr* which names him as our biographer's father. Al-Damiri himself identifies the Maliki chief judge Muhammad ibn 'Abd al-Karim ibn Ahmad ibn Siddiq al-Damiri as his grandfather, leaving no doubt that Kamal al-Din was in fact his great-grandfather. It is unclear whether our biographer inherited the profession of his patriarchs, but his sympathies with the Cairene judiciary are plainly evident. He never sides with an Ottoman chief judge against members of the Egyptian judiciary and is, in that sense, as partisan a reporter as Ibn Iyas. Nonetheless, his narrative provides invaluable insight into the identities of the individual Ottoman chief qadis as well as the professional rivalries that marked their encounters with Egyptian judges. Read in tandem with Ibn Iyas's history, al-Damiri's account challenges two predominant assumptions in the secondary literature: one, that the Ottoman state tampered with the legal process but not the law produced; and, two, that the conflict between the state and local jurists was a limited, post-conquest tussle.

Other primary sources consulted include the chronicles of Shaykh al-Islam Muhammad ibn al-Surur al-Bakri al-Siddiqi (d. 1676), *al-Nuzha al-zahiya fi dhikr wulat Misr wa-l-Qahira al-mu'izziya*; Muhammad ibn al-Mu'ti ibn Abi al-Fath ibn Ahmad ibn 'Abd al-Mughni ibn 'Ali al-Ishaqi al-Manufi (d. 1580), *Akhbar al-awwal fi-man tasarraf fi Misr min arbab al-duwal*; and finally, 'Abd-al-Wahhab al-Sha'rani's (d. 1565) writings as found in M. Winter, *Society and Religion in Early Ottoman Egypt: Studies in the Writings of 'Abd al-Wahhab al-Sha'rani*.[23]

As a final disclaimer, it should be noted that this is a study of Ottoman Cairo, giving us little insight into how courts functioned, or were even defined, in the thousands of rural towns and villages which dot the Nile Valley. Nonetheless, it provides an interesting point of comparison with the research on Aintab, Jerusalem, Damascus, Istanbul, Ederne, Bosnia, and Cyprus, to name a few of the places on which studies have appeared, and gives scope for drawing broader conclusions on early modern law and society.

Conclusion

From an internal and subjective (private) perspective, the topic of custom sheds light on whether certain practices are to be considered 'Islamic' or 'un-Islamic' and throws into relief the rich variety of stimuli, both local and translocal, at work in the complex, lived reality of Muslim culture. From an external and objective (public structural) perspective, it explores the *sijill* as an institution (an appendage of the court or *mahkama shar'iya*) and as a historical text, where *qanun*, local custom, and Islamic legal theory intersect to produce, expunge, and reproduce culture.

To continue to assume that the law produced in the Ottoman era was unaltered by the Ottoman administration of justice is simply untenable when what was once a private law had become a public enterprise; when what was once a universal religious law had become geographically bound for all subjects, without religious distinction; when what was once a plural law based on the principle of the coequality of the *madhahib* was becoming a unitary law under the aegis of a state *madhhab*; when what was once a culture of *millet*s (communities) was becoming a mass culture of individuals, or proto-citizens.

While the Ottoman administration of justice consciously molded society to a more homogenous system of rights and obligations, it was far more cognizant of the distinction between sins and crimes than its successors. Nonetheless, its conflation of religious and political authority foreshadowed the current struggle over the role of religion and state in post-Mubarak Egypt. The instruments which accelerated the bureaucratization of the law in practice were the archive, the *sijill*, the legal document (*hujja*)—and the paycheck with which we began.

In the next chapter, we examine the theoretical hindrances that 'secular critique' and its historicist framework pose to this view of history.

Chapter One
The Empire in Theory

Introduction
Rarely can one claim that any aspect of Islamic Egyptian history is understudied by comparison with its neighbors. The country's status as a so-called 'heartland' Islamic state, and as a repository of historical memory and center of cultural production, has earned it a place at the center of Islamic studies. But as a category of study, 'custom' has not generated much research in the field of Islamic studies, even less in the case of the heartland states. This remains true in spite of the fact that custom's fate is inextricably interwoven with the consolidation and decline of empire, and with the rise of the modern nation-state.

The steady growth of research on Ottoman *sijill*s has made enormous contributions to our knowledge of the economic, municipal, and, to a more limited extent, cultural history of the Islamic city. Social and economic histories based on these sources have received the lion's share of attention. Yet, while a proliferation of works on gender, minorities, and slaves in the Ottoman *sijill*s have broadened and deepened our understanding of the nuances of everyday life,[1] they have not yielded much insight into the one area for which the *sijill*s hold enormous potential—legal practice.

An unfortunate consequence of this neglect has been the inhibition of research into legal theory and legal praxis and their osmotic influence on one another in a given political setting.[2] Moreover, scholars working on custom limit themselves to the so-called geographic 'peripheries' of

Southeast Asia, as represented by Indonesia and Malaysia, South Asia, or in the case of Arab states, subgroups like the Berber or the Bedouin.[3] Their aim has been to measure the qualitative distance between peripheral and heartland practices and between heterodoxy and orthodoxy in Islam. Those living on its geographic peripheries, such as in the Ottoman hinterlands, are believed to exist along civilizational fault lines where Islam has yet to penetrate institutionally and where customary, nominal Islam prevails.[4] Heterogeneity, heterodoxy, and peripheralization are then measured against a counterparadigm of homogeneity, orthodoxy, and centrism.

One need not diminish the importance or prestige of Egypt's legal institutions to question the presumed ethnic homogeneity or religious orthodoxy of its premier city. Cairo hosted various Arabic-speaking, Turkic, Circassian, Mongol, and Abyssinian troops, political elites, merchants, slaves, and scholars of diverse social backgrounds. The number of "foreign" Muslims equaled, and at times surpassed, the number of Coptic Christians, Egypt's large religious minority. Moreover, they played key roles in the political, military, and judicial governance of the state. Merchant and scholarly classes contained sizable communities of Moroccans, Syrians, Arabians, Yemenis, and Persians, to name a few. J. Hathaway notes that, throughout the sixteenth and seventeenth centuries,

> Caucasian Mamluks were evidently still flowing into Egypt, [and] the province was receiving an influx of military and administrative personnel from the Ottoman Empire's Anatolian and Balkan regions. . . . Meanwhile, Turcophone bureaucrats of various ethnic origins arrived in Cairo to staff the provincial administration, and the Ottoman governors transported their own sizable entourages to Cairo.[5]

Commenting on the size of these entourages, Raymond says:

> In Cairo in the sixteenth and seventeenth centuries, the militias (the most important of which were those of the janissaries and 'Azab) must have numbered 15,000 men not including the households of the Mamluk emirs. Toward the end of the eighteenth century, the ruling caste numbered about 10,000 men, not

reckoning the families and servants, and was still therefore an important part of the Cairo population.[6]

By the end of the eighteenth century, Jomard, one of the authors of the *Description de l'Egypte*, estimated Cairo's population at 263,700.[7] Of these, 25,000 were non-Egyptian Muslims, including 10,000 Turks, 10,000 North Africans, and 5,000 Syrians. An equal number of non-Muslims are also found: 10,000 Copts, 5,000 Syrian Christians, 5,000 Franks, 3,000 Jews, and 2,000 Armenians.[8] It can be assumed that the numbers were even higher in the seventeenth century when, according to Raymond, Cairo's total population exceeded 300,000. Underscoring this diversity, Winter writes that "travelers were deeply impressed by its size and the heterogeneity of its population. All the accounts of Cairo, whether written by the Turks Mustafa 'Ali and Evliya Celebi, by the Maghribi visitors, or the many Europeans, describe their authors' astonishment at the sight of this great city with its large number of foreigners, merchants and other segments of society."[9]

One might also add that the wider Egyptian population was equally heterogeneous: northerners, who straddled the ethnic, religious, geographic, and civilizational fault lines of the Mediterranean peoples, and southerners (*sa'idi*s), who straddled the fault lines of the Nile Basin peoples. But instead of probing these cultural worlds, studies of the 'heartland' have generally adapted culture to a Marxist analysis. Culture becomes the hallmark "of the rulers, of the scholars, of the wealthy merchants and bureaucrats."[10] 'Consumption' studies abound, detailing the rise of a bourgeoisie and its shaping of artistic, architectural, and intellectual trends. Undeniably, class and consumption are pivotal to culture, but when considered alone they invite an essentialist perspective unable to admit the complex of elements (religious, ethnic, linguistic, gendered) that thrived alongside class. It prevents us from asking when, and under what conditions, does communal identity trump class? When, and under what conditions, does it change? What role does the rise of the individual, as a legal personage, play in this history? The evolving relationship of customary law to Islamic law and *qanun* provides an appropriate framework for probing the ways in which different communities modulated their distinct ethnic, professional, religious, and class affiliations within the confines of a legalistic, 'universalizing' state.

The Empire in Historiography

The bloc of scholars known as 'Arab Ottomanists' have produced the most promising, albeit fragmented, research on the role of custom in the seventeenth and eighteenth centuries.[11] But the subject is not infrequently alluded to, albeit marginally, as part of the broader discussion on the 'decline and readjustment' of the Ottoman state in the late sixteenth century. Concurrently, one broad thesis has emerged in which custom is seen as an expanding source of law.

Taking their cue from the thesis forwarded by scholars in *The Cambridge History of Islam*—that local 'capitalist classes,' or provincial elites, emerged to challenge the central authority of the state in the seventeenth century—many scholars have produced what may be described as a general theory of custom's role in the rivalry between the Ottoman center and periphery.[12] R. Jennings, A. Marcus, and N. Hanna argue that the seventeenth century heralds the "triumph" of local custom in sharia courts across the empire, from Bursa to Aleppo, Damascus, and Cairo, over its rival, the imperial *qanun*.[13] Awed by the strength and lineage of the Egyptian judicial establishment, Winter argues that the Ottomans limited their reforms to the legal process and avoided tampering with the laws produced: "The Ottomans did not infringe upon the religious or scholarly life of Egypt. Indeed, they limited their interference to material things."[14]

Hanna adds that by the end of the sixteenth century, the Egyptian judiciary had asserted its autonomy from the state and was able to shape the law produced. She writes: "The way justice was carried out was to a large measure left to the discretion of the magistrates working in the courts . . . the qadi administered justice according to the rules of the *madhhab* as he saw fit."[15] The thesis of Ottoman 'political decline' is a cornerstone of this analysis.

Like many of the legal histories of Ottoman state and society in the seventeenth and eighteenth centuries, Hanna's is based on the thesis of 'political decline,' which exaggerates the local judiciary's autonomy and overestimates the influence of local custom on provincial society. Thus, in the first instance, Egyptian nationalist sentiments have shaped the view of the Ottoman era as "foreign, obscurantist, responsible for the decline of Egypt and Cairo."[16] In the second, nationalist theory has informed our analyses of the economic and political forces fueling the rise of provincial elites in those centuries.

D.R. Khoury has challenged the thesis of political decline, if only by pushing back its date to the eighteenth century.[17] Identifying two types of elites in the Arab provinces—those descended from Mamluks and those descended from appointed Ottoman officers—Khoury argues that the latter represented 'local Ottomans' who were invested in, and loyal to, the state. These are to be distinguished from the local elites which emerged toward the end of the eighteenth century, such as the Wahhabi movement in Arabia, who sought independence from the state. The implicit link forged in Ottoman studies between nationalist theory, the rise of provincial capital classes, and the expanding role of custom is thus disrupted, at least for the seventeenth century.

Challenging the entire thesis of 'political decline,' Gerber writes that "the theory about the decline of the center is exaggerated for the entire polity."[18] Many of the so-called characteristics of decline, he concludes, "are simply pervasive characteristics of past centuries."[19] Gerber suggests that the notion of 'decline' first arose in sixteenth-century Ottoman *nasiha* ('advice to the ruler' or 'mirrors for princes') literature, in which the fifteenth century was idealized as a utopic golden age. But this, he argues, should be read as a sign of dramatic change, not of decline.[20] In a similar vein, Fleischer writes that one such writer described his own times so disparagingly because "he was the child of an age in which the few who were literate and learned could hope . . . for a rewarding career as a judge, teacher or member of the expanding bureaucracy . . . he lived into another age in which the government ranks were crowded, when basic literacy was more commonly available."[21]

To see political decline "in the Ottoman custom of coopting local elites into positions of authority" is to base the theory of decline on an "optical illusion," concludes Gerber. Many of the changes seen as characteristic signs of decline are in fact signs of adaptation to the empire's rapidly expanding frontiers. It would be both paradoxical and "absurd," he argues, "to claim that the growth of the empire was a symptom of decline."[22]

Increasingly, the practice of coopting local elites is seen as a cornerstone of Ottoman statecraft. Examining the manner in which the Ottomans established control in the fourteenth and fifteenth centuries over a largely Orthodox Christian population in the Balkans and the Aegean basin, H. Lowry bases their success in ruling a multiethnic, multiconfessional state less on military coercion than on granting a wide variety of concessions and privileges to their subjects.[23] The absence of ideology, or, as he calls it, "strict religious orthodoxy," contributed to the Ottoman state's tolerance of local customs, while earning it the support of this diverse populace. Bolstering this concept, C. Kafadar and R. Abou al-Haj note that the more ideological narratives would only be written in the sixteenth century to buttress what had become the self-image of the dynasty after the conquest of the Islamic heartlands and holy sites.[24]

The Muslim conquest of Constantinople was, for example, later portrayed in various apocalyptic traditions as one of the portents of the end times. An Ottoman mystic, Ahmed Bî-cân, voiced these apocalyptic fears and expectations soon after the Ottoman conquest in 1453. His narrative, expressed in the Turkish vernacular, would be used to showcase the Ottoman enterprise within the final tribulations and to cast Sultan Mehmed II as an apocalyptic warrior.[25]

By the sixteenth century, imperial history was an important component of universal history. L. Peirce and S. Buzov paint evocative pictures of a new hegemony under Sulayman Qanuni ('the lawgiver'), a new social contract in which ideology is anything but absent.[26] In a comparative study of the *qanun* in Egypt and Bosnia, for instance, Buzov claims that "no sultan before or after Sulayman undertook changing *kânûn* law and replacing it by law that disregarded completely the local legal practices and customs."[27]

Peirce's work on the *sijill*s of Aintab of 1540–41 concludes that "the new hegemony of the Ottoman sultanate as the standard-bearer for Sunni Islam meant a replacement of the colorful cultural palette of the empire's youth by a more sober social orthodoxy."[28] At the same time, Peirce qualifies her conclusion with the statement that "legal culture was heavily influenced by local participation and local customary law." She further qualifies that the new "sober social orthodoxy" was limited to "cities in the orbit of the capital" while "in the provinces which were, in fact, the bulk of the empire, regional cultures inevitably infused the practice of the law."[29] In a similar vein, B. Ergene argues that in the provincial Anatolian courts of Çankiri and Kastamonu, customary law was influential because "Ottoman courts were responsive to social, political, and cultural pressures in their localities."[30] Both he and Peirce acknowledge that Ottoman courts were rule-based, while underscoring the importance of local custom in shaping the rules. In other words, the state had retreated from its own hegemonic legal model.

Winter and Buzov find that the retreat of the state, or its 'Islamization,' has taken place by the middle of the sixteenth century. Both see the source of this retreat in the sultanates' confrontation with the formidable judicial classes in Egypt.[31] As the relationship between the universal sovereign and the *umma* (community of believers) "was determined and established in the lands hitherto known as the Sultanate of Rum, it was necessary to present proof of the existence of a distinctively Ottoman knowledge and juridical tradition. Sulayman could not speak for that."[32] The elite jurist, Abu al-Su'ud (Turkish: Ebu's-Su'ud), however, could. His intervention, generally seen as making *qanun* conform to *fiqh*, restored legal authority to the jurist classes such that the law and its administration were no longer "controlled and directed exclusively by the state," but by a judicial class organized into a corporative Hanafi guild.[33]

In other words, the argument holds that as the movement toward Islamization accelerated, the caliph's authority was diminished. What is overlooked in this analysis, however, is that the role of the bureaucratic state, if not the office of caliph, was far from diminished. Though Abu al-Su'ud was a representative of his Hanafi guild, he was, more importantly, a representative of the state, its chief judicial bureaucrat, and the first in a new breed of powerful 'state jurists.' We should distinguish, therefore, between the sultanate as an embodiment of the individual ruler, and the sultanate as an embodiment of the bureaucratic state. The age of absolute monarchy may have dimmed, but the future of the centralized bureaucratic state was bright.

The reposing of legislative authority in the hands of the Anatolian judiciary, or more precisely its corporative Hanafi bureaucrats, did not herald the abandonment of Ottoman legal orthodoxy and should not impede our view of the subtle but powerfully inhibiting forces brought to bear on local custom, even after Abu al-Su'ud's ascendance. Over the course of the sixteenth century, customary law increasingly confronted a breed of orthodoxy that cleaved one's essential personhood from one's communal identity. The task falling to the judicial staff of the sharia courts was the arbitration of points of conflict between the *qanun*, custom, and Islamic law as they affected the *individual*. The discretion they exercised in limiting, modifying, or negating customary practices was impressive, and raises serious questions about the extent to which custom was mitigated, altered, and reconstituted through their efforts.

In spite of the claim that Abu al-Su'ud opened the door to a "new Ottoman cultural identity . . . [that saw merit] in preservation of the cultural and religious systems"[34] of the empire, the evidence suggests that it neither reversed Ottoman policies nor ended the juristic debate, not only on *qanun* and *fiqh*, but over the sharia as an abstraction. Is the sharia limited to the laws derived from the jurisprudential hermeneutic *(fiqh)* of the jurist? Who has the authority to uncover sharia laws? The radical reimagining of this abstraction, before and after the reign of Sulayman, produced not just a consciously Ottoman *qanun*, but a consciously Ottoman sharia, to be distinguished from that of rival Sunni powers, past and present. With its implicit categories of orthodoxy and heresy, therefore, the thesis of Islamization fails to account for the dynamics of appropriation and reinvention underlying the discursive construction of a distinctly Ottoman orthodoxy.

Due to what has been termed "a history of imprecision and collusion in theological ax-grinding," the words 'orthodoxy' and 'heresy' have held a vexed position in Islamic studies.[35] Broadly speaking, the term 'orthodoxy' alludes to the importance of 'correct opinion,' whereas 'orthopraxy' emphasizes 'correct conduct.' The concept of orthodoxy seems more appropriate to the study of Catholicism or Shi'ism, where a clerical hierarchy possesses the religious authority to make definitive pronouncements on 'that which is inside' and 'that which is outside' the tradition. In the case of Sunni Islam, however, M. Hodgson, W.C. Smith, W.M. Watt, and I. Goldziher, to name but a few, have described the association between orthodoxy and Sunni thought as a liability rather than an asset. Even within Sunnism, the term invariably encourages the view that one school is more doctrinally 'correct' than another.

A staple conceptual trope encountered in much of the foundational secondary literature on the Ottoman state, for example, presumes that the Arab heartland is/was the bastion of 'Sunni orthodoxy.' The objections of Arab ulama to Ottoman reforms are persistently framed in this literature, therefore, in terms of a rivalry between *qanun* 'heterodoxy' and sharia 'orthodoxy.' It is well known that Ottoman judicial reforms triggered opposition from Syrian and Egyptian jurists, who bemoaned what they regarded as the demise of Islam under the Ottomans. But the tendency to view one side of the conflict as heterodox, and the other as orthodox, suggests the existence of a clearly delineated orthodoxy, usually legalistic and even then bereft of any nuance, to be measured against an equally obvious heterodoxy.

Predictably, for modern scholars it is the objections of Egyptian or Syrian ulama that are viewed as templates for Muslim orthodoxy.[36] But would the Ottomans have shared this view? Writing in the 1950s, M.

Hodgson concluded that "the moral tone of the centralizing empire was already deeply set by the time that Salim's conquest in the Arab lands (1517) gave it a first-line role in Islamdom as a whole."[37] Inalcik argued that as early as the fourteenth century, Islamic legitimation and questions of Islamic orthodoxy were of growing importance to the Ottoman state, which considered the defense and spread of Islam its most important role and aspired to uphold the sharia. This was made possible by the "sharia–military alliance" that "associated the major civilian institutions relatively closely with the central government."[38] Many of these notions derive from P. Wittek's *gaza* (Arabic, *ghazw* or *ghaza*) thesis, which held that the Ottoman Empire's raison d'être was to expand the borders of Islam by perpetuating jihad against the lands of unbelief, or *dar al-harb*.[39]

In the intervening years, many facets of the *ghaza* thesis have been criticized on the grounds that a jihad ideology against Christendom was an insufficient motive for Ottoman policies, including the recruitment of Byzantine subjects into the ranks of the Ottoman military and the waging of war on other Muslim states.[40] This critique threw the very 'Muslimness' of the *ghazi*s into question, with R.P. Linder going so far as to suggest that "Osman and his followers were holy warriors in another just cause, that of shamanism."[41] But C. Kafadar argues that "refutations" of this thesis based on discrepancies between *ghaza* ideology and Ottoman practice miss the point, since the *ghaza* thesis is not bound to idealized and anachronistic definitions of *ghaza* based on standards of 'orthodox' or 'true' Islam.[42] Kafadar's point is well taken, particularly his objections to the terminology employed to capture these developments: the heterogeneous and fluid boundaries of the frontier, he writes, simply defy the labels 'heterodox' and 'orthodox.' "Taskoprizade, an eminent Sunni scholar of the sixteenth century," he explains, "was probably much more conscious of the distinction between orthodoxy and heterodoxy than his fourteenth century Ottoman forebears."[43] I. Ataseven also warns:

> In a society where the population is Sunni, Shii, or both or none, and where many are Sufis, then distinctions between these words cannot be perpetually upheld. In a struggle to legitimize a position of power and where orthodoxy is a means towards such legitimation, this orthodoxy is everything and nothing at the same time. It is the perspective of power that refuses to see a complex reality. It

dresses difference in an orthodox vocabulary that often gives the illusion that the heterodox of society and the orthodox are arguing against each other.[44]

The import of Kafadar's point extends beyond the frontier culture of the *ghazi* state. One might question orthodoxy even in the heartland itself. Furthermore, one might question the categorization of Islamic law as a font of orthodoxy. If anything, *fiqh* (jurisprudential theory) is distilled through a discursive tradition emphasizing formulas of 'correct conduct,' over and above the formulation of 'correct opinion.'[45] Human interpretations of God's will are subject to fallacy and error, which means that legal opinions can only be mere approximations. This is not to suggest that authoritative opinions within the *madhhab*s were not whittled down over time, but to assert that the *madhhab* system, and indeed the very structural rationale of jurisprudential theory, is orthoprax.

Within the boundaries of the four Sunni schools of law, the circulation of multiple normative opinions is not only possible, but actual. And while each school may hold its own views on what constitutes correct conduct, given sufficient consensus within the discursive parameters of the *madhhab*, all opinions are equally sound. Indeed, the only orthodoxy one may speak of in Islamic law is methodological. A consensus on the methods by which the law is derived *(usul al-fiqh)* exists, but not necessarily on the legal opinions derived from them. If, therefore, the corporative Hanafi guild's fatwas deviate from those of Shafi'i scholars, which is to be considered more orthodox? Which represents 'Islamization'?

A less subjective paradigm for framing the conflicts under study is thus proposed in this text—'antagonistic sharias.' The sharia of the Cairene jurists upheld legal pluralism through the coequality of the *madhahib* (schools of law) as well as the legitimacy of local custom. The Ottoman sharia, on the other hand, promoted orthodoxy through the primacy of one official *madhhab*, the Hanafi, and the primacy of one body of universal customs, *qanun*. By subtle inhibition rather than blunt force, therefore, it was the state, rather than the jurist-author classes of Cairo or Damascus, that was the agent of 'orthodoxification.'

For too long, historians of Islamic law have identified the mufti (jurist) as the sole agent of legal change, while ignoring the role of the state and its judiciary in accommodating and legitimating change. M. Hoexter argues that scholars have been searching under the lamppost, poring over fatwa collections and legal treatises, and neglecting the role of judges and rulers, despite the fact that the latter were heavily involved in producing a distinctly innovative, Ottoman sharia.[46] But 'innovation' *(bid'a)* was never the word used by the empire's spokesmen. Rather, this was the label applied to it by its opponents in Arab judicial circles, many of whom openly charged the state with innovating to the point of heresy.[47] But too often we have taken the claims of Arab jurists at face value, neglecting to ask how the empire projected itself. As shown in the next chapter, the language of 'renewal,' or *tajdid*, is most often used to describe imperial reforms, while the language of *takfir*, or charge of unbelief, is used to confront even the most esteemed of its critics.

In view of this claim, the static polarity created by the labels of juristic 'orthodoxy' and state 'heterodoxy' that are generally attached to such questions serves no purpose but to entrench the general mold in which the rivalry between jurists and the Ottoman state has always been cast—as a 'tension' between *qanun* and sharia.[48] In the Ottoman Empire, however, the tension is more aptly described as a rivalry between two 'antagonistic' sharias, one leaning toward an orthoprax model that legitimated local custom, and the other toward an orthodoxy that *de*legitimated it. By definition, orthodoxy is predatory. It brooks no rivals and abhors pluralism, whether ideological or structural. In the discourse of natural law, it strives to reshape 'morality as it is' into a singular vision of 'morality as it should be.' In the sixteenth century, it was the state, rather than local jurists, that was the progenitor of this vision.

The new social orthodoxy, forecasting the rise of mass culture, the individual, the bureaucratic state, and codified law, was a fundamental component of the early modern political venture.

The Empire in Theory

It will be noted that nowhere in the secondary literature is theory of any kind discussed. And while it may not be readily apparent why a work on law and society in sixteenth-century Ottoman Cairo should be prefaced by a discussion on political modernity and its handmaiden, secular critique, several reasons may be given. The most obvious of these is that the writing of history is itself a product of two methodological modernist paradigms: secular criticism and historicism.

Historicism

In the academy, secular criticism generates, arranges, and interprets historical data based on given assumptions and categories. Historicism then affixes that history onto a modernist calendar where historical time becomes a yardstick of the "cultural distance (at least in institutional development) that was assumed to exist between the West and the non-West."[49] In the new historicist calendar, time itself is recast. Once conceived of as circular, it straightens into a linear arrow plotting the course of human progress and betterment in a singular trajectory forward. The historicist calendar is thus preoccupied with plotting the 'points of origin' of modernity, making it appear, as D. Chakrabarty argues, "not simply global but rather as something that became global *over time* . . . this 'first in Europe, then elsewhere' structure of global historical time allowed Marx to say that the 'country that is more developed industrially only shows, to the less developed, the image of its own future.'"[50] Political modernity thus comes to non-Europeans as "someone's way of saying not yet," consigning "Indians, Africans, and other 'rude' nations to an imaginary waiting room of history. In doing so, it converted history itself into a version of this waiting room."[51]

But if the postmodern critique has adeptly disposed of the historicist waiting room, it has been far less perspicacious in its critique of the other pillar on which political modernity stands: secularism, and its cognitive arm, secular criticism. Even Chakrabarty's devastating critique of modernization theory concedes that political modernity has a peculiarly European genealogy, since

> everything we associate with "political modernity," from the rule by modern institutions of the state, bureaucracy, secularism and capitalist enterprise, concepts such as citizenship, public, private, civil society, democracy, popular sovereignty, popular/mass culture, equality before the law, social justice, scientific rationality—all bear the mark of a peculiarly European genealogy of concepts and traditions.[52]

Chakrabarty's goal, to show that the continued internalization, (re)assimilation, and application of these concepts in the present by non-Europeans generates "alternative modernities," liberating the modern from the fetters of the historicist calendar. But what of the past? Does it remain consigned to the generic 'premodern' world of 'tradition?'

Is there room for a consideration of the political inheritance of non-Europeans as constituent elements of Chakrabarty's 'alternative modernities'? The 'early modern' paradigm now current provides a way forward, if only by adjusting the chronology of Europe's rise and throwing into question the modernist timetable. Emerging out of Wallerstein's world-systems theory, the 'early modern' label emerged as a postmodern rejection of modernization theory's claim that all nations were destined to follow the same path of evolutionary development, and of this theory's excessive focus on nationalism.

In Wallerstein's view, three kinds of societies have existed across human history.[53] The first consists of 'mini-systems,' composed of tribes and small chiefdoms. The other two are 'world systems,' either politically unified, as in the case of single-state world empires such as Rome or the Ottoman Empire, or not, as in the polities engaged in the silk-road trade. None of these systems is national. The 'modern world system,' considered to have emerged between 1450 and 1550, is only the latest expression of the latter type, but unique in being the first, and only fully capitalist, world economy to have expanded across the entire planet by about the twentieth century.[54]

Janet Abu-Lughod agrees with the first half of Wallerstein's statement but challenges the last as excessively Eurocentric. The title of her monograph, *Before European Hegemony*, is self-explanatory.[55] An extensive, premodern world system existed across Eurasia in the thirteenth century, she argues, prior to the formation of the modern world system identified by Wallerstein.[56] Furthermore, she challenges the view that the 'rise of the West,' beginning with the intrusion of armed Portuguese ships into the relatively peaceful trade networks of the Indian Ocean in the sixteenth century, was a result of features internal to Europe rather than external circumstance, namely the collapse of the previous world system.[57] This older world system, forged by the Mongol empire and its successor states, fostered trade links across the Eurasian land mass, enabling a high degree of economic, political, and social synthesis while fueling artistic and cultural efflorescence.[58]

While Wallerstein and Abu-Lughod disagree on a number of issues—he dismisses her claim that the Mongol Empire and its successors constitute a 'world system,' while she derides the suggestion that these conditions only developed in Europe in the sixteenth century due to "her internal inventiveness and the virtues of her unique entrepreneurial spirit"—they are both in agreement that modernization's claims to autogeneration during the Enlightenment are patently at odds with the historical record.⁵⁹ Abu-Lughod's analysis, however, allows scholars not only to extend the appellation 'early modern' to the study of Ottoman society, but to rethink the very roots of economic and, by extension, political modernity in its successor states.

To do so cogently, however, the boundaries, assumptions, and limitations of political modernity's master idiom—secularization theory—would have to be suspended. Why, and is this even possible?

Secularism

"Even with the help of Stirner's egoism, Adorno's negative dialectics, and Derrida's deconstruction," it is impossible, in Pecora's words, "to imagine a world *entirely* liberated from dominant conceptions, and many of these conceptions—or so I will argue—cannot be divorced from the complicated exchange, translation, and contest of ideas that have occurred under the name of secularization."⁶⁰

It is necessary, however, because secularization theory mutes the historical contest of political ideas that occurred under the name of religion. It conjures a static and undifferentiated picture of religious life in Islam based on a refracted image of religious life in European history. The reticence of historians of Islam to engage with critical theory can be partially attributed to the theory's insistent parochialism. But there is another fear that prevents scholars committed to the progressive ideals of secularism from deconstructing secular critique: the very real fear that such a critique potentially challenges the values of secular liberalism and could arm the counterdiscourse from the religious right. But ceding religion to the religious has proven even more dangerous.

The casting out of 'things religious' from 'things secular'—if only by asserting the former's 'retreat' from public life—has in fact facilitated the modern fundamentalist project. If historicism produced the 'not yet' discourse among exponents of modernism, the secular critique has provoked the 'not *that*' discourse among the exponents of religious revivalism, *that* being the cluster of political ideals grouped together under the secular umbrella. *That*, variously imagined, is what the revivalist in Islam and in other religions defines as the politically alien, imported 'other.' A quintessentially reactionary answer to the question of "What is 'religious'?" is thus born, not in opposition to modernity, but on its terms.

The field has yet to heed S. Mahmood's calls for "a serious engagement with the historical relevance of [key Islamicate ideas] and practices in the present."[61] It has yet to produce the conceptual tools necessary for such an undertaking. It continues to empty out Islamic history, particularly legal history, into 'secular' and 'religious' piles, producing a stilted, even incoherent, binary between 'things spiritual' and 'things worldly,' 'things dogmatic' and 'things rational.' The 'nonsecular' state merges into a quasi-theocratic construct based on 'religious' laws that govern through divine political sovereignty. But while 'religious' states *can* be theocratic, they can also be civil, bureaucratic, monarchic, or military-conquest states. Islamic political history abounds with all of them, save one: theocracy is virtually unknown in Islam. It would be left to twentieth-century Islamist moderns to invent it.

All too often, what passes in the academy for a discursive treatment of political modernity vis-à-vis religious political history, certainly Islam's, lacks all critical nuances, and is almost always distilled into the inadequate lexical idioms of secular critique. Abstracted into a "system of signs and symbols" which imbue the believer with "powerful, pervasive and longlasting moods and motivations,"[62] religion is at once defined broadly enough to capture the totality of human religious experiences, yet too broadly to capture any of its critical nuances.

The stark binary between things 'secular' and 'nonsecular' is at the base of R. Bellah's conclusion that what separated the political development of the west from that of the Muslim east was the revival of the classical, Greco-Roman notion of citizenship encased in the dominant conceptions of secularism found in early modern western Europe.[63] Secularism and citizenship, he offers, were avenues of political development that were closed to the Islamic world, as the latter's political resources had always been limited to the powerful, but necessarily utopian, fusion of religion and politics. The category of identity that could transcend clan and familial bonds in the Muslim world was "not that of a citizen," but of an "adult male believer."[64]

Bellah's secularism, categorized as the moment when belief (religious dogma) gives way to ideology (rational doctrine), is, of course, no less utopian.[65] Since Max Weber, secularization has been credited with enabling the ephemeral process known as economic, social, and political modernity. The preponderant view on which Bellah's secularism rests is anchored to two suppositions about modernity: (a) the retreat of religion as a dominant sphere, and (b) the reconstruction of institutions on a rational basis.

The 'retreat of religion' signifies the abandonment of religious dogma and the adoption of a rational, even irreligious, worldview by the masses. But as C. Brown counters, this would mean that "all our ancestors were literal Christian believers, all of the time."[66] There was, he argues, "no 'ideal state' in which religion grasped the total worldview of the people, and which has been dissipating for the history of mankind."[67] Brown's own thesis, that increasing urbanization (a feature of modernization) can be correlated with lowered church attendance, fares no better, however, and is contradicted by the evidence of the history of Scotland and the United States. In fact, rapid urbanization has provoked *increased* religiosity and is often cited as the primary cause not only of higher church or mosque attendance, but of powerful revivalist and fundamentalist trends.[68] The notion that increasing affluence prompts secular behavior is another way in which the concept of secularization has been yoked to capitalism, forming the crux of one of the more important debates in the discourse on globalization.

An older and more viable thesis held that religion was never cast out, as such, but served as the engine of the Enlightenment. In his *The Protestant Ethic and the Spirit of Capitalism*, M. Weber identified the Protestant Reformation as a shaping force in the creation of the modern world, and a catalyst for the Enlightenment. Religion did not suddenly disappear as a result of the Enlightenment, but continued, in both spirit and practice, to haunt and inhabit the modern world.

The earliest spin-offs of this Weberian discourse defined secularism *through* religion rather than *against* it. Part Christian apologetics, part postmodern critique, the argument of scholars like P. Berger was that Christianity "carried the seeds of secularism within it from the beginning."[69] Echoing the views of Berger, B. Lewis went further to argue that the intertwining of secular and religious authority in the Roman period was a de facto rejection of a Christian, Biblical call to secularism. "We could contend that here lies the great historical irony in the relation between religion and secularization," concludes Berger, "an irony that can be graphically put by saying that, historically speaking, Christianity has been its own gravedigger."[70]

Secularization continued to be seen as a consequence of transformations within the Christian tradition, such that Hans Blumenberg, in *The Legitimacy of the Modern Age*, could dismiss secularization's claims to autogeneration as fantasy. Secularization occurs by "*by* eschatology," he argued, when "the failed expectations of an end-time forced instead a turn to an increasingly extended sense of human temporality."[71] For Nietzsche, 'scientific Truth,' the crowning achievement of the Enlightenment, had itself sprung from the religious ideal of metaphysical 'Truth.' But does this mean that secularism can simply be reduced to a secular version of Christian eschatology? For Löwith, who spoke of the secularization *of* Christian eschatology, the answer was negative.[72] Secularism may indeed be a consequence of Christian thought, but it is so only as a formal "reoccupation" of past and now "vacant" theological "answer positions."[73] In other words, it is theology without religion.

For all of the above, secular modernity entailed the transfer of schemes and models elaborated in the field of religion to the field of the secular. Christianity continues to nourish modernity "unconsciously," while the latter lives

> only as something consisting of a bequest and an inheritance, despite the negations and illusions of autofoundation. Modernity would not be a new time, founded and conscious of its foundation, but would only be the moment where there is effected a change of plane, a *'worlding'* of Christianity.[74]

"A divine parent," in T. Asad's sardonic summation, Christianity morphs

> into its human offspring (modernity), as transcendence embodying itself in worldly life (secularity) . . . Christianity alone, of all religions, gives birth to a plural democratic world, of all religions, it begets unfettered human agency. The elemental human dispossession that characterizes all religions is paradoxically overcome by and through a unique religion: Christianity.[75]

Pecora and Asad dismiss the claim that this is a uniquely Christian phenomenon. The former argues that secularism, as "transcendence embodying itself in worldly life," is pre-Christian. It is found in ancient Greece where reason and revelation were cleaved into distinct disciplines—philosophy and theology—and where a system of civil government existed that was neither theological nor quasi-theocratic. Nonetheless, Pecora struggles to outline possible alternative scenarios of religious 'worlding,' lending his voice to Asad's call for a new anthropology of secularism by which we may critique the "enabling myths, the disavowed violence, and the redemptive, universalizing attitude toward the rest of the world underwriting the idea of secular liberalism."[76]

Nonetheless Pecora finds fault with Asad's analysis for providing a civilizational and thus polarizing approach to what secularization represents in Islam.[77] This may seem an odd assertion coming from someone who has already acknowledged the absence of any unifying representation of secularism, even in the west. But Pecora is concerned with representations of 'secularity' as something uniquely, and impermeably, civilizational. It not clear to this writer, however, that this is Asad's intention. Unlike Pecora, who adopts a historical approach to these questions, Asad is concerned with analyzing the ontological roots of the *current* polarization between political Islam and western secularization theory.

The debate on whether certain elements of the secular critique, or secularization theory, possess or lack universal qualities is important, but as yet open-ended. My concern is for the way in which secularization theory, as a binary of opposites, skews our perspective on religious life in history and severs its links to the present. For Asad, who shares this concern, secular critique obscures the natural or organic categories that exist within individual religious systems. In the case of Islam, for example, it ignores "the line between *morality* and *manners* (a crucial distinction for the worldly critic)."[78]

In his discussion of blasphemy in Islam, Asad argues that matters of belief (even unbelief) were historically 'private,' assuming a legal dimension only when employed 'publicly' (through writings, lectures, or other forms of activism) in potentially seditious political behavior. Here, he draws parallels with the hegemony of the modern state in England, which criminalized blasphemy in the seventeenth century when 'national' courts replaced ecclesiastical courts. There were no conditions, however, under which the Islamic state could interrogate private beliefs in the hopes of taking them to a public jury.[79]

While Asad's binary is useful from a host of sociological perspectives, it lacks the precision of Islam's jurisprudential concepts. One would hardly recognize 'manners' and 'morality,' for instance, as two divisible categories in Islamic legal theory. Rather, one encounters a more precise dissection of morality into 'sins' and 'crimes.' In the tenth century, judicial theory disentangled temporal and spiritual authority in Islam, producing two ontological categories of sharia law: 'the rights of God,' (*huquq Allah*), from which *'ibadat* (law pertaining to worship) is derived, and the 'rights of humans' (*huquq al-'adamiyyin*), from which *mu'amalat* (laws pertaining to the conduct of men and women among themselves) emanate. The former was rooted in the theological interpretations of the Qur'an and Hadith as they related to liturgy, ritual, and moral conduct (sin), while the latter was rooted in jurisprudential methods relating to social conduct (crime). While sins could also be crimes, they remained a separable category from the latter when touching on *huquq Allah*, such as belief, liturgy, and other aspects of piety or ritual practice. To be certain, the interrogation of the boundaries between the two was, and remains, a point of contention, but the maxim which held sway for the duration of the Islamic state's history was that the 'rights of God' "are claims of God, and God has no need of a human agency to execute His will."[80]

Islam's 'moment of worlding' had come to pass, therefore, long before the European Enlightenment and long before the rise of the Ottoman Empire. Islamicate schemes and legal models had decriminalized grave sins, including unbelief, homosexuality, prostitution, and the selling or consumption of intoxicants. And while contending views could be found within Islamic legal theory, the predisposition toward given *madhhab*s meant that dissenting views could be overcome in practice. Secularization theory can neither speak to nor adequately compartmentalize this bifurcation in Islamic concepts of morality and justice. It cannot acknowledge it as an instantiation of a much older religious worlding, long preceding that of Christianity's under the aegis of Calvinist philosophy.

Comparing the Ottoman state, supposedly the last in a line of Islamicate premodern states, with its Calvinist contemporary in Geneva, the lauded forerunner of the modern secular state, helps demonstrate the inadequacies, and the inherent biases, of the secular critique. Both states arrive at the early modern juncture from disparate positions on the question of sin and crime. But the comparison leaves the forerunner of European secularism looking far more theocratic, politically and socially, than its so-called traditional counterpart.

Considered a political milestone, Calvin's *Institute of the Christian Religion* distinguished between "the spiritual kingdom of Christ and civil government [as] things very different and remote from each other."[81] His rule over Geneva represented the first Protestant experiment paving the way for the reformed Protestant church and the ideal of civil government. The bedrock of secularization theory, civil government, was the Calvinist movement's gift to the Christian political reformation. Addressing himself to the French monarch, King Francis, he writes: "The civil magistrates may not assume to themselves the administration of the Word and the Sacraments; or the power of the keys of the kingdom of heaven."[82] In other words, the state had powers stemming from religion but no power *over* religious doctrine, the very nucleus of the separation between state and religion that stands at the heart of Europe's secular moment.

Calvin's caveat, that the legitimacy of civil government rests on its ability to uphold religious practice, is not unlike the Islamic maxim that political legitimacy rests on the state's ability to uphold the sharia. But sins and crimes were far more dangerously and consciously conflated in Calvin's state. Christian Rome had provided ample historical precedent on which to draw, and, like Constantine and Justinian before him, Calvin understood the fulfillment of this duty to mean the *enforcement* of religious orthodoxy and the rooting out of heresy. In practice, this meant the categorization of sins as de facto crimes.[83]

In 1536, Calvin was invited to remain in Geneva to enforce a proclamation issued for the purpose of regulating moral and religious life. It prohibited blasphemy and profanity, cards and dice, the protection of adulterers, thieves, vagabonds, and spendthrifts, excessive drinking, and all holidays except Sunday. It also commanded all inhabitants to attend worship services and forbade the Catholic sacraments.[84] Calvin's state punished 'sins against God' as surely as it did 'sins against man.'

Like the Ottoman Empire, Calvin's state held a deep-seated hostility to custom. Chapter 5 of the *Institutes*, titled "The Appeal to 'Custom' against Truth," prefaces an attack on both Catholic and Protestant thinkers and their "sophistic brawls" and "speculative theology," in whose hands "the private vices of the many have often caused public error, or rather a general agreement on vices, which these good men now want to make law."[85] While the Ottoman state treated custom with equal suspicion, it was motivated less by the question of its moral iniquity than by its potential for fostering competing identities and competing sources of legal authority.

The above is not to suggest that Islamic history is free of any confusion regarding the separation of sins and crimes. To the contrary, Islamic history abounds with Muslim rulers who saw it as both their prerogative and their duty to enforce the 'rights of God.' The point to be made, however, is that the tradition had not produced the systemic institutional or philosophical basis for sustaining such regimes.[86] Political Islam and political Christianity thus arrive at the early modern juncture from two opposing trajectories. And yet, Calvin's quasi-theocracy and its maxim that the legitimacy of civil government rested on the state's ability to uphold religious practice are seen as mitigating conditions of secularism, while in Islam, a comparable maxim—that the legitimacy of the ruler rested on his ability to uphold the sharia—continues to be read as emblematic of the 'religious' state.

The modern historical narrative about Islam, a history that is reduced to the sum of its encounter with the 'novel' and autogenerated ideals of European political modernity, is thus an impoverished one. And while the role of the west is inescapable in any rendering of this history, it is far from being the determinative role. The sixteenth-century juncture, where the Calvinist and Ottoman state meet, imposed its own internal economic and political logic on both societies and stands at the root of their respective modernities. For the Ottomans, the century of 'crises and readjustment' posed numerous internal and external challenges, as well as opportunities. Notably, these include the challenge of new European capitalist formations such as the corporation and the practical demands of administering an integrated economy in a vast multiethnic and multisectarian empire. But if the impetus for legal reform was economic and political, its outcome was social. In pursuit of reform, the balance between religious and political authority, between jurists and society, and between sins and crimes would be permanently reconfigured.

Not unlike Calvin's state, but very *unlike* its predecessors, the Ottoman Empire made "public morality more generally" a state enterprise.[87] In the first chapter of the *Qanunnama* (legal codes issued in the name of Ottoman sultans) of Salim I and Sulayman, where *zina'* (illicit extramarital sex) is discussed, Ottoman law transformed the physical punishments found in the sharia into a fixed fine-based system of penalties; physical punishments for *hadd*-based crimes (*hadd* being a Qur'anic criminal penalty) were generally excluded from the *qanunnama*s.[88] But even as it lowered the penalties, it lowered the bar of proof for sins such as *zina'*, making it easier to charge and convict people for the offense. Sins were becoming crimes.

Nonetheless, it bears repeating that while the conflation of religious and political authority in the Ottoman and Calvinist states, respectively, was motivated by similar ends, they yielded very different moral orders. While Ottoman jurists continued to sweep more and more sins under the discretionary authority of the state, they also worked to commute their harshness, transforming grave sins into criminal misdemeanors. Moreover, it should be said, the sins under scrutiny, such as the discussion on *zina'*, were related to public law and to *mu'amalat* on prostitution, rape, and paternity claims. Calvin's moral state, on the other hand, is more evocative of the Islamic Republic of Iran (the first theocracy in Islamic history) or the Wahhabi Kingdom of Saudi Arabia than its own contemporary, the Ottoman Empire. The irony for the historian of Islam, however, is that Islamist currents have, since the eighteenth century, moved steadily in the direction not only of conflating sins with crimes, but of reversing their order in modern political life, while the Christian west has continued to forge greater degrees of separation between them.[89]

Should this imply that the historical Islamic state was already secular? Far from it: it should instead confirm the futility of the idiom. The Roman, Byzantine, Abbasid, Calvinist, and Ottoman states were all nonsecular, but that did not prevent an astonishing variety of political configurations from arising within them—the 'modern secular' state being only the latest expression. In each, as in the present, the jostling of spiritual and temporal authority, of religious and political authority, of state law and jurisprudential law, of sins and crimes, produced uneven and perpetually variant models of state and society. What they shared, however, was a will to consolidate political authority *through* religious authority.

Rome adopted Christianity as an antidote to the empire's decline, when it could ill afford the fissures produced by the Christological debates of the fourth and fifth centuries. To secure its grip on the reigns of empire, it played a well-documented role in the construction of Christian orthodoxy and in the prosecution of deviance from it. A comparable, though ultimately futile, venture was attempted by the Abbasid state, followed by the less radical, but more effective, Ottoman venture under study.

The success of this venture may be measured by its political resonance in the present. In Egypt, Ottoman policies continued to be amplified into the nineteenth and twentieth centuries as the association between political and religious authority grew more, not less, intimate. In 1835–36, in line with centuries of preference for the official *madhhab*, "Egyptian muftis were forbidden to give fatwas according to other *madhhab*s and only Hanafi law was enforced."[90] By 1892, the plurality of jurisdictions under Hanafi hegemony was abolished. In the twentieth century, the cooption of religious institutions by the bureaucratic state accelerated. In 1961, Gamal Abd al-Nasser's revolutionary government nationalized al-Azhar and granted its Grand Shaykh the rank of minister. Henceforth, the Grand Shaykh would be appointed by, and answerable to, the president.[91]

Endowed with its new religious authority, the 'secular' republic of Egypt has pursued a series of bizarre and well-publicized crusades against sinners. In 2001, for example, it waged a legal war on the gay communities of Cairo, raiding a floating Nile nightclub, the *Queen Boat*, and unleashing a public wave of arrests and trials.[92] It was not under Islamic law that these charges were filed, but under the modern Egyptian legal code, a hybrid of 'secular,' French-inspired principles, Egyptian customs, and lastly, sharia (defined as Hanafi code) laws. In many respects, the twentieth century represents the triumph of political authority over religious authority in Islam, with disastrous results for society at large.

From its inception, the crystallization of judicial doctrines in Islam has been a politicized venture.[93] F. Vogel has shown that Hanafi jurists under the Abbasid Empire were trying to ensure that their interpretations and methods would survive and compete against contending interpretations offered by Abbasid authorities.[94] S. Jackson has argued that jurists could restrict the power of the state by preserving the sharia's authority over communities who adhered to *madhhab* rules.[95]

By the sixteenth century, the conflict had been revisited in favor of the state. More directly involved in day-to-day legislative activity than its predecessor, the Ottoman state coopted the judiciary and abolished the four offices of *qadi al-qudah*, or chief judges representing the four schools of law. It replaced the latter with the office of chief Hanafi qadi, and concentrated judicial authority in the hands of the official state *madhhab*. In so doing, it achieved what the Abbasid state could not: it made law a public enterprise. Its moment of structural and philosophical reformation is thus an important one in the history of Islamicate conceptions of self and moral sovereignty. The growing intimacy between the individual and the state, and between individual rights and codification, are hallmarks of this reformation.

The rise of the bureaucratic state, of public law and of the individual, should not be seen as Islam's own 'autogenerated' modernity, however. Rather, the period should be regarded as a logical extension of a religious and political tradition that was, by its very nature, perpetually coalescing. Nor should the separation of sins and crimes be seen as a marker of the system's secular credentials. A principal difference between the modern west and Islamic political history is that in the former, secularism provides the dominant intellectual conceptions. In the latter, however, secular principles are encased within dominant religious conceptions.

For all their shared political conundrums (defining and limiting the reach of temporal and spiritual authority) and their common origins in Hellenism and Hebrew scripture, European Christendom and Islamic societies have yielded very different interpretations of the master ideas at play in each religion. Arguments from historicism and secular critique cannot account for this variance. But, more importantly, we are left with the inescapable irony that Islamic society does not come to modernity or secularism through the west, but rather becomes estranged from them through the empirical lens of western cognition.

Conclusion

The most basic historiographical problems pertaining to the view of the Ottoman state as 'premodern' or 'early modern' are rooted in historicism and secular criticism. The deconstruction of these two critical approaches made it possible to to reposition the Ottoman state as both the last in a long line of Islamic empire-states and, simultaneously, as the first in a new breed of Islamic states. Then, as now, the consolidation of law, culture, and, by extension, political identity, in a multiethnic, multiconfessional state, provoked antagonistic discourses. On its way to becoming a universal state, the Ottoman Empire coopted the religious establishment, created new spaces for the dispensation of a bureaucratized justice, and subverted the authority of clan, community, and sect. Under bureaucratic law, subjects came closer to achieving citizenship with all its individual (albeit as yet unequal by modern standards) rights and obligations.

The ideological components of this venture brought into question the broad labels, including 'orthodox' and 'heterodox,' generally used to define the tension that marked the relationship of the judiciary in Cairo to its Ottoman counterpart. In their stead, I have proposed the concept of 'antagonistic sharias' as a means of shifting the focus away from the relationship of the *qanun* to sharia and to that of rival sharias. From this perspective, the judicial conflicts of the sixteenth century emerged as a discursive and contextual debate on the increasing hegemony of the state, its universal *qanun*s, and its disregard of local communities and local practice.

Chapter Two
Custom in Sharia and in the *Siyasat-i ilahi* (Divine *Siyasa*)

Introduction

Each stage in the development of a theory of custom represents a transitory moment in the history of Islamic society, a moment of disengagement with the past and a conscious reinvention of the present. Occurring in three distinct stages, the development of a theory of custom began in the formative period, from the seventh to the ninth centuries, as Muslim society transitioned from pre-Islamic *jahiliya*, or 'age of ignorance' (before revelation), to the Islamic age of moral knowledge (after revelation). The second stage occurred during the eleventh century when the Mongol conquests devastated the classical caliphate. Reconstituted on its ruins, Islamic society buried the universalizing claims of the Abbasid caliphate and reemerged as myriad empire-states stretching from the Maghreb to the Turco-Persian, Indic, and Southeast Asian worlds of Islam. By the fourteenth to sixteenth centuries, the universalizing state was born again.

But what does each stage in the transformation of theory mean for custom in practice? Does theory work to legitimate custom, or to circumscribe it? G. Libson has argued that the incorporation of custom as a secondary source of law alongside the primary sources of *fiqh* (Qur'an, Hadith, *qiyas*, and *ijma'*) worked to legitimate it.[1] Conversely, I. Netton regards the same theory as a limitation on custom in practice.[2] Increasingly subjected to the aegis of the jurists, he argues, custom came to be aligned more closely with Islamic law. I adopt the position that the theory of custom represents an amalgam of sometimes competing opinions that reflect the political and social exigencies of their day. In other words, they are not moving in a single and straight trajectory forward, either toward or away from custom. To fully comprehend the limits, challenges, and concerns of this judicial discourse, however, it must be contrasted with its counterdiscourse from political philosophy.

Because custom encompasses both the practice of the local community and the practice of the state though *siyasa*, it is automatically political. The judicial discourse on custom is a dialogue on the moral limits of *siyasa*, and an endeavor to compete with the state and its counterdiscourse from political philosophy. At the heart of this philosophical discourse was an ancient Greek concept, the *nomos* (*namus* in Turkish), originally signifying 'revealed divine law,' which became, over time, delinked from its anchor in prophetic revelation and assimilated to *siyasa*—a higher *siyasa*, or to be more precise a *siyasat-i ilahi*, a little-understood doctrine which aimed at the moral perfection of man in the material world. Significantly for the law, the divine *siyasa* promoted the *qanun* to something greater than it had been. *Qanun* was no longer an expression of sultanic custom; it was an extension of the perfected moral cosmos. In all, this 'higher *siyasa*,' embodied in *qanun* and anchored in natural morality, made it possible for the state to universalize its new orthodoxy while deflecting juristic criticism.

In turn, the development of the theory of custom by Ottoman Egyptian scholars like Ibn Nujaym reflects a keen awareness of this looming political hegemony. Ibn Nujaym relied on the scholars who came before him and who elaborated theories of *istihsan* (juristic preference based on notions of the greater good) and *maslaha* (public welfare). But his focus was tellingly different from that of his predecessors. While forbidding changes in *'ibadat* stemming from the rights of God, scholars like Shatibi allowed for change in *mu'amalat* based on local custom.[3] Ibn Nujaym, on the other hand, forbids innovation in both.

From the beginning, jurists who accepted 'secondary sources' of law such as *maslaha* and *istihsan*, including Ibn Taymiya (d. 1328), were generally wary of political custom. In I.R. Netton's view, conservative jurists like Ibn Taymiya only accepted these devices as a means of subordinating *siyasa* legislation to the authority of the *fuqaha'*.[4] Nevertheless, the juristic debate remained focused on the validity of custom itself, as a normative source of popular and political practice. But by the time the Egyptian jurist Ibn Nujaym was writing, the parameters of the debate had shifted.

While the Mamluk Ibn Taymiya wrote from the imperial center, the Ottoman Ibn Nujaym wrote from its provincial fringes. In the Mamluk era, custom was a signifier of local practice. In the Ottoman era, it had come to signify translocal customs compiled and manufactured in a 'foreign' capital. The debate was no longer about the legitimacy of custom per se, but about the legitimacy of local versus translocal custom. Furthermore, while his predecessors appear concerned with the impact of custom on *'ibadat*, Ibn Nujaym is more urgently preoccupied with its impact on *mu'amalat*.

As the product of *siyasa* legislation, *qanun* bore directly on both the 'rights of God' and the 'rights of humans,' something the secular critique obscures in translating it as 'secular' law. *Siyasa* has two dimensions in Islam, one being conceptually tied to political custom[5] and the other to religious authority. Because all Islamic jurists delegated the enforcement, if not the adjudication, of the 'rights of God' to the state, *siyasa* had a religious function too. In view of this overlap, a reinterpretation of the moral limits of *siyasa* gives the state new purviews over the 'rights of God.' Precisely because of the close association between *mu'amalat*, *'ibadat*, and *siyasa*, there are extensive jurisprudential works preoccupied with controlling state practice. What is less well understood, however, is how the state counteracted such efforts.

A survey of the discourse on morality and its relationship to custom is our starting point in exploring the Ottoman state's use of religious and secular law in asserting its hegemony.

The 'Good' and the 'Detestable' in Islamic Legal Theory

What is the status of an act before revelation assigns its value? Reinhart argues that the relevance of this question, posed by Muslim jurists themselves, was all but ignored by Islamicists who viewed it as an exercise in jurisprudential 'thought experiments.' As all Muslims lived after the era with which these scholars were concerned—that is, after revelation—scholars have dismissed the entire discourse as an intellectual polemic with little bearing on reality. In his discussion of Islamic legal theory, for instance, S. Hurgronje dismissed the relevance of the question of whether all acts are forbidden by nature except for those allowed by the divine law, concluding that while such musings may have been of importance to the Imam al-Haramayn (the imam of the two great mosques at Mecca and Medina), they added little to a correct understanding of Islam. Reinhart, however, argues that the polemicists were not just asking about acts "before revelation" but also "reflecting upon the important epistemological questions in the background. They were asking about the importance of 'revealed' knowledge against other sources of knowledge." In other words, are acts good or bad because they have an intrinsic value that is recognizable to the *'aql* (reason), or because of the value assigned to each by revelation? Reinhart concludes that "what was being determined through reflection on such topics as these was the relation between morality and culture."[6] Is there a natural morality, and are human beings innately capable of apprehending it through reason?

The answer to this question determines how jurists assess the status of an act as 'obligatory,' 'proscribed,' 'permitted,' 'disapproved,' or 'indifferent.' It also represents a rational attempt to "ground the valuations in something more than legal hermeneutic," that is, more than the rulings (*ahkam*) derived from scripture.[7] K. Abou El Fadl notes that because these acts were assessed on the basis of "higher-order/lower-order values [they] did not just refer to the five values of sharia, but also to moral imperatives."[8] These imperatives influenced the relationship between legal hermeneutics (or the relationship between jurisprudence and scripture) and the normative laws (custom) that predated them. This is made apparent when we consider that the phrase used for 'before revelation,' *qabl wurud al-shar'*, can mean 'before the *shar'* arrives,' 'before it is met with,' or 'before it takes effect.'[9]

Whether the customary laws that predate Islam are seen as valid or invalid is dependent, therefore, on how one answers the question, 'Is there a universal morality?' If the answer is affirmative, then a 'lie' told in pre-Islamic times is as sinful as a 'lie' told in Islamic times. If, on the other hand, morality can only be uncovered through revelation, and has no meaning outside of revelation, it *cannot* be determined that a 'lie' in pre-Islamic times was a sin at all. If, therefore, 'acts' have no status outside of that assigned to them by revelation, then the customary laws governing these 'acts' cannot have any determinate status and are neither valid nor invalid.

When this question was first raised in the ninth century, purportedly by Abu Hanifa himself, it elicited three responses: one, the view that proscribed the use of what came before, including the appeal to non-Muslim scripture; two, the view that permitted the use of what came before; and three, the view which held that acts had no status outside of that assigned to them by revelation, championed by Ibn Hanbal. Attributions made to Shafi'i reveal a similar ambiguity and hesitation about appealing to what came 'before revelation.'[10]

From the point of view of Muslim jurists, customs possess a dual identity. On the one hand, they represent 'positive laws'; on the other, they contain within them a 'positive morality.' The latter is generally of two types: 'morality as it is' without regard to its merits, and 'morality as it would be' if it conformed to the eternal or divine law. Custom fits into the first category of 'morality as it is.' The reason that some scholars ignore the distinction between 'morality as it is' and 'morality as it should be' is because they use sharia and *fiqh* interchangeably when referring to Islamic law, ignoring a jurisprudential distinction between the former as perfected divine law and the latter as a human approximation. The distinction is an important one, however, and goes to the heart of jurisprudential attitudes in Islam toward customary law.

At the heart of this juristic discourse, asserts Reinhart, is the debate over the "limitations of human moral-epistemological capacity" and "the nature of acts themselves."[11] Abou El Fadl adds that "the core logic of the debate focused on a hierarchy of normatives according to which lower-order values are evaluated in light of higher-order values."[12] As an example he points to the sharia requirement of justice, which would compel jurists to determine 'what is necessary for justice.' In other words, 'morality as it should be' is constantly informing, shaping, or potentially abrogating 'morality as it is.' Concepts of *maslaha* (utility/public good) and *istihsan* (juristic preference), which derive from the ethical determination of what is good (*husn*) and what is ugly/reprehensible (*qubh*), provide the legal tools by which this is actualized in practice.[13] For example, Shatibi uses the criterion of *husn* and *qubh* to argue that the practice of covering the head is a custom (*'ada*) subject to change, as it may be good in Muslim societies but not so elsewhere.[14] In other words, covering the head is a feature of 'morality as it is' in Muslim societies, not of 'morality as it should be.' Implicit here are notions of 'natural law' or a universal morality (perfected divine law) that can be 'uncovered' by qualified jurists.

Concepts of 'natural' morality have influenced the way in which Muslim jurists assessed the status of acts arising from custom, both 'before' and 'after' revelation. Islamic jurisprudence is often described as 'natural law,' or alternately 'positive law.' Since these are western terms, it may be helpful to outline the development of these concepts in the works of western jurists. Natural law, in Thomas Aquinas's view, "is nothing else than the rational creature's participation of the eternal law."[15] The 'rational creature,' being endowed with a share of divine providence and, therefore, of 'eternal reason,' is ably equipped to uncover the eternal law. In other words, a universal morality, containing within it an eternal law, exists and may be discovered through the application of human reason. This is akin to the Islamic concept of sharia, which, appropriately, translates into 'the way/path to the watering well.' 'The way,' the correct path to correct outward conduct, can be uncovered through both revelation and reason. The relation between law and reason is unmistakable, as in Aquinas's view "the participation of the eternal law in the rational creature is properly called a law, since a law is something pertaining to reason." Like Muslim jurists, he denies that the rational creature can ever hope to attain "a full participation of the dictate of the divine reason, but according to its own mode, and imperfectly." Positive law, on the other hand, is "law set by political superiors to political inferiors."[16] The source of 'positive' legislation is neither scripture nor revelation, but the concept of 'utility.' This is roughly correspondent to the concept of *siyasa* legislation. A second class of positive laws is set by "sentiments felt by an indeterminate body of men in regard to human conduct." These sentiments are "mere opinions" shaped by "positive morality."[17] Hence, if the sharia represents 'morality as it should be,' *fiqh* represents an imperfect, human approximation of it. 'Positive law,' on the other hand, represents 'morality as it is,' and is, in the Islamic context, shaped by local custom and *siyasa*.

Returning to the question posed at the outset, therefore, one must conclude that the status of an act arising from custom, either 'before revelation' or 'after revelation,' was well considered and assigned a definitive value. This value, derived from a consideration of what is 'beautiful' and what is 'ugly,' found expression in the twin judicial instruments of *istihsan* and *maslaha*. We may now explore the idea that the criteria by which this value was assigned served not only to legitimate, but also to delegitimate custom, when and where it failed to meet the sharia's criteria of 'morality as it should be.'

Custom in Islamic Legal Theory

The relationship of morality to custom receives considerable attention in the legal literature because the latter serves as a broad rubric under which the various social and normative standards associated with a given community, individual, or state are grouped. Yet, in spite of the attention given to the status of acts 'before revelation,' custom was never incorporated as a primary source of law alongside the Qur'an, Hadith, *qiyas*, and *ijma'*.[18] It was, however, accepted as a secondary source of law and eventually, in Libson's assessment, as a formal, albeit subsidiary, source of law.[19] The term 'custom' serves as a very large umbrella under which the various normative practices associated with a given culture are grouped. Because Islamic jurisprudence refused to make custom an official source of law, no matter how much it may have contributed to the law jurisprudents produced, scholars have argued that this is evidence of the dissonance between theory and practice. But instead of dissonance, it conveys the effort expended to keep 'morality as it is' from overshadowing 'morality as it should be.' Moreover, as Libson has shown, Muslim jurists did eventually confer a measure of recognition on custom in the eleventh century, classifying it as imperative law in some of the major Maliki and Hanafi works, a trend that continued to gain momentum from the fourteenth through the sixteenth century.[20] Prior to the ninth century, however, Libson writes that "so long as the literary redaction of *hadith* collections was still in progress . . . new customs and practices could find refuge in the *hadith*-literature and there was no special need to grant them formal, independent recognition, that is to accept custom as a source of law."[21]

By the beginning of the Abbasid period most of these terms had undergone technical specification and further individuation into distinct categories of custom. From the eleventh century on, jurists incorporated custom under the maxim that "what is known by custom is equivalent to that which is stipulated," giving it the force of imperative law.[22] The Hanafi jurist al-Sarakhsi (d. 1097) recognized it as a material source of law, a view that prevailed in his day, giving it the force of a written stipulation. Anything dictated by custom, in this view, equals that dictated by text, and therefore custom, whether general or specific, did constitute a basis for judicial decisions.[23] Sarakhsi and others were able to do this by bringing *'urf* (customary law) under the umbrella of other secondary sources of law, such as *istihsan* and *darura* (necessity), paving the way for the next generation of jurists.[24]

K. Masud argues that "the foundations of modern renaissance in Islamic legal thought were laid in the fourteenth century by the Muslim jurists who wrote on the methodology and the ends of Islamic law."[25] And while Hanafis worked to incorporate custom into the law, it was a Maliki who built on Sarakhsi's ideas to develop the theory of *maslaha* as a 'secondary' source of law alongside the primary *usul*. A judicial theory of *istihsan* and *maslaha* was constructed by Shatibi to give the concept of *tahsiniyat* ('embellishments') legal teeth.[26] A legal principle relating to custom was developed, stipulating that if the side of *maslaha* predominates, the matter is considered *maslaha*; if it does not, it is *mafsada* (public detriment).[27] Shatibi and others could do this because they believed "in the relationship of *shari'a* to *'ada* (custom) more than in the relationship between *shari'a* and *'aql* (reason)."[28] In other words, 'morality as it is' was a more reliable indicator of 'morality as it should be' than a reason-based approximation of the latter would be. As Shatibi saw it, "the values of good and evil already existed" within *'ada* but they were often confused.[29] The sharia never rejects custom entirely since the sharia of Muhammad confirmed many, if not most, of the *'adat* (pl. of *'ada*) of *jahili* Arabia. But if Shatibi was flexible on the topic of custom in *mu'amalat*, he was notably less so when it came to the influence of the latter on the 'rights of God' (*'ibadat*), calling it a 'negative innovation.'

The next generation of sixteenth-century scholars undertook the first serious attempt to incorporate practical custom into the law without granting it formal recognition. By this point, argues Libson, Hanafis frequently appealed to it as an independent source of law. In an attribution to Qadi Husayn, "probably by al-Marwazi al-Shafi'i (d. 1070) by Ahmad Muhammad al-Qastallani (d. 1517)," we read: "Resort to custom is one of the five foundations on which the law *(fiqh)* is built."[30] In a work of the same title, *al-Ashbah wa-l-naza'ir*, al-Suyuti (d. 1505) writes: "Know that the consideration of *'ada* and *'urf* is referred to in jurisprudence on so many questions that they rendered it a source of law in the chapter on the [moral] truths which may be uncovered through deduction and custom."[31] The conclusion to his investigation delivers the maxim, "What is proven by *'urf* is equivalent to that proven by a *shar'i* proof."[32]

Significantly, Ibn Nujaym (d. 1563), an Egyptian Hanafi jurist, was the first to devote a separate chapter *(bab)* to the topic. According to him, the sixth principle of *fiqh* holds that "custom is authoritative" because "what is good in the view of Muslims is good in God's view."[33] The seventeenth-century historian Hezafenn Husayn, expressing the common sentiments of his time, said, "Every age has its *orf* and every *orf* its requirements. . . . He who does not know the *orf* of his contemporaries is ignorant *(jahil)*."³⁴

All of the above seems to indicate a growing inclination to afford custom recognition, or what Libson calls its eventual acceptance as a formal source of law. However, one should not assume that the more recognition afforded custom, the more authority it held in practice. A closer examination reveals that with each stage in the development of these doctrines, custom became more narrowly defined and limited in practice. By the time it was accorded written confirmation in the eleventh century, for example, custom had been deprived of the broad and fluid features it possessed in the ninth century. It was no longer a term encompassing the practice of the Prophet, the ancestors, the general community, and the practice of other religious communities: now it referred to an amalgamation of broadly related and clearly delineated concepts—*'urf*, *'adat*, *'amal* (customary practice), *adab* (prescribed Islamic behavior, manners, or etiquette), and *siyasa/qanun*. By the time it was recognized as a 'secondary' source of law in the sixteenth century, centuries of discussion on what constituted *husn* and *qubh*—on what was acceptable innovation and what was not—had helped define the boundaries of Muslim moral thought ever more precisely.

In the same way that Ibn Taymiya's work helped bring *siyasa* under the aegis of the jurists, Shatibi's development of the theory of *maslaha* brought popular custom under the aegis of *fiqh*-based legal devices. Thus, while it is true that the theories of *maslaha* and *istihsan* allowed for the admission of custom, they also provided firm criteria by which to assess what could *not* be legitimately admitted. In the final analysis, it was the theory of the legists, and their discourse on the limits of *siyasa* and *'ada* (valid or invalid custom), that made it possible for Egyptian jurists to challenge the legality of codified state custom, or *qanun*.

Muslim scholars considered every aspect of state administration, be it *siyasa*, *qanun*, or bureaucratic administration, to be a branch of custom.³⁵ Heyd writes that "synonymous with kanun in meaning is 'adet," and that the regulations of Uzun Hasan are also sometimes called *'adat*.³⁶ The term is also used interchangeably with *yasa*.³⁷ Ibn Taymiya used the term *al-'ada al-sultaniya* (sultanic practice or custom), in a manner equivalent to the Ottoman *örf-i padisahi*,³⁸ while officials who carried out the sultan's orders were called *ehli-i 'örf*.³⁹ But there remained separate branches of custom (based in community practice) alongside *siyasa*. Heyd explains that

> In many cases, the expression *şer' ve örf* [sharia and *'urf*] may have the same meaning as *şer' ve kanun* ... indeed, in some contexts *'örf* is still used in a meaning close to its original significance, reflecting the fact that the Ottoman *kanun*, like the *kanun*s of other rulers, often confirmed existing local practice.[40]

Fleischer does not hesitate to place *qanun* firmly within the domain of custom:

> The cumulative character of dynastic law was such that the ascription of a *qanunnama* to a particular sultan did not affect its legality; the two greatest lawgivers of the empire, Mehmed II and Sulayman, were compilers of custom as much as promulgators of new regulations, required by new circumstances.[41]

But *siyasa* in Islam has two dimensions: the first is 'secular' in that it grants rulers or states the authority to promulgate laws derived from customs, while the second is religious, obliging rulers or states to enforce the rights of God against wine drinkers, fornicators, adulterers, and thieves, or to enforce the *hudud*. Sarakhsi assigns exclusive authority over the fixed penalties of the *hudud* to the sovereign.[42] Imber argues that this division and "the classification of these offences and the penalties for them does not in any sense arise out of the structural logic of the law, but solely out of scriptural authority."[43] *Siyasa* yields, therefore, to non-qadi adjudication, otherwise known as *mazalim* courts, supported by *shurta* (paramilitary or police forces) in cases of criminal law.[44]

The close association between custom and *siyasa* is evident from the fact that scholars such as Ibn Taymiya use the terms *maslaha* and *siyasa* interchangeably. It is precisely this close association that sparked a general juristic movement after the advent of Mongol rule,

> when states adopted or imitated the Mongol practice of dynastic laws and customs called *yasak* or *yasa*, and often applied the term *siyasa* to these rules. ... Makrizi went so far as to claim that "*siyasa*" in Mamluk military-class usage was not Arabic at all, but derives from *yasa*.[45]

To curb this tendency, a staunch opponent of syncretic popular and state customs like Ibn Taymiya was willing to accept the limited application of *maslaha*, if only because it brought *siyasa* under the aegis of the ulama.[46] Shatibi, on the other hand, opposed all forms of 'innovation' arising from custom, but only in the area of *'ibadat*, and sought thereby to avoid any repetition of the 'confusion' in pre-Islamic *jahili* times between *'amal* (customary practice) and *shar'* (practice stemming from sharia).[47]

Shatibi rejected adaptation to social change in ritual and worship, family, and trusts (all falling under *'ibadat*), but he showed flexibility with respect to taxes (an area of *mu'amalat*). Out of forty cases of religious/social 'innovation,' Shatibi accepted social change in fourteen and rejected twenty-three.[48] Thus he distinguished between two kinds of obligations, those which are absolute and not subject to change, consisting of *'ibadat*, or the 'rights of God,' and those which are relative and subject to change, consisting of *'adat* and including *mu'amalat* or the 'rights of humans.' The former are liturgical *(ta'abbudi)* and the latter utilitarian *(maslahi)*.[49] Although both sharia and *'adat* are closely connected and both willed by God, the latter "belongs to the creative will," while the former "belongs to the Legislative." Any changes in custom must consider, therefore, "the intent of the law" *(maqasid al-sharia)*.[50]

Shatibi also identified two basic categories of living customs: 'universal customs' *(al-'awa'id al-'amma)*, that do not change with time, place, or state (including very limited biological activities such as eating, drinking, and feeling joy and sorrow), and those customs associated with a particular region or culture *(al-'awa'id al-jariya)*, which do change with time, place, or state (including forms of dress, dwelling, and so on). Here change occurs in five ways: 1) differences in *husn* and *qubh* based on social norms, such as covering the head; 2) change resulting from technological shifts; 3) differences in *mu'amalat*, such as giving a dowry before marriage; 4) differences arising from considerations external to the act in question, such as determining the age of maturity on the basis of either puberty or chronological age;[51] and 5) those 'irregular' *'awa'id* which are associated with an individual, for example, habits, hobbies, and the like.[52] But even those *'adat* which could, in theory, change were conditional upon three things: first, custom could not work retroactively—in other words, valid *'adat* must represent a common and recurrent phenomenon; second, it could not contravene the principles of a contractual agreement; and third, custom should not violate scripture *(nass)*.[53]

'Adat belong to the physical world and are constant. Shatibi uses the term in the sense of habits and behavior as well as custom, "as an opposite

term to *'ibadat.*"⁵⁴ When an event happens contrary to *'ada* it is considered a "breach in custom" *(kharq al-'ada)*. The enormity of this violation is underlined by the fact that only the prophets are allowed to breach customs.⁵⁵ This is not to suggest that all *'adat* are constant, however, for only "universal customs" are perpetually so *(al-'awa'id al-mustamirra)*, but, Shatibi argues, change in custom should occur gradually.⁵⁶ Furthermore, change could only be permitted in areas of *mu'amalat*, but never *'ibadat*, where it was always considered negative innovation *(bid'a)*.⁵⁷ Not so for the sixteenth-century Ibn Nujaym, who argued that *bid'a* could occur in both realms of law.⁵⁸

Ibn Nujaym's departure from Shatibi can only be understood in the context of his Ottoman-Egyptian setting, where innovation in matters of both *'ibadat* and *mu'amalat* was a source of strife. In the former, for example, the reform that most outraged local scholars was the *qanun* of 927, when the Ottomans imposed a marriage tax *(rusum)* of sixty nifs for a virgin and thirty for marriage to a widow or divorcee. A portion was to go the *'aqid* (notary), some to the *shahid* (witness), and the rest remitted to the governor.⁵⁹ The *rusum*, a customary tax levied on judicial services throughout Anatolia, was universalized via this decree and levied across the empire. Qadis were given little choice but to "follow *al-sayq al-'uthmani*" [the Ottoman laws]. Seeing it as a penalty against marriage and divorce, the people, writes Ibn Iyas, refused and "the *sunna* of marriage was discontinued" for a time.⁶⁰

Al-Azhar protested against the Ottoman marriage tax, and about a hundred jurists descended upon the governor, Khayrbek (who only met the most senior among them), to voice their opposition. Objecting to the marriage tax on *shar'i* grounds, they argued that it violated the Sunna of the Prophet, who was married by exchanging a simple silver ring, six ansaf of silver, and the reading of a verse from the Holy Book. They also argued that it made the costs of marriage too prohibitive, as the couple also had to pay the witnesses as well as the *muqaddimin* (civil servant who represented the sultan in court). Quoting numerous Hadiths contradicting the new Ottoman marriage tax, the jurist attempted to shake the governor's resolve. However, indicating that the decision was not his to make, the governor proclaimed: "Who am I? *Al-Khundikar* [the Ottoman sultan] has decreed such. . . . In Egypt you are to follow *al-sayq al-'uthmani* [the Ottoman laws]." To which the Azhari shaykh 'Isa replied: "This is the *sayq* of *kufr* [laws of the unbelievers]." This comment led to the shaykh's incarceration until a group of *amir*s interceded on his behalf.⁶¹

But, undaunted, other jurists continued to debate the marriage tax until, finally, the governor indicated his powerlessness to deviate from the *qanun* by conceding to the Maliki Shaykh Shams al-Din al-Laqani, "I fear for my own neck more than I fear for yours. Go in God's name."⁶² They left, but not before threatening to send an official delegation to inform Sultan Sulayman himself of the injustices occurring in Egypt and to close the mosques and schools. Taking their threats seriously, the governor sent an emissary to Istanbul, presumably to seek further instructions. The fact that no changes or revisions were made to the *qanun* is indicative of the Sublime Porte's unyielding response.

By the end of the century, opposition to the law could still be found, judging by Sha'rani's warning: "Pay willingly the money due to the *qanun* and the *qassam* [tax collector for mariage contracts]. If one does not give of his free will, he will give in spite of himself. He is wise who knows his time."⁶³ We have already seen how jurists argued against this law, namely that it had no basis in *fiqh*, and might actually have violated the Sunna by taxing one of the 'rights of God' and introducing unnecessary hardship and cost.

Ibn Nujaym's willingness to label changes in *mu'amalat* as *bid'a* is a naked critique of Ottoman *siyasa* and its codified, universal *qanun*.⁶⁴ A 'universal *'urf*,' he reasoned, can be never be promulgated on the basis of a local custom. Quoting Bukhari's ruling that *'urf* always represents the 'particular' *(khass)* and can never serve as the basis of a universal practice, he defends the legitimacy of myriad local customs against Ottoman standardization.⁶⁵ He also uses this same maxim in a barely veiled critique of the Ottoman marriage tax and the co-option of the local judiciary into a state bureaucracy. Asking, "Is it permissible for a judge to accept gifts?" and "Does a judge receive pay on his holiday from *bayt al-mal* [the state treasury]?" he concludes that only "the customs of a people" can determine the answer.⁶⁶ Judges are permitted to receive an amount not to exceed that which is stipulated by local *'ada*.⁶⁷ If the amount received exceeds that established by custom, the difference should be returned. The distance between Ibn Nujaym and Ibn Taymiya and Shatibi reflects the distinct political and social geographies of their days.

Winter alludes to the controversy in Cairo over the legality of *qanun* in quoting Sha'rani:

> The father of our Shaykh said, I asked Ahmad Ibn Yusuf al-Hanafi while he was serving as a *qadi* in Damascus about the legality of the *yasaq*, that is the fee that the *qadi* collects. The legal 'provisions are derived from the Qur'an, the Sunna, the consensus or the analogy: from which of the four do you take this *yasak*?' He was quiet and then said: 'No by God, it is according to the ways of the clients (*mawali*).' I said to him: 'Ignorance should not be a model.'[68]

Winter also comments that

> Nothing the Ottomans did provoke as much anger as their legal and juridical innovations, particularly in the sensitive area of personal law. . . . The most offensive legal change was a tax on marriage contracts called *yasaq*. . . . A Maghribi *'alim* . . . cried into the governor's face: "This is the infidels' law!"[69]

R. Repp views similar conflicts across the empire as symptoms of 'tension' between *qanun* and sharia explained in terms of the "universal, systematically developed character of the *şeriat* and . . . the limited, pre-eminently pragmatic and applied nature of the *kanun*."[70] I would argue that it was exactly the opposite. If by sharia he means Islamic jurisprudence, then it is the latter which allows for *ikhtilaf* (judicial disputation), through a multiplicity of schools and a jurisprudential methodology which can, in theory, yield a multitude of opinions. The *qanun*, on the other hand, may be pragmatic but it is delimited rather than 'limited,' modifying aspects of *'ibadat* as well as *mu'amalat* to reflect a universal 'perfected' law. A familiarity with the juristic criteria for assessing what is valid and what is invalid innovation (*bid'a*) may help clarify the fulcrum of debate.

For their part, the Ottomans never employed the term *bid'a* to refer to their legal reforms, not even positive *bid'a*. Innovation could only originate in non-sultanic custom and could be classified as 'recognized custom and innovation' (*bid'at-i ma'rufa*) and 'rejected innovation and custom' (*bid'at-i marduda*), also called *hayf* (injustice), *zulm* (oppression), and *sena'at* (fabricated).[71] Heyd writes that it "is to be noticed that the *shari'ah* term *bid'at* in official Ottoman usage signifies not only innovations contrary to the religious law but also those in contravention of the *kanun*."[72] Innovation through *qanun* was only referred to as *tajdid* (renewal). In the Cairo *sijill*s, the *qanun* standardizing weights and measurements is called "oppressive renewal" *(tajdid muzlim)*.[73] In the *Qanunnama* of Baghdad of 1527, the same *qanun*s are referred to as "recognized customs" *('adat-i ma'lum)*, and "illegal innovations" are abolished.[74]

Needless to say, from the perspective of Arab jurists such as Ibn Nujaym, the application of the *qanun* came at the cost of a 'breach' in local customs, and as such qualified as *bid'a* rather than *tajdid*. In Anatolia, the legality of Ottoman *qanun*, which met the sharia's conditions and conformed to established local norms, was not in doubt. In Egypt and other Arab provinces, the *qanun* (originating in and flowing from Turco-Islamic traditions) represented the universalization of a particular *(khass)* *'ada*. It neither conformed to local practice, nor shied away from penetrating private spaces, the rights of the bride, women's attire, and freedom of movement. When, therefore, local ulama charged that Ottoman *qanun* violated the sharia, they were referring to its invalidity as a translocal corpus of 'foreign,' 'imported' customs. Imported custom, they argued, is invalidated by the first rule governing the validity of *'ada/'urf*: that it must represent a common and recurrent, local phenomenon.

The rebuttal to jurists like Ibn Nujaym was the *Siyasat-i ilahi*, an inventive work of Islamic political philosophy not merely suited to the regionally bound changes of the day, but ringing in the emerging modern international order. Although variously refracted by the expansion of European power in the late modern period, the reflection of these intellectual and institutional trends demands further study in much of the Islamic writing and activism of the late modern period, particularly given the resonance of appeals for a return to the caliphate even in the present. But from a legal standpoint, it is the doctrine of *namus* that stands at the core of this rebuttal.

The *Siyasat-i ilahi* and *Namus* Laws

The *Siyasat-i ilahi*, an innovative synthesis of juristic, philosophical, and Sufi thought, concocted by state bureaucrats and jurists, redefined the Ottoman caliphate in the sixteenth century. Although these intellectuals emphasized dynasticism, the philosophy underwriting their form of caliphate lessened the role of ethnicity in determining candidature for the highest political office in Islam. It also employed the legislative authority accorded only to 'classical' caliphs in earlier juristic political philosophy to legitimate and promote bureaucratic states ultimately legislated by reason, in the interests of constructing ethnically and religiously inclusive political identities in the process.

It is widely noted that the account of Salim I's (r. 1512–20) acceptance of the robe of universal caliphate from the last in the Abbasid line is a myth. That the tale originated in the late modern period, a time when Ottoman claims to the highest office were broadly trumpeted, suggests that Salim and his immediate predecessors bore caliphal titles in keeping with the broader conventions of the day. The same cannot be so easily argued in the case of his successor, Sulayman I (r. 1520–66), and Sulayman's successors.

Colin Imber argues that Sulayman claimed "not merely the title but also the office of Caliphate with its implications of universal sovereignty."[75] His thesis is based on a close reading of the fatwas and other writings of the scholar and jurist Abu al-Su'ud (d. 1574). This son of a prominent scholarly family of ulama and Sufis, who had long been close to the premier personages of the political realm, was a highly regarded madrasa professor and judge before he assumed the highest judicial post in the state, that of Shaykh al-Islam, which he held from 1545 to 1574.[76] His writings are presented as confirmation that, beginning in Sulayman's reign, "the Ottoman use of the title [caliph] acquired a doctrinal as well as a rhetorical significance" by according the sultan a role as "both the interpreter and the executor of the sharia"—a function of the 'classical' caliphs alone in established juristic political philosophy.[77] As for the problem of non-Quraysh lineage, Abu al-Su'ud ignores the longstanding perspective entirely to proclaim, as in the law books of Buda, Skopje, and Thessaloniki, that Sulayman is the "inheritor of the Great Caliphate from father to son." Not only is the entire Ottoman dynasty thus established as the holder of universal sovereignty, but "God Most High" is credited with having "bestowed the Caliphate of the Earth" on the Ottomans in direct succession from the four Rashidun ('rightly guided') caliphs who followed the Prophet.[78] Why the Ottomans? Abu al-Su'ud's response, at least according to Imber, is that the "imperial magnificence of the Ottoman Empire at its height was itself proof that God had appointed the Ottoman Sultan as Caliph."[79]

There was, therefore, consensus among scholars, but the issue hinged on how significant the office of the caliphate was. As Hodgson puts it, "the special Ottoman synthesis of state and Shari'ah . . . did support the idea of Caliphate. But it did so only by the standards of Faylasufs [philosophers] and the later Falsafah [Greek philosophy]-inspired legists, in the same manner as the other great monarchs of the time: all were Caliphs within their own territories."[80] The universal sovereignty of 'classical' caliphs, not to mention their legislative role, remained an unjustifiable leap from the perspective of juristic political philosophy. The fact that the Shaykh al-Islam was willing to make that leap, however, preferring the "standards" of philosophers to those of jurists to confer the "caliphate of the world" on the Ottomans, is indisputably significant. Imber links this audacious move to the broader bureaucratic reforms initiated in the reign of Sulayman. The literally universal sovereignty exercised by the 'classical' caliphs is incidental to Abu al-Su'ud. The true goal is the legislative authority as both the "interpreter and the executor of the sharia" that comes with the caliphate of old. Particularly since the decline of the Abbasids and rise of non-Quraysh sultans, legislation was bifurcated into *siyasa* (the domain of the state) and sharia (the realm of the jurists). The common adoption of caliphal titles did not alter this binary. Only as caliphs in the 'classical' sense could the Ottomans endow the codified *qanun*s (sultanic law books) of the *siyasa* with a cloak of sanctity.[81] Universal sovereignty alone could limit the authority of the jurists, while enabling the bureaucratization of the legal establishment, by allowing the state to choose which of several competing juristic opinions would be enforced as a standardized 'sharia.' This suggests that Ottoman claims of universal sovereignty were spurred by the very 'crises' of the sixteenth century, reflective of the early modern condition, that required the state to transform itself, as most Ottomanists agree, "from a military conquest state into a bureaucratic state and bastion of Sunni Islam."[82]

While motives for attributing universal sovereignty to the Ottoman caliphs abounded, the justification of this position remained problematic. Even as the Shaykh al-Islam of a major world power, Abu al-Su'ud's mere assertion of the Ottomans' divine right to universal sovereignty, even given their 'imperial magnificence,' appears wholly insufficient in influencing enduring doctrinal development. As Hodgson argues, Abu al-Su'ud's evasion reflects his dependence on the "standards" of philosophers, the latter no less representative of old ways than jurists.

Studies of specific political philosophers reflect the same assessment. For example, Antony Black follows the lead of both Heyd and Fleischer to credit Tursun Beg (d. 1491)—who rose to the rank of state treasurer (*diwan* secretary and *daftardar*)—with the composition of "the first Ottoman essay in political thought."[83] In his *Tarikh-i Abu al-Fath*, Tursun Beg writes of two realms of legislation: the *siyasat-i sultani* (sultanic government), identified with *'urf* (custom) and the need to maintain order in the "material" *(zahir)* world, and the *siyasat-i ilahi* (divine government, in Heyd's reading), to ensure that "not only the order of the material world, but also that of the 'hidden' *(batin)*, i.e., spiritual, world is instituted."[84] Black goes on to explain that, in Tursun Beg's estimation, jurists identify *siyasat-i ilahi* with sharia and name its "legislator" *(sari')* as the Prophet. Philosophers, however, speak of its "institutor" *(wazi')* as the *namus*. Black, Heyd, and Fleischer recognize the juristic definition in Tursun Beg's writing and conclude that the author intended to "subordinate *qanun* to *shari'a*."[85] Nevertheless, this conclusion depends on how *namus* is translated and *siyasat-i ilahi* is defined, by others besides Tursun Beg.

Heyd sets the tone for Black and others to translate *namus* as "rational law."[86] This reflects the philosopher Ahmad Miskawayh's (d. 1030) usage, for one, in which *namus* is understood in the original Greek manner as "*siyasa* and *tadbir* [administration]."[87] But according to M. Plessner, *namus* more widely connoted "divine law," "with or without the addition of *ilahi*," as revealed through the prophets.[88] For example, Ibn Sina (d. 1037) based his definition on Aristotle, using it in the sense of revealed law in his discussion of the rational sciences. "The *Falasifa* mean by law *(namus)*," he wrote, "the *Sunna*, the permanent, certain pattern, and the revelation sent down."[89] E.I.J. Rosenthal adds the important insight that both strands were tied together by Nasir al-Din al-Tusi (d. 1274), who wrote that justice is served by three things: the *namus ilahi* (divine law), the ruler, and currency.[90] Thus, although maintaining the philosophical perspective in stating "the greatest *namus* is the *shari'a*," al-Tusi asserted that "the second [*namus*] is the *sultan* who obeys *Shari'a*—for *din* and *mulk* are twins—and the third *namus* is money."[91]

Jalal al-Din al-Dawani (d. 1503)—a contemporary of Tursun Beg based in Iran—is widely recognized to have carried forward al-Tusi's conception.[92] His work was also favored by Ottoman jurists like Abu al-Su'ud. It is therefore of utmost significance that in his *Akhlaq-i Jalali*, all references to *namus ilahi* were replaced with the word 'sharia,' and the ruler was preserved as "the second *namus*."[93] Thus al-Dawani denied the jurists' hermeneutical schematic, *usul al-fiqh*, sole custody of the divine law, whether defined as *namus ilahi* or sharia. The ruler was the second *namus*.

This does not suggest that al-Dawani ceased to view the sharia as the greatest *namus*, only that he asserted the coequality of *siyasa* (derived from the ruler) and *fiqh* (the method of jurists) in establishing the sharia's overarching cosmology of moral perfection. Like the jurists' law, state law was also capable of apprehending, and enjoined to enforce, that "permanent, certain pattern" of divine law. The only condition al-Dawani interjected was that it must be the *siyasa* of a "caliph" or the author's innovative institution of "imamate"—one whose head upheld the qualifications and authority of a 'classical' caliph, but was not of Quraysh lineage.[94] And regarding universal sovereignty, al-Dawani also broke with the past by resolving that there could be more than one imam. The essential qualification raising an individual ruler to imamate was government with "equity" *(insaf)*.[95] As M. Arkoun clarifies, the philosopher's concept of *insaf* is rooted in Aristotelian thought, meaning "to grant rights" or to "assure others the same right that one claims for one's self."[96] The concept is further expressed particularly in Hanafi *fiqh* (the school most prevalent in Ottoman and Mughal contexts) through the juristic tool of *istihsan* (juristic preference), allowing "a more flexible and circumstantial conception and practice" of law than that produced by *qiyas* (analogical reasoning).[97] The opposite of government with equity, in the work of al-Dawani and other jurists and philosophers, is "false government," or any that adheres "to the principle of force" and treats its constituents as "slaves."[98] Al-Dawani, therefore, equated the Platonic philosopher-king with a 'classical' caliph or imam, while placing the sultanate and all other modes of government essentially among three classes of the unjust state, the highest of which was only partially redeemed even when adhering to the jurists' sharia.

By Sulayman's era, al-Dawani's conception of *siyasat-i ilahi* is evident in various writings other than Abu al-Su'ud's. A prime example is the *Akhlaq-i 'Ala'i* of 'Ali Chelebi Kinalizade (d. 1572), a philosopher, Sufi, judge, and eventually chief judge of Anatolia. As Black shows, Kinalizade "reproduces" al-Dawani's celebrated work on the same topic "point by point," but in a manner "adapted . . . to Ottoman circumstances."[99] Kinalizade not only praised Sulayman as a philosopher-king who had established the Platonic "virtuous city," but lauded his enforcing the sharia and "his own institutes from *shari'* principles." Thus, in Kinalizade's opinion, Sulayman successfully "integrated rational and revealed law" (that is, *siyasa* and sharia), so his government was deserving of the "true Caliphate."[100] The argument is further echoed in former *wazir* Lutfi Pasha's (d. 1563) assertion that the Ottoman sultan was "imam" and "caliph"—that is, the imam "who maintains the Faith and governs the kingdom of Islam with equity" and the caliph "who commands the good and prohibits the evil." Furthermore, his heirs possessed the same authority by means of inheritance alone.[101]

While al-Dawani's concept of imams and caliphs clearly underwrites Ottoman usage, to Black and others these writings imply nothing more than evidence of the stasis of Ottoman political thought, indicating not only a dearth of thinkers, but that those present were no more than "classical Falsafa dried and reconstituted."[102] Leslie Peirce, on the other hand, makes a fuller assessment in recognizing these Ottoman works as innovations extending from "Islamic religious texts, Greco-Islamic political philosophy, traditions of ancient Persian statecraft and eschatological and esoteric doctrines."[103] This leads Peirce to conclude that "Imam" was "probably the more important title" as the "title of Caliph was in common use" by the sixteenth century.[104] Given the innovations represented by specifically Ottoman works, however, a definitive conclusion on the Ottoman caliphate requires a closer consideration of the eschatological and esoteric doctrines to which Peirce refers.

The influence of Sufism in various spheres of Muslim societies, including politics, is not disputed anywhere. Although Sufis were organized into multiple orders (*tariqa*s) by the sixteenth century, Muhyi al-Din ibn al-'Arabi's (d. 1240) concept of *wahdat al-wujud* (unity of being) had achieved virtual hegemony as the central theosophical concept of Sufi thought. Although rooted in neo-Platonic concepts of emanation, its sociopolitical implication for Muslims was that when all 'Being' is 'united,' the categories of Muslims and *dhimmi*s upheld by *fiqh* appear difficult to maintain. Ibn al-'Arabi confirms this throughout his *Fusus al-hikam*, but nowhere more succinctly than in the following lines: "Men may be divided into two groups. The first travel a way they know . . . which is their Straight Path. The second group travel a way they do not know . . . which is their Straight Path."[105]

For Sufi orders, founding *shaykh*s or *pir*s were that Perfect Human. Furthermore, in the more politically oriented Sufi literature, the Perfect Human assumed the role of the Platonic philosopher-king. As such, the various interpretations by the Perfect Humans promoted differing perspectives on the centrality of the jurists' sharia, ranging from absolute conformity (the ultra-'Sober' view) to absolute disregard (the ultra-'Intoxicated' perspective).[106] Beginning in the fifteenth century, Mehmed II (r. 1444–46 and 1451–81) broke deep Ottoman bonds to the Intoxicated Khalwatiya order to establish enduring ties with the Sober Naqshbandiya order, ostensibly due to the former's public popularity and connections with political opponents, but also as a function of their aversion to civil authority and rival claims to caliphal authority as Perfect Humans.[107] In their stead, Mehmed reached out to the likes of the Naqshbandi Nur al-Din al-Jami (d. 1492), whose celebrated *al-Durra al-fakhira* he commissioned. The work is most significant for the manner in which it argues for the "uncreatedness" and "createdness" of the Qur'an, thus ameliorating the claim of jurists to sole interpretive rights, while opening the door to civil power.[108] By the time of Sulayman, the Naqshbandiya's place in Ottoman state and society was well established, extending, but not restricted, to their support in wars with the Shi'a Safavids.

The Ottomans' Sober relationship with Sufism confirms the importance of the imamate, al-Dawani's philosophically-inspired juristic model. Peirce is quite right to conclude that this institution also most "effectively countered" a Safavid ideology wrapped in the Shi'i concept of imamate. But Shi'ism in general was not the specific reason caliphal claims were important. The ideal of the universal caliphate lingers in the manner in which the esoteric doctrines of philosophers and Sufis are placed within the eschatological significance of the late sixteenth century—the turn of the second Islamic *(hijri)* millennium. S. Subrahmanyam's argument that millenarianism, a "Eurasian" phenomenon, formed an essential component of early modernity applies to the Ottoman case. The Safavids rose to power as the "perfect masters" *(murshid-i kamil)* of a Sufi order and ruled as representatives of the Hidden Imam and the promised *mahdi*.[109] C. Fleischer emphasizes strongly that the messianic and apocalyptic movements of the time bred a similar preoccupation with renewal and a reborn universal caliph/*mahdi* for a new age in the Ottoman context. Millenarianism, in fact, played a crucial role in justifying a non-Quraysh universal caliph in Ottoman literature.[110] Although S. Buzov makes a case for the ebb of millenarian literature by the end of Sulayman's reign, the persistence of Safavid rivalry, the continuous use of a 'classical' caliph's titles and legislative authority, and the Eurasian scope of millenarianism at the time, implies that its importance to bolstering universal claims cannot be so easily dismissed.[111]

Returning to the insufficiencies of Abu al-Su'ud's proclamations, it appears that in light of the growing influence of the concept of *siyasat-i ilahi* and the changing definition of *namus*, the Naqshbandiya connection, Safavid Shi'ism, and the prevalence of millenarian expectations, the Shaykh al-Islam could afford to be nonchalant toward established juristic political philosophy. Jurists were not the sole group with doctrinal claims to the sharia, and juristic political philosophy was not the only legitimate expression of Islam. Thus, although Sulayman and his heirs were not universal sovereigns according to established juristic political philosophy, the non-Quraysh Ottomans bore the titles and exercised the authority of 'classical' caliphs through a synthesis of al-Dawani's *siyasat-i ilahi*, Naqshbandi doctrines of Perfect Humans, and al-Jami's perspective on the ruler's relationship to the Qur'an. The waves of millenarian expectation added fuel to their claims. These were 'early modern caliphs,' promulgating the *siyasat-i ilahi* through direct access to the *namus*, exercising the intuition of Sober Sufis to legislate, bringing the millenarian order promised by *mahdi*s. That Abu al-Su'ud and Kinalizade were themselves jurists of the highest rank precludes the idea that no more than old tensions between jurists and bureaucrats were being replayed. Rather, they represent a tug of war between state and nonstate jurists. They attest to the doctrinal and ideological innovation occurring among state jurists, writing and instituting an early modern Islamic polity in which philosophical and Sufi political doctrines were deployed to challenge the nonstate jurists' last line of defense against the state's increasingly dominant legislative authority.

Although the enduring influence of this enterprise will be discussed in subsequent chapters, evidence of the recognition of (at least) Sulayman's universal claims provides an appropriate transition from nonstate juristic reasoning. As long as a nominal Abbasid caliph had resided in Cairo, sultans far and wide had sought legitimacy by means of his investiture.

This had even been the case for the expansive and longstanding Delhi Sultanate (1206–1526).[112] By the fifteenth century, however, intensive diplomatic exchanges between the Ottomans and Delhi's rivals, the southerly Bahmanid Sultanate (1347–1527), opened a new chapter in relations between Mediterranean and South Asian polities.[113] In the sixteenth century, Ottoman expansion into Egypt and Portuguese threats to their Indian Ocean trade elevated the level of interaction to a formal alliance and joint naval operations with the Sultanate of Gujarat (1407–1583). A contemporary account of these exchanges can be read in the Ottoman admiral Sidi 'Ali Reis's (d. 1562) *Mir'at al-Memalik*, which covers the author's experiences from 1553 to 1556. He is not only amazed to hear that the *khutba* is read in the Ottomans' name in the mosques of the "Khakan of China"—a caliphal prerogative—but records various expressions of deference to the Ottomans from Baluchistan to Gujarat.[114] Particularly in the sultanate of Gujarat, he meets a strong pro-Ottoman faction of officials, including a *wazir* who refers to Sulayman as the "Padshah of Islam," and another who hopes "the land of Gujarat will soon be joined to the protected domains of the Ottoman Empire."[115] That these are all allusions to Ottoman claims of universal sovereignty as caliphs, not merely imams, is confirmed by the admiral's encounter with none other than the Mughal emperor Humayun (r. 1530–56), who sent Sidi 'Ali home to Istanbul with a letter addressing Sulayman as "Caliph of the World."[116]

The Ottoman caliphate collapsed the barrier between worldly *siyasa* and religious law. It would not be incorrect to speak of an assimilation between *siyasa* and sharia, and of the Islamization of *qanun*. However, the implied subordination of *qanun* to *fiqh* in this schematic is grossly misleading. A measure of alignment between Islamic jurisprudence and state legislation took place, but on the latter's terms. There was a dialectical shift in the relationship between *fiqh* and *siyasa* that placed both on the same ontological footing. The *siyasat-i ilahi* was not subordinate to juristic *fiqh* so much as its political counterpart, grounded in the same perfected moral cosmos. In other words, natural morality was as accessible to the ruler as to the jurist.

Sixteenth-century Egyptian scholars used the words *namus* and *qanun* interchangeably. According to al-Damiri, Muhammad Shah ibn Hazm, the Ottoman chief judge of Egypt in 1563, was known for implementing the *namus* until heads were "bowed" *(ta'ta'at)*.[117] In a discussion with Sha'rani, the sixteenth-century Egyptian Sufi, concerning the legitimacy of Ottoman *qanun*, Shaykh Khawwas conveys this same understanding:

> The spirit of the revelation consists of the world order. If religious laws disappear, the rule of *namus* replaces them in each generation in which they are lacking. This is what is meant now by [the term] *qanun* in the Ottoman state. Its application, however, is lawful only in countries that have no religious laws. As for Egypt, Syria, Baghdad, North Africa and the other lands of Islam, the application

there of the *qanun* is unlawful, because it is not infallible and it may have been set down by the kings of the infidels.[118]

By implying that the *namus* is valid only "if the religious laws disappear," Khawwas dispels any doubt that the term is now used exclusively in contradistinction to the "religious laws."

At the same time, Khawwas's statement is a strong rebuttal to the Ottoman attempt at 'universalizing' state customs, voicing the open suspicion that the *qanun* of the Ottomans embodies the values and customs passed down by "infidel kings." Again, the implication is that the customs of former 'infidels' should not have precedence over the customs of 'real' Muslims. But given that all Muslims are, by definition, the descendants of former infidels, Khawwas's misgiving would invalidate all customary laws. Clearly, this was not what was he was advocating. Rather, he was objecting to the imposition of Turkic/Ottoman customs on non-Turks, and his most effective means of doing so was to attack the 'orthodoxy' of his opponents, implying they had misapplied the *namus* in lands where the "religious laws" already prevail. On the surface, this seems to suggest that the conflict is between sharia (religious laws) and *qanun* (secular laws). But Khawwas's argument is more subtle: it is the hegemony of *qanun* over *all* forms of custom, and its presumed universality, that is in contention.

Qanun had become interchangeable in Ottoman usage with all categories of custom, or *'ada*. If the assimilation of *siyasa* to concepts of natural law made this possible, it was the abolition of the *mazalim* court and the reassignment of its duties to the sharia court that gave it practical expression. As J. Nielsen puts it, the *mazalim* court was "the structure through which the temporal authorities took direct responsibility for dispensing justice."[119] The initial combination of the role of judge and ruler in the Prophet and in the early caliphs ended by the eighth century, when a rapid expansion in the empire's frontiers made this solution untenable. From that time forward, the development of a jurisprudential system, with qualified judges at its center, produced a rival legal authority to that of Muslim rulers in judicial affairs. Nonetheless, the state continued to exercise a measure of legal authority outside the bounds of the sharia law in the *mazalim* venue.

The origin of the institution can be traced to the Abbasid caliphs al-Mahdi (r. 775–85) and al-Hadi (r. 785–86), although it may have existed in an earlier time. However, the institution remained controversial with the religious scholars, who viewed its work as an infringement on their jurisdiction. Nevertheless, scholars reconciled themselves to the presence of these courts and attempted to guide as well as legitimate their practices. Al-Mawardi (d. 1058), for example, has a lengthy chapter on *mazalim* in his book on the ordinances of government *(al-ahkam al-sultaniya)*, where he states:

> The redress of wrongs involves persuading the contending parties by the awesome presence and dignity of the person in office to accept an equitable settlement and end their dispute. The official concerned must, therefore, be majestic, authoritative, and imposing, as well as manifestly honest, free of avarice, and eminently pious. Since his office calls for a combination of the charisma of those in power with the serenity of judges, he must enjoy the qualities proper to both categories, and show by his courtliness the ability to command the obedience due to each.[120]

By the time al-Maqrizi was writing in the fifteenth century the institution was well established, as was the practice of housing the procedures in a building designated for this purpose. The 'House of Justice' *(dar al-'adl)*, as it was known, was

> moved inside the citadel by Sultan Qalawun (r. 678–89/1279–90) to the *iwan*, a large columned room used as the principal audience hall, which he had rebuilt. His son Sultan al-Ashraf Khalil (r. 689–93/1290–93) renovated this structure, before finally his brother, another son of Qalawun, Sultan al-Nasir Muhammad (r. 693, 698–708, 709–41/1293, 1299–1309, 1310–41), had the building torn down and built his impressive *iwan/dar al-'adl* in the citadel, whose remains were still encountered by European visitors of the early nineteenth century.[121]

While the *mazalim* court was formally abolished by the Ottoman state, its structural characteristics (that is, a physical space designated for the hosting of legal proceedings) were physically imposed upon the once spatially delimited network of the sharia courts. As shown in chapter three, this assimilation changed the conceptual and spatial parameters of the Islamic court, while collapsing the physical barrier between spiritual and temporal authority.

Conclusion

While 'acts' in Islam were assigned a definitive value based on the criteria of 'ugliness' and 'beauty,' this value was never fixed. It is precisely this elasticity that allowed jurists to both legitimate and delegitimate custom. The discussion above illustrates that the judicial attempt to define 'acts' arising from custom was an endeavor to delimit the latter's broad scope in the classical period. The preoccupations of *fiqh* with the limits of *siyasa* and popular religious customs in the fourteenth and fifteenth centuries stemmed from a judicial apprehension that 'negative innovation' (*bid'a*) based on custom would eventually infuse and distort Islamic doctrines.

The need to claim caliphal legitimacy was most acute, given the degree of legislative authority persistently exercised by the state, well beyond the reign of Sulayman. The typical adoption of caliphal titles by non-Quraysh sultans of the day by no means endowed the *siyasa* of those states with such authority. According to established juristic political philosophy, only 'classical' caliphs of Quraysh lineage, exercising universal sovereignty, could choose between the opinions of jurists, let alone issue new orders of their own—that is, until al-Dawani.

When al-Dawani introduced the idea of non-Quraysh imams in the fifteenth century, legitimating their state laws as the second *namus*, he rewrote the book, so to speak. There can be no doubt that al-Dawani's influence on the Ottoman capital reflects the analogical extent to which his juristic and philosophical conception of Plato's 'virtuous city' was synthesized with Sufism and millenarianism under the Ottoman aegis. In the process of overcoming their non-Quraysh lineages to assume the legislative authority of universal caliphs, state bureaucrats and jurists wrote a new Islamic political philosophy. The Ottoman and Mughal states remained dynastic, to be sure, but the implication of their intellectual regimes was to lessen the role of ethnicity in Islamic political philosophy, while promoting the bureaucratic state legislated by reason. Blood was subordinated to ideology, and historical cycles superseded by a new age.

These are revolutionary changes in Islamic political philosophy. The historical breadth and longevity of this line of thought, even when represented by no more than titles, confirms that the move was more than a passing fancy. Regimes headed by non-Quraysh caliphs and imams as heads of bureaucratic states were here to stay.

It is no surprise, then, that Ibn Nujaym, who lived in a state which purported to apply "the best *nizam* [order] in God's way," was foremost in his generation to decry 'innovation' in the rights of humans *(muʿamalat)*. He, and others like him, viewed Ottoman claims to *siyasat-i ilahi* and to 'perfected moral law' *(namus)* as a license for innovation in corners of the law previously off limits to the ruler. As such, his development of the theory of custom delegitimated the 'universal' pretensions of Ottoman *qanun*.

We are now poised to investigate who would win, and who would lose, this discursive war of wills.

Chapter Three
The Construction of Orthodoxy:
Renewal *(Tajdid)* and Renunciation *(Takfir)*

Introduction

Did the economic and political landscape of the 'long' sixteenth century foster a judicial climate that enhanced or diminished the force of customary law *('urf)* in Ottoman sharia courts? Based on the evidence of the *sijill*, a limited number of scholars have answered the question by characterizing the seventeenth century as one in which local custom played an integral role in informing the judge's ruling. In the case of Bursa, H. Gerber argues that the fluidity of legal sources at the qadi's (judge's) disposal resulted in 'informal' proceedings in which local custom was often upheld in contravention of imperial orders.[1] In the case of Aleppo, A. Marcus confirms this hypothesis, but delinks it from the question of 'arbitrary' justice to argue that judges regularly enforced "established custom because it gave legislative expression to local interests."[2] In the case of Cairo, N. Hanna notes a "preponderance" of custom in the *sijill*s of the seventeenth century, characterizing it as "a feature of the Ottoman judiciary system."[3] Like Marcus, she views it as a tool for grassroots legislative expression.

In other words, local jurists had spearheaded a return to 'orthodoxy,' contributed to the 'Islamization' of Ottoman law and society, and were victorious in their confrontation with the state. As will be shown, the secondary literature gives readjustment three broad forms over the 'long sixteenth century': 'economic growth'; 'decentralization' (or 'political decline'); and 'Islamization.' All three of these trends, said to accelerate by the end of the sixteenth century, represent the dominant paradigms through which the evidence of the *sijill* is filtered. In this analysis, patterns of 'economic growth' and 'political decline' stimulate the rise of 'local capitalist classes,' in turn promoting the rise of a provincial elite that could assert local custom. This is, however, a speculative conclusion at best, as it is drawn, not from a quantitative survey of the *sijill*, but rather from a qualitative assessment of the nature of society and state in this century.

The most glaring problem with the paradigm of 'Islamization' is not its overarching economic thesis, but its exaggeration of the thesis of political decline. The Ottoman state is characterized as a 'military conquest state' which responded to the 'crises' of the mid- to late sixteenth century by transforming itself into a belated 'bastion of Sunni Islam.' A counterview links ideological and religious currents in the early sixteenth century to fundamental social and legal change, but continues to fall back on the thesis of Islamization by announcing the ultimate failure of this venture. That is to say, it prevents us from seeing the long sixteenth century as a watershed in the history of Islamic law.

Far from presenting itself as a military conquest state, the Ottoman Empire presented itself as a 'renewer' of the faith and the instrument of 'Sunni reunification,' even draping the conquest of Egypt in the language of *tajdid* (renewal) of the state, and *takfir* (excommunication) of rulers who had strayed from religion. Not since the classical Abbasid state had the Muslim world been politically unified, even nominally, into one state. Between the thirteenth and fifteenth centuries the devastation of the Mongol conquests accelerated the political fragmentation of this world, giving rise to a host of reconstituted mini-states. By the sixteenth century, the reunification of this contiguous Sunni territory was the undeclared aim of Ottoman sultans. A survey of the rhetoric of the intra-Muslim jihad amply demonstrates how the impulse for 'Sunni reunification' translated into a sustained campaign of *takfir* against the Mamluk state.[4] But the rhetoric of 'Sunni reunification' was far from limited to the battlefield; it also permeated the internal struggles over law and society. This is well documented in the sources cataloging the myriad conflicts that erupted between state and local ulama throughout the sixteenth century and well into the seventeenth. These sources also reveal the extent to which the state sought to unify the 'legal process' and, more importantly, the 'law produced' by unifying Cairo's cultural palette.

Three policies characterized this effort. One was the making of a state judiciary and an official *madhhab* possessing procedural and substantive authority over the other Sunni schools of law. The second was the evolution of Ottoman *qanun* from a 'locally bounded' set of customary state laws to a 'universally unbounded' legal code. The third was a policy of judicial purges that included a general prohibition on *ijtihad* (independent reasoning) and calls for the *tajdid* (renewal) of local doctrines. *Ijtihad* has been a key area of scholarly inquiry into the sharia's ability to adapt to novel circumstances. In the Ottoman era, the prerogative of exercising independent judicial reasoning had fallen to the state jurist, a composite character in a corporatist guild. Thus, even if we accept the arguable claim that the state had declined in political authority by the end of the sixteenth century, we must still ponder the degree to which the movement for legal unification had already molded judicial trends over the course of this century. At the very least, the questions raised above invite a more nuanced reading of the evidence of the *sijill* and of the dominant paradigm of 'Islamization.'

Inter-empire Trade and the Rise of Local Capital

Revisionist economic and political histories advocated by Ottomanists, and by scholars of the Mediterranean more widely, have overturned early twentieth-century paradigms of 'Arab economic decline' under the Ottomans. The new thesis, that the era ushered in a period of 'spectacular economic growth' and sparked the rise of a local capitalist class, has allowed scholars to reconceive of the long sixteenth century as a period of 'crises and readjustment' rather than 'decline.' The old view of the Ottomans as responsible for the decline of the Arab provinces was supported by the general thesis that the Mediterranean region as a whole suffered an economic depression in the sixteenth century. Stemming from the work of Fernand Braudel, this thesis held that the 1590s witnessed the beginning of a depression in European economies. That date was modified by later research on the 1650s–1680s.[5] While some scholars rejected the idea of an economic depression for England, France, Belgium, and Holland, for the Mediterranean in general, Faroqhi writes that "a long-term economic crisis has frequently been linked with the circumnavigation of Africa by heavily armed Dutch ships."[6] As part of the revisionist school challenging this paradigm, O.L. Barkan, H. Inalcik, A. Raymond, N. Hanna, J. Hathaway, S. Faroqhi, and others have allowed us to reconsider the thesis of economic decline.⁷ In the case of Anatolia, Faroqhi casts the period between 1500 and 1600 as one of "unusual growth and crises," arguing that during the course of this century, the population of the Anatolian tax-paying urban population almost doubled.⁸ Parallel developments in Spain, southern France, and Italy are also observable in the sixteenth century, and point to what researchers have termed a broad period of demographic upswing.

In the case of Ottoman Cairo, Raymond's research set the stage for a reassessment of the view of Ottoman rule as responsible for the decline of Egypt and Cairo and framed the discussion in terms of the "continuity," "change," or "growth" that occurred in the shift from one Muslim dynastic state to another. Refuting the claim that Ottoman rule precipitated economic decline, Raymond argued that the economic decline of Arab cities was well underway by the time of the conquest. Baghdad, for example, never fully recovered from the Mongol invasions, while Damascus, "ransacked by Tamerlane in 1400," was in the grip of an economic slump. The Hijaz, Palestine, and Syria, under Mamluk rule, had also begun declining in the fifteenth century, while the contemporary Maghreb "was already going through a dark period."⁹

If anything, this argument suggests, the conquests breathed new economic life into Arab cities. The assimilation of the Arab provinces into the empire meant the unification of vast stretches of territory, resurrecting the old borders of the Roman Empire and allowing "subjects of the emperor . . . [to] go from the Danube to the Indian Ocean and from Persia to the Maghreb without ceasing to be submitted to the same laws."¹⁰ The "easy circulation of men and goods" allowed by this territorial unity, Raymond argued, facilitated the rise of "a huge market" that was open to the great cities of Egypt and Syria.¹¹ If the distant trade to and from the Far East and Southeast Asia began to be diverted toward the "great European places of market," the opportunities provided by inter-empire trade more than compensated.

Contributing to the economic boom "was the presence in the capitals of the provinces of a large class of persons with a high level of consumption of luxury goods," numbering in the tens of thousands. Added to the fact that tribute paid to the central Istanbul treasury was small—"in Egypt the hazina never went beyond 30 million paras"—this meant that the bulk of the levies was spent in local markets. The vigorous economic activity fostered in this climate is something "to which the number of trade guilds [estimated at 250] bear witness."[12]

Combined, the paradigms of 'economic growth' and 'political decentralization' have fostered the argument that judicial institutions were increasingly autonomous. Hanna, for instance, argues that the "indigenous" Egyptian judiciary was able to reassert its domination over the 'law,' if not the 'legal process,' by the late sixteenth/early seventeenth century.[13] More than that, she stresses that even at the height of its political power, the Ottoman state only controlled the 'legal process,' never the 'law produced.' "The way justice was carried out," she concludes, "was to a large measure left to the discretion of the magistrates working in the courts . . . the *qadi* administered justice according to the rules of the *madhhab* as he saw fit."[14] A linchpin of her argument is that local deputy judges, who often remained in their posts for life, were more influential than the Ottoman chief judges, whose average period of tenure was between one and three years.

However, Hanna's reasoning does not account for the frequent Ottoman campaigns purging local courts of their local deputy judges (*na'ib*s), witnessed for the better part of the sixteenth century. Ottoman court purges were justified on the grounds that corruption was endemic to the Cairene judiciary. Unless we accept the Ottoman charge that the judiciary in Cairo was permeated with corrupt and inept officials at face value, another motive must be sought for the termination of *na'ib*s, *wakil*s (representatives), and *shahid*s (professional witnesses).[15] Winter suggests that "in the organization of Egypt's system of justice, the Ottomans adopted an approach of trial and error, but ultimately aimed at Ottomanization and centralization."[16] Like Hanna, however, he makes a distinction between the 'legal process' and the 'law produced,' suggesting it was only the former that came under state auspices: "The Ottomans did not infringe upon the religious or scholarly life of Egypt. Indeed, they limited their interference to material things. . . . It stands to reason that the Ottoman *'ulama'* were awed by the strength and depth of the Islamic scholarly tradition of Egypt."[17]

Winter's assumption is not supported by the evidence, which suggests that the Ottomans were not so "awed" as to be dissuaded from challenging the rulings *(ahkam)* of prominent local judges. Even where he finds evidence of such confrontation and of efforts at *tajdid*, he dismisses it as the capricious whim of "[a] certain arrogant chief *qadi* [who] declared upon his arrival that he would renew *(yujaddidu)* the Egyptians' religion."[18]

The distinction erected between the 'law produced' and the 'legal process' allows Hanna to assert the impenetrability of the former and, what is more, to claim that the state's hold on the latter was diminished by the end of the sixteenth century, when the powers of the chief Ottoman judge were "drastically curtailed."[19] As an example of his declining authority, she writes that the orders issued by the chief Ottoman judge 'Abd al-Wahhab al-Rumi (1600), directing deputy judges to reduce the number of people working in the courts, were reversed upon his departure.[20] But, as may be gleaned from Ibn Iyas's early-sixteenth-century accounts, it was far from unusual for a judge to issue such orders, or for them to be reversed.[21] The point to be made, however, is that such campaigns were applied with enough consistency to intimidate and cajole local jurists.

Moreover, al-Damiri's biography of late sixteenth- and early seventeenth-century Ottoman chief judges gainsays Hanna's portrait of the toothless Ottoman judicial figurehead. Husayn ibn Muhammad Husam al-Din Qaraçli-Zada, appointed in 1579, was well respected and liked by the communities of Cairo because he exercised strict control over the governor and his men *(al-hukkam al-siyasiya)* such that they were unable to "deviate from his orders and rulings."[22] Well into the seventeenth century, 'Abd Allah ibn 'Ali Jan Zada, who took office in 1611, was best known for confronting Mustafa Bek when the latter blocked a prominent gate near the Khan al-Khalili market to build himself a shop. The judge ordered it demolished and the gate returned to its original structure. He "was a degree above *hukkam al-siyasa*," concludes al-Damiri.[23] Another demonstration of the political authority of the state comes in 1607–11 when, after decades of failed attempts, the state was finally able to eradicate the *tulba* (an illegal tax imposed by rural landlords/administrators on the peasantry).[24] None of this hints of 'political decline' or of decentralization.

Challenging the entire thesis of 'political decline,' H. Gerber writes, "the theory about the decline of the center is exaggerated for the entire polity."[25] Many of the characteristics of decline to which scholars point, he concludes, "are simply pervasive characteristics of past centuries."[26] Gerber suggests that the notion of 'decline' first arose in sixteenth-century Ottoman *nasiha* literature, when the fifteenth century was idealized as a "utopic golden age." But this, he argues, should be read as a sign of the dramatic changes overtaking society in the late sixteenth century, not as decline.[27]

The theory of political decline dovetails into (and bolsters) the argument that local institutions resisted 'Ottomanization' and retained their Mamluk features.[28] In general terms, Winter states that "the survival of Mamluks and their eventual resumption of prominence and power is the most obscure but intriguing question," and that overall Egypt continued to be governed by a "provincial administrative system [that] was still based on Mamluk methods and traditions."[29] The appointment of Khayrbek (d. 1522), a Mamluk *amir* who had collaborated with the Ottomans against the Mamluks, as governor of Egypt allowed him to "resurrect several customs and ceremonies associated with the Mamluk Sultanate."[30] P.M. Holt, another proponent of the Mamluk continuum theory, has argued that the post of *sanjak bey* in Ottoman Egypt was a resurrection of the Mamluk office of *amir mi'a* (an officer who held an *iqta'* that supported one hundred horsemen). Holt and others have extended this theory to elite households in Egypt, which they regard to be modeled on those of the Mamluk sultanate.[31]

Sounding a more cautionary note, J. Hathaway points out that a process of decentralization begun late in the sixteenth century led to an "empire-wide political culture based on households, up to and including the household of the Ottoman Sultan himself in the Topkapi palace."[32] Without cognizance of this fact, she continues, "the competition between *bey*s and officers in seventeenth-century Egypt is too easily interpreted as a confrontation between traditional Mamluk institutions and Ottoman innovations." Hathaway's analysis implies transformation and continuum, linking local conditions in Egypt to empire-wide political and economic trends.

D. Ayalon, who has researched the question of 'continuum' and 'transformation' in the Mamluk army, finds more evidence of the latter. Noting that the Ottomans compelled Mamluks to abandon their Turkic names and to adopt Arab ones, he concludes that "one of the main differences between the two societies under discussion, which had far-reaching effects on their respective destinies and structures, was that the earlier Mamluks bore almost exclusively Turkish or other non-Arab names, whereas the Mamluks of Ottoman Egypt bore, with quite a limited number of exceptions, only Arab names."[33]

Effectively contrasting the politics of identity in both states, Ayalon's observations have broad implications from the perspective of ideology and culture. In the Mamluk system, non-Arab names bestowed a prestige on their bearer and underlined the exclusivity of the Mamluk ranks. Sultan al-Zahir Timurbugha and his predecessor Yalbay, for instance, withheld the payment of the *nafaqa* (allowance) from the children of Mamluks, or *awlad al-nas*, "for they hate whoever is called after the name of a prophet or of the companion of a prophet."[34]

Under the Ottomans, however, Arab names became the yardstick of Ottoman culture, signaling a disavowal of excessive differentiation based on ethnic pride in favor of more universal trends based, in this case, on prophetic Sunna. The outward appeal to prophetic Sunna was one strategy by which to remedy the divisive politics of identity within a multiethnic army. The symbolic nature of Ottoman military and political reforms should not diminish their practical significance. Whether promoting 'prophetic Sunna,' or 'Ottoman custom,' unifying impulses based on universal principles pervaded Ottoman statecraft.

Gerber, too, underscores the argument that "Ottoman bureaucracy was permeated with universalistic principles to a greater extent than is usually allowed for," implying that an expanding state and a mushrooming bureaucracy necessitated the "creation of a relatively unified court system."[35] And in addition to the unified court system, the state also pursued the "standardization of *qanun*, particularly as the sixteenth century progressed."[36] R. Repp's and C. Imber's combined research on the office of chief mufti of Istanbul sheds light on the latter's growing authority in the mid-sixteenth century, and on the rigorous process of harmonization between *qanun* and sharia that followed. *Qanun* had been thoroughly 'Islamized.'[37]

It was not until Sulayman Qanuni (1520–66), writes Imber, that "the Ottoman use of the title [caliph] acquired a doctrinal as well as a rhetorical significance."[38] Spurred by his apocalyptic ambitions and the 'crises' of the sixteenth century,[39] the state transformed itself "from a military conquest state into a bureaucratic state and bastion of Sunni Islam."[40] Most notably, it accorded the sultan a role as "both the interpreter and the executor of the *Shari'a*."[41]

C. Fleischer has emphasized the fluid and shifting parameters of authority, legitimation, and ideology during Sulayman's (r. 1520–66) reign, describing its first three decades "as extraordinary for the multiplicity of competing or contradictory cultural and social ideals and assumptions they managed simultaneously to contain as for the growth of dynastic power and of an ever more grandiose imperial culture."[42] Fleischer contextualizes this venture within the messianic and apocalyptic expectations of the era with its emphasis on renewal and on a reborn universal caliphate.

For S. Buzov, Ebu's Su'ud's appointment to the office of chief mufti in 1545 signified the venture's failure.[43] The production of sultanic *qanun* was slowed and that which existed was harmonized with sharia through a process of 'Islamization.' Buzov attributes this reorientation to the sultanate's confrontation with the formidable institutional strength and legal traditions of the judicial classes in the newly conquered Arabic-speaking provinces.[44] Because the relationship between this universal sovereign and the *umma* "was determined and established in the lands hitherto known as the Sultanate of Rum, it was necessary to present proof of the existence of a distinctively Ottoman knowledge and juridical tradition. Sulayman could not speak for that."[45] The elite lawyer Ebu's-Su'ud, however, could. His intervention restored legal authority to the jurist classes such that the law and its administration were no longer "controlled and directed exclusively by the state," but by a judicial class organized into a corporative Hanafi guild.[46] Buzov's thesis fits into the paradigm of 'Islamization,' alongside Imber's, Repp's, and Winter's works, the latter concluding that tensions between Ottoman officials and Egyptians eased "as the sixteenth century progressed, [and] the empire was increasingly orthodox."[47]

The conceptual limitations of the thesis of Islamization have already been outlined in the introduction. But there is another fundamental problem with its timeline. Restricted as it is to the events of the mid- and late sixteenth century, the thesis is excessive in its focus on Sulayman's reign. It treats the Sulaymanic period as an anomaly, neither shaped by, nor relevant to, what came before or after. R. Abou El-Haj's research, however, throws some doubt on the uniqueness of the Sulaymanic era, showing that "the designation [sultan] is interchangeably used with caliph" in the early sixteenth century as well.[48] There is no doubt that the conquest of the Arab provinces gave Ottoman caliphal claims new weight, but this does not negate the existence of similar 'rhetorical' and 'apocalyptic' discourses at a much earlier date.

Moreover, even though the *qanun* was modified to reflect the growing authority and input of state ulama in the mid-sixteenth century, its essential form and organization were established in the fifteenth century. Between the years 1451 and 1481, Mehmed issued the first two *qanunnama*s intended for "universal" application. The first initiated the bureaucratic era for which the Ottoman state is so renowned. It organized the ulama into bureaucratic state offices beneath the office of sultan. The second was chiefly concerned with taxes and land laws, feudal holdings, and criminal law. That the document was not abolished but later subsumed under a new title, *Qanunnama Osmani*, in 1501 by Bayezid II (1481–1512) is a testament to the stability of Mehmed's legacy.[49] Sulayman's stature as 'Qanuni' (lawgiver), the honorific title bestowed on him by his official biographers, consciously exaggerates his role as a legislator. Sulayman's claim to caliphal authority may have been more infused with apocalyptic and messianic language, but it was used to instantiate Mehmed's laws. That there was such a need speaks of the state's desire for legislative authority and legitimacy. The quest for legitimacy would become more acute after the conquest of Egypt and Syria.

Similarly, the post-Sulaymanic era is not as different from Sulayman's time as is presumed. Buzov is correct to conclude that Sulayman could not speak to the judicial wall he confronted in the Arabic-speaking world. The wall, founded on the ruins of the tenth-century Mihna, held fast to the principle that it was the credential, rather than the office, that bestowed legitimacy on law. Insofar as the ascendance of Abu al-Su'ud signified the victory of the credential over the individual ruler, the thesis of Islamization stands. But its concurrent claim, that Arab legal orthodoxy was 'discovered' and faithfully harmonized with *qanun*, stands uncomfortably amid the evidence.

The universalism which permeated Ottoman statecraft and law is expressively conveyed in the laws promulgated by Mehmed, upheld by Sulayman, and legitimated by Abu al-Su'ud. And in spite of the claim that the latter opened the door to a "new Ottoman cultural identity . . . [that saw merit] in preservation of the cultural and religious systems"[50] of the empire, the debate on the very definition and function, not only of *qanun* and *fiqh*, but of the sharia as an abstraction, had only just begun.

While outward conformity to 'continuum' was often professed for the Mamluk era, judicial institutions in Ottoman Egypt were administered by an ideology that demanded a minimum degree of substantive conformity to the Ottoman model. A close examination of the conflicts underpinning relations between state and local jurists, throughout the long sixteenth century, exposes the limitations of the thesis of Islamization in explaining their persistence. If the reforms were merely administrative, and Ottoman laws had been steadily Islamized, what accounts for the clashes that transpired well into the seventeenth century between local jurists and their counterparts from among the corporative Hanafi guild? It becomes even more inexplicable given Ibn Iyas' claim that the local judiciary was willing—too willing, in his view—to accommodate its new overlords. What explains it, I argue, is their unwillingness to oblige the state's repeated calls to 'renew their faith' and by extension their legal doctrines.

Before turning to the issue of *tajdid*, the Ottoman state's claim to 'universal sovereignty' will be demonstrated through the rhetoric of *takfir* employed on the eve of war.

Takfir: The Intra-Muslim Jihad

Careful to avoid the charge that they were perpetrating *fitna* by initiating a Muslim civil war, the Ottomans initiated their hostilities against the Mamluk regime in Cairo by dipping their sword in the religious idiom.[51] The conquests of Egypt and Syria in 1517 were presented not as an attack upon the Sunni peoples of the Arab heartland, but as a jihad to check the tyrannical rule of the despotic Mamluk sultan, al-Ghuri. It was not a conquest, but an Islamic *fath* (opening) akin to the early Arabian *futuhat*.

Salim had to be acutely conscious that a conquest of the Sunni Arab heartland would catapult him in stature from a mere *ghazi* (invader) on the frontiers of the Muslim world to 'the protector of Mecca, Medina, and Jerusalem' and 'official guardian of the pilgrimage routes.' No doubt he was also aware that credentials such as these carried more weight than the title of caliph, claimed, at the time, by a number of rulers in the Muslim world.[52] But before moving on his prize, Salim first had the difficult task of legitimating war against the other great Sunni power. Legitimation was a necessary precursor to any war, but it was especially important in the context of a looming war with the largest Sunni Muslim state, one that encompassed the holy lands of Mecca, Medina, and Jerusalem as well as the great centers of Arab learning. Framed by Salim as a battle between just Islamic rule and the unjust oppression of a military caste, the looming war adopted the language of jihad, theoretically forbidden against fellow Muslims. But in this, the Ottoman state had ample historical precedent on which to draw.[53]

The Qur'an (4:92) forbade the shedding of Muslim blood, and the theory of jihad only recognized holy wars launched in the path of Allah (*fi sabil Allah*). Legal theory provided no special rules for the regulation of intra-Muslim warfare. Without forsaking the notion of a universal *dar al-Islam*, jurists could not elaborate a formal branch of legal literature that would recognize the de facto breakup of the political *umma* (religio-political community) by establishing rules to govern intra-Muslim wars and treaties. In theory, writes Har-El, intra-Muslim war remained illegal.[54] But the absence of theory did not of course reflect practice, where intra-Muslim warfare was far from uncommon. In the absence of a theoretical basis from which to conduct such wars, the *siyar* (literature governing relations between Muslim and non-Muslim states) became a practical guide for the regulation of both intra-Muslim and international relations. For all intents and purposes, this permitted Muslim states to launch wars of jihad upon one another. Generally, however, these wars were given the added designation of *muqatala* (conflict), *fitna* (strife), *harb* (war), or *qital* (battle).[55]

Because the welfare of the *umma*, and not the state, was paramount in Islamic political philosophy, the transgression of the sharia by one Muslim state empowered another to intervene in its restoration. In practice, intra-Muslim jihad was conducted on two levels: jihad against political dissension, usually involving rebellion or secession, and jihad against religious dissension.[56] Moreover, the intra-Muslim jihad differed from the jihad conducted in *dar al-harb* in one important respect: the Muslim armies and populations which were conquered were to be accorded their full rights as Muslims under the sharia. Thus, the property of a Muslim could not be confiscated as part of the spoils of war, nor could he/she be enslaved. The same applied to the property of non-Muslim *dhimma* (protected minorities) who resided in Muslim territories.

Baghdad's destruction in 1258, and with it the seat of the universal Muslim caliphate, exacerbated the conditions which generated the intra-Muslim jihad. From the moment of its inception in 750, the Abbasid state faced secessionist challenges, but the notion of an Islamic political center to which all looked, even nominally, for political investitures and for spiritual authority had not diminished with the growing number of independent Muslim states. Only after 1258 was this notion more or less extinguished. By the time Ibn Taymiya, the Hanbali jurist, was writing (d. 1328), the *umma* could be classified as "a natural confederation of states" and the caliphate as an unnecessary fiction.[57]

At the same time as this de facto 'confederation of Muslim states' was being intellectualized, the political landscape of the thirteenth, fourteenth, and fifteenth centuries was becoming an arena in which intra-Muslim jihads were now as common as the jihad against *dar al-harb*. New patterns of conquest, expansion, and annexation within *dar al-Islam* asserted themselves at an unprecedented rate. Squarely at the center of this phenomenon was the Ottoman state. Relatively novel, and certainly unanticipated by classical *fiqh*, this Muslim-over-Muslim form of conquest gave rise to a host of doctrinal paradoxes for the ruling and intellectual elite.

It is not without significance that the earliest state petitions to Ottoman muftis were in the form of questions on the legality of the intra-Muslim jihad.[58] Used to legitimate and reinforce state actions, the fatwa features prominently in the preparatory stages of intra-Muslim war, for unlike regular jihads directed against *dar al-harb*, jihad against Muslims had to be carefully justified. Notably, the authorizing of such a war was always preceded by *takfir* (excommunication/charge of unbelief) against the Muslim foe.[59] Other charges, such as *fasad* (corruption), *zulm* (oppression), or *jawr* (tyranny), usually preceded or accompanied the charge. But *takfir*, concludes Har-El, is the only legal tool that legitimized this type of war.[60]

Soon after his ascension to power in 1362, Murad I (1362–89) consulted his ulama on "whether, in the face of threats from Anatolian rulers, troops collected for the purpose of the *gaza* against the unbelievers in Rumeli might be used to meet the threat in Anadalu first [against the Muslim principalities] and the *gaza* consequently delayed." In Murad II's reign (1421–51), fatwas on the legality of the punitive expedition against Karaman on 24 Safar 848/12 June 1444 were sought from the ulama of Egypt.[61] Thus as early as in Murad I's reign, the fatwa had become an important instrument in the authorization or denial of punitive military action against other Anatolian Muslim states.[62]

Typically, the fatwas condemned the 'duplicitous' conduct of Anatolian kings who were accused of exploiting the Ottoman preoccupation with the jihad in the Balkans and raiding its undefended borders.[63] Şükrüllah expressed this sentiment in canonical terms, voicing the ulama's consensus that Murad I should, "before embarking on *gaza* against Serbia and Hungary . . . make war on the neighboring Muslim kings who planned to attack Bursa in his absence."[64] *Gaza*, according to the ulama, was a communal obligation, whereas the prevention of injury to Muslims was the individual obligation of the monarch.

It is significant that Muslim states resorted to the concept of jihad when fighting one another and conformed in rhetoric to its terms of engagement.

Har-El writes that "both the Mamluks and the Ottomans followed a policy of Sunni religious revivalism and Islamic political unification."[65] In the eyes of the protagonist states, therefore, an effective expansion into *dar al-harb* could only be achieved if "a reborn universal caliphate" existed. To achieve this, however, the state had to be committed to prolonged warfare against other Muslim states, a policy that could potentially cost it its legitimacy.[66]

It follows, therefore, that the links which bound *ifta'* to intra-Muslim jihad and to the state would be most visible when the Ottoman state came to a head with "the extremely difficult problem of justifying war against the other great Sunni ruler."[67] More than that, it was the seat of the Abbasid caliph, the Arabic-speaking heartlands, and the Hijaz. Turkish chroniclers report that before launching his war against the Mamluk army at Marj Dabiq (1516), Salim awaited the authorizing fatwa of Ali Çemali, the chief mufti of Istanbul, on the battlefield.[68] It can be assumed, however, that the operation "had [already] been thoroughly canvassed," writes Repp, implying that some kind of "consensus of the *'ulama*'"[69] had been achieved long before Salim left Istanbul. He writes that "if Salim did, as Çelalzade Mustafa says, seek his advice individually even if only to confirm an already established policy, the fact would not be without significance as it would constitute perhaps the first demonstrable instance of a sultan's having applied exclusively to the *mufti* on a point of public policy."[70]

As war loomed, the indictments against the Mamluks grew more severe. Years before the conquest, Bayezid II (r. 1481–1512) had waged war against Qaytbay (r. 1467–68), accusing the latter of being an "infidel Circassian" for having supported his rival, Prince Cem.[71] Most of the Anatolian ulama were said to be in favor of the war, even resisting Bayezid's efforts to secure a *modus vivendi* with the Mamluks. Instead, the ulama justified jihad against him and "the heresy, oppression and rebellion of the rulers of Egypt and Syria *(ilhad va zulm va 'isyan li-muluk Misr va Sham)*."[72] The Mamluks may have been heretics, but they were not as yet *kuffar* (unbelievers).

The last Mamluk sultan, al-Ashraf Qansuh al-Ghuri (r. 1510–16), is accused of spoiling the 'father–son' relationship between himself and Salim I by establishing relations with the heretic Safavids, and by harboring intentions to attack the Ottomans. A fatwa was issued by the chief mufti stating that war with Circassians (Mamluks) was no less than a religious obligation, because they educated their children in infidel Circassia and allowed their coins, which bore the *shahada* (Islamic declaration of faith), "to be spoiled in the hands of unclean members of the world's 72 nations."⁷³ The Mamluks were now infidels.⁷⁴

Military-state propaganda justifying the intra-Muslim jihad demonstrates the extent to which Islamic doctrine and symbolism, in this case *takfir*, were wielded in the service of a 'universalist' ideology, cloaking expansionist impulses within the rhetoric of unification. Post-conquest, those impulses are expressed through the doctrine of *tajdid*.

Tajdid: The Social Conquest

In 517, on 18 Ramadan, the state called on Circassian Mamluks who had resurfaced in Cairo to dress according to Ottoman custom. But the order was soon rescinded, writes Ibn Iyas.⁷⁵ A few years later, however, remnants of the Mamluk army were again ordered to 'Ottomanize.' After dismissing a thousand Mamluks and *awlad al-nas* from active military service in December 1521, Khayrbek personally cut off half the beards of several Mamluks during a public military parade and handed them to their former owners, saying: "Follow the Ottoman rules in cutting your beard, narrowing the sleeves of your dress and in everything that the Ottomans do."⁷⁶

All of these efforts, writes Winter, were intensified after Mustafa Pasha, Sultan Sulayman's brother-in-law, replaced Khayrbek in 1522. What is most notable about these changes is that they signal an abrogation of the symbols of the Mamluk army.⁷⁷ On a note of resignation, Ibn Iyas marks the passing of an era by advising Mamluk soldiers to adapt to the new customs of the age:

> Walk with time, oh wronged one,
> and shed the processional clothes *(mawakib)*
> and follow the Sultan in robes *(suqman)* or hats *(tartur)*
> and be among the political community *(qawm)* and the nations
>   *(al-awtan)* in dress.⁷⁸

More importantly, Ibn Iyas was also conceding that the *qawm*, now defined as the Ottoman polity, demanded a set degree of cultural conformity among the various 'nations' *(al-awtan)* it embraced. General trends over the course of the sixteenth century confirm the persistence of this universal ideal and, judging by Ayalon's conclusions, its success in the military.

In the Mamluk sultanate racial rivalries played a most prominent part, and many a time they silenced the rivalries of the various factions of the Mamluks. The hostility of the Circassians to the other Mamluk races and their feeling of superiority is well documented in the contemporary sources. . . . In the period covered by al-Jabarti and ad-Dimurdashi, the picture is entirely different. The racial problem simply does not exist.[79]

Even beyond military etiquette, many of the most prominent symbols of the Mamluk state, especially those associated with religious festivals, were also abrogated. Ibn Iyas writes:

And so ended the parades which would proceed during the *'id al-nahr*, as though that system *(nizam)* had never been. And so lapsed *(battal)* many of the symbols of the kingdom enacted for sultans past during the *a'yad*, until Egypt became bereft of any *nizam* that once was.[80]

Also abolished was the Mamluk practice of distributing meat *(adhiya)* on the occasion of *'id* to the jurists, *amir*s, soldiers, and even the Sufi monasteries and graveyards. When, in 924, the people complained to the governor, he replied, " I follow only Ibn 'Uthman's ways in all matters."[81] Ibn Iyas was especially chagrined however, at the fact that the Mamluk tent, purchased for 30,000 dinars by Qaytbay, was sold to the Moroccan community for a pittance at 4,000 dinars, writing, "it was one of the symbols of the kingdom."[82] He also condemned them for forsaking customs associated with the *mawlid al-nabi* (public celebration of the Prophet's birthday)—an 'innovation' and a source of juristic debate for centuries—such as giving gifts to preachers, jurists, and Qur'an reciters *(qurra')*.[83] The neglect of Egypt's customary religious festivals *(a'yad)*, and the end of the famous processions which proceeded on "land and water," prompted the mournful words: "Oh, my sorrow *(lahfi)* for Egypt's festivals, how they have perished."[84] Only the Hajj (pilgrimage to Mecca) procession continued as per "the old customs."[85]

Like the theory of 'decline,' the theory that local institutions, especially judicial ones, resisted 'Ottomanization' may originate with the Ottomans themselves. It was expedient for the Ottoman state to portray itself as a continuum with the Mamluk order for reasons of political legitimacy—something it assiduously cultivated. Rhetorically, it bowed before the concept of 'precedent,' encapsulated in the Islamic ideal of Sunna. In official discourse, Egypt and its administrative institutions are referred to by the biblical expression *al-diyar al-Yusufiya* (the abode of the Prophet Joseph) and *al-takht al-Yusufiya* (the bench of the Prophet Joseph) in homage to that principle.[86]

Other nods to local custom were made in the early years of the conquest, when rapid, often fundamental, changes were first introduced. In such an environment, outward appeals to continuum and claims to universal sovereignty were vital rhetorical weapons in the bid to consolidate power. These claims are aggressively asserted in the *Qanunnama Sham* (intended for greater Syria), composed in 1519, two years after the conquest. Here the acquisition of Egypt and Syria is recorded as "an assignment from God."[87] Moreover, the document draws parallels between the Prophet's *khilafa* and the reign of the Ottoman sultan.

But even claims to universal sovereignty were not enough to stem social discontent. The relative stability that the province had enjoyed under Khayrbek ended with his death, writes the Turkish chronicler Uzunçarsili, when a steep rise in the number of rebellions was recorded.[88] Khayrbek's successor, the Ottoman officer Mustafa Pasha, had intensified efforts to 'Ottomanize' local institutions by imposing Ottoman taxes in place of Mamluk ones. In so doing, he lit a social fuse that was only defused when the new laws were packaged as extensions of the 'old.'

In 1524, Sulayman's secretary (*tazkarji*, also called *tawqi'i* or *nashanji*) Ibrahim Pasha was commissioned to investigate the source of the unrest gripping Cairo. He found that the army had not participated in a single uprising, and that the principal antagonists were the *'azban* (a militia stationed at the citadel)[89] and the *ahali* (communities).[90] The demands of the communities were threefold: a reduction in Ottoman taxes, a return to Mamluk *qanun*, and a repeal of Ottoman *qanun*, which "did not suit the conditions of *al-Diyar al-Misriya*."[91] Significantly, they did not ask for a repeal of Ottoman *qanun* and a return to the sharia, as is often implied in the secondary literature, but for a return to "Mamluk *qanun*." Popular anger was also directed at the Egyptian *fuqaha'*, who were accused by Ibn Iyas of fearing for their "seats" instead of safeguarding the "rights of Muslims against these edicts *(rusum)*."[92]

According to the *Qanunnama Misr*, Sulayman sent Ibrahim to Egypt to negotiate with the *ahali* in 1525. The latter immediately availed himself of a copy of Qaytbay's (d. 1468) *qanun* and, soon thereafter, compiled the *Qanunnama Misr* (reportedly penned in his own hand), a document which claimed to amend Ottoman *'askeri* and *qada'i* laws in line with the *qanun* of Qaytbay.[93] His efforts produced one of the most important pieces of Ottoman literature, at once a judicial document and a political manifesto. Buzov has ably shown the preamble to the *Qanunnama Misr* to be a philosophical proclamation of caliphal authority as "Shadow of God on Earth," and the awaited *mujaddid* (renewer).[94] It is also a very telling, albeit deliberately ambiguous, judicial document. U. Heyd noted that it contained the first explicit statement justifying Ottoman *qanun* and its application.[95] However, part of the justification rested on the document's claim to harmonize Ottoman *qanun* and Qaytbay's *qanun*.

Naturally, scholars have wondered why the laws of Qaytbay should have been chosen over the laws of a more recent Mamluk sultan, like al-Ghuri or Tumanbay. H. Inalcik speculates that a "codex of Qaytbay's laws" must have existed.[96] Behrens-Abouseif, however, dismisses the possibility, arguing that there is nothing to indicate that Qaytbay was a legislator of any importance.[97] A careful reading of the text of the *Qanunnama* supports Behrens-Abouseif's position, for nowhere does it actually refer to a 'codex of Qaytbay,' but to "the *'ada* (custom) and *qanun* that were applied in the time of Qaytbay."[98]

The question persists, why Qaytbay? It will be remembered that in waging his jihad against the last Mamluk sultans, Salim had labeled them *kuffar*, a charge which stripped them of legislative authority. Bayezid II (1481–1512), it should be mentioned, had also accused Qaytbay (d. 1468) of 'heresy' *(ilhad)*, but that was a lesser charge made by a different sultan. The doctrinal paradoxes that would have been generated by enacting the *qanun* of a declared *kafir* like al-Ghuri are multiple—they were less numerous in the case of a remote 'heretic' like Qaytbay.

The Ottomans were not making special concessions to the Egyptians by developing a customized law for them, but following their own established policies. Imber writes:

> When a sultan conquered new lands, he would order the compilation of both a new cadastral survey and a new law-book for the

area. The new law-book would, as a rule, simply list pre-conquest taxes and note whether these had been confirmed or abolished. In the provinces of eastern and south-eastern Anatolia, for example, which Salim I (1512–1520) conquered between 1514 and 1516, the first Ottoman law books for the area normally state in their preambles that they are compiled 'in accordance with the qanun of Hasan Padishah,' a reference to the laws in force in the days of the Akkoyunlu Sultan, Uzun Hasan, who had died in 1478.[99]

Heyd makes the important observation, however, that they referred to the imposition of their "law-books" as *tajdid*, rather than *'urf/'amal/jadid* (*jadid* means 'new').[100] Making pretence to a continuum between their rule and that of predecessor dynasties was thus of some importance to the Ottomans. The question is, was it enough to dissuade them from promoting a new hegemony under the guise of 'renewal?'

In the case of the *Qanunnama Misr* it is clear that the Ottoman claim to "enacting the laws of Qaytbay" was more fictive than genuine. On the one hand, the *Qanunnama Misr* speaks of activating the laws of Qaytbay, and on the other, of enacting in Cairo the *qanun* that is "applied *(ma'mul bihi)* in the province of Rum," indicating that "copies of it [should] be preserved in the *Diwan Misr*."[101]

A double movement is thus at work in the *Qanunnama Misr*. In the first instance, it appears to acknowledge that past precedent confers authority on local *qanun*, and in the other it exhibits a notable impulse to replicate the application of imperial *qanun* from one territory to another. A survey of the judicial reforms initiated immediately after the conquest will demonstrate the extent to which the so-called movement to 'harmonize' the laws of Salim and the laws of Qaytbay was a legal fiction.

The Demotion of the Local Judiciary

The impact of the conquest on the legal process, on the laws produced, and on lawmakers was both immediate and profound. Even before the conquest of Egypt, it was rumored that Sultan Salim planned to abolish all legal schools in Syria, after its fall in 1516. In 1517, the rumors were partially confirmed as all but the Hanafi school were suspended in Damascus *(abtal min al-Sham)*, as per the "custom in his [Salim's] lands" *('adatih fi biladih)*.[102] In 1519, news of the unfortunate fate of the Shafi'i *qadi al-qudah* (chief judge), Shihab al-Din Ahmad ibn Farfur al-Dimashqi, at the hands of the new Ottoman governor of Damascus, Amir Janbirdi al-Ghazali, further alarmed jurists in Cairo. Purportedly, the Shafi'i judge had been mercilessly persecuted by al-Ghazali and given an ultimatum to rule according to the Hanafi rite, or forfeit his office (and even his life, according to other reports).[103] Ibn Farfur fled Damascus to Aleppo, from where he wrote directly to Sultan Salim complaining of the indignities he had suffered at the hands of al-Ghazali. Salim responded with a *marsum* (sultanic decree) conferring on Ibn Farfur the position of qadi of Aleppo, where he permanently resettled with his wife and children.[104]

Whether exaggerated or not, the main events surrounding Ibn Farfur's career, his exile and demotion from the chief judgeship of Damascus to the chief judgeship of a provincial town, symbolize the very real tribulations of the elite Damascene judiciary. The Cairene judiciary felt the impact of the conquest no less profoundly. The first to feel the force of the reforms were the four chief judges *(qudat al-qudah)* of the four schools of law, who were summarily dismissed from office in the reign of Salim. It would be a full four years before they were reinstated by the Ottoman *qadi al-qudah* Muhammad Halabi in 1521, early in Sulayman's reign. But they no longer served as four coequal chief judges of the respective schools. Instead, they were demoted to the status of 'deputies' of the Ottoman chief judge.[105] A year later, in 1522, a *marsum* announced the bifurcation of the Ottoman chief judge's position *(qadi al-qudah)* into two offices, that of *qadi 'askar* (chief of the military courts) and that of *qadi al-'arab* (chief of the civilian courts). Both positions were reserved for Ottoman Hanafis.[106] Yet again, the four *qudat al-qudah* were dismissed and formally reinstated in August 1523 of the following year—this time as the deputies of *the qadi al-'arab*. The point to be made is that the demotion of Egypt's chief judges to the status of deputies of the chief Ottoman judge was both immediate and permanent.

It was the mainstay of the Egyptian judiciary, however, the deputies *(na'ibs)* of the chief judge of each school, who fared the worst. In the year of the conquest, 1517, the Shafi'i chief judge, Kamal al-Din al-Tawil, was ordered to dismiss all but four of his deputy judges.[107] No explanation was given for the targeting of the Shafi'i deputies. However, two years later, in 1519, the governor ordered all four chief judges of the local *madhhab*s to reduce the number of deputy judges in their *madhhab*s. The Shafi'i qadi was allowed to retain five, the Hanafi two, the Maliki seven, and the Hanbali three. The following year, in Dhu'l Hujja 1520, the governor was still unsatisfied with the conduct of the remaining deputy judges, and warned the "four *qadi*s to control their *nuwwab*."[108] On the heels of this latest warning, each *madhhab* was allowed to retain seven *na'ib*s and two *shahid*s, in line with the demands of Ottoman *yasaq* (taxation).

The campaign to reduce the number of deputy judges from all the schools of law was an obvious attempt to bolster the authority of the Hanafi Ottoman chief judge and of his guild members, while constraining the only element in Egyptian society that could impede reform. Nonetheless, the governor's order of 1520, insofar as it allowed for higher numbers of Maliki, Shafi'i, and Hanbali *na'ib*s than the previous edict, is perhaps indication enough that the attempt to exclude local members of the judiciary was simply untenable.

Moreover, the Egyptian judicial establishment, which jealously guarded its authority and privilege, was anything but passive in the face of this campaign. Ibn Iyas notes that no sooner would an order arrive stipulating a reduction in the number of *na'ib*s than their numbers would once again be multiplied. But Cairo's chief judges, as well as their deputies, were hardly the only targets. The net was cast even wider to include *wakil*s (loosely translated as attorneys or legal representatives) and *shahid*s (a permanent body of court-accredited witnesses), all of whom were dismissed in unprecedented numbers. The charge against them, as individuals and as a class, was that they were "corrupt."[109]

Court Purges
Court purges were a by-product of the state's wish to exert its dominion over the law and of the local judiciary's will to resist such dominion. The obdurate refusal of the Cairene judiciary to abide by sultanic edicts, and the heavy-handed manner in which the state penalized certain members of the profession for their intransigence, explains both the frequency and the duration of these campaigns. It seems unlikely that the state ever intended to permanently displace the local judiciary. Rather, it only sought to enforce minimal compliance with its directives. But such compliance was often difficult to garner, as demonstrated by the example of the sultanic edict banning marriage between Ottoman soldiers and Mamluk women *(nisa' al-atrak)*.

The ban, passed in the early years of the conquest, sought to forestall potential alliances between the imperial soldiery and local elites, thereby minimizing the risk of provincial secession. But such marriages continued to occur as "none of Egypt's judges paid [the sultan] heed, nor did the witnesses."[110] To reinvigorate his edict, the sultan personally called on his soldiers to divorce the women of *ahl Miṣr*, or face immediate execution by hanging. Only some complied, reports Ibn Iyas, failing to elaborate on the fate of the non-compliant. He does, however, describe the humiliating punishment meted out to judges who were guilty of violating the ban.

In 1517 a noncompliant Shafi'i judge was made an example of and censured by the Ottoman authorities. But surprisingly, he was not charged with violating sultanic law. Rather, the charges against him centered on the claim that he had violated a basic principle of *fiqh*. According to the chief Ottoman judge, the latter had ratified the marriage of an Ottoman soldier to a widow without first ascertaining that she had fulfilled her obligatory waiting period (*'idda*). As an example to others, the offending judge was beaten and paraded around Cairo saddled backward on a donkey.[111]

It is significant that the Ottoman chief judge used a *fiqh*-based pretext for punishing the Shafi'i judge rather than citing the real reasons for his censure—the violation of sultanic law. What might appear to be a circuitous process of conviction suggests that Egyptian jurists were articulating their objections to the edict on the grounds that preventing two Muslims, who were otherwise eligible to marry, from entering into marriage was in direct conflict with Islamic law. Presumably unwilling or unable to assert the coequality of *qanun* and *fiqh*, the Ottoman judge found fault with his adversary's ruling on the very same basis. He, too, had failed to meet the criteria of Islamic law.

Further proof of the state's willingness to banish rebellious judges from legal practice came in Ramadan 1519, when the Shafi'i chief judge, Kamal al-Din al-Tawil, attended the monthly *majlis* (state assembly) to plead the case of his *na'ib*, Nur al-Din 'Ali al-Maymuni, who had been exiled by the governor of Cairo to Damanhur. Al-Tawil petitioned for the latter's right to return to Cairo, but only partially succeeded. While al-Maymuni could return to Cairo, he was "never" to practice law again.[112] And so, concludes Ibn Iyas, "the rulings *(rasm)* of Islam's judges have been effaced."[113] While we learn little of the particulars of the case, its conclusion is revealing. In the eyes of the Ottoman chief judge, al-Maymuni had 'misused' his legal authority and his license to practice was revoked accordingly.

The assumption that such incidents exemplify the vagaries of conquest alone is put to rest by al-Damiri. In 1591, the chief Ottoman judge, al-Efendi Hasan, earned widespread condemnation in Cairo for instructing his acting deputy to dismiss *na'ib*s and *shuhud* from the courts even *before* his arrival from Istanbul. Mercifully, writes al-Damiri, he died at sea "and so the Muslims were spared his evil-doing."[114] But even in the face of al-Hasan's premature death, the damage done by his deputy warranted the following verse from al-Damiri:

Oceans have crashed upon the *fuqaha'*,
    especially its judges and our witnesses.[115]

While the judge who was appointed in Hasan's stead was a more conciliatory figure, the worst had yet to come. In 1600, eight years after al-Hasan's ill-fated appointment, one of the most infamous chief judges, 'Abd al-Wahhab ibn Ibrahim al-Rumi al-Hanafi, arrived with a similar mandate. Al-Rumi's first order of business was to purge the courts of most of their witnesses and deputy judges.[116] They remained barred from service for the remainder of his yearlong tenure. Al-Damiri noted that 'Abd al-Wahhab's 'offenses' in the eyes of the local judiciary were not limited to court purges. In a throwback to the kinds of excesses described by Ibn Iyas, 'Abd al-Wahhab also interfered with the administration of *awqaf* (endowments) and imposed a harsh criminal code, meting out severe punishment for the slightest of crimes. In particular, he exceeded the penalties prescribed by the sharia for theft or intoxication. Moreover, he would not allow the remaining court staff to collect more than three *ansaf* for their services, thus bringing added poverty on those who remained in judicial service. Egypt, concludes al-Damiri, had not seen a judge of his kind since the Ottoman conquest.[117] Not surprisingly, poems satirizing 'Abd al-Wahhab were numerous and biting:

Cut, cut, you cut the livelihood of the *shuhud*
you swapped known customs *(al-ta'aruf)* with denial *(juhud)*
[brought] death to rain *(al-mughith)* and that which is known/good
    (al-ma'ruf).[118]

News of his *'azl* (termination of tenure) arrived in 1601.

It is worth noting that al-Damiri ends this long litany of charges and complaints by stressing that Abd al-Wahhab was not without personal merit, for he never accepted bribes. This is a recurring theme in al-Damiri's biography. Ottoman judges, who were on the receiving end of the most scathing, seemingly personal attacks, are redeemed in the end as "persons of integrity." One can only conclude, therefore, that the rivalries described were never personal in nature, but firmly grounded in antagonistic legal doctrines. The doctrines in question, whether pertaining to legal processes or substantive law, were never static, however, and neither were relations between local jurists and Ottoman judges. It is not uncommon to find an exceedingly unpopular judge replaced with a more conciliatory figure who would temper or even reverse his predecessor's policies. To some extent, this reflects the personal discretion that individual Ottoman judges exercised in dispensing the duties of their office. But it also suggests that the Porte's threshold of tolerance for judicial conflict was not limitless.

'Abd al-Wahhab's volatile tenure, for example, was followed by that of the conciliatory 'Uthman ibn Muhammad Pasha, known as Rawa Zada, who had the sole distinction of presiding over the chief judgeship of Egypt three times—in 1593, in 1595, and finally in 1601.[119] Rawa Zada's first undertaking was to reverse his predecessor's policies by ordering the witnesses and judges back to work, earning both the gratitude and support of their ranks.[120] Typically, each of his appointments followed on the heels of a particularly confrontational episode in Ottoman–Egyptian judicial relations.[121]

In describing these clashes and purges, neither Ibn Iyas nor al-Damiri does more than voice their chagrin and sympathy for the injustices suffered by local judges. Neither, however, describes the impact of these purges on the day-to-day functioning of the courts. Who officiated over the courts in the absence of local judges, witnesses, and notaries? Did the Ottoman chief judge's Hanafi deputies (and their personal coterie of notaries and witnesses) replace local judges? Or were the neighborhood courts closed for the interim of these campaigns? If they were closed, was the Bab al-'Ali court (seat of the Ottoman chief judge) the only court open to the public? There are no obvious answers to these questions. But, given the logistical problems inherent in the closure of all but one of Cairo's courts, we can safely discount that possibility. The high court alone could not have met the legal needs of one of the empire's most populous cities. In describing a purge in the late sixteenth century, al-Damiri does mention, however, that the only venue in which people had access to non-Hanafi judges was the high court, suggesting that other courts continued to function, but under the auspices of Hanafi judges alone. Presumably, these would have been members of the chief Ottoman judge's personal entourage rather than local Hanafi judges. The next question that comes to mind is, what impact did this have on the law produced? The obvious answer is that it would have greatly hampered the application of the non-Hanafi law for the duration of the campaign.

The link between court purges and a decline in the authority of the *madhhab*s is most apparent in the late sixteenth century. Al-Damiri reserves his harshest criticisms for the progenitor of this policy, the same 'Abd al-Wahhab who purged the courts in 1600 of judges, witnesses, and notaries. During his yearlong tenure, 'Abd al-Wahhab not only purged the courts of their staff, he also formally suspended the non-Hanafi schools of law.[122] In effect, Cairo's various communities, most of whom were *not* adherents of Hanafism, had no recourse to Shafi'i, Hanbali, or Maliki law for the better part of a year.

Subversive *Ijtihad*

Court purges notwithstanding, there were other means by which the local judiciary's independence was curbed. A policy impugning the capacity of judges to exercise independent *ijtihad* was one such method. As a prerogative that could undermine the state's bid to shape the law produced, *ijtihad* was viewed as potentially subversive. This is especially true in the first decades of Sulayman's rule and at the peak of his venture in messianic kingship and aspiration to the position of supreme *mujtahid*.[123] The example of al-Laqani, a Maliki judge who refused to accept the position of deputy *(na'ib)* to the chief Ottoman judge in 1524, clearly demonstrates the political liability of assuming the title or role of a *mujtahid*. Soon after being coerced into the position of deputy to the chief Hanafi judge, "as per the custom *('adat)* of the Anatolian judges *(qudat al-arwam)*,"[124] Laqani found his rulings challenged on the grounds that they were based on weak Hadith *(qawl)*. His rebuttal to the chief Ottoman judge reminded the latter that he was an independent scholar, entitled to engage in unfettered, independent reasoning *(ijtihad mutlaq)*.[125]

> Among us [we hold] the principle that if a judge issues a ruling on the basis of a weak opinion, he renders that opinion strong and it enters into practice *(ma'mul bihi)* and I have attained a station [that will

not permit] my rulings to be contradicted when I am the expounder (*sharih*) of the *madhhab*. I have no need of the post [deputy judge] and have exiled myself . . . exiled myself . . . exiled myself.[126]

Each time Laqani proclaimed his own exile, the chief judge interjected, "I have reinstated you." Al-Laqani's insistence on his right to *ijtihad* and his reluctance to accept a demotion in rank (as deputy to the chief Ottoman judge) tells us that one was linked to the other. In other words, a deputy judge lacked the right to engage in *ijtihad mutlaq*. While al-Damiri never tells us what substantive issue or ruling was at stake in this dispute, he does imply that Laqani's ruling was overturned as the latter died of "fever" (a euphemism for "heartbreak") soon after.

The story appears to be cross-referenced in Sha'rani's chronicle, however, where the latter describes the opposition generated by the imposition of a certain *qanun*. Sha'rani commends the early sixteenth-century Fakhr al-Din al-Sunbati, who resigned his post as judge when he learned that the *qanun* (in this case the court fees/*rusum*) would be imposed on judges. He retired to his village, writes Sha'rani, where he heard cases as a *fard kifayya* (a religious obligation which one or more individuals may undertake on behalf of the community), free of charge.[127]

The *rasm* in question was the *qanun* of 1521, already discussed in chapter two, which imposed a marriage tax of sixty nifs for a virgin, and thirty for a widow or divorcee. As shown, qadis were ordered to "follow *al-sayq al-'uthmani*,"[128] and the protests of almost one hundred Azhari scholars, including al-Laqani, were insufficient to stop it. Nonetheless, the marriage tax continued to gall local jurists, earning mention in several chronicles, and receiving extensive treatment in one of the most important sixteenth-century juridical works.[129]

During the same period, Ottoman chief judges who imposed the *qanun* with vigor were posthumously disparaged. Muhammad Shah ibn Hazm, for example, arrived in 1563 and soon gained notoriety for his rigid and stern application of the *qanun*. His authority was so absolute, writes al-Damiri, that even the governor was subordinate to him. He implemented the *namus* (alternative name for *qanun*) till heads were "bowed" (*ta'ta'at*). Extremely unpopular, this judge inspired many a satiric poem against him and his "*siyasa*." Al-Damiri accuses him of "ignorance" of the ways of the communities of Egypt (*ahali misr*), who are used to "lenience and unaccustomed to his ways."[130] But a description of the rewards bestowed upon Hazm when he returned to Istanbul undermines the claim that he was merely acting out of ignorance. It bears repeating that Hazm was rewarded, not for his individual initiative, but for pursuing a broader agenda that enjoyed a measure of consensus and support in the imperial center.

Again, such confrontations were not limited to the first quarter of the century, but were a consistent feature of the first hundred years of Ottoman rule. Muhammad Ibn Ahmad Najm al-Din al-Ghiti (d. 1573/74), who held the prestigious post of teacher at al-Salihiya al-Najmiya (the pre-eminent madrasa of Cairo), defended Sha'rani (d. 1565), a Sufi and an *'alim*, when the latter was accused of engaging in *ijtihad mutlaq*.[131] Laqani's unfortunate fate, and Shar'ani's brush with Ottoman officials, illustrates that jurists who were perceived (or who perceived themselves) as great *mujtahid*s could be found in the sixteenth century, and more importantly, that their activities often courted confrontation with the state.

Even without engaging in *ijtihad*, local jurists could earn the censure of the state merely by challenging or critiquing Ottoman judicial policy. An example is the important Hanafi scholar 'Ali Nur al-Din al-Tarabulsi, who rose to prominence when he challenged the chief judge Muhammad ibn Ilyas, or Jevizada's, right to allow the 'exchange' of *waqf* for property or cash.[132] Al-Tarabulsi was dismissed from service and prohibited from practicing law, but continued to show defiance and to issue fatwas until an order of execution was issued against him. "He died the day it arrived."[133]

Incursions into the domain of personal morality (or the rights of God) were part and parcel of the application of Ottoman *qanun*. Both Ibn Iyas and Damiri describe episodic bouts of puritanical zeal meant to bolster the flagging moral rectitude of Cairo's civilian population.[134] Intoxication figured prominently in these campaigns, as did the conduct of women and of *dhimmi*s. That said, the bounds of 'ideal' morality were in a constant state of flux. Coffee, for example, went from an illicit brew to a staple drink and source of commercial enterprise by the early seventeenth century.

Similarly, intoxicants such as alcohol appear to have been tolerated in one era and prohibited unequivocally in another. From al-Damiri's manuscript, we learn that in 1579 the chief judge, Husayn ibn Muhammad Husam al-Din Qaraçli-Zada, was a strict prohibitionist and "no scent of intoxicant was smelled in Cairo in his time."[135] Well into the seventeenth century, the governor, Husayn Pasha (r. 1637), banned all forms of smoking, and subsequently killed fifty men caught violating the ban, on the spot.[136] Nonetheless, Qaraçli-Zada was well respected and well liked by the communities of Cairo because he exercised strict control upon the governor and his men such that they were unable to "deviate from his orders and rulings."[137] The same praise is heaped upon his deputies (*na'ib*s). Locals, both jurists and laypersons, were willing to overlook their discomfort with the strict moral codes propounded by certain Ottoman judges if they could be assured that random and illegal taxes and punishments imposed by *al-hukkam al-siyasa* on the ordinary people would be lifted.[138]

The *qanun*'s foray into private morality was decried by ordinary people, but it does not appear to have stoked any serious conflict with local judges, who were far more concerned with the long-term impact of the *qanun* dispensing the first salaries to the ulama of al-Azhar.[139]

The Co-option of the Judiciary

Sparking one of the most incendiary episodes in Ottoman–Egyptian judicial relations, the edict promulgating the bureaucratization of the local judiciary was implemented between the years 1552 and 1554 by the *qadi 'askar* 'Abd al-Baqi ibn 'Ali al-'Arabi al-Rumi. Not since the conquest had an imperial edict ignited such a crisis. At issue was the independence of the Cairene judiciary from the state.

C. Imber has shown that the muftiship of Istanbul "had emerged from relative obscurity in the fifteenth century to become, by the mid-sixteenth century, the supreme office in the Ottoman judicial hierarchy."[140] In the case of Egypt, G. Nahal has argued that by the seventeenth century, the judiciary in Egypt was hierarchically organized and, while free from the interference of other branches of provincial government, reported directly to Istanbul.[141] In other words, the judiciary in Egypt was now hierarchically embedded in an empire-wide bureaucracy culminating in the supreme judicial office of state—that of the chief mufti of Istanbul. It is unclear, however, why this transformation is viewed as a seventeenth-century development. Indeed, al-Damiri's narrative suggests that the attempt to bureaucratize the local judiciary in Cairo occurred at least a half century earlier—at exactly the same time as the muftiship of Istanbul was coming into prominence as the "supreme [judicial] office."

According to our biographer, the ulama viewed the distribution of state pensions to al-Azhar scholars as a calamity. Inevitably, a serious altercation ensued between al-Rumi and the prominent Egyptian scholar Shams al-Din Muhammad al-Hanbali, reaching its zenith when the latter penned a derisive poem attacking his nemesis. So popular was the poem, writes al-Damiri, that donkey drivers *(rukban)* recited it in and around Cairo:

> Were the ceiling made of silver,
> a fire would he wish upon the house.
> Were graves piled high with gold,
> death would he rush.
> Alone with the beloved
> love is forgotten
> but her jewelry remembered and stolen.[142]

The incidental poem might have been forgotten had al-Hanbali not delivered it to the qadi of Giza, who was heading to Istanbul, with explicit instructions that it be read aloud to Sultan Sulayman by the grand mufti of Istanbul himself, the famous Shaykh al-Islam Abu al-Su'ud. We may speculate about al-Hanbali's intentions. Did he wish to draw the Porte's attention to the fact that al-Rumi was personally disliked? If so, why make the added demand that it be read to the sultan by none other than the chief mufti of Istanbul? Let us consider the first question. Al-Damiri cites numerous examples of Ottoman chief judges deemed corrupt by their counterparts in Cairo, but for whom no special emissary was dispatched to the sultan. Furthermore, at no time does al-Damiri impugn, directly or otherwise, al-Rumi's character, something he readily does with other Ottoman chief judges. It seems unlikely, therefore, that al-Hanbali's grand gesture was motivated by personal animosity. Instead, the poem is a metaphor for the state and its rapacious drive to co-opt a sacred duty into a profane bureaucratic structure. What better way to highlight these objections than by handpicking Abu al-Su'ud, the individual who personified this new bureaucratic trend, to read it to its progenitor, the sultan?

But the contents of the letter never reached the sultan. Learning of the plot, the *qadi 'askar* hastened to the governor, 'Ali Pasha, complaining that a certain Shams al-Din al-Hanbali had "attacked us" in his poem and had sent it to the sultan with a certain Muhammad al-Manshi. Intercepted in Alexandria, al-Manshi was brought before the *diwan*, "poem in hand." The offending poet-jurist, al-Hanbali, was then summoned from his post at the prestigious Madrasat al-Zahiriya for interrogation. Leading the interrogation was the governor, who asked, "O Shaykh, are these your words insulting the *shaykh al-Islam, qadi Misr*?"

"Yes!" he answered.

"Were you not afraid of what might befall you writing such things?"

"I merely relayed the events as they unfolded," he replied.

At which point the Ottoman judge interjected, "The principle among Hanafis [holds] that to insult a *qadi* is *kufr* [unbelief]."

Demanding his detractor's execution, and rebuffed by the governor who refused to endorse the request,[143] al-Rumi threatened to "shut the courts of Egypt and leave the country."[144]

In the end, the courts remained open and Shams al-Din remained among the living. Nonetheless, he was imprisoned and visited on a daily basis by the governor's emissary, al-Daylami. The poignant exchange that is alleged to have transpired between the latter and the jailed shaykh demonstrates the use of religious ideology in the campaign to 'renew' legal practices. For days al-Daylami beseeched Shams al-Din: "Renew your Islam" *(jaddid islamak)*. With equal consistency, Shams al-Din replied, "I am a Muslim, and nothing has emanated forth from me that contradicts Islam or [the rulings of] its Shaykh, al-Qarrafi."[145]

Without giving us any indication of how long Shams al-Din was incarcerated, al-Damiri reports that he was eventually released. Nothing more is written of this incident, except for a footnote indicating that, years later, when news of al-Rumi's death in Anatolia arrived, al-Hanbali was moved to pen two lines eulogizing his former nemesis:

> How our differences caused tears of blood!
> Now that he is gone we weep for him.[146]

Barring sarcasm, which seems unlikely under the circumstances, it is not surprising that Shams al-Din would write these conciliatory lines about a man he had depicted as a vulgar materialist. Again, it bears repeating that these conflicts were rarely personal in nature. Al-Hanbali speaks of their "differences," an unexpected choice of words for an accused thief from his accuser. What transpired in the *diwan* between the men only confirms that the "differences" of which Shams al-Din wrote, though couched in personal language, were, in reality, ideological. His attacks on Rumi can only be read, therefore, as a critique of judicial policies enforced through imperial directive, not by the capricious whim of an individual judge.

Al-Damiri's biography ends in the early seventeenth century, with several more anecdotes suggesting that tensions between Ottoman judges and local judges continued to flare. Among the complaints directed against qadi Salih ibn Sa'id (ten. 1612–13) was that he delegated too much authority to his *atba'* (followers) and allowed them to exert too much influence in judicial matters. They, in turn, were corrupt and abused their powers, says al-Damiri.

While the above may suggest a clear delineation between Egyptian jurists and members of the Ottoman Hanafi guild, al-Damiri's biography of the chief Ottoman judges in Egypt reveals a far more complex relationship. Many an Ottoman chief judge won the admiration of Cairo's communities by shielding them from *qanun*, upholding the principle of judicial disputation *(ikhtilaf)*, respecting the *madhahib*, and legitimating local customary laws. Some did this without drawing the Porte's ire, while others paid a heavy price for their discretionary tactics.

In 1549 Salih ibn Jalal was praised for his opposition to *hukkam al-siyasa* and for upholding the *shar'*. The chronicler writes that he was renowned for his "expertise in lifting the harm from Muslims," an allusion to his reliance on the jurisprudential principle of *maslaha*, or public interest. In practice, this could mean a more hospitable environment for local custom under the pretext of "lifting the harm" *(izalat al-darar)*. He was also praised by Sultan Sulayman Qanuni, writes the author, implying that these more lenient measures were in accord with the Porte's directives. In 1569, the chief judge Muhammad ibn 'Abd al-Qadir was praised as a scholar of Sufism whose knowledge of religious sciences *('ilm)* and of the 'customary practice' of the people *('amal)* was impeccable.[147] In the case of another chief judge, Muhammad ibn Shaykh Muhammad ibn Ilyas, who left office in 1570, al-Damiri writes that he was "praised by the people of knowledge *(ahl al-ma'arif)* for his knowledge," a reference to the scholar's Sufi credentials.[148] Al-Damiri commends the judge's inclination for consultation with Egyptian jurists and for correspondence with jurists from many *madhhab*s, "of which he was highly knowledgeable."[149] Significantly, he was also well regarded for looking into the welfare *(masalih)* of Muslims.[150] Pervez al-Rumi, who took office in 1574, was also commended for resorting to *maslaha*.[151] 'Abd al-Ghani ibn Mir Shah, who assumed the chief judgeship of Egypt twice (first in 1576–78 and again in 1585–86), was another well-regarded scholar who was inclined toward *awlad al-'Arab* (the Arabic-speaking masses) and the *fuqaha'* and paid heed to *maslaha*.[152]

But the stories of many a popular Ottoman chief judge illustrate that they were praised not for their lenient interpretations of Ottoman law, but, sometimes, their blatant disregard of it. One such figure is Fayd Allah ibn Ahmad, known as Qaf Zada, who took office in 1591. Our biographer al-Damiri praises him for consciously disregarding important aspects of the *qanun*, notably the collection of the stipulated court fees. Qaf Zada was responsible for "ending the deterioration of the divine laws of the venerable *shar'*."[153] Al-Damiri goes so far as to credit him with leading an intellectual renaissance so that "people counted his days as a dream."[154] More than that, Qaf Zada attempted to correct some of the excesses of his predecessors by restoring to the judicial classes some of the privileges they had enjoyed prior to the conquest. He wrote to Shaykh Badr al-Din al-Qarafi, chief judge of the Maliki school, for example, reassuring him that "we issued the order that none but you shall issue fatwas for the Maliki *madhhab* without your consent."[155]

One cannot fail to note, however, that the most popular Ottoman judges in Egypt, like 'Ali ibn Yasin al-Tarabulsi al-Hanafi (date unknown) in the early seventeenth century, were often held in low regard by their Ottoman peers.[156] Considered a very pious individual who personally performed the *adhan* five times a day, al-Tarabulsi was loathed by the ulama of Rum. When he was alive they condemned him to the sultan, writes al-Damiri, and when he died they denied the validity of his fatwas. They attacked his "popular/weighty *madhhab*," demeaned his rulings, and vigorously implored the sultan to exile or execute the miscreant judge. In time, the campaign was successful in securing a sultanic edict *(marsum)* proclaiming a death sentence on Tarabulsi and, as always, it arrived in Cairo on the same day he died of natural causes. Finally, as if to encapsulate the judicial wrangling he has described, al-Damiri makes a point of recounting the good example of his own grandfather, the Maliki chief judge Muhammad ibn 'Abd al-Karim ibn Ahmad ibn Siddiq al-Damiri, who only implemented those "*qawanin* that did not contravene the *shari'a*."[157]

Conclusion

In the past few decades, a new and expanding line of inquiry into the Ottoman Empire has overturned once stable historical paradigms. In no small part thanks to the rich documentary and archival evidence available to us, a uniquely textured history of Ottoman law is emerging, allowing for an intimate portrayal of society and legal culture. Within this tide of revision, however, a paradigm of exceptionalism permeates scholarship on Ottoman Egypt. Due to its size, wealth, and Islamic pedigree, Egypt occupies a unique status within the wider Ottoman narrative, a status which exaggerates the impenetrability of its legal institutions and its local customs. Ibn Iyas' and al-Damiri cast doubt on this stoic narrative.

The history presented above warrants a reexamination of the idea that the Ottoman state tampered only with the administration of justice. It invites a reassessment of the belief that judicial tensions eased after the shock and vagaries of the conquest and of the claim that the local judiciary was able to reassert its independence from the state. The language of *takfir* and *tajdid* amply demonstrate the rhetorical means by which this independence challenged, and paradoxically highlighted, the Ottoman self-perception as 'renewers' of the faith. The renewed 'Ottoman sharia,' emphasizing 'orthodoxy' in its pursuit of universalism, codification, and homogenization, stood in antagonistic rivalry with that of the Cairene jurists, among whom a traditionally orthoprax and pluralistic legal model prevailed. The latter upheld the traditional juristic paradigm that local custom/practice held precedent in the microcommunity's affairs, while the state challenged this assertion by endowing the *qanun* with a 'universal legitimacy.' This intervention was not limited to *qanun* law, however, but extended to the critical discourse on judicial and legislative 'authority' in Islam. The political appropriation of this authority, whether through caliphal claims to the supreme right of *ijtihad*, or through the diminution of the coequality of the *madhhab*s, implies that the center of gravity for the production of communal/local culture had shifted to a 'transcommunal' judicial body. Where *fiqh* had left room for local custom to resolve gray areas of the law, the *qanun* and the official *madhhab* now attempted to take its place.

The emphasis on the construction of 'orthodoxy' notwithstanding, it should be made clear that this in no way implies a rigid, authoritarian, or static ideal. The renewal project remained perpetually discursive and transformative. Almost unanimously, the secondary literature on court registers from the sixteenth and seventeenth centuries suggests that in practice the Ottoman sharia courts functioned with a commendable professionalism, serving as equitable venues where "a woman or a slave" could win rulings against *amir*s; where the qadi's judgements were expeditious and enforced with the assistance of the *shurta*; where *dhimmi*s preferred to have their cases heard; and, where sharia courts handled a broader range of cases than ever before.[158]

Next, we will consider how the renewal project enhanced the autonomy of the individual, and how it was connected to the status of the document in Islamic law.

Chapter Four
"This *Sijill* is a *Hujja*!"
Mass-producing Legal Documents in Ottoman Cairo

Introduction

The standardization of record-keeping via the written legal document (*hujja*), and the centralization of records via the public archive, were key factors in the changing relationship between subjects and their state. They were also the key innovations separating the Ottomans from their predecessors. Neither the Ottomans, nor any other political moderns, can claim to have invented either the written legal document or the archive. Nonetheless, there is a systematization at work in Ottoman judicial life which gives them a new vibrancy and application—for the first time in memory, legal documents were produced, notarized, indexed, and archived for the common man and woman. The sixteenth century can thus be characterized as the site of a mass production of legal documents. The political impact of this documented life on Muslim conceptions of self and moral sovereignty is the subject of this chapter. But first a word on the innovations that made it possible.

While there is enormous textual evidence that record keeping, by any name, was a long-established Islamic practice, some scholars, impressed by the fact that the only complete, extant *sijill*s date from the first two decades of Ottoman rule—in the case of Egypt, from the Mahkama al-Salihiya—have suggested that the practice of compiling registers of legal documents (*sijill*-keeping) was an Ottoman innovation.[1] This is not a view endorsed by most scholars, who agree that the practice of *sijill*-keeping long predates the Ottomans and is, in all likelihood, pre-Islamic in origin. Indeed there is virtually no evidence to support the claim that the Ottoman state was the first to invent the *sijill* (as a legal register) or the archive.² After all, the discovery of a compilation of Mamluk legal documents in the Haram collection (*sijill* documents or fragments of an archive of Mamluk documents found in the Haram sanctuary in Jerusalem), representing fragments of an archive, lays to rest any such notion. Moreover, the variety and names of Haram documents share much in form and content with their counterparts in the Ottoman *sijill*. A. Sonbol cautions that even the practice of recording contracts in courts, "usually seen as regulated under the Ottomans, actually existed since Ancient Egyptian times, and was traditional for Islamic Egypt before the arrival of the Ottomans."³ All that changed under the Ottomans was that registration became compulsory. And finally, even the formulaic clichés encountered in the *shurut* (model contracts) manuals share a strong affinity with those found in the *sijill*s of both Mamluk and Ottoman states.⁴

But if there was nothing innovative about the Ottoman system of record-keeping and archiving, why is it the only archive in Egypt to yield "millions" of perfectly preserved legal documents?⁵ One obvious explanation is that the Ottoman era is the most recent and, therefore, the most likely to yield the largest number of surviving documents. As ordinary records documenting purchases, marriages, divorces, and so on became archaic, they were likely disposed of, or retained within private collections, as in the Khalidi family's *daftar*. But the sheer contrast between that which survives from the Ottoman and the pre-Ottoman periods suggests the need for a fuller explanation. The lack of a comparable cache of documents surviving from either of its Muslim contemporaries, the Mughal or Safavid states, further weakens the argument that the records of the Ottoman archive survive only because they are more recent.

What explains the discrepancy, I will argue, is a transformation in Ottomans' attitudes to the document. It was certainly not the first or only Muslim state to produce and archive important legal documents, but it was the only one to mass-produce them. It generated millions of documents pertaining to the lives of ordinary men and women—their marriages and divorces, their property disputes, their personal disputes and claims—and it alone preserved them in their millions. It was not the first Islamic state to grant important documents (state edicts, inheritance and tax registers) the status of an 'authoritative legal proof' *(hujja)*, but it was the first to bestow this designation on a mass of mundane civil documents. It did not invent the Islamic court, but it invented one of its most identifiable, bureaucratic symbols—the courthouse. No longer embodied in the person of the judge (who previously held court in any number of changing venues), the 'court' became associated with a predesignated, fixed, and public place. It did not invent the practice of registering a document with the court, but it was the first to make such registration compulsory for marriage and divorce. We must be careful, therefore, when speaking of documents being registered with the pre-Ottoman 'court,' for what exactly designates a court in Mamluk, Fatimid, or Roman times? Not only does the conceptual and practical definition of the 'court' change under Ottoman administration, but so do the protocols associated with the custodial guardianship of court documents (*sijill*s).

In the Ottoman system, judges, who traditionally retained custody of their *sijill*s, were alienated from their own records by a series of new protocols transferring custody of the *sijill* to a professional class of bureaucratic archivists. The Ottomans could now boast of a central, state archive, and what is more, of what is arguably the first public archive in the history of the Islamic state. As a consortium of public and private documents dating back generations, the archive functioned as a public repository of memory to be accessed under restricted conditions. Without the public archive, it would not have been possible to mass-produce authoritative legal documents, or *hujja*s.

The Document Triumphant

It is not yet clear when a precise lexical vocabulary denoting a legally sound document emerged. In theological and classical judicial usage, the term *hujja* was used in the sense of a 'proof' or 'sign.'[6] In Ottoman usage, a written *hujja* (Turkish: *hüccet*) constituted any document that was approved and signed by jurists, containing the confession of one party and the acceptance of another.[7] Generally speaking, Ottoman courts treated three types of documents as 'sound' or 'certain' in the absence of memory or witnesses. The first was that important body of documents that every state designated as authoritative, namely state edicts, endowments (*awqaf*), and taxation and inheritance records. The second was a free-floating body of documents that circulated in private hands, such as Numjarawi's, and which, more often than not, were copies of an original archived document. The third was the *sijill* itself, an unprecedented designation for a judge's complete records.

According to the tenth-century Hanafi jurist, al-Tahawi, certain documents could be regarded as *hujja*s, in an interpretation that long predates the Ottomans. In the example of a contract of sale that has been canceled, "Abu Hanifa and others call for a separate document *(hujja)* that specifically cancels the sale."[8] Thus, *hujja*s could be documents, but more often than not, the theological and legal literature uses the word in the sense of a 'proof' provided in the form of a 'sign,' oral testimony or, by Tahawi's time, a document.[9]

Wakin sees in this a positive indication of the importance of having "written documents in one's hands,"[10] a need which had become acute in the late sixteenth century, judging by the fact that more and more documents were being given the designation of *hujja*. *Hujja*s circulated across geographic boundaries within the empire, as demonstrated by one issued for a merchant from the court of Aleppo in 1607, naming the merchant's legal representative *(wakil)* in Egypt.[11] Moreover, documents circulated across temporal boundaries, such that 'old' documents *(hujja qadima)*, which could no longer be verified by living witnesses, were also accepted as sound.[12] Almost all cases pertaining to *waqf*, for example, are *'ilam*s (complex documents) with references to multiple legal documents, going back to the date of the *waqf*'s establishment, the testamentary bequest stipulating its distribution (indicated over multiple generations), and its administration.[13]

That said, there were also definite conditions stipulating when an 'authoritative' document could be used, and when it could not. In Cairo, for example, such documents could only be endorsed in the Bab al-'Ali court, seat of the Ottoman chief judge. Deputy judges were strictly forbidden from ruling on the basis of written *hujja*s issued by other judges, from adding their seal to any document issued by another court, or from signing a *hujja* without the signature of the original witnesses.[14]

By the end of the sixteenth century written *hujja*s were commonly cited in the Cairo *sijill* and registered as *hujja shar'iya*, a "*shar'i* proof," *hujja musattara*, simply indicating a "written proof,"[15] or even *hujja shar'iya musattara*.[16] A typical example of a 'sound' written *hujja*, like the one issued in 1562 in the Qisma 'Askeriya to the wife of a prisoner of war seeking to annul *(faskh)* her marriage, reads: "This is a *shar'i hujja*, and a sound *(sahiha)*, sheltered *(mar'iya)* document, made public and composed in the presence of our lord the *qassam*."[17]

The above heading precedes an itemized catalogue of the wife's (conspicuously modest) earthly belongings. Another example reads: "This is a clear *shar'i hujja* and a sheltered, forthright *(sariha)* document, the contents of which are known, and the text [of which] is interpreted according to our lord *fulan*'s understanding."[18]

In both documents, the term *mar'iya* (sheltered, guarded, or protected) is an explicit reference to the document's authenticity and an implicit reference to its archival credentials. How the written document attained such status, particularly in view of Islamic law's preference for oral testimony, is the subject of this chapter.

Before any technical innovations in the collation, authentication, and indexing of documents could take place, a formidable theoretical legal tradition would have to be overcome. Scholarship has generally regarded the position of documents in Islamic society as its longest-standing legal fiction. Documents remained extralegal in theory, but widespread in practice. But the radical transformation of the legal document in Ottoman practice, and indeed the very answer to the riddle of its survival, can hardly be understood in the absence of the dialectic between legal theory and practice.

The Document in Theory

A copy of the manumission of Mustafa al-Numjarawi, the original stored in Constantinople *(surat 'itqnama Mustafa al-Numjarawi, al-asl maktab bi-Qustantiniya)*, reads as follows:

> This is a sound and *shar'i hujja* (legitimate proof), and a clear, protected writ/deed, its content conveying *(yu'rib madmunniha)* that which *('an dhikri ma)* was decreed and acknowledged in the honourable *shar'i majlis* and the seat of the Hanif faith [which is] sheltered against change or corruption.[19]

In spite of centuries of Islamic legal ambiguity toward written documents, this particular document, recorded in the presence of the Ottoman chief judge *(qadi al-qudah)* of Cairo in the court of the Bab al-'Ali, is declared a "sound and *shar'i* proof" *(hujja)*. The status of al-Numjarawi's document of manumission, issued by the chief judge of Istanbul, would seem to contravene some of the basic tenets of Islamic legal theory, which shunned the written document as a "suspect" and weak *hujja*, and maintained the primacy of oral testimony through witnessing. What is more, the document in al-Numjarawi's possession is not the original, but a "copy" of the original document, issued and housed in the Maktab (archive) of Constantinople.

This was hardly innovative, as the transmission and multiplication of important documents was commonplace even early in Islamic history. The Ottoman state's predecessors noted differences between a draft, an original, and a draft copy *(musawwada)*.[20] But they almost certainly reserved such protocols for documents pertaining to important matters of state or society. By contrast, Numjarawi's document was neither a religious fatwa nor a state edict, but an unremarkable certificate attesting to the manumission of an ordinary slave. It, and millions like it, signified a transformation in the status of written documents in Islamic legal practice. The question is, does it also reflect a widening breach with legal theory?

An enduring paradox for the historian of the *sijill* is the 'unofficial,' and, by some arguments, even 'extralegal' status they, and all written documents, occupy in Islamic legal theory. Muslim jurists are sympathetic to the ancient view expressed by Socrates:

> Once a thing is put in writing, the composition, whatever it may be, drifts all over the place, getting into the hands of not only those who understand it, but equally those who have no business with it; it doesn't know how to address the right people, and not address the wrong. And when it is ill treated and unfairly abused, it always needs its parent [living speech] to come to its help, being unable to defend or help itself.[21]

These cautionary words would resonate in Islamic society, where the rules of evidentiary procedure served to undermine the document in legal theory. Thus, in spite of a clear Qur'anic conjunction to write down contracts, B. Messick argues, Islamic law "emptied the Qur'anic command of all binding force, denied validity to written documents, and insisted on the evidence of eye witnesses."[22] In F. Rosenthal's words, Muslim society was "peculiar" in adhering to a never-abandoned fiction—very soon to be enshrined in the very center of Muslim intellectual life, the science of Hadith—of the primacy of the spoken word.[23]

Nonetheless, the sheer necessity of documentation, and the fact that jurists of the ninth and tenth centuries, such as the Hanafi al-Tahawi, were "deeply concerned" with the legal status of the documents, provides an important area of contact between theory and practice.[24] After all, writes J. Wakin, documents remained "crucial to the everyday conduct of affairs."[25] It is not surprising, therefore, that the continued use of written documents became the subject of a rich legal literature. But the importance of this genre is diminished by Messick, who writes that while "the manuals do envision witnessing acts associated with the preparation of written instruments," they do not take further steps to legitimate the written document as a source of evidence independent of the former.[26] Even Wakin contends that in spite of the attention given by jurists to the question of documents, the status of the 'written word' remained "ambiguous."[27] T. Turan, who concedes that there *was* a noticeable transformation in Ottoman attitudes to the document, concludes that the sluggish response of Islamic legal theory proved an insurmountable barrier to the necessary changes and, as a result, hardly reflects the use of documents in practice.[28]

The conclusion that theory stagnated, while practice continued to evolve unbridled, ignores a long tradition predisposed to viewing documents which were 'well-guarded' (kept in safe storage) as 'chaste' and therefore sound. Wakin's work shows that the Hanafi school took a leading role in "cultivating" the practical literature on *hiyal* (legal devices or evasions) and on *shurut* (model contracts) as well as the works on "the *mahadir* and *sijillat*, formularies containing model documents for use of the qadi and his clerks."[29] The literature on legal documents and their formularies "grew," she argues, "out of an "attempt by jurists to bring ideal theory and practices together."[30] While noting the contributions of the other schools to this literature, she also mentions that they were considerably smaller, and "a later synthetic creation made possible largely by the success of the Hanafi works."[31]

Hanafi theory did, therefore, provide set criteria by which to assess a document's chastity and, provided it met the criteria indicated, was prepared to accept it as a *hujja sahiha*, or sound evidence. The Ottoman civil code of 1877, the *Mejelle*, conveys this recognition, "albeit in a negative way," in Wakin's conclusion, as "the witnessed document had no value in itself—unless it met those requirements mentioned above."[32] A central problem with this perspective is its underlying assumption that legal theory should reflect, positively, changes in practice. In other words, it neglects the fact that practice is aligning itself with theory.

Centuries before the *Mejelle*, the *Fatawa 'Alamgiriya*, an enormous compendium of Hanafi law, composed in 1664–72 by order of the Mughal emperor Aurangzeb, demonstrates the extent to which the assimilation of practice and theory had already occurred. For the most part, the arrangement and selection of subjects in the *Fatawa* follows the *Hidaya* of al-Marghinani (d. 1196), itself adopted from the classical works of Hanafi *fiqh*, and is considered largely unoriginal. But the work does contain evidence of originality in the addition of five new chapters not found in the *Hidaya*.[33] Significantly, one is on *mahadir* (formularies) and the other on *sijillat*.[34] More evidence that Hanafi doctrines had already absorbed and assimilated the written document is found in the *Fatawa 'Alamgiri*'s proclamation that "this *sijill* is a *hujja* for the recipient of this judgment *(mahkum lahu)*."[35] In other words, "this register is a de facto *hujja*."

This important transformation had broad and penetrating consequences for Muslim society, which will be considered in chapter 5. For now, I wish to provide further evidence of this transformation in judicial and diplomatic practice. It stands to reason that a predilection for seeing written legal document as proofs would render obsolete a variety of older formulary styles signifying an 'authoritative document.' In the selection at my disposal, a document known as the *tawriq* is encountered in five records from the Bab al-'Ali court in 1005–1006. Originating from the root *waraq* (paper) designating a copy of a document, the label is encountered on the top right-hand corner of the page.[36] In the fifth document, however, it appears in the body of the opening statement: "[T]his is a certain, *shar'i* motion and a clear *tawriq ta'aqud* (duplicate contract)."[37] Each of these documents pertains to high-ranking individuals, including members of the judicial and merchant elite and officials from the *diwan*. Two pertain to the same individual, an *amir* and a merchant by the name of Khawaja Isma'il, one being an *iqrar* (legal acknowledgment) and the second a purchase.[38] Another involves the *multazim* and the chief mufti in a document pertaining to the rent of a portion of a *waqf* property.[39]

Fifty years later, by 1055–56, the *tawriq* as an authoritative copy appears to have lapsed from usage. It is not encountered even once in a much larger sample of documents from the same court. Was the *tawriq* rendered obsolete by the phrase, "this *sijill* is a *hujja*?" Before we can answer this question, we need to understand the archive's role in generating the authoritative written *hujja* and in fueling its mass production.

The Public Archive

If legal documents were to be mass produced as *hujja*s, there would have to be a mechanism for their mass authentication. Insofar as it discouraged the free circulation of documents in the public domain and in individual hands, the archive appears as a mechanism created to do just that. This is what Derrida wants us to realize before we even begin to contemplate the archive: the nature of an archive is to be both authoritarianly transparent (i.e., accessible to the public under restricted conditions) and authoritatively concealed.[40] The concerns of jurists like Tahawi could thus be assuaged by the presence of a mechanism minimizing the risk of forgery or interpolation, while contributing to the preservation of millions of documents.[41]

From the Greek *arche*, which means 'the beginning,' the word for archive (*arkhein*) means 'to begin, command, or rule.' Certainly not an Ottoman innovation, the practice of archiving was already customary in the ancient eastern Mediterranean, and it may be assumed that the Arabs knew of this institution at an early date. Indeed there is "a short précis on the back of some papyri, intended to facilitate storing and reference. But there is no evidence of the existence of a central archive, as there was in Greek times."[42]

But there was a central archive in Fatimid times, and Ibn al-Sayrafi calls the archivist a *khazin*, while praising the Baghdad archive, *al-khizana al-'uzma*, as a model. The function of an archivist was to "file the originals of incoming documents, and the copies of the outgoing ones according to months, in folders with headings. A certain decline in this practice seems to have set in in Mamluk times, and there were periods when the *dawadar* of the confidential secretary sufficed as an archivist."[43] But whether the central archives of the ancient Greeks or the Abbasids were ever equivalent to the Ottoman public archive is questionable. Whether they mass-produced and archived documents on the scale of the Ottomans is unknown and must remain a mystery.

The Courthouse

The building of a mass archive was contingent on a radical reimagining of the court in Islam. The spatial contours of the Islamic court (*majlis al-hukm)* had always been physically embodied in the person of the judge, who held his sessions in a number of changing venues. Mosques and certain madrasas, which generally functioned as places of arbitration, were likely the main depositories for important judicial registers or documents. The fact that the Haram documents were found "within the precincts of the al-Haram aš-Šarif in Jerusalem, the third most holy place in the Muslim world," suggests as much.[44] However, a great many more registers would have been circulating in the private homes of individual judges or their descendants for, in homage to a tradition dating from the classical period, it was established juridical etiquette for an outgoing judge to surrender *(taslim/tasalum)* his registers to the incoming judge.[45] What is to be emphasized here is the absence of a central archive in which to store and preserve said documents (explaining the dearth in complete pre-Ottoman registers) and the private nature of the judge's role as the embodiment of the 'court' *(majlis al-shar')* and as the principle custodian of its records.

Debunking the Weberian assumption that no rational system of law, let alone court system, existed in the Muslim world before modernization, scholars such as N. Hanna and A. Sonbol estimate that thirty-seven courts and sub-courts served Cairo in the eighteenth century.[46] But were we to ask what exactly was being counted, the differences between the Ottoman and pre-Ottoman eras should become immediately apparent. Had this been a tally of the courts in Mamluk Cairo, we would be counting the number of licensed judges and deputy judges in the city, not the number of 'courthouses.'

Seven years after the Ottoman conquest of Egypt (1522), Cairo's legal landscape was reshaped by a network of fixed 'courthouses' that covered the city.[47] From a structural perspective, a geographically fixed courthouse changed the playing field. A fixed, rather than free-floating, court also reanchored the *sijill* to the courthouse and, by extension, to the public archive. This is substantiated by the fact that the archive preceded the fixed courts. Ibn Iyas writes that in the early days of the conquest, the governor called on all local judges and witnesses to surrender their records, particularly marital contracts, to the deputies of the Ottoman *qadi 'asker*. None complied, and the order went unenforced until a *muqaddim* was dispatched to confiscate them by force.[48] Perhaps for this reason, the "first four pages of the first volume of the sijill [Shari'ah court records] of the Ottoman archives for the Shari'ah court of the Mediterranean port town of Dumyat date back to 1505 while the Ottoman invasion took place in 1517. The format of the individual entries in the first four pages—mostly marriages—is followed in the later entries dating after the Ottoman invasion."[49]

Sonbol takes this to mean "that registration of cases in court took place before the arrival of the Ottomans and the practice was continued by the Ottomans."[50] The assumption that people deposited their important papers in the qadi's *diwan* (as his private *sijill* was known) is of course true, and must not be forgotten. At the same time, however, this is no seamless transition from Mamluk to Ottoman court systems. In the first place, there was no physical courthouse with which to register documents in the Mamluk era, nor a unified *sijill* (encompassing all marriage documents), handed down from generation to generation, to be relinquished into Ottoman custody. The likely reason there are records predating the conquest in the Ottoman *sijill*—especially marriage contracts—is that they had been confiscated by the *muqaddim* in an unprecedented incursion on judicial sovereignty.

A *muqaddim's* job was to attend and observe the court's proceedings, and at day's end, to collect all marriage contracts to be deposited in the governor's *diwan*. Thereafter, they were stored according to rules ordained by Ottoman law (*yasaq*).[51] Writing in the seventeenth century, al-Bakri al-Siddiqi (d. 1676) described the same judicial routine persisting into his day. But in addition to the presence of a *muqaddim*, the *qadi 'asker* also had his records examined every three days.[52] Again, this is a significant departure from past precedent, when only suspicion of forgery or wrongdoing could justify inspection of the judges' records. The days when a judge surrendered his *sijill* only on death or retirement, or stood as the personification of the court, had drawn to an end.

The opening clichés encountered in Mamluk and Ottoman *sijill*s testify to the subtle but profoundly transformative shifts overtaking the spatial conceptions of the Islamic court. Every court record contained within the Mamluk Haram collection begins with the statement, "*Hadara fulan ila majlis al-hukm al-'aziz al-fulani*" ('So-and-so attended the honorable assembly of judge so-and-so').[53] The wording is significantly different in the *sijill*s of Ottoman Cairo, where the term *majlis al-hukm* is dropped in favor of the name of the courthouse. For example, "So-and-so attended the Bab al-'Ali (*hadara al-Bab al-'Ali fulan*),"[54] indicating nothing more of the judge's identity. Others use the formulaic cliché, "Before *mawlana* al-Hanafi, *fulan* alleged" to identify the judge's *madhhab*.[55] But, in a fixed court with fixed judges representing the four schools of law, referring to the judge by name would have been redundant. The only exception made is in the case of 'deputy' judges, who often stood in for the chief judges of their schools. In that eventuality, the name of the deputy was provided in the opening address.

In sum, the variant clichés employed by Mamluk and Ottoman scribes highlight the distinction between the judge's court *(majlis al-ḥukm)* and the courthouse *(maḥkama)*. *Majlis al-ḥukm* denotes an assembly embodied in the person of the judge. The Ottoman *sijill*, where the name of the courthouse and the *madhhab* of the presiding judge is given, provides a clear indication that the *sijill* was no longer anchored to an individual qadi, but rather to a physical space, populated by various judges and their deputies.

The continuities with earlier eras noticeable in Ottoman judicial practice should not, therefore, detract from the real innovations they introduced to the spatial geography of the courtroom and to the parameters of a judge's jurisdiction over his own register. But, as important as the courthouse and the public archive were in harmonizing theory and practice, and in contributing to the preservation of documents, they were not the only innovations to contribute to the document's triumph. Another was the series of reforms affecting the protocols by which *sijill*s were arranged, handled, and authenticated.

The *Sijill* as Text and Testament

The precise history of the *sijill* as an institution, its bureaucratic roots, and its evolution in form and function have yet to be determined, leaving serious questions as to the general and the particular in Ottoman administrative practice and historiography open-ended. Such as it is, the evidence suggests that documents in general, and legal formularies (model contracts) in particular, were part and parcel of the Near Eastern pre-Islamic tradition.[56] The evidence is less clear when it comes to the names and types of documents contained within the judicial registers of the pre-Ottoman period.[57]

In Qur'anic and early Arabic usage, F.C. De Blois writes, the word *sijill* denotes documents of an official or juridical nature.[58] Deriving from the Latin *sigillum*, meaning 'seal' in classical usage, it denoted in medieval Latin a document with an affixed seal. Filtering into Byzantine vocabulary, the word eventually passed into Arabic via Aramaic. In Arabic, De Blois notes, the word does not mean 'seal' but does denote a written document.

In classical Arabic it is "frequently used for a document containing the judgments of a kadi and in various other technical senses."[59] In *Mafatih al-'Ulum*, al-Khawarazmi indicates that it denotes a "credit note given to official messengers exempting them from the costs of their journey."[60] D. P. Little writes that in *Subh al-A'sha*, the Mamluk scholar al-Qalqashandi used the word in reference to documents issued by Fatimid caliphs, and "[o]therwise, he used sidjill once to designate a document issued by a judge to certify (isdjal) the legal integrity of his son."[61] In *shurut* works (model contracts), the term *sijill* was given "technical denotations and was defined in contrast to two other types of documents or records"—*nuskha* (an exact copy of a document) and *mahdar*.[62] Wakin and Little describe the *mahadir* as written records of the proceedings before the judge (or the minutes of the court), and the *sijillat* as the written judgments containing the judges' decisions.[63] The *Fatawa 'Alamgiri* confirm this usage but also indicate that the *sijill* is to contain an exact copy of the original *mahdar* of the case.[64] This is a format faithfully adopted in the Ottoman *sijill*s.

While "the precise denotation of sidjillat in this context of various kinds of decrees is not yet clear,"[65] in Ottoman usage, the terms "*kadi sidjilleri*" or "*sher'iyye sidjilleri*" referred exclusively to the complete register from an Ottoman court.[66] Underscoring the striking similarity of legal documents found from one era to the next is Salameh's description of the Ottoman Jerusalem *sijill*s as encompassing "records of marriages, divorces, alimony, guardianship, inventories of estates, buying, selling and trading, prices of commodities, construction, documents related to the villages of Jerusalem with regard to the purchase of land and documents related to murders [or reports]."[67] S.A.I. Milad provides an appendix of the types of documents found in Cairo in the court of the Salihiya al-Najmiya, which includes all of the above as well as documents pertaining to reconciliation between spouses, adoption, appointments of wet nurses, embezzlement of public foundations, embezzlement more generally, imprisonment, and release from prison.[68]

A. Bayinder finds much the same in Anatolian courts, but adds another type of court document, the *i'lam*. The latter is a summary of an extended case, settled over many days or weeks, and includes all the statements of the plaintiff, the defendant, relevant proofs, and finally, the judge's ruling.[69] An equivalent to the *i'lam* is the Mamluk "complex document," described by Little as containing "a bill of sale accompanied by at least six other documents," encompassing *ishhad*s and *iqrar*s.⁷⁰ In the selection at my disposal, examples of all such documents are found, excepting those relating to adoption, embezzlement, or vouchers.

By the beginning of the sixteenth century, the compilation of registers "formed part of the established routine at least in the larger cities."⁷¹ Special registers for inheritance were established in the bigger cities like Bursa or Cairo, but these were not the responsibility of the judge, and "were kept by a special official known as the '*askeri qassam*."⁷² But again, this may not have been an innovation, as the Diwan al-Mawarith (Ministry of Inheritance) for the allocation of inheritance was itself an established institution which, one would assume, required the keeping of 'special registers.' Little writes:

> In the Mamluk and other periods the state often confiscated parts or the whole of estates as a means of securing public or private gain. This aspect of the Islamic laws of inheritance were in fact institutionalized in the Ayyubid and Mamluk empires in a Diwan al-Mawarith (Ministry of Inheritance), which undertook to monitor the estates of deceased persons and to collect the portion due to the state, called *al-mawarith al-hashriya* (or escheat estates). In fact we know from one of the Haram documents (#535) that a bureau called Diwan al-Mawarith al-Hashshiya was operative in Jerusalem during the eighth/fourteenth century.⁷³

Because a complete judicial register is lacking for the Mamluk period, very little can be said about the former's structural organization. But the abundance of Ottoman *sijill*s from various corners of the empire allows for a comparative look at various regional courts. Like the Anatolian *sijill*s described by Faroqhi, the first half of the Cairene *sijill* generally gathers contractual agreements witnessed and preserved in the local court, such as sales, loans, marriage and divorce contracts, and the manumission of slaves.⁷⁴ The second half of the Cairo *sijill* is taken up with orders issued by the sultan's council. Similar to modern circulars, some are general orders directed at governors while others are specifically addressed to the chief judge of the courts. Most are written in Ottoman Turkish. Again this is reflected in the records of Ottoman Jerusalem from the Khalidi family *daftar* where, D. Little and A.U. Turgay write, "in contrast to the documents written in Ottoman Turkish, almost all are connected in some way or another, as we have seen, with royal affairs, the Arabic documents, with one exception, deal with private affairs."[75]

At the beginning of each *sijill* is a confirmatory page documenting the name of the judge and clerk assigned to the court. Both the Jerusalem and the Cairo *sijill* open with virtually the same confirmatory statement, the former distinguished by its brevity:

> This page was prepared to ascertain the events that occurred in the time of . . . Muhammad Efendi, the *qadi* at that time in the city of Jerusalem, along with his deputy 'Abd Allah ibn 'Umar, beginning at the end of Rabi' II 1122/24 September 1710.[76]

The *sijill* of the Bab al-'Ali in Cairo is an elaborated version:

> Thanks and prayers and peace be upon the prophet Muhammad (SAAWS). This jubilant *(sa'id) sijill* is blessed in its commencement, gracious in its conclusion, prepared *(al-mu'id)* to ascertain the *shar'i* events which originate from the court of the Bab al-'Ali in Misr al-Mahrusa to eradicate *(izalat)* its sins by *qanun* in the reign of [the judge] *sayyiddina mawlana* Shaykh al-Islam, *sadr al-mawali al-kiram*, pride of the times . . . Muhammad Efendi ibn al-Mawla, son of the late Shaykh al-Islam Hasan Efendi __? and the deputy [Hanafi judge] Mawlana, pride of the *'ulama'*__? al-Efendi ibn Mawlana Darwish Efendi, on the blessed day of __? in the year 1055/1646. Khatam.[77]

Text: Formulary Structure

Another notable feature of documents contained within the *sijill* is their adherence to strict formularies, another factor critical to the document's 'integrity.' Faroqhi's presumption that the senior scribes of the Ottoman courts "put the claims of plaintiff, defendant and witnesses into the appropriate legal formulas" has been proven correct.[78] Nahal and Salameh note that deciphering the script of the early sixteenth-century scribes is sometimes possible only because of the preponderance of legal clichés. Bayinder goes further to assert that "[t]he rules of court registration took place within the '*es-Surut*' and '*al-Mahadir ve's-sicillat*' parts of the Islamic law Books."[79] Again, in keeping with the desire to minimize the risk of forgery, and to standardize the law produced, the Ottomans adopted what conformed with these objectives from their predecessors—in this case, the use of model *shurut* contracts.

Lest we assume that the adherence to strict formularies was an Ottoman innovation, it should be noted that a highly formulaic style of writing is also a feature of the Mamluk legal documents. Little has shown that of the 333 recorded inventories listing the possessions of a dead or dying individual in the Haram collection, the majority begin with the phrase "*hasala l-wuquf 'ala,*" (X's inventory was itemized), another thirty-four contain the alternate phrase "*waqafa 'ala,*" with the same meaning, while eleven begin with the phrase "*dubitat hawa'ij fulan*" (the possessions of so-and-so were recorded).[80] While no inventories for a dead or dying individual are found in the sample at my disposal, witnessed inventories were common in the records of the Qismas in Cairo and generally begin with the phrase "*hadarat al-hurma fulana lithubuti ma laha*" (the woman *x* attended [court] to establish what is hers/what is owed her). *Ishhad*s in the Haram documents always began with the phrase "*ashhada 'alayhi fulan*" (so-and-so testified for him) or "*hadara ila shuhudihi wa-ashhada 'ala.*"[81] The documents on which this research is based include a total of thirty-three *ishhad*s, none of which deviates from this strict formula.[82]

Within the Ottoman Empire, the stability of formulaic clichés is consistent across geographic boundaries. In the sijills of Ottoman Jerusalem, Salameh notes that "the beginning of each document differs depending on the topic. In general the topic can be understood by reading the first two lines."[83] Examples of identical formulaic clichés for legal contracts such as sales, rent, acknowledgments, and marriage from both the Jerusalem and Cairo *sijill*s abound. Providing samples from the former, Salameh lists the following formulaic opening lines:

> Muhammad ibn Muhammad alleged . . . The renter our Lord . . . Before our lord the Efendi . . . Was purchased . . . The woman testified against her[84] . . . The husband *fulan*, the wife *fulana*, *al-sadaq* amount X, received in hand by her deputy *fulan (al-maqbud bi yad wakilaha fulan)* amount Y, and the rest *(wa-l-baqi)* amount Z, owed to her on the death of or separation [from] her husband.[85]

Comparison with the Cairo *sijill* confirms the procedural conformity of Ottoman courts to the same formulaic clichés.[86] Forty-nine documents in the collection under study begin with the lines "*fulan* alleged," fifteen rental contracts begin "the renter *fulan*," and seven marriage contracts are identical to the contract Salameh described.[87] Out of thirty-five *khuttuba*s (the custom of signing a marriage contract but delaying the *dukhla*, or date of consummation, to a later time), for example, the identical formula appears abridged variously as "Before our Hanafi lord, *fulan* attested *(asdaq)* to his engagement," or simply, "*fulan* attested."[88]

In seventeen cases of *istifta'* and *futya* (where people sought and received a jurist's legal opinion) the document is always composed of two parts, the first containing the question, and the second the mufti's reply: "The woman asked . . . and he answered her query."[89] This brief sample indicates some stability in the formulaic clichés encountered in witnessed depositions from Mamluk to Ottoman documents. It also demonstrates symmetry between formularies from the mid-sixteenth to the mid-seventeenth centuries in two Arab cities within the empire.

The combination of a legible and formulaic *sijill* facilitated the unification of the legal process by ensuring adherence to strict contractual 'models.' In the final analysis, it also made the task of extrajudicial review that much easier while minimizing the risk of forgery. The priority made of the latter is reflected in the self-referential terminology found in the Cairo *sijill*: "The assembly of the honorable *shar'* and the circle of the *hanif* faith, [which is] protected from *alterations (taghyir)*"[90] [emphasis added].

But if the formulary models remained stable, the rules of documentary authentification were about to change.

Abbreviated Diplomatics

In Mamluk times, a written judgment issued by one judge could only be transmitted to a second judge through the supporting oral testimony of at least two witnesses. The testimony of the witnesses *(ikhbar)*—including the scribe who wrote the document—was certified through a special judicial annotation known as the *i'lam* or *raqm*, inserted by the judge beneath the signatures of witnesses. But the "contamination" of the *isghal* (judicial stamp) in only one *sijill* brought an end to this complicated procedure in the middle of the sixteenth century.[91] Thereafter, a simplified procedure was adopted that did away with the authentication of the *ikhbar*. Thus, by the mid-sixteenth century, the "form of the *isghal* . . . and the form of authentication changed as well. The rather complicated procedure which was used among the Mamluks was abolished and the *'unwan* was introduced in its place."⁹² The *'unwan* contained the judge's name and was supplemented with the imprint of his stamp. This was the case for both two-part instruments and simple instruments.

Numjarawi's manumission document is illustrative of this truncation. A number of further inferences can be made about the legal system which upheld it as a *hujja sahiha*. One, the document fails to identify any designated court or judge as the recipient of said document, indicating that it was valid in any 'high' court in the empire. Two, the role of witnesses in ascertaining the veracity of the contents of this document is nil. Numjarawi was unaccompanied by any witnesses—and certainly not the original scribe—who could testify that they were present at the moment of the document's composition in Istanbul. The only signatures are those of the designated witnesses who were present at the document's incorporation into the Cairo *sijill*, not to its drafting in Istanbul.

But the high number of designated witnesses officiating over its incorporation into the Cairo *sijill* suggests the adoption of a compensatory strategy of authentication. In a *sijill* where the usual number of witnesses per document rarely exceeded three, the signatures of seven designated witnesses, as well as "a number of those present" in the court *('adad min al-hadirin)*, were incorporated under the document.⁹³ These are not, however, the secondary witnesses of which Wakin wrote. As she herself explains, the latter were often the designated witnesses of the court, and their principal role was to ascertain the authenticity of the handwriting of the original signatories to the document. But in this particular case, there were no signatories to Numjarawi's original document, or at least none that were reproduced in the Cairo *sijill*. Finally, the reader will note that Numjarawi's document was not an original, but a copy *(sura)* of the original document archived in Istanbul, indicating that the validity of *hujja*s hinged as much on the existence of a master copy archived in the safe depots of Constantinople as it did on the signature of witnesses.

A final factor in the *sijill*'s evolution into an entity "protected from alteration" was the grafting of 'writing' onto 'speaking' through a synthetic blend of judicial responsibilities (expert witness, notary, and court scribe) that destabilized the primacy of the spoken word and formally privileged the document in Islamic evidentiary procedure.

The Fusion of Speaking and Writing

As the embodiment of 'presence,' the authority of the witness and the spoken word had always trumped the authority of the written word in Islamic law. Until, that is, the sixteenth century, when witnessing and writing were assimilated in judicial practice. Providing another important point of contact between Islamic legal theory and legal practice, the assimilation of speech and writing led to the grafting of the functions of the 'witness' onto that of the notary.

Historically, there had always been a degree of overlap between the role of the notary and the witness, the latter arising with the spread of script and the proliferation in legal documents during the classical era when judges, unable to process the vast number of legal instruments demanded by the public, delegated part of this responsibility to a professional class of private notaries.[94] Significantly, notaries had always been recruited from the ranks of professional witnesses and were distinguished as "clerks who practice their profession outside of the court."[95] In practice, the notary acted as a private "assistant to the judge," while the latter maintained final authority over the adjudication process.[96]

Like the notary profession, witnessing was an institution with long roots in the pre-Islamic, Near Eastern tradition. To ascertain the *'adala* (integrity) of witnesses "a regulated system of screening and formal certification" was formalized.[97] A permanent body of accredited witnesses eventually arose whose function was to furnish the court with expert testimony.

R. Jennings identified a permanent body of accredited witnesses, identified as *shuhud al-hal*, who oversaw the incorporation of all legal documents into the Kayseri *sijill*.[98] S. Faroqhi refers to a similar body attached to the Anatolian courts, the *ahl al-'urf*, a merchant and scholarly elite equated with "the governor's men (ehl-i 'orf)," and with "oppression," both being "presented as two closely allied terms."[99] In the case of Cairo, G. Nahal was the first to identify this body as the *ahl al-khibra*, comprised of technical experts in the fields of engineering, commerce, or the like.[100]

The early fusion of the spoken and written words is reflected in the practice of grafting the notary profession onto that of the designated witness. C. Petry describes witnesses and notaries as having overlapping functions in medieval Cairo, and uses the terms 'witness' *(shahid)* and 'notary' interchangeably himself.[101] Pointing to the degree of assimilation which had already taken place between witnessing and notarizing, R.

Vesely notes that witnesses served as *katib*s (writers or scribes), *muwaththiq*s (drafters of instruments), *shuruti*s (instrument adepts or drafters of formularies), or *shuhud 'adl* (just witnesses).[102]

E. Tyan has argued that Islamic legal theory and practice would only be harmonized in the twentieth century, when Maliki theory officially grafted the role of witness onto that of notary. While this is not entirely inaccurate, the embedding of these stipulations in the legal codes of twentieth-century nations is a function of positive codification. As a system of case laws, even one more inclined toward codification in the early modern centuries, Islamic law yields negative evidence of a coherent and unified strategy of assimilating theory and practice, as we saw in the *Mejelle* and the *Fatawa 'Alamgiriya*. But Tyan also disregards another earlier innovation critical to the role and function of scribes, witnesses, and notaries: their transformation from private to public guilds.

In 1521 the chief judge of Cairo shut down the "shops of the witnesses,"[103] also known as *hawanit al-ta'dil*, the designated chambers where notaries awaited their clients on benches.[104] At the same time, writes the chronicler al-Bakri, designated witnesses were barred from work. Some, having obtained the permission of the Hanafi chief judge, were allowed to continue in service, but most were barred and strictly prosecuted for violating the stop-work order.[105] If the state's goal was to promulgate new procedural rules with respect to the composition and storage of legal documents, such a policy made eminent sense.

What Vesely described as the notary's traditionally 'private' role is a distinction utterly lost in Ottoman administration.[106] Numerous textual indications convey the impact of this transformation on notarial procedures. A notarized document from the first half of the sixteenth century, for example, is always transcribed in the name of the notary himself. By the mid-sixteenth century, however, documents were notarized in the name of a specific judge or court. What is also immediately apparent is the high degree of symmetry between the job of a notary *(shuruti/muwaththiq)* and the job of a court scribe *(katib/'adil)*. Nahal described the latter as "acting notaries," with an expertise in drawing up various model contracts.[107] There is evidence to support this conclusion. In document 821, dated 1055 (1646) from the *sijill* of the Bab al-'Ali, the words *"min khat al-Shaykh Ahmad al-Sha'rawi,"* or "by the hand of al-Shaykh Ahmad al-Sha'rawi," are found at the bottom of the text.[108] In the Cambridge

University Genizah Series, the authors indicate that "[w]hen the witness wrote the witness clause himself he generally indicated this by adding the phrase *bi-khattihi* ('in his writing')." And more often than not, notaries were one of the designated witnesses *('udul)* because they "acted as one of the witnesses to the documents they drew up."[109] But there is reason to believe that Sha'rawi was more than a notary and a designated witness—he was also the principal court scribe. As there is nothing to distinguish Sha'rawi's penmanship from that of the principal scribe for pages 1–20 and 160–178, we may assume that the latter played the roles of notary, witness, and most importantly, court scribe, simultaneously. But it bears repeating that what was innovative in the Ottoman system was not simply that Sha'rawi could be scribe, notary, and court expert in one, but that he held these positions *formally* as a bureaucratic official. The net effect of these systemic reforms was an official document increasingly authoritative over and against oral testimony.

'Awad ibn Salim was accused of failing to pay a portion of the *sadaq* owing his wife Saliha, daughter of al-Shaykh Taj al-'Arifin, to whom he had been married by his father's *wikala*. An agreement, signed by the groom's father and presented by the father-in-law, stipulated that the groom would pay the remaining portion of the *sadaq* on his return from the Hajj to Mecca. But when he returned, complained the bride's father, he delayed payment, providing only verbal oaths to pay the *sadaq*. As of this moment, neither written contract nor verbal promise had been fulfilled. For his part, the reluctant groom swore that he was neither aware of, nor a willing party to, the contract. But Salim's father, the signatory to the marital contract, disputed his son's testimony. Faced with conflicting oral testimonies, and a document to which the principal protagonist was not a signatory, the court ruled in favor of the holder of the document and against the groom.

There are two possible explanations for the court's decision. To consider the first possibility, Wakin explains that fathers who concluded contracts for their children when they were minors resorted to 'primary witnesses' who could "testify to the minority of the boy, [and] to his father's guardianship." This is because a father's unfettered authority to act as *wakil* for his children (especially his sons) was no longer absolute once they reached legal maturity. But Salim's father presented no such witnesses, suggesting that his son was not a minor at time the contract was signed.[110] In other words, Salim's father no longer had unfettered powers over his son. It would appear, therefore, that it was the combined testimony of Salim's father and father-in-law, in tandem with the document, that carried the day. But the highly unusual procedure adopted in the transcription of this document is a textual clue to the weight accorded the document in the judge's ruling.

By binding Salim to a written contract which lacked his signature, the court had generated a dilemma for itself. Lacking Salim's oral or written acknowledgment of the marriage, the court abandoned its usual stratagem of posing a singular question and receiving, or at least recording, a singular answer (a formula encountered in hundreds of documents). Rather, the record reads that the judge pressed the groom "over and over again, time after time" *(marra ba'd marra, fatra ba'd fatra)* on whether he had verbally agreed to the terms of the contract.[111] Salim's denial was consistent but ultimately futile. The weight of the document tipped the scales against him.

Conclusion

The mass of people who came to the sharia court seeking written records, ranging from contracts to amicable settlements *(sulh)*, or to list their earthly belongings, no matter how meager, reflects what scholars like Hanna, Gerber, and Sonbol term the "easy accessibility" of the Ottoman court. But while "accessibility" was one important element in this dynamic court culture, the other was necessity. Documents, specifically official documents approved and signed by jurists, were no longer the preserve of the elite, and archives were no longer just stocked with important state registers (such as tax and land surveys). Documents were now a public currency, and the archives brimmed with the personal, even intimate, artifacts of private lives. It was this inherent tension between public and private that inaugurated documentary preservation in early-modern Ottoman society.

The archive defines memory institutionally; it is not just a data bank, but a system of political legitimation and a blueprint for the construction of political identity. In the next chapter, I examine how the mass production of documents changes the histories produced.

Chapter Five
The Documented Life

Introduction

> The archive . . . names at once the commencement and the commandment . . . the principle according to the law, there where men and God command, there where authority, social order are exercised, in this place from which order is given.[1]

The "order" arising from the "commandment" in Derrida's analysis of the archive is an appropriate lens for viewing the social and political ramifications of an increasingly documented early modern life. Possessing all of the prerogatives of record keeper—setting acquisition policies, institutionalizing the link between scholarship and information—the archivist produces knowledge by providing tangible evidence of memory for individuals, communities, and states. But it is an institutional memory, defined within a prevailing political order that commands 'forgetting' as well as 'remembering.'

The history of archiving is yet to be written in full, and while the archivist has received a limited amount of attention in Ottoman research, one aspect of the early modern archive has been ignored: its role in generating mass culture through the mass production of documents. The enormous data bank that is the Ottoman archive creates a paper trail for the lives of the countless, faceless masses, providing the foundations for a subaltern history rarely glimpsed in premodern historical sources. More than the archive, therefore, it is the millions of individual documents contained within it that provide the textual footprints of an 'early-modern individualism,' or proto-citizenship.

In Europe, individualism has meant many things: originality in art, individual separation from divinity, or individualism *through* Protestantism's direct access to God. Modernization theory cast the medieval era as the age of conformity and the Renaissance as the age of individual expression. Politically, modern individualism is contingent on the promise of citizenship and constitutionalism. The latter marked the onset of a new covenant between individual-as-citizen and the state, and defined the former as a legal identity, transcending religious, ethnic, class, and gender identities. Early-modern individualism in the Ottoman state is not dissimilar.

The individual is certainly no stranger to pre-Ottoman Islamic law, but the sixteenth century marks a critical turning point in the sharia court's rational and procedural definition of 'essential personhood.' V. Aksan and D.S. Goffman's recent edited collection of articles, by scholars such as L. Peirce and N. Qattan, points to the birth of the "individual," "linkages with the European and Mediterranean worlds in the construction of physical and mental boundaries," including "new group consciousness," the preservation of "a local sense of the past," and "broad appeal to political ideology through the popularization of scholarly discourse" as examples of the "Ottoman movement toward the modern."[2]

A necessary precondition of this early-modern individualism was the 'territorialization of the law.' Cleaving essential personhood from local identity, territorialized laws privilege territorially based identities, subjecting "individuals and communities that may be otherwise diverse to one and the same law."[3] For Qattan, it is the archive which is principally responsible for this transformation. Because it contains official documents, which relate to the public and are at its limited disposal, the archive 'commences' the moment of transference from private to public spaces, from religious universal law to a civil law, for all subjects.

Bringing us back to the question of commandment, archival documents embody power both as entities in stasis (such as preserved records in a fixed archive), and entities in motion (such as a copy of an original *hujja* like Numjarawi's which circulated freely in society). As a document in stasis, the *hujja* lives within the archive, a preserved, albeit selective, memory to be accessed under restricted conditions. In motion, however, the transportable *hujja* carries one's rights forward in society at large.

The social relevance of the transportable *hujja* is made amply apparent by its popular demand. People came to the courts in droves requesting nothing more than the issuance of a written *hujja*. This makes some sense given the importance of having written documents in hand, but it hardly accounts for the number of people seeking *hujja*s not merely as a record of a property right or contract, but as official writs of their status as freed slaves, as divorced women, as urbanites versus peasants, and so on. Backed by the force of the state and recognized in any high court in the empire, *hujja*s penetrated the whole of society to erect new categories of personhood by deflecting, deterring, and regulating the conduct of others toward a person according to the documented status of the latter.

The Document in Stasis: Territorializing Sharia

As the study of Ottoman law and society expanded, it drew a vivid portrait of the sharia court as a unified legal venue for Muslim and *dhimmi* alike. But it was A. Fattal who described this as a process of territorialization, specifically of Hanafi law, which consciously expanded notions of political sovereignty to include judicial control over non-Muslims.[4] Qattan has added to this thread by directly linking territorialization to "the institutionalization of the record-keeping process and its housing in a public space—a court." Because the qadi's court was the "locus of the authenticated and sanctioned record," Qattan sees in this "a further embodiment of authority" for the qadi who "already stood to implement a territorialized gloss of shari'a law."[5] The connection made by Qattan between 'archiving' and 'territorializing' the law is a vital one. Her assessment of record-keeping as a quintessentially political act, and her reading of the archive and the *sijill* as twin factories of political identity, brings much-needed stimulus to the scholarship on Ottoman *sijill*s. Nevertheless, Qattan's view of the qadi as judge and archivist simultaneously is not, in my view, borne out by the evidence.

In the first place, rather than a "further embodiment of the judge's authority," the initiation of the 'fixed court' frequently signaled the symbolic moment of a judge's *disembodiment* from both his court and *sijill*, as described above. Second, while I am indebted to Qattan's textual approach to semantic political identities and their shifting perimeters in the *sijill*, I find that her argument overlooks the manner in which the *sijill* transformed Muslim as well as non-Muslim political identity through textual manipulation.

Qattan argues that "reflecting socio-economic integration across religious communities as well as its limits, the court refracted religious identity through the prism of state authority, and in the process both highlighted and erased it."[6] Her conclusion that *dhimmi*s were becoming Ottoman subjects misses, however, the equally innovative processes by which the identity of the Muslim majority—those who were already subjects—was also being reshaped.

The *sijill*s 'flag' all sorts of people, most of them Muslim. For example, the courts distinguished between 'foreign Muslims,' 'slaves,' 'freed slaves,' those sentenced to prison, or those about to be released from prison. Even more, race and phenotype were used to describe the latter categories, including skin, eye, and hair color, or distinct physical markings (such as scars). But it is what is *not* flagged which is of greatest import. Cairo was a multiethnic city comprising Turkic, Circassian, Bosnian, Nubian, Syrian, Maghrebi, and Persian communities, to name but a few, yet the massive data bank that is the Ottoman *sijill* is striking in its consistent and stubborn silence on the ethnic or racial identity of its freeborn, local Muslim population.

The *sijill* does not flag and integrate religious differences alone: it also reconstitutes Muslim identity. A willful amnesia when it comes to the geographic origins, ethnicity, or linguistic identities of the *sijill*'s Muslim inhabitants projects a false gloss of homogeneity onto their heterogeneous backgrounds. It also suggests that, more than the transformation of *dhimmi*s into subjects, we are witnessing a broader shift from 'subjects' to 'proto-citizens.'

Occurring in several stages, the territorialization of law was 'commanded' through a form of 'archival violence'—in this case, what I am calling the civil marriage law of 1521.

Archival Violence and Memory

> Naturally destined to serve the communication of laws and the order of the city transparently, a writing becomes the instrument of abusive power; of a caste of "intellectuals" that is ensuring hegemony, whether its own or that of special interests: the violence of a secretariat, a discriminating reserve, an effect of scribble and type.[7]

The archive is at once "revolutionary and traditional," because it preserves, but in a contrived way which Derrida perceives as "the violence of the archive itself."[8] There is no greater, more potent symbol of Ottoman archival violence than its coercive role in transferring marriage from the private to the public sphere. Marking the dawn of civil marriage, and the transformation of Islamic law into a territorial-civil law for all subjects, the *qanun* of 1521 is one of the most important and overlooked laws ever to be promulgated in the history of Ottoman and Islamic social history. Part of the program of 'renewal,' described in chapter three, the law of 1521 kicked off a century of antagonism between local and state jurists. I defer further discussion of its broader social and political implications to the next chapter, where an extensive analysis of the history of civil marriage, and its role in transforming the 'rights of God' in Islamic law, is found. For now, suffice it to say that the law marked the expansion of the public sphere by transferring records of personal law from private to public spaces. The impact, on Muslim and non-Muslim alike, was dramatic.

The *sijill*'s textual memory of the law, and its transcription through a process of conscious manipulation that reconstituted political identities, preserved it as an 'always already' textually shaped reality. Forgetting was as integral to this process as remembering. This is what Derrida meant by saying that the archive "shelters itself from memory which it also shelters: which comes down to saying also that it forgets."[9] If we are to treat the *sijill* as more than "a quarry of facts in the reconstruction of the past," we must begin, therefore, with what is forgotten.[10]

Unlike minorities, slaves, foreigners, peasants who had abandoned the land, or convicts, the vast majority of Muslims who inhabit the text of the *sijill* do so "by virtue of almost total semantic omission and silence."[11] Here the unflagged religious identity of the Muslim majority is posited as a natural category, a derivative of the discourse of power that naturalizes an otherwise arbitrary category. But here too, the absence of textual markings is a process not just of 'naturalizing' religion, and thereby omitting 'Muslimness' as a flag, but of expunging other markers of identity. Casting a homogenizing gloss atop a diverse cultural urbanscape, the *sijill* expunges difference to project Muslim society as an integrated monolith. Recalling earlier descriptions of Cairo as an open center of migration in the sixteenth and seventeenth centuries, one would expect the *sijill* to be an ethnographer's dream. Instead, it communicates almost nothing about the ethnic or communal identity of its tenants. The *sijill* never flags the skin color, ethnicity, or linguistic affinity of its freeborn Muslim constituents.

Clues to the Muslim litigant's identity can of course be found in things which are flagged: name, place of residence, gender, and profession. But little else in the *sijill* indicates whether the individuals in question belong to the North African (Maghrebi), Syrian, Arabian, or Yemeni community. No discriminatory flags are used to distinguish Arabic-speaking communities *(awlad al-arab)* from the Turkic, Slavic, Georgian, and Circassian human waves flowing into the city. All inhabit the *sijill* side by side, blanketed in the textual silence of a selective amnesia.

The silence of the *sijill* on the Muslim religious majority is thus deeper and more startling than is realized by scholars. Omitting all references to 'Muslimness' as well as ethnicity, it produces a 'generic Ottoman-Muslim,' increasingly defined through the territorial laws of a bureaucratic state. Take the example of the marriage contract in Ottoman Cairo, where mention of race, regional origins, or even linguistic affinity can scarcely be found. In what was, even by the standards of the day, an international city, this is quite a feat. It compensates, however, by providing an enormous amount of socioeconomic data on its generic 'Ottoman Muslims.'

Out of thirty-eight marriage *(zawaj/nikah)* and engagement contracts *(khutuba)*, six include the marriage of *'askeri* (military) men to women of the *ra'aya* (civilian population), usually the daughters of local merchants (like the *sukkariya*) or scholars.[12] Another ten men from Cairo also wed women from Cairo,[13] one *khawaja* wed his cousin,[14] and fifteen *'askeri*s wed the daughters[15] or ex-slaves/concubines of higher ranking *'askeri*s.[16] At first glance, inter-*'askeri* marriages appear to be ethnically homogenous unions, as most slaves, concubines, and soldiers in the Ottoman Empire were recruited from the Balkans. But the ethnicity of the *'asker* became increasingly difficult to identify as "the distinction between the Ottoman military and Egyptian civilians broke down, probably from about the middle of the 10th/16th century when merchants and artisans in Cairo enrolled in greater numbers in the Janissaries and 'Azban."[17] Moreover, there is also no way of identifying the ethnic origins of the "daughter of the *'askeri*" in the marriage contracts (more will be said on the ex-concubines below). The absence of markings thus becomes a negative device for expunging, erasing, and rescribing political identity in an otherwise culturally, racially, and linguistically diverse city. However, the *sijill* also makes important exceptions. For example, it consistently identifies particular battalions, such as the Mutafarriqa or the Inshikariya *askeri*s, as 'Rumis' and others as 'Circassians.' How may we explain this?

Ayalon has shown that in the Mamluk sultanate, racial rivalries played a prominent role in the competition between various factions of Mamluks. The hostility of the Circassians to the "other Mamluk races and their feeling of superiority is well documented in the contemporary sources."[18] Curiously, and in spite of an Ottoman military policy that discouraged ethnic pride, military divisions continued to be identified as Circassian or Rumi. Still, the idea that this is a hangover of identity politics from the Mamluk era does not explain why the Ottoman *sijill* perpetuates this tradition.

From an administrative military perspective, ethnic flags can operate as markers of troop identification, distinguishing between troops of Egyptian-Mamluk origin (incorporated after the conquest) and Ottoman recruits. But what served the purposes of a military bureaucrat can be misleading to the historian. In Ottoman Egypt, 'Circassian' was the label bestowed on remnants of the Mamluk military, and on their descendants. Alternatively, the term 'Rumi' is ethnically opaque and most often used to designate a geographic point of origin. We do not know if the Rumi soldier is a Slav, a Bosnian, or a Georgian. 'Ethnicity,' in this case, may not be an indication of ethnicity at all.

But there is another explanation for these ethnic markers. The *sijill* is simply following standard textual protocol in describing slaves. While the number of military slaves drastically declined from the mid-sixteenth century on, slavery is deeply embedded in Islamic military history. What we may be witnessing, therefore, is a residual effect, not of Mamluk protocol, but of slave protocol. There are, therefore, categories of Muslims for whom the silence is broken, including the two unusual examples below.

The first case comes from a rare document, in which a man and a woman, both Muslim, are identified by ethnicity. Cutting across class and ethnic lines, the document is an inventory of possessions belonging to a woman identified as a "Bedouin" married—in a customary ceremony—to a "Circassian" *'askeri*. Apart from being unusual in listing the ethnicity of both parties, the document is also unusual in its mention of "customary marriage," the term now applied to any unregistered marriage. Indeed the very notion of customary marriage (*zawaj 'urfi*) in modern Egypt, like common law in English jurisprudence, developed in contradistinction to the idea of marriage as a public institution after the law of 1521. But to the return to the question at hand, why has the woman been flagged as a Bedouin? The simplest and most straightforward explanation is that she is a stranger to Cairo.

Outsiders, those passing through on commercial or personal business, are always flagged, usually by region, village, town, or city of origin. For example, one finds references to the "Faiyumi," the "Halabi," and in the case above, a "Bedouin." Residency is thus established as primary marker of identity alongside class for the Muslims who inhabit the *sijill*. Both intersect in the nuptials of an *'askeri* of the Mutafarriqa militia to the daughter of a *khawaja*[19] and of a man from the Faiyum to the daughter of a *khawaja*.[20] But there are further layers of demarcation and flagging that disrupt the *sijill*'s textual silence on Muslims. The most startling is skin color.

The second case is found in a marriage document, where the groom is identified as a man from Cairo and his bride described as the "white" (*al-bayda'*) "daughter of the slave of Allah" (*bint 'abd Allah*).[21] Out of thirty-eight marriage documents culled in this research, fifteen unite military men (*'askeris*) with the white daughters of "slaves of Allah."[22] These were the former slaves and concubines, usually of men of higher military rank than the grooms.[23] As mentioned, skin color was a textual indicant of one's status as slave, or former slave. "One had to be fair-skinned," writes Ayalon, "to be (in most cases) an inhabitant of the area stretching to the north and to the north-east of the lands of Islam; to be born an infidel; to be brought into the Mamluk sultanate."[24] The Ottoman Empire recruited most of its "*kullar* from the Christian peoples living within its boundaries," or the Balkans and the Black Sea regions.[25]

While the temptation to see the flagging of skin color as reflexive of its essential role in defining personhood is strong, it may also be essentialist. There is no way of excluding race as a conscious category of textual identity and personhood, but it is so as a secondary attribute of personhood. Essential personhood, that which meets the conditions of 'normalization' and commands the *sijill*'s 'silence,' is determined not just by one's status as a member of the Muslim majority, nor by one's color, nor even by one's status as a resident or outsider, but by one's status as freeborn or (ex-) slave. Like religious identity, one's birth or sale into slavery was an inescapable mark of one's social and political standing. If in the case of religious minorities it meant an implicit recognition of their marginal but protected status, in the case of slaves, it could mean either marginality or, alternatively, privilege.

Perhaps no society has developed as complex, or bizarre, a system of slavery as Muslim society. Here we encounter the kind of domestic slavery found elsewhere, but not the industrial slavery associated with the American plantation model. We also encounter a uniquely Muslim institution: the slave ruling caste. Mamluks, literally meaning 'those who are owned,' were an elite caste of military slaves, owned by the sultan and at his command alone. High-ranking Mamluks, manumitted on retirement, and their civilian descendants, constituted an important element of the aristocracy. Depending on the slave's status, therefore, the flagging of a slave can be a strategy either for integrating marginality, or for institutionalizing privilege.

The final category of Muslim to be flagged and physically objectified in the manner of a slave were those on the cusp of a criminal conviction or on the cusp of release from prison. Shaykh Nahiyat al-Basatin came to court to charge his son-in-law, and cousin, with defaulting on providing his daughter her promised *kiswa* (wardrobe) over a three-year period. He was able to produce the original marriage contract, signed in the court of the mosque of Qawsun (?) in 1641, and was corroborated in his testimony by several witnesses.[26] Eventually, the husband's confession was obtained. What follows immediately thereafter is a physical description of the husband—a blond man, clean shaven, medium build with a space between his brows *(mafruq al-hajibayn)*. This is the *sijill*'s way of signaling that the defendant has been found guilty. The delinquent husband's sentence is allocated separately, maybe a fine or prison time, and remains unknown. His rank (temporary or permanent) among the silent textual majority has expired.

There are, as such, outbursts of chatter, rather than an absolute textual silence maintained on ethnicity and phenotype in the *sijill*. Proto-citizenship, however, hinges on the predictability and exceptionalism of the document's selective amnesia. In other words, the criteria by which silence and chatter are maintained cannot be arbitrary or unpredictable. Equally, it hinges on two other characteristics: its embodiment of power, and its transportability. Allowing people to assert their rights before any chief judge in the empire, the transportable *hujja* was a 'mobile bill of a given right.'

The Document in Motion

The expansion in the authority of documents brought about an expansion in the autonomy of the individual who consciously wielded them as certificates of a given claim, right, or exemption. Overwhelmingly, it was women, former slaves, and members of religious minorities who asked the court for *hujja*s. And each and every time an individual did so, they bypassed the customary arbitration of their community. But the secondary literature, particularly that on minorities, has been reluctant to relinquish its romantic belief in the 'autonomous local community.'

A. Raymond, B. Braud, and B. Lewis have all made strong arguments for the autonomy enjoyed by Ottoman communities.[27] More recently, Cohen has offered a more nuanced view of Jewish Ottoman communities, in which certain aspects of Jewish communal life, such as internal taxes, a system of mutual assistance, or regulations and covenants can simply be "assumed to have existed," but where Jews also frequently appealed to the sharia courts.[28] This is true in matters that concerned only Jews, even marriage and divorce (which, according to Jewish law, were forbidden from being presented to gentile authorities), because they "viewed the court as an important part of the fibre of personal and community life."[29]

But "there was always a tension," writes A. Shmuelevitz, "between mild pressure and open conflict, between the desire to preserve the principle of [community] autonomy and the pressure for more integration, which arose chiefly from a variety of activities and demands in the administrative, legal, economic and, to some extent, even social fields."[30] Citing numerous strategies of resistance, including a Jewish community ban on resorting to the Islamic court, Shmuelevitz's work challenges the assumptions of older paradigms. Shmuelevitz's and Cohen's arguments, drawing on the *sijill*s of Jerusalem, are confirmed in this and countless other emerging works. But we have yet to correlate the decline in communal autonomy to proto-citizenship.

One need only look to Napoleonic France, and to the guarded reaction of Jewish leaders to the promises of citizenship and assimilation, to understand the correlation between citizenship and a new breed of individualism that threatened to eclipse communal identities. Like their counterparts in Europe, the religious minorities of the Ottoman Empire were loath to accept their newfound status during the constitutional era,[31] preferring the *jizya* (poll tax on non-Muslim *dhimma*, or protected minorities) to some of the duties and obligations of citizenship, such as military service in the Ottoman armed forces. But more importantly, like the Jews of France and Germany, they feared that the substitution of religious authority with political authority would lead to the dilution of their communal cohesion, solidarity, and identity. One finds the same unease expressed by Jewish community leaders in Jerusalem and Cairo in the fifteenth and sixteenth centuries, who admonished their flock for mimicking mainstream cultural behavior and imposed a ban on resorting to the Islamic courts.[32] Various strategies of resistance accompanied the ban, some quite ingenious.

Cohen writes that there were times when Jews appealed to the authority of Muslim courts, even in private matters such as marriage and divorce, matters forbidden from being presented to gentile authorities by Jewish law. Indeed, many Jews came voluntarily to the Muslim qadi for rulings, even in matters that concerned only Jews. Cohen provides examples of civil suits in which Jews brought other Jews to court over petty affairs and criminal charges, and even on claims dealing with movable property and real estate. This was because they "viewed the court as an important part of the fibre of personal and community life," not because they considered the Jewish courts ineffectual or inferior. Furthermore, the Jewish community had every reason to trust the Muslim courts because "greater weight was often attributed to the testimony of Jews than that of Muslims, not only in actions of Jew against Jew, but also of Jew against Muslim, or Muslim against Christian."[33]

Christian and Jewish men sometimes resorted to Islamic courts to circumvent the obligations of traditional marriage contracts. When two Christian men claimed to be married to the same woman, it was the person in possession of a *hujja* who triumphed.[34] In one case, Dawud claimed he had recently wed Tuffaha through her brother's *wikala*, while 'Abd Rabb al-Masih claimed he had been wed to her in childhood through her father's *wikala*. Even though they had never cohabited, al-Masih claimed that he had paid her father the dower as well as her maintenance expenditures for eleven years. While Dawud was able to produce a written marriage contract, al-Masih was not and, predictably, lost his case. The closing line read, "'Abd Rabb al-Masih was not believed." But was al-Masih lying? Such verbal agreements were customary, although judging by such cases, increasingly risky. But the validity of the arrangement is not at issue. What is at issue is proof of the arrangement. Neither the girl's father, nor any other member of the community, was on hand as a witness in this case. The decision was reached on the authority of the *hujja* presented. But why did al-Masih not summon witnesses? If he were telling the truth, surely someone could vouch for the agreement, and for the money he claims exchanged hands. The case which follows might explain why al-Masih had no witnesses.

The parents of a Jewish woman alleged that their daughter was wedded to Ishaq ibn – (?), and that the latter had failed to pay them the remaining half of the dower. When questioned, Ishaq denied that he had ever wed their daughter, and challenged them to produce oral evidence *(bayyina)*, or witnesses, in support of their claims. The parents left, but returned later (it is not clear whether it was later that day, that week, or the next) without the requisite evidence. Ishaq then took an oath upon the Torah that no marriage had ever taken place. The case was then summarily dismissed.[35] What jumps outs of this text is Ishaq's challenge to the parents to produce a witness. The question is: from where does his confidence stem?

Ishaq's confidence can only stem from one of two things; one, he is telling the truth, or two, he knows that Jewish witnesses would be reluctant to testify in a sharia court. Several clues within the document in fact lend credence to the parents' claims. In the first instance, it will be noted that the parents were asking for the payment of the deferred dower, generally given only in the event of a divorce or the husband's death. Proving or disproving such an allegation would be a simple matter of providing neighbors, relatives, and friends to testify that X was married to Y and cohabited at address Z. In fact, the parents did go on a search for witnesses, but returned empty-handed. Not a single relative, neighbor, or friend could be persuaded to testify to their daughter's marriage and divorce. The persistence with which the parents went in search of witnesses, and the fact that they returned empty-handed, suggests either a very incompetent lie, or a desperate couple throwing themselves on the mercy of the court. The absence of Jewish witnesses is emblematic of the strategy of resistance adopted by the community and of its limited success in forestalling the legal integration of its individual members in the sharia courts. Equally, however, the presence of a persistent and growing number of individuals—such as the couple above—in the sharia court, is indicative of the strategy's limitations.

The social or even physical cohesion of a minority community, something which can be seen in any North American or European city with a large immigrant population, is thus to be separated from the question of its legal autonomy. Muslim immigrants to the west, for example, maintain tight social and physical communities and yet lack an autonomous legal venue, or sharia court, for arbitrating family law. Like members of any other community, they are subject to the unified law of the land without religious distinction. We must be careful, therefore, not to equate the physical cohesion of Cairo's communities with their cultural or sociolegal isolation from Muslim society at large, while recognizing the link between a unified, territorially bound law for all subjects and the hallmarks of citizenship.

We may now examine the impact of this legal movement on the majority (Muslim) population, paying special heed to the role it plays in reassigning gender, class, and communal identity on an increasingly individualistic basis.

Among Muslim women, most sought *hujja*s of divorce, of marital conflicts, or even *hujja*s ordering a romantic suitor to cease and desist.

The freed concubine of al-Hajj 'Ali the Qahwaji (also her legal *wali*), Khatun bint 'Abd Allah, "of white complexion," charged al-Zayni 'Abd al-Rab al-Haqan with "confronting her" and demanding that she cohabit with him, "as wives do . . . without legal justification."[36] At issue in this case is a woman's right to consent to marriage. The defendant admitted to making such demands, but claimed that he had "married her" through al-Zayni Muhammad Ibrahim al-Yankashari's *wikala* and produced a written document indicating that he had paid the advance dower and agreed to the amount of the deferred portion. He also claimed that she had received her dower in hand. When the judge sent a court-appointed witness to take Khatun's testimony (outside of court), she took an oath denying that she had authorized al-Zayni Muhammad to act as her *wakil*, or that she had received a dower in hand. Haqan's case was summarily dismissed for, as far as the court was concerned, his dispute was now with al-Zayni Muhammad to the exclusion of Khatun bint 'Abd Allah. Khatun was not a signatory to the written contract.

Another woman in need of *hujja* deflecting the unwanted advances of a suitor, this time her ex-husband, was 'Abida. 'Abida came to court accompanied by several witnesses from her neighborhood to testify that her husband Hijazi had divorced her and was now denying the divorce and (re) claiming his conjugal rights.[37] Without documentation supported by eye-witness testimony, 'Abida's legal status, and that of thousands of women, remained dependent on the testimony of community members, and subject to repeated challenge. 'Abida thus came to the court of her own accord to request that it block Hijazi's claims and, more importantly, that it issue a written *hujja* of the divorce preempting such claims in the future. When and if she should need it, the *hujja* allowed 'Abida to assert her legal rights without further need for witnesses.

Like women, manumitted slaves were a vulnerable constituency, often needing documented proof of their status to ward off unwarranted aggression. Al-Zayni Yusuf, for example, complained to the chief Ottoman judge in 1646 that Abu Bakr ibn 'Isa al-Rumi, a merchant from the Khan al-Khalili market, had publicly "struck" him and derided him as a slave. Having been formally manumitted by Muhammad Halabi, the complainant not only produced the document of manumission but demanded the judge implement the law by commanding Abu Bakr to refrain from harassing him. He then requested a *hujja* to that effect. In some ways, al-Zayni was asking for the equivalent of a restraining order. He was also seeking a more definitive proclamation of his legal new status than the manumission document—a *hujja* repudiating the infringement of his rights as a free man. The judge complied with both requests.[38] One could seek legal shelter in the document, therefore, to stem abusive or unwanted conduct, from private individuals or public bureaucrats.

We see the same in cases of *iltizam*, where a public bureaucrat, the *multazim*, pursued those accused of abandoning farming *(filaha)*.[39] In two cases, two merchants, obviously wealthy, were accosted by the *multazim* and accused of having "*athar* (traces of) *al-filaha*" about them.[40] The judge ruled in both men's favor, and issued *hujja*s preempting the *multazim* from confronting or fining them.

In all, the *hujja*s obtained by the men, women, and manumitted slaves described above ensured that whatever infringement of their rights had taken place, it would not be repeated in the future.

Conclusion

The documented life is an altered life. It is altered through the textual manipulation of identity on the one hand and through the text's mediation between the world and the individual on the other. Both redraw the perimeters of essential personhood, and of political identity, to produce an early modern individual more detached from local custom than at any time in recorded history. The archive territorialized Islamic law, mediated its transmission from private to public spaces, and negotiated its conversion into a Muslim civil code for all subjects, thereby remapping the relationship between state and society. One law for all citizens meant a negation of the mediation of the community.

Building on Fattal's conception of Islamic law as a 'territorialized' law in these centuries, and on Qattan's interpretation of this process as a means of 'secularizing' sharia through the integration of non-Muslims, the argument follows that the great leap forward is not from *dhimmi* to subject, but from subject to proto-citizen.

Chapter Six
The Rights of God *(Huquq Allah)*:
"A Moral Transgression but Not a Crime"

Introduction

> Life without *khala'a* (licentiousness) is a life deprived;
> Only an expert can tell you.
> By the *'uluwi* (celestial) world
> I swear I have rebelled against the *salafi* (pious ancestors') world.
> How many nights did I unload my worries in the pond *(birka)*?
> And around me, young men,
> all like me,
> spoken of well by those who are good,
> called ignorant by the people of ignorance.
>   Shihab al-Mansuri[1] (translated by author)

The boundaries of moral sin, and the degrees to which the state or society enforced those bounds through censure or coercion, are the subject of poetic laments, juristic polemic, political theory, and modern Islamist conflict in the twenty-first century. In this chapter, we explore these bounds through an examination of an all-but-forgotten distinction in Islamic law between the 'rights of God' *(huquq Allah)* and the 'rights of humans' *(huquq al-adamiyyin)*, as developed in legal theory and as interpreted by the state. The term 'rights of God' encompasses the basic ordering of key social institutions like marriage, inheritance, and religious endowments, as well as the fixed penalties *(hudud)* governing adultery, fornication, intoxication, and theft, all of which are examined in this chapter. Because jurisprudential theory allowed branches of custom (*siyasa* and *'ada*) to play a 'refining' role in the institutions arising from these rights (such as the determination of the bride price or dowry), the link between the 'rights of God' and custom is both tangible and permanent.

The debate over what constituted 'correct conduct' preoccupied the Sunni heartland no less than the so-called 'peripheries' of Islam. Furthermore, under the pressures of Ottoman religious renewal, the increasing authority of written documents, and the theory of the legists regulating custom, the bounds of Muslim morality became ever more rigid. This orthodoxy was pursued through multiple strategies. Foremost among them was a *qanun* marking the onset of civil marriage in Islamic legal practice. The registration of marriage in the sharia court, a compulsory policy by 1521, turned what had once been an informal contract, signed in the presence of two witnesses, into a formal civil union. That is, state jurists were now partners in the marriage contract, its principle witnesses and primary custodians. More than that, its courts were now positioned as final arbiters in negotiating its terms or, if the case warranted, its dissolution. Whether by accident or design, however, the version of civil marriage that emerged in early-modern judicial practice fundamentally altered Muslim and non-Muslim conceptions of self and moral sovereignty.

As argued in chapter five, the 'documented life' enhanced the autonomy of the individual who consciously wielded documents as certificates of a given claim, right, or exemption. The document not only enhanced the legal status of the individual, it helped the state carve out a place as supreme arbiter of the link between custom and the rights of God.

The Ottoman *sijill*s reveal a more stable, standardized approach to the rules governing marriage and divorce, in which marriage was so systematized that the influence of local custom and communal practices is negligible in the *sijill*.

The codification of the substantive laws produced was one strategy by which the rights and obligations of marriage were systematized, and proto-citizenship was promoted at large. The courts redefined the links between 'essential personhood' (with all the rights and obligations that this entailed) and local identity, with its peculiar ethnic, religious, or regional variations. Codification is a two-lane road here: one lane for custom and the other for jurisprudence itself. Custom is unified through a process of redaction that opts for the 'best' of custom, even non-sultanic, and the 'soundest' of judicial opinions, even non-Hanafi.

Among the most important non-Hanafi opinions to become incorporated into the universal *qanun* was the Egyptian and Syrian practice of dividing the dower (the *mahr*, or dowry paid directly to the bride by the groom) into advanced and deferred portions. Deemed the most 'morally perfected' opinion, it was enforced even in the Sublime Porte of Constantinople.[2] Another, even more vital to the institutions of civil marriage, was the 'conditional stipulation' in the marital contract allowing women to 'prohibit what is permitted [*ma'ruf*]' for their spouses by custom or, even more remarkably, by Sunna and law.

It should be noted that the Ottoman understanding of the 'rights of God,' and the attempt to manufacture a legal orthodoxy around them, does not imply a static Ottoman ideal. Indeed, the chronicles and *sijill*s reveal that the moralizing tone of the state and its jurists repeatedly defined and redefined the bounds of Muslim morality over the course of the sixteenth and early seventeenth centuries. In some cases, this implies a narrowing of the definition of what was 'permissible,' and in others, a relaxation. In all cases, however, it reflects the 'orthodoxy' of the day.

We begin with the core penalties of the Quranic *hudud* (fixed penalties) and their transformation over the course of the sixteenth century from a system of corporal punishments (such as flogging or amputation) into a system of fines and imprisonment.

The *Hudud*

Before presenting the evidence of the *sijill*, a few words on the interpretation of the 'rights of God' under the Ottomans, particularly the fixed penalties *(hudud)*, will shed light on the state's understanding of the scope of its jurisdiction in the area of *'ibadat*.

Imber argues that although the state was responsible for enforcing the *hudud* in theory, the only real crime to fall under its purview was highway robbery:

> For most offences of violence committed within a community, Hanafi law makes the community itself responsible for bringing assistance and, in cases of homicide where the killer is unknown,

for defraying the blood-money paid to the heirs of the victim . . . In practice, the infliction of the punishments for fornication and theft is impossible since the rules of procedure are so strict. . . . With the exception of highway robbery, therefore, the fixed penalties are not legal realities.[3]

The jurists, he argues, adopted the attitude that the fixed penalties "are claims of God, and God has no need of a human agency to execute his will."[4] At the same time, however, jurists delegated to the state the right of *ta'zir*, or discretionary punishment, in areas that did not include blood money, compensation for damage, or the fixed penalties.[5] Because jurists do not define what constitutes a discretionary offense, Imber argues that, ironically, they pushed more and more offenses under the category of discretionary punishment: "Ebu's-Su'ud, for example was able to bring coffee-drinking into this category. . . . The result was to bring the punishment of most offences under the authority of the ruler to deal with as he wished, with no judicial constraints."[6]

Even though the fixed penalties were not under the discretionary authority of *ta'zir*, L. Peirce's work suggests that "in the Aintab records for 1540–1541, we are observing an aggressive effort to punish zina."[7] Ibn Iyas also provides abundant evidence to suggest that such offenses were vigorously prosecuted in Cairo in the first quarter of the sixteenth century. Not only did the Ottoman state enforce the fixed penalties (including punishment for intoxication), but it often exceeded them. Moreover, there is evidence to suggest that such policies were not limited to the years immediately following the conquest, but echoed well beyond the sixteenth century. The official intolerance for intoxication, for example, is noted in the works of latter-day biographers such as al-Damiri, who provides numerous examples of it by the end of the sixteenth century. Whether this was also true of the intervening years is uncertain. Suffice it to say there is no mention of anyone's incarceration or release from prison on the grounds of intoxication in the documents at my disposal. This does not, however, rule out the possibility that it continued to occur. *Siyasa* justice, meted out at the command of the governor, was often swift and deadly, bypassing the formal courts altogether. Nonetheless, as shown in chapter one, an important juridical innovation occurred in Hanafi law at this time, suggesting a clear-cut policy of activating the fixed penalties while limiting their severity.

Starting with the Ottoman conquest of Egypt, Ibn Iyas' account provides detailed examples of *siyasa* justice in the first years of Ottoman rule, documenting the manner in which penalties frequently exceeded the limits of the sharia. In one case, an Ottoman soldier apprehended a commoner when he "caught the latter's hand in his pocket," stealing four *ansaf*.[8] Taken before the governor, the culprit had his hand amputated, followed by a public humiliation in which he was paraded through the streets, the offending hand "hanging from his neck." The people, writes Ibn Iyas, were saddened for the man and for the severity of his fate over a measly sum. Even more severely, another individual was put to death by hanging for stealing cucumbers from a field, something Ibn Iyas describes as a "repugnant *(shani')* event,"[9] that extinguished the life of a husband, father, and son over a trifle.[10] Other examples of hangings for 'trifling' infractions are given, as well as the hanging of several people he describes as innocent of any crime.[11] In the year 1520, four more thieves were hanged, leading Ibn Iyas to accuse the governor of presiding in judgment while "drunk" and of being an oppressor *(zalim)*.[12] When the Ottoman currency was introduced, he continues, many more people were threatened with hanging for refusing to trade by the new currency.[13]

Ibn Iyas' shock, and that of the general populace, arises from the fact that such measures exceeded the limits of the *hudud*. In the case of theft, Ibn Taymiya's position is that a person's right hand must be amputated, but only if the theft exceeded three dirhams,[14] while al-Mawardi points out that that there are differences of opinion on minimum amounts for amputation, the nature of the property that warrants amputation, and the person due amputation if the crime is committed in a group.[15] In all cases, however, a death sentence for stealing cucumbers would have been seen as a great miscarriage of justice.

The social unrest which gripped Cairo as a result of these policies soon reached the Sublime Porte for, in 1519, a *qasim* (judge overseeing the division of inheritances) arrived from Constantinople bearing edicts *(marasim)* from Sultan Salim addressing Amir Kamshbigha, the governor of Cairo. Citing the numerous complaints against the *mazalim* he had opened in Cairo, it terminated the governor's tenure and ordered his return to Constantinople.[16] Ibn Iyas calls Kamshbigha a "murderous Rumi," and is pleased by the edict terminating his service.[17] But the departure of this governor did not imply a termination of *siyasa* justice, or *mazalim*.

Al-Damiri reports that in 1534–36, Khusrev Pasha suppressed crime so effectively that merchants left their stores unlocked.[18] Later still, Masih

Pasha (1575–80) ordered the arms and legs of thieves cut off and thrown in the street.[19] The *Qanunnama Misr*, it will be remembered, eventually abolished the *mazalim* and delegated all substantive law to the sharia court, a measure which scholars believe helped to ensure that criminal penalties stayed within the bounds of the sharia, but which did not, obviously, end the imposition of *siyasa* justice altogether.

Another feature of the early and late sixteenth century was the application in practice of the laws governing *dhimmi* life, including the dress codes found in Islamic legal theory. Al-Damiri wrote that in Hassan Pasha al-Khadim's day (1580), the Jews wore red hats *(taratir)* and the Christians wore black ones. Indicating that dress codes were already in effect, however, he writes that before Khadim's time, the Jews wore yellow hats and the Christians blue ones.[20] It does appear, therefore, that dress codes were at times enforced, though how consistently remains unclear.

Intoxication is another 'sin' which becomes a de facto crime, on and off, for much of the sixteenth and the first half of the seventeenth centuries. Underscoring the severity of early Ottoman attitudes, Ibn Iyas reports that in the year 1519 a merchant, al-Mahalawi, of bad repute for charging interest *(riba)*, was arrested on the charge that he had sold alcohol and *ma'jun* (paste, presumably narcotic) to the Turcomans during the month of Ramadan. The Governor ordered that the individual be charged and hanged after the *'id* festivities. But a group of the defendant's friends and clients from among the militias *(inshikariya)* prevented the order from being carried out. His supporters followed this up by going to the *suq al-waraqin* (the paper-makers' market) and assaulting those who had informed on al-Mahalawi. When the merchants complained to the governor, he ordered that the defendant be crucified on Bab al-Midan.[21]

Stories such as this are repeated throughout the century. As mentioned in chapter three, the chief Ottoman judge Husayn ibn Muhammad Husam al-Din Qaraçli Zada, appointed in 1579, was described by al-Damiri as a strict prohibitionist, and that "no scent of intoxicant was smelled in Cairo in his time."[22] Well into the seventeenth century, Husayn Pasha (1637) banned all forms of smoking, and subsequently killed fifty men caught in violation, on the spot.[23]

Coffee quickly became another source of immense controversy when "under Sufi auspices the use of coffee as a beverage spread in the Near East in the fifteenth century."[24] It became an integral part of *dhikr* gatherings, a practice said to have been started by the Shadhili Shaykh, Abu'l-Hassan 'Ali ibn 'Umar (d. in Yemen 1418).[25] Opponents of the new product obtained fatwas and medical opinions against it while supporters did the same. These debates preoccupied the members of the judiciary as much as it did the state, and often, the 'popular mob,' who frequently attacked coffeehouses at the behest of the shaykhs.

Winter writes that the Egyptian shaykh Ghazzi believed that an *ijma'* had been achieved on this issue: so long as the drinking of coffee was not accompanied by wine drinking, music, and mixing with adolescents and women, it was permitted. But his contemporary, 'Abd al-Haq al-Sunbati, was of a different opinion, and frequently incited listeners at al-Azhar to attack the coffeehouses.[26] Sha'rani, a prominent Egyptian Sufi, regards these as trifling issues on which one should waste little time as the ulama were themselves undecided.[27]

The *sijill*s shed light on this debate on intoxication, providing useful information on its legal trajectory in practice. There are no records of coffee traders or coffee shop owners (*qahwaji*s) in any of the records at my disposal prior to the seventeenth century. However there are four such documents dated thereafter. In 1614, the *sijill* of al-Bab al-'Ali records that a *qahwaji*, al-Manfaluti, was released from jail after paying a debt of ten dinars.[28] It is unclear whether the fine was levied on account of his profession or whether it was unrelated. It is only by the mid-seventeenth century, however, that the first case involving a commercial contract for the wholesale purchase of coffee is found.[29] In that same *sijill*, there are two other references to coffee shops as part of the description of a given neighbourhood (*hayy*). In one, a coffee shop is said to be in an area adjacent to the tomb of a holy Sufi, Sayyid –? 'Uqb. In another case pertaining to *waqf*, the neighborhood is described and identified by two names, 'al-Haramayn al-Sharifayn' and 'Qahwat Timsah,' indicating the degree to which coffee shops had become normalized fixtures in local neighborhoods.[30] The proximity of Sufi shrines to the coffee shops mentioned, indeed the fact that streets were often named after the shrine and the coffee shop simultaneously, is indicative of the continued association between Sufism and coffee.

Again, when it came to consumption of intoxicants, judicial opinion varies. Ibn Taymiya argued that flogging was due to anyone who consumed any intoxicant.[31] Al-Mawardi, however, suggested that punishment might not only vary from flogging to public humiliation, but that some scholars considered 'inebriation,' rather than consumption, to be the crime, while others argued that only wine, or only alcoholic intoxicants, were banned, not inebriation itself.[32] The subtleties of this debate are lost in the interpretation of the 'rights of God' by the Ottoman state. But as demonstrated by the example of coffee, presumably because it had become a staple source of trade within the empire, the bounds of 'ideal' morality were in a constant state of flux. As such, coffee went from an illicit brew to a staple drink and source of commercial revenue, with the full backing of the state, by the seventeenth century. In point of fact, Abu al-Su'ud's categorization of coffee consumption as a matter for discretionary punishment gave the state wide license in deciding whether to criminalize or decriminalize the 'sin' of intoxication.

The debate on coffee and the reformulation of the fixed penalties hinged on the relationship of sin to crime. The threshold of Muslim morality, once defined by the partnership between the jurists *(fiqh)* and communities of Cairo, now included the state. The *qanun* and official *madhhab*, which oversaw the standardization of women's rights and obligations in marriage and divorce, their access to public space, and their freedom of movement, attest to this presence. What is more, they attest to the rise of a fourth party to this partnership—the individual.

The Threshold of Morality

In the early years of the conquest, a draconian code of moral conduct was imposed on the women of Cairo by both the governor and the Ottoman chief judge. Almost a hundred years later, this code appears to have disappeared. The sharia courts of the late sixteenth to the mid-seventeenth century operated under a new code, reflecting a new ideal with respect to women and their right to freedom of movement. The question is: does the new hegemony indicate the authority of local custom, the 'Islamization' of the laws, or the transformation of Ottoman orthodoxy? The distinctions are important, as they reflect the success or failure of the Ottoman venture.

The argument made here is that Ottoman rule in the early sixteenth century is notable for the conflation of sins and crimes. As the century progressed, a greater effort was made to separate the two. The point to be made, therefore, is that the boundaries of moral conduct, whether restricted or delimited, had little to do with local custom. Neither extreme in the moral pendulum represented the normative standards sanctioned by local practices. In other words, while the Ottoman moral ideal fluctuated and changed, the state's basic drive to unify legal practice and social conduct did not.

Ottomans officials had a clear notion of the role or place of women in society, including a variant threshold of sexual modesty from their Egyptian counterparts. This is amply demonstrated by the numerous examples of *siyasa* justice meted out to women accused of unchaste conduct. In the year of the conquest, on 9 Ramadan 923 (1517), four women accused of consorting with the Turcomen and of introducing them to women "strange to them" *(ajanib)* were paraded around town on donkeys, their faces "exposed and smeared in black."[33] In 1518, another woman was accosted in an alley by soldiers *(asbahaniya)* who charged that she had been consorting with a Christian. She and the Christian were arrested and brought before the governor, who decreed that the woman be stripped of her clothes, her hands and legs bound, her feet attached to the back of a donkey, and her body dragged through the streets, "face first," from al-Kadashin to Bab Zuwayla, where she was to be hanged. Some said that she died before reaching the Bab, while others said the soldiers drowned her in the Nile around the "middle Island."[34] Ibn Iyas laments her death and her terrible suffering. He does not, however, inform us of the fate of the Christian.

In 1519, another Muslim woman was apprehended consorting with a Jewish man, and when the matter became known, was arrested alongside her consort and the *makari* (donkey driver) who provided her transport. A 'middle person,' who introduced the two, was also arrested. The governor ruled that the *makari* was to be beaten, the woman jailed "in a room," and the Jewish man jailed in the Daylam prison.[35] One can only speculate about the background of the women and the nature of these rendezvous. Was it the sin of prostitution or the sin of an illicit cross-communal relationship that fueled these incidents? Based on the number of *qanun* targeting the mobility and public access of *all* women in Cairo, it could be said that the general moral conduct of Cairo's female population was, itself, a source of concern.

On the heels of these incidents, the Ottoman chief judge had town criers call on the women of Cairo to remain within their homes. This included a ban on going to the markets or riding donkeys, at penalty of being tied to the tail of a donkey *(ikdish)* by the hair and paraded in the streets. Unbeknownst to the residents of Cairo, the custom in Istanbul punished prostitutes by placing them on the backs of donkeys and parading them through the streets. It struck Ottoman officials as unseemly that the women of Cairo rode donkeys of their own free will. The *makariya* (donkey drivers) were forced to sell their donkeys and to purchase mules and carriages with rugs for the women to sit atop. And this adaptation persisted, writes Ibn Iyas, as donkeys disappeared, and women rode in the tradition and style of Istanbul. This is a wonderful examples of the culture clash that often marked encounters between Ottoman officialdom and Egyptian society, and of the antagonistic sharias they embraced.

But a total prohibition on women appearing in public places suggests that beyond differences over preferred modes of travel, the Ottomans had more general concerns about the outward conduct of Egyptian women. Ibn Iyas links the ban on women appearing in public to a day when the *qadi 'asker* ascended the citadel and saw a group of local women chatting with a group of *asbahaniya* (soldiers) in the middle of the market. This affected him deeply, and he complained to the governor that "the women of the people of Egypt have corrupted the soldiery of the *khundikar*," and that the troops were no longer good for anything.[36] This, concludes Ibn Iyas, troubled the governor to such an extent that he was persuaded to ban the women of Cairo from appearing in public. The ban appears to have been rigorously enforced, for soon after the governor's order, a woman found riding a donkey on a desert road was forced down, beaten, and had her "buttons broken," escaping the fury of the soldiers only through the "intercession" of "others" and the payment of a fine in the amount of two ashraf.[37]

Underscoring a deep cultural unease among the *ahali* (people) of Cairo with the threshold of Ottoman morality, the rulings of the chief Ottoman judge were met with increasing antagonism. An appeal to the *qadi 'asker* to relax the ban by allowing women to visit the *hammams*, relatives, and graveyards was eventually agreed to, but with the caveat that only elderly women were allowed to visit the graves, and that all other women were to be accompanied by their husbands to visit relatives or the baths. A poem satirizing the Ottoman judge accuses him of putting *qanun* above the *shar'* of Ahmad.[38] Once again, the direct criticism made is that the Ottomans had exceeded the bounds of *fiqh* and prophetic example in banishing women from public life. On the day of the chief judge's final departure from Cairo, the "women of Cairo" gathered for his sendoff, satirically chanting: "Come to whoring *(quhb)* and intoxication *(sukr)*, the *qadi 'asker* has left us."[39]

None of the measures adopted by the *qadi 'asker* lasted very long, however. While Ibn Iyas writes that donkeys disappeared from Cairo, the phenomenon was far from permanent. By the late sixteenth century, the practice was revived and the courts were plainly unconcerned. When he visited Cairo, Mustafa 'Ali, the late sixteenth-century Turkish chronicler, described his horror at this custom.

> Their women, all of them, ride donkeys. Even the spouses of some notables ride on donkeys to the Bulaq promenade. . . . This unbecoming behavior constitutes a serious defect to the city of Cairo, because in other lands, they put prostitutes on donkeys as punishment. In Cairo the women mount donkeys of their own free will and expose themselves to the public; therefore, it appears appropriate that as a punishment, they be put on camels.[40]

Further evidence of these different moral economies is found in the writings of another Turkish chronicler who visited a local hospital, the Bimaristan al-Mansuri (named after the Mamluk sultan al-Malik Qalawun), which "included a department for mental patients and one for women, with attendants who were also women." But he was astonished that the male doctors entered the women's quarters in the hospital "without shame to treat them."[41] Reflecting local attitudes, the Egyptian writer Sha'rani haughtily dismisses the opinion that women should not receive male guests at home in the husband's absence as a "Bedouin custom" unworthy of emulation.[42]

By the end of the sixteenth century, the state's moral pendulum had swung back again. The modification of Ottoman *qanun*, reflected in *sijill*s of the late sixteenth century, indicate a dramatic relaxation in the bounds of gendered morality. This is most evident in the freedom of movement and the freedom of lawful association that the courts consistently bestowed on women. There are two documents touching on the issue of women and their freedom of movement and access to public space. One is from 1045 (1635) (doc. no. 66) and evokes a very different portrait of the Ottoman chief judge from that of his early-sixteenth-century predecessor. In this document, the judge appears as the guarantor of given rights, including a woman's right to appear in public and her right to legitimate association with members of the opposite sex.

The document begins by identifying the Hanafi judge and the woman as Hijaziya bint Zaynab bint 'Atiya.[43] Hijaziya came to the court seeking to rectify the wrongful imprisonment of her suitor Jum'a. His imprisonment, she argued, flowed from the false testimony of her brother, Hijazi ibn 'Atiya, the stockkeeper at the bakeries, who had attacked her and blocked her opportunity for marriage *(wuquf 'ardiha)*. Maligning her honor, the brother had gone so far as to accuse her of an illicit affair with a 'strange' *(ajnabi)* man, the aforementioned Jum'a, before calling upon the *muqaddim* to arrest them both. The record indicates that Jum'a was arrested, and that Hijaziya appeared in court to appeal his incarceration as well as to affirm her desire to "retain him" *(li-l-tamassuk bih)* as a suitor. She concluded by asking the court for a *shar'i hujja* prohibiting the brother from further interference.

Having heard her appeal, the judge turned his attention to the brother, Hijazi, who confirmed that he called the *muqaddim* when "news reached him" that a man named Jum'a sat *(jalis)* with his sister in her "private quarters." Rushing to her quarters, Hijazi was able to confirm the truth of the report and to see them cloistered in her rooms with his own eyes. He then "closed the door upon her," and called the *muqaddim*, who arrested Jum'a in her rooms.

Refuting his testimony, Hijaziya denied the charge that she had ever met Jum'a in her rooms. She did, however, freely confess to meeting with Jum'a in public (in the alley in which she lived) to discuss his proposal of marriage. And contrary to her brother's claims, she continued, the *muqaddim* had not arrested Jum'a in her rooms but "in the middle of the road."

Placing the burden of proof on Hijazi, who had not produced "*shar'i* witnesses" *(bayinat shahd)* to back his claims, the judge proved unwilling to accept his version of the events. Hijaziya then asked the judge to enforce *(ijra')* the honorable *shar'* and "he responded to her request" by informing the brother that his testimony lacked corroborative evidence, and closed the session until such time as one or the other of the claimants could bring witnessed proof of their claims.

After an unspecified interval of time, both Hijaziya and her brother Hijazi returned to the court accompanied by witnesses from her quarter, among them Ahmad al-Jawish and Shaykh 'Abd al-Basit ibn Badr ibn al-Faqir Ahmad from the *ahali* of Saqt Maydum(?) and Ahmad ibn 'Ali from Kum Abu Khilla and ibn 'Ali ibn Muhammad. All of the men testified that the *muqaddim al-shubashi* had arrested Jum'a "on the road," near the hospital *(bimaristan)*, and that he was not arrested in Hijaziya's home. Moreover, they served as character witnesses for Hijaziya, informing the judge that she was "among the virtuous and the upright of worldly women and that they know of nothing but that," and that her brother's charge had no veracity and lacked the status of a *shar'i* report. "And when the matter *(amr)* was found to be thus, this was precisely recorded," reads the *mahdar*. But the case does not appear to be closed, as the document concludes by requesting a *talab wa su'al* ('question and answer'), "to be reviewed as need dictates [at some future point]." The terms *talab* and *su'al* indicate the court's request for a final fatwa on the subject. Until such time as Hijaziya obtained one, a judgment was still pending. Nonetheless, the fatwa appears to be a final formality as all indications are that Hijaziya had won her case.

There are several points of interest raised by this case that warrant comment. First, Hijaziya's right (as an adult who requires no *wali* to broker a marriage on her behalf) to meet her suitor in a public place was clearly not in dispute. It is well documented that patriarchal customs, though not Islamic law, generally delegated such authority to male relatives, a prerogative that Hijazi, her brother, seemed bent on preserving. Second, at no time did he seek to impose his will through community arbitration, or take the law into his own hands. Instead, he followed the letter of the law, filing a formal complaint leading to Jum'a's arrest by the appropriate state officials and remaining at all times within the bounds of *qanun* and sharia. But more importantly, his testimony, contradicted by eyewitnesses from the neighborhood, appeared contrived. The allegation that Hijaziya and Jum'a were cloistered in her rooms (an illicit setting) suggests that Hijazi was trying to deflect the issue away from her *fiqh*-based rights to accept a marriage proposal, and toward her 'moral conduct.' In effect, this implies that he was aware of the fact that the courts would uphold her right both to consent to the marriage and to meet potential suitors in a *shar'i* setting.

As a social document, the case is illustrative of the fact that all claims, no matter how private or sensitive, were brought before the courts and, what is more, that moral conduct was the business of the state (Jum'a was, after all, arrested) and its sharia court. The role of the community is central to establishing the facts of the case and the reputation of the claimants, but it plays no role whatsoever in determining the judge's ruling. But even more importantly, it demonstrates Hijaziya's individual agency before the law. She had a certain status as a member of a community, and her standing within that community determined the level of support she received from its important constituents in the courtroom. The collective testimonials of her neighbors formed the keystone of her case.

But the question remains: was it the normative morality of her community and its customs that determined what was licit or illicit in this case? Could it even be assumed that the community had a homogenous moral outlook? Apart from being asked to testify to her character, the witnesses were asked to provide corroborative evidence—where the meeting took place, and the exact location of Jum'a's arrest. They were not asked to arbitrate between the siblings, give an opinion on Hijaziya's blocked betrothal, or suggest a remedy based in communal practice. Rather, her prerogatives under the law established the terms of the suit and its settlement, give her the right to meet a potential suitor in a suitable venue, and to challenge the authority of her closest male kin—an authority deeply rooted in custom. But more importantly, this case illustrates Hijaziya's individual autonomy from those customs. Her request for a *hujja shar'iya* to that effect demonstrates the close association between those individual rights and the document.

If anything, therefore, Hijaziya's case demonstrates the limited reach of custom in regulating public morality. It also demonstrates an expansion in moral boundaries such that women were free to associate with men, provided they had legitimate reasons for doing so, and a legitimate venue in which to meet. Another example of the expanding bounds of morality and of individual agency is found in a case from S.A.I. Milad's article on the *sijill*s of the Salihiya al-Najmiya in Cairo. In 1627 Zayna bint Muhammad ibn Shams al-Din, known as bint Turabi, alleged that her husband, al-'Allali 'Ali ibn 'Abd Allah, a *qassab* (maker and seller of sugar-cane drinks), frequently beat her and locked her within the house by "closing the door upon her," intending by such behavior "to do her harm." Al-'Allali did not deny the accusation but justified his conduct by claiming that "she had a long tongue," that is, was verbally abusive. The judge commanded both of them to refrain from wronging one another, and further instructed the husband to "refrain from closing the door upon her," forbidding the latter from impeding his wife's freedom of movement and access to public space.⁴⁴ Again, it bears repeating that this is a far cry from the early days of the conquest, when women were officially prohibited from leaving their homes unless accompanied by their husbands.

What is more, Zayna was not petitioning the court for a divorce. Rather, she sought the court's intercession in and mediation of an ongoing marital conflict. The question is: why did she not seek the community's arbitration instead? Conceivably, the community, its elders and respected members, could have brought pressure to bear on al-'Allali. Is it possible that she *had* appealed to the community and encountered indifference? Or is it that the court was the venue of first choice? Given that communal arbitration lacked the writ and force of law, it stands to reason that the vague injunction, that both were to refrain from verbal and physical abuse, ended with a binding legal injunction against the husband, forbidding him from "closing the door upon her." Zayna's actions culminated, therefore, in the issuance of a *hujja* asserting her physical freedom to come and go. What is more, she had formally documented her husband's behavior and strengthened her own hand within the marriage by preparing the ground for future litigation, or even divorce.

Coupled with the fact that the sheer variety of cases brought to the court in the late sixteenth and mid-seventeenth centuries far exceeds anything found in the mid-sixteenth, it becomes difficult to overlook the link between the expanding authority of the document and the expanding autonomy of the individual. The one made it possible for the other to emerge as the shaping force of a new, translocal, transcommunal social orthodoxy. No clearer, or more glaring, example can be found than the introduction of civil marriage.

Civil Marriage

> Question: Now that a Sultanic decree has been issued commanding that no marriage be concluded without the cognisance of a judge, is a marriage [concluded] without such a cognisance valid? Answer: No, lest it give rise to dispute and litigation.⁴⁵

An imperial decree issued in the time of Abu al-Su'ud made the registration of marriage before a court judge compulsory. With a single stroke of the pen, marriage, which in the Islamic legal tradition required no more than the signing of a document between the couple in the presence of two witnesses,[46] had become a civil institution. As this important institution was placed squarely within the purview of the bureaucratic courts, its boundaries were now delineated by state jurists.

Marking the dawn of civil marriage, and the transformation of Islamic law into a territorial-civil law for all subjects, the *qanun* of 1521 is one of the most important and overlooked laws ever to be promulgated in the history of Ottoman and Islamic social history. Coming almost three centuries before the adoption of civil marriage in the west, the *qanun* of 1521 compelled all subjects, without religious distinction, to register marital and divorce contracts in the court of the Ottoman chief judge. The process of registration was also accompanied by a series of new levies or a 'marriage tax'—sixty nifs for a virgin and thirty for marriage to a widow or divorcée—apportioned in court fees to the notary (*'aqid*), the witness (*shahid*), and the governor.[47] In spite of enormous and virulent opposition, Ibn Iyas writes that judges were given little choice in the matter, and forewarned to "follow the Ottoman law" (*al-sayq al-'uthmani*).[48] On a popular level, the edict was widely rejected and seen as a "penalty" against marriage, an illicit means by which to generate state revenue, and for a time "the *Sunna* of marriage was discontinued."[49]

For its part, al-Azhar vehemently protested the marriage tax, and over a hundred of its most eminent scholars surrounded the governor Khayrbek's residence demanding its repeal. Quoting numerous Hadith, their spokesmen argued that marriage in the Sunna of the Prophet required nothing more than the exchange of silver rings, six pieces (*ansaf*) of silver, and the reading of a verse from the holy book. As such, the new tax had no basis in, and indeed violated, the tenets of Islamic law by imposing prohibitive and undue costs on people. What the judges were describing was marriage as it had always been—an informal institution to which the state was not party.

To be certain, written marriage contracts had always existed, and some people even registered them in the qadi's *diwan* (pre-Ottoman register). But this was probably done very unsystematically as qadis did not draw up the marital contracts themselves. This was the job of a specialized notary (*ma'zun*), who may have deposited the records with the qadi, kept them himself, or given them to the married couple. However we look at it, the great difference between the pre- and post-Ottoman procedure is the private nature of the former and the public nature of the latter.

First noted by M. Winter, the law of 1521 and the judicial confrontation it provoked has been downplayed as an administrative, post-conquest tussle between Egyptian jurists and the new political overlords—a naked Ottoman attempt to control the legal process, but not a grab for substantive judicial authority. A. Sonbol takes more note of its importance, concluding that the requirement "that all marriages be registered in court" was a "change" that "made the court a direct player in personal and family relations."[50] Nonetheless, in Sonbol's analysis, the institutional strength of the Egyptian judiciary, its *madhahib* and local elites, combined to stabilize the administration of justice and to provide a continuum in legal practices from Mamluk to Ottoman times. But the links between the administration of justice and the production of justice are lost in this analysis. Egyptian jurists in the sixteenth century, on the other hand, never seemed to lose sight of the connection. Bombastically claiming that the house of the law was crumbling at the hand of the 'infidel' Turk, jurists lamented the fate of Muslim law and society after the law of 1521. In truth, the house was not crumbling, it was being remodeled.

Islamic law, which had stood for centuries as the epitome of a private, nongovernmental, self-regulating institution (in revenue generation, accreditation, licensing, and appointment), was becoming incrementally 'governmentalized.' Local jurists understood the weight of the moment, with its unprecedented bureaucratic intrusion into private spaces, as a moment of transference for the law itself. The law of 1521, which had rendered marriage a public institution, was a first step in the transformation of Islamic law into a growing public entity. No small procedural adjustment, therefore, the law of 1521 represents a revolutionary social and political transformation, heralding the onset of what modern Europeans would call 'civil marriage.'

Defined as a secular contract drawn before a civil magistrate that unites a man and woman in marriage, civil marriage became compulsory in modern Europe incrementally, over the course of the eighteenth, nineteenth, and twentieth centuries. But its roots also lay in the sixteenth century, when the Protestant Reformation rejected the Catholic view of marriage as a sacrament. Martin Luther declared marriage to be "a worldly thing . . . that belongs to the realm of government," and a similar opinion was expressed by Calvin.[51] But in most of Europe, marriages continued to require a religious ceremony until the French Revolution of 1792 introduced civil marriage—also by compulsion. In England, Lord Hardwicke's Marriage Act of 1753 required that, in order to be valid and registered, all marriages were to be performed in an official ceremony in a religious setting. In 1836, the requirement that the ceremony take place in a religious forum was removed, and registrars were given the authority to register marriages conducted by a nonreligious official.[52]

In theory, civil law is secular in that it does not recognize the obstacles erected by religion to marriage. In practice, notwithstanding recent challenges from the gay community, the dominant conception of marriage in the west continued to be defined by Christian precepts of monogamy and heterosexuality. Nonetheless, it opened the door to interfaith marriage and to nonreligious ceremonies in which one or both parties professed no religion. The differences and similarities between this and the conception of civil marriage which developed in Islam are striking.

To begin with the differences, the classical marital contract in Islam, and Judaism for that matter, has never been a sacrament, never more than a worldly legal contract between two individuals. An ancient forerunner of the Protestant marriage contract, it nonetheless shares one important feature in common with its sacramental counterpart in Europe: in its pre-territorial stage, Islamic family law extended to the universal religious community—an Islamic law for Muslims. This would formally change with the edict of 1521, which made no distinction between Muslim and non-Muslim thereafter.

Aside from pushing people into the courts, the new law had several consequences on marriage in practice. We cannot say for certain how many marriages remained 'unregistered,' or customary (*'urfi*), as they were now called. On rare occasion, however, one can find a reference to "*zawaj bi-l-'urfi*."

Cutting across class and ethnic lines, one document, an inventory of possessions belonging to a woman identified as a "Bedouin," describes her as "married by custom" to a "Circassian" *'askeri*.[53] Apart from being unusual in listing the ethnicity of both parties, the document is also unusual in its mention of "customary marriage," the term now applied to any unregistered marriage. Indeed the very notion of customary marriage (*zawaj 'urfi*) in modern Egypt, like common law in English jurisprudence, developed in contradistinction to the idea of marriage as a public institution after the law of 1521.

As the formal definition of marriage took root, it facilitated the convergence of legal theory with (largely Hanafi) legal practice, while regulating and inevitably diminishing the influence of local customary arbitration. In addition to standardizing the rights of individuals within marriage, the courts also unified the substantive laws produced by eliminating any deviation based in custom in the practice of giving the dowry, and providing this reformulation with the force of a *qanun* injunction. But most importantly, they encouraged brides and their families to avail themselves of a *fiqh*-based right to the conditional clause—a device which enhanced the wife's autonomy within the marriage.

The Conditional Clause

The earliest conditional stipulations I have encountered seem designed to resist the application of a *qanun* from the early sixteenth century. In Rajab 928 (1521), the *qadi 'asker* reportedly declared, "I wish to make the women of Egypt follow the ways of the women of Istanbul in dealing with their husbands. It is our custom that when a husband enters marriage, the wife returns to him half her dowry, and he is not responsible for providing a *kiswa* (wardrobe) or *nafaqa fi-sadaqiha* (marital maintenance) but provides her with a *jawkha* (credit ledger) and two blouses once a year, and feeds her as little or as much as he sees fit." Naturally, writes Ibn Iyas, this had the effect of making the men of the *a'wam* (masses) happy and the women miserable.[54]

The *sijill*s indicate, however, that neither the *kiswa* nor the *nafaqa* were ever replaced by the *jawkha*. With regard to the third clause, that he may feed her as little or as much as he likes, there is negative evidence to suggest that its potential enforcement remained a concern for women. Almost forty years after the *qanun*'s issuance in 1521, two marital contracts from the court of Ibn Tulun (1557–58) contain the conditional clause that it is incumbent on the husband to ensure that his wife enjoys a wide variety of foods corresponding to the variety he consumes. In the first document, the Hanafi judge ratifies a contract of 'return' (spousal reconciliation) conditional upon the wife "eating a variety of foods with him [the husband]."[55] The second is a contract of engagement *(khutuba)* conditional upon the same clause from the same year.[56] It would seem, therefore, that the force of the *qanun* continued to be felt, and resisted, into the mid-sixteenth century. Based on these two documents alone, however, it is impossible to speculate on the extent to which people adhered to, or ignored, the order of 1521, only to conclude that it was not unheard of for wives to fear a husband availing himself of it. Nonetheless, the fact that a conditional clause was allowed to neutralize the *qanun* is perhaps an indication of the state's commitment to the *qanun* as, qualitatively speaking, a male privilege that fell short of a right. This seems an apt assessment given that the conditional clause also worked to neutralize male privileges enshrined in Islamic jurisprudence, such as polygyny, as falling short of an unqualified right.

Preventing the Harm: Polygyny and Spousal Abuse

On first seeing the frequency with which marital contracts in the Ottoman period contain conditional stipulations, Sonbol writes: "The first thought that comes to the mind of a researcher reading this marriage contract is, 'What do I do with it?'"[57] While Sonbol demonstrates the distance between these Ottoman-era contracts and their modern counterparts, I should like to focus on the ways in which they refract essential personhood in the context of a public court, archive, and increasingly surveilling state. Effectively allowing women to stipulate set conditions by which the marriage was to function or end, the conditional stipulations are most remarkable for allowing them not only to reject behaviors rooted in personal or group customs, but to reject behavior sanctioned by Islamic law, such as polygyny.

Out of thirty-eight marriage contracts ratified between the mid-sixteenth and the early seventeenth centuries, six contain the conditional clause that "if he marries other than her, or purchases a concubine of any race, by direct action or through the agency of another, she is pronounced divorced through one *talqa*."[58] Beyond this basic formula, the writing and elaboration of such clauses vary considerably from document to document. Some empower the woman to dissolve the husband's new marriage, others to dissolve only her own, while still others fine the husband monetarily. Sonbol has noted this phenomenon extensively, as has Salameh in the Jerusalem *sijill*, though the latter takes "repetition in the conditions of marriage that the husband should not marry another woman" to mean "that the practice of polygamy [sic] was common in Jerusalem."[59] Assuming, however, that polygyny proved too costly for the lower classes, and given that almost every elite marriage includes in "repetition" this condition, would it not be more logical to assume that plural marriages were, in fact, uncommon?

Not one of the contracts representing the daughters of commoners—thirty in total —makes any stipulations against polygyny or concubinage. Six out of eight contracts for the daughters of notables, merchants, high-ranking military, and even the concubines of deceased notables, on the other hand, include such a precondition. Given that a full six out of eight elite marriages contain this proviso, can it still be assumed that polygyny was common, even among the elite? A much larger sample of documents would need to be examined before we can answer this question, but the sheer prevalence of this clause, whether in Jerusalem or Cairo, indicates that monogamy was judicially enforced and socially preferred in many elite marriages. But is this an indication of the law's 'Islamization' or its de-Islamization? How could the marital contract be allowed to abrogate the Islamic laws and Sunna, which legitimated polygyny?

Not surprisingly, the validity of such stipulations was disputed among different schools of thought. The Hanafi, Shafi'i, and Maliki schools regarded these conditions as illegitimate, while the *nikah* contract containing them could itself remain valid. Among those who considered these stipulations invalid were 'Ali Sa'id ibn al-Musayyab, Hasan al-Basri, Sufyan al-Thawri, Abu Hanifa, Malik, and Shafi'i.[60] Meanwhile, the Hanbali school considered them to be valid and binding.

Ibn Taymiya (d. AH 728/CE 1328) argued that things which are prohibited cannot be covenanted, while *mubah* or permissible matters may be agreed upon.[61] In other words, a contractual condition cannot permit that which has been forbidden by the law, but can proscribe that which has been permitted by law. According to Ibn Qudamah (d. AH 620/CE 1223), it was also not correct to say that stipulations against the taking of a second wife 'prohibit[ed] the legal' or distorted the *nikah* agreement, for restraining a married man from taking a second wife, or maintaining a wife in her paternal home, were declared valid by the Caliph 'Umar. By way of analogy, all the schools of law allowed a man to delegate the right of divorce either to his wife or to a third party, even though this is usually conceived as the man's exclusive right in Islamic jurisprudence.

The Hanbali position was, therefore, most in keeping with the notion of the marital covenant as a civil contract requiring both parties to fulfill their stipulated obligations. Nevertheless, this was the position of the Hanbalis, not the Hanafis, who at this juncture denied the validity of conditions that could 'prohibit the legal,' such as a wife preempting her husband from remarrying during her tenure as his wife. Consider the following excerpt from the *Fatawa 'Alamghiri*:

> When anything is stipulated in a contract of marriage which is contrary to law, as, for example, that the husband shall not marry another wife during the lifetime of the party with whom the contract is made, nor privately entertain a woman as his concubine, the condition is void, and the contract valid together with the dower.[62]

But by the time the Ottoman Law of Family Rights—the first-ever official code of Islamic family law—was enacted in 1917, the position had changed. It states that where a woman stipulates the husband will not marry another wife, if he does so, she or the second wife would stand divorced, the contract of marriage shall be valid, and the condition enforceable.[63]

Clearly this is not a process of de-Islamization, or more absurdly a "novelty for Islamic law," as some of the literature on gender and modern legal reform in the Ottoman Empire would suggest.[64] It is, rather, a gradual distillation of a Hanbali opinion into the Hanafi *madhhab*, an early form of the process that would come to be known as *talfiq*. A modernist method for "patchworking" legal codes out of opinions derived from all the schools of law, *talfiq* is generally seen as a twentieth-century phenomenon. In all but name, however, the conditional stipulations preventing polygyny in the court of the Ottoman chief judge represent an early form of *talfiq*.

Given that polygyny and concubinage predate the rise of Islam, one may count them among the many pre-Islamic customs that were eventually incorporated into Islamic law. The use of the conditional clause, a device which allows for the abrogation of such practices (even though neither is proscribed by the law), is a vivid example of how jurists continued to modify 'morality as it is' to reflect 'morality as it should be.' In other words, while polygyny was sanctioned for men, it was hardly viewed as an absolute right. Rather, the courts appear to have treated it as a privilege conditional upon the first wife's consent.

The conditional stipulations banning polygyny seem to have entered the Hanafi school (or at least the courts) by the back door, through the provisions on 'harm' *(darar)* rather than through the debate on contractual agreements, where it is found in Hanbalism.

'Harm' was defined more broadly than polygyny, to encompass more basic concerns, such as physical abuse. In two marriage contracts found in the Cairo *sijill*, the bride insisted on the conditional clause that she would be divorced by one *talqa* "if he should beat or mark her." Class was not a factor in these two particular documents, as one certified an elite marriage and the other a lower-class one.[65]

As we have seen, the attempt to unify practice, based on 'the best of customs' and on the best judicial opinion, was most evident in the example of marriage. We may now examine the examples of the deferred dowry, where a very similar process is underway.

The Deferred Dowry

Every marital contract in the *sijill* records I collected, numbering thirty-eight in total, lists the amount of the bride price, the advanced and deferred portions, and, if the woman is represented by an agent *(wakil)*, it also names the person who received the dowry on her behalf. The case of the deferred dower, originating in pre-Islamic custom, makes it clear that Ottoman courts were not opposed to custom in and of itself, merely to the competing legitimacy of variant customs. Its incorporation into Ottoman law also demonstrates that state jurists were less concerned with universalizing Anatolian or Turkic customs than with unifying practice on the basis of one custom, without regard to its origins.

The dowry (*mahr* or *sadaq*) is the only marriage gift required by Islamic law, although the actual amount of the marriage settlement is decided on the basis of custom. In the earliest Islamic marriage contracts found in the Egyptian papyri, the groom gave a *sadaq* that was divided into advance and deferred portions, payable on the husband's death or divorce, and brides brought to the marriage a counterpart dowry (*jihaz* or *shiwar*). Rapport speculates that the practice originates in Byzantine law, a conclusion drawn from the fact that the practice was common to Muslims, Copts, and Jews, and resembled the Egyptian marriage contracts of late antiquity.[66]

The Islamic legal literature preserves the objections of classical jurists, including Malik, to what they term objectionable, 'Egyptian' innovations. But eventually, concludes Rapport, "the local traditions were incorporated, albeit with modifications, into the legal discourse."[67] The Andalusian jurist al-'Utbi (d. 869) relates that "the *sadaq* in the marriage of the Egyptians is deferred to the time of death or divorce. And Malik used to invalidate it before consummation."⁶⁸ In the ninth century, the jurists from Medina ruled that a woman could demand the deferred portion of her dowry at any time. But Syrian and Egyptian jurists continued to rule that she could do so only in the event of death or divorce. Other prominent jurists apart from the Malikis condemned the practice, including Sufyan al-Thawri and Shafi'i.⁶⁹ Between the ninth and eleventh centuries, however, a compromise was attained such that the deferred dower was accepted in modified form. All marriage contracts from that time forward refer to the deferred *sadaq*, and all include a specific time, usually ranging from one to ten years (although one contract specifies five nights), in which the remainder would be paid to the wife.⁷⁰

But the compromise may have been more official than real, Reinhart reasons, as there is nothing to indicate that wives demanded the deferred *sadaq* within the specified time.⁷¹ The custom of the deferred dower was designed to give women leverage over their husbands, and so prevent careless divorce. Shaybani considered it a "fine or penalty on husbands and a deterrent against violations of the marital arrangements that were not formally inserted in the marriage contract."⁷²

Over time, the deferred *sadaq* would become fully incorporated in its original form, such that specific dates for its payment were dropped by the Ottoman period, if not long before. Rapport suggests that this may be explained by the fact that it replaced the *mut'a*, a Qur'anic gift of an unspecified sum given to women on divorce. "Consolation payments disappear from the divorce deeds of the third/ninth century through the fifth/eleventh century . . . at least in Egypt, the *mut'a* payment became obsolete when it became common practice to defer a portion of the *sadaq* until death or divorce."⁷³ Thus here we have an example of a *fiqh*-based ruling being displaced by the customs of the urban centers of Egypt and Syria, such that

> it became the custom, seemingly throughout the Islamic world, to divide the dower into two portions, the advance dower payable on marriage, and the more substantial deferred dower payable to the wife on widowhood or divorce, or to her heirs if she pre-deceased the husband.⁷⁴

By the latter half of the sixteenth century, this 'heartland custom' had been assimilated into the judicial Ottoman discourse—but not before a fight. In the beginning, the Ottomans appeared to abjure the practice, repeatedly warning court officials to ensure that the *mahr al-mithl* (full dowry) was delivered to women.⁷⁵ Eventually, however, Abu al-Suʿud incorporated this practice of deferred dowry into Hanafi *fiqh*, and called for its implementation in Anatolian cities. Referring to the giving of gifts upon betrothal or engagement, and outlining what happens to the money in the event of the couple's separation, Abu al-Suʿud goes through a variety of legal opinions before redacting them into one 'correct' opinion. When asked, "Can Hind in law demand and receive her deferred dower when her husband is alive?" he replied, "In the custom of this land, if the term is not fixed, she does not receive it before death or divorce."⁷⁶ In Imber's view, "Ebu's-Suʿud is here redefining and regularizing a popular custom. *Kalin*, the earnest-money which the husband pays on betrothal, is refashioned [in the juristic language of the Egyptians and Syrians] as an advance dower, making it part of the marriage contract itself."⁷⁷

In the *sijill*s of Cairo, all marriage contracts, without exception, contain the same formula stipulating the deferred and advance portions of the *sadaq*, and clearly stipulating that the payment of the former is contingent upon death or divorce. A typical example reads:

[A] dowry, in the amount [stipulated] by custom (*qadrahu min al-ʿurf*) amount X received (*maqbud*) by brother/father on her behalf by way of *wikala*, amount Y paid up front, and the [deferred] remainder lawfully hers (*tahilu laha*) in the event of divorce or husband's death.⁷⁸

The case of the deferred dower aptly illustrates that the Ottomans were not simply collating and imposing Anatolian/sultanic customs on others. Rather, they were motivated, for economic, political, and ideological reasons, to unify the law produced. Beyond the dowry, the *sijill* reflects this drive at standardization of a wife's economic rights, and a stringent policy of enforcement.

Shaykh Nahiyat al-Basatin sent his son-in-law and cousin to prison for failing to provide his daughter's *kiswa* over a three-year period.⁷⁹ What follows is a physical description of the husband—a blond man, clean shaven, of medium build, with a space between his brows (*mafruq al-hajibayn*). It will be remembered that only two types of people were physically described in court—slaves/former slaves and those about to be jailed or released from prison. In another document, a father sues his son-in-law for appropriating his daughter's money and jewelry. The husband denies the charge, but witnesses confirm the father's testimony.[80] He is ordered to return both the possessions and the money to his wife.

When presented with complaints lodged by wives or their families, therefore, the courts appear to have worked to delimit any encroachment on women's property rights. It bears mentioning that Great Britain and France would not grant women similar rights until the late eighteenth and early nineteenth centuries, respectively. It was no small feat, therefore, for the courts to confront the force of one of the more enduring traits of patriarchy, the appropriation of women's wealth, and the customs that sanctioned it. An alignment between theory and practice was thus at work in Ottoman society with translocal application.

From the perspective of the unifying state, the alignment of practice with Islamic legal theory was an expedient route to cultural standardization. In this respect, it is not inappropriate to speak of an 'Islamization' taking place. But this is only one element in the process of becoming orthodox. The case of the deferred dower illustrates that custom was another thread. Confronted with a number of variant customary practices for the giving of the dower, the state and its jurists consolidated them into one. 'Ottomanization' through codified custom, as much as 'Islamization' through innovative patchworking, was a byproduct of the new orthodoxy.

Similarly, the march toward unification is nowhere more evident than in the area of divorce laws, especially those pertaining to annulment *(faskh)*. Here, we witness not only a movement to eradicate customary practice, but also to redact the multiple legal opinions of the various schools into alignment with the official *madhhab*.

Divorce *(Talaq)* and Annulment *(Faskh)*

> *Question:* "Hind's husband disappears, and she is unable to obtain maintenance. Is it permissible for her to act as a Shafi'i and marry another man?"
> *Answer:* "It is permissible, so long as there is a need for maintenance."[81]

Probably after 1552, Imber writes, a sultanic decree "rendered this solution impossible," and Abu al-Su'ud, the original author of the above, revised his response to state, "There has been a Sultanic prohibition, forbidding the practice of acting as a Shafi'i in the lands of Rumelia and Anatolia."[82]

Shortly after this ruling, however, the chief judge of the *qisma 'askeriya* in Cairo ratified a *hujja shar'iya* annuling the marriage of an abandoned wife. To complicate matters further, this was the wife of a soldier *('askeri)*, and a prisoner of war in the "Christian lands." The original *hujja* was signed by the *qassam al-'askeri*, a military judge who presided over the specialized courts for military personnel, primarily inheritance, property divisions, and, in this case, divorce. The woman had come to the Bab al-'Ali court to make a testamentary bequest, listing her worldly possessions and naming a guardian for her three sons by her ex-husband. The *hujja* of her annulment, presented by way of contextualizing the stipulations of the will, begins by citing a "sound *shar'i hujja* issued publicly *(sadara al-'ishhar bi-ha)*" by the *qassam al-'askeri* of the Egyptian lands *(diyar)* annulling Maryam bint 'Abd Allah's marriage to a Muslim prisoner of war.[83] The soldier, from the area of Sullala, is "known as a trustworthy individual in the Egyptian lands," and is believed to be a prisoner of war "in the Christian lands." Given the circumstances, reads the document, "God had made permissible her divorce from him." As mentioned, the *hujja* was a preamble to Maryam bint 'Abd Allah's will and, as such, the remainder of the document lists her earthly possessions and names her new husband, Ibn 'Abd Allah al-Rumi, "a worthy guardian" over her three sons, Muhyi, Hasan, and Ramadan, "in the event that she meets her fate [death]." The latter, it reads, is also responsible for meeting both her and her sons' financial needs during the marriage while concluding "it is in her best interests and in her aforementioned sons' best interests that this should happen *(ahsan ma yuf'al)*."[84] This is the last annulment presided over by a Hanafi judge in the documents at hand. From this time forward, all other records of annulment from the Bab al-'Ali reflect a very different procedure, one that was meant to be less accommodating and utilitarian in its attitude to annulment.

Thereafter, one could only obtain an annulment on the basis of abandonment from the Hanafi chief judge's court, the Bab al-'Ali. But the ruling could not be delivered by the Hanafi judge himself. Rather, the matter was delegated to the Hanbali chief judge. In the year 1596, a perfunctory formula delegating permission to the Hanbali deputy is provided and mimicked in four other documents of annulment. The shortest period of absence found in this collection is eight months and the longest is four years.[85] One, from the year 1645–46, grants a woman permission to declare herself divorced, after providing proof of harm *(darar)* stemming from her husband's yearlong absence.[86] In the same *sijill*, another *faskh* is granted after a two-year absence, on the basis of *darrura shar'iya* (*shar'i* necessity).[87]

An annulment document from the year 1055–56 (1645–46), based on the longest period of absence—four years—reads:

> 1. With the kind permission of his eminence the Shaykh al-Islam [extended] to our lord the Hanbali judge; established *(thabat)* before him [was] knowledge *(ma'rifat)* of the woman 'Asakir, the lady bint Muhammad al-Banna and knowledge of her husband Khatir ibn Sulayman and of his absence from Misr and its suburbs, a *shar'i* absence
> 2. which permits the hearing of a motion *(da'wa)* and a ruling in absentia *(al-hukm 'ala al-ghayib)* shar'an, a period of four years.[88]

During these four years, it continues, 'Asakir had been without maintenance *(nafaqa)* or a *shar'i* provider, as her husband left nothing and sent nothing from which she could spend on herself "and there is naught which obligates her to remain under his protection *('ala dhimmatih)*, and he has no special status *(martab khass)* for his continued absence to date." After the perfunctory testimony of several witnesses who corroborated this state of affairs, 'Asakir took a *shar'i* oath "upon God almighty" that her claim was true and requested the aforementioned judge "to enact *(yaf'al)* the *shar'* and enable her to annul *(faskh)* her marital contract *(nikah)* from her husband's *'isma*, for her harm." Thereafter, the judge enabled her to utter *(tasrih lafziha)* the phrase "I have annuled my marriage from my indicated husband."[89]

It is unknown why Abu al-Su'ud referred to the practice as Shafi'i when only Hanbali judges granted such annulments in the Cairo *sijill*. Nonetheless, it is interesting that a *qanun* consciously prohibited the practice only in the "lands of Rumelia and Anatolia." The fact that courts in Cairo continued to grant annulments is not evidence of the triumph of Egyptian custom, however, but of the principle of judicial *ikhtilaf*. Nonetheless, the procedural steps followed in such cases demonstrate the degree of control exercised by the courts of the chief Ottoman judge over variant practices. No motion for *faskh* could be filed outside of the Bab al-'Ali, indicating that the state judiciary continued to oversee, if not actually grant, annulments, thereby ensuring that the practice met the strictest and most restrictive criteria.

It should be noted that custom plays no role in the Hanbali judge's decision, formulated on the basis of 'lifting the harm' or 'necessity.' The fact that the period of absence ranges from eight months to four years suggests that the length of time lapsing between a husband's absence and a wife's motion for divorce rested on the wife's individual choice. The community's idea of an 'appropriate' length of time was a moot consideration once the case reached the court. The *sijill* neither mentions the *ta'ifa* (community) to which these women belonged, nor hints at what their community's sense of propriety dictated. Maryam bint 'Abd Allah, it will be remembered, was the wife of a prisoner of war. One would imagine a degree of public censure befalling women who failed to remain loyal to such men. But the courts entertained no sentimentality for the circumstances which brought about the husband's absence. The only issue of concern appeared to be the degree of harm, largely economic, suffered by the woman, and her children, as a result of her husband's absence. Judicial tools such as 'lifting the harm' or 'necessity' (based on considerations of *maslaha* and *istihsan*) could, therefore, be used to overcome social pressures rooted in custom. The very fact that the practice was banned in Anatolia is proof enough that such attitudes existed.

In summary, all aspects of marriage and divorce were strictly managed and diligently streamlined by the courts. But, as demonstrated by the example of *faskh*, the courts were often more successful at streamlining custom than redacting *fiqh*. Undoubtedly, however, the restrictions imposed on the practice had an inhibiting effect on women seeking annulments.

Indeed, it is only where legal theory makes explicit caveats for it, as in the determination of the amount of the bride price, that custom is allowed to exert an influence on the social and religious institution of marriage. The same can be said of the administration of religious endowments *(awqaf)*, another critical religious institution.

Waqf

One of the many justifications given for the Ottoman conquest was the alleged abuse of the sacred tenets governing *waqf* under the Mamluks. Al-Damiri wrote that Sultan Salim invaded the Mamluk state in order to correct the abuses resulting from the exchange of *waqf*. Even if based in some vague historical truth, the account relayed by al-Damiri lacks credibility. Before the Ottomans, he writes, the violation of *waqf* through 'exchange' *(istibdal)* had reached dangerous levels under the Egyptian Mamluks. As a concerned Muslim, Sultan Salim sent a delegation of ministers to Cairo to investigate the veracity of these reports. When they met with the Shaykh al-Islam of Cairo, the Ottoman ministers asked him if it was permissible for them to 'lease' the most sacred *waqf* in Egypt—the mosque of al-Azhar—telling him that it "impressed us more than anything in the rest of Egypt and [that it] is airy and close to other residences." They were astonished to hear him say: "This is a simple matter," as, he explained, the *waqf* had yet to be legally registered *(yuthbat)* and was considered the property of the state treasury *(bayt al-mal)*.[90] When the ministers relayed this conversation back to Salim, his outrage was such that he resolved to conquer Ghuri's state, then and there.

The above narrative paints the Mamluk state as a degenerate polity where nothing, not even the revered *waqf* of the mosque of al-Azhar, was beyond the state's rapacious grasp. Even worse, the corruption is so widespread it extends beyond the state to include the country's ulama, for even Egypt's top Islamic scholar, the Shaykh al-Islam, is complicit. But Ibn Iyas describes the Ottomans as the rapacious ones, charging them with meddling in the *awqaf* and bringing impoverishment to its beneficiaries: men, women, and even orphans and widows.[91] One point on which both al-Damiri and Ibn Iyas agree, however, is that the Ottomans brought all large *awqaf* under the jurisdictional and administrative authority of the Ottoman chief judge. Only he could make appointments to *awqaf*, introduce changes, or sanction existing practices.[92]

The chroniclers provide detailed accounts of some of the conflicts that erupted between state jurists and local jurists over the administration of *awqaf*. In one prominent dispute, the Ottoman chief judge Nur al-Din al-Tarabulsi was challenged by the Maliki chief judge Muhyi al-Din Yehya ibn al-Damiri, when he overturned a judgment made by 'Abd al-Bir ibn al-Shuhna (Maliki chief judge under al-Ghuri) concerning the *waqf* of Amir Yashbek ibn Mahdi al-Diwidar. The latter had stipulated that control of his *waqf* should go to Amir Taghribirdi, but when the latter died, Yashbek's daughter received a judgment from judge Shuhna overturning the previous judgment and surrendering control of the *waqf* to her. When she died, some of Yashbek's men petitioned to have the *waqf* ruling, which effectively placed it in the hands of her descendants, overturned yet again and 'restored' to Yashbek's militia. Tarabulsi granted their wish, leading Judge Shuhna's relatives as well as other notable judges to denounce his ruling openly. The former recanted his ruling almost immediately, leading Ibn Iyas to deride him for his lack of judgment.[93]

Again the *sijill*s shed more light on such disputes, revealing the core issues at stake, while confirming the general thesis of this work. At its heart, the conflict over *waqf* hinges on the control of vast sums of money. Sultanic decrees or *qanun*s, which sought to eradicate many local practices, did so for the purposes of maximizing taxation. Any exceptions to the strict regulation of religious endowments were garnered at the highest level of state and entered into the *sijill*. This is demonstrated in document 33 from the year 1645, which begins by proclaiming that an "honorable sultanic order was issued," publicly proclaimed, and "complemented by the honorable scholars." The contents, "which are directed by the hand of the eminent Sultan . . . champion of the sharia of the lord of the messengers, the greatest of the sultans of 'Uthman," it instructs, "should be enacted," such that none "violate" its tenets. Read in the presence of eminent jurists and state officials, including the chief Ottoman judge and Ibrahim Agha-dar al-Sa'ada, the "honorable sultanic decree" outlined that what prevails (*jari*) in the *waqf* of the deceased Mustafa Agha Qullar Aghasi in Bulaq, the "custom of selling comestible products from the northern and southern *wakayil* [caravanserai or market]," is licit. None of the products, it stresses, should be sold outside of the mentioned *wakayil*, and no one should confront them on this from the *hisba* or the *shubashi*'s office nor from among *hukam al-siyasa*, in conformity with the "honourable sultanic decree pertaining to such and the guidelines of the honourable *qanun* prohibiting confrontation or interference in such."[94]

The current practice, it continues, of selling such products outside of the indicated *wakayil* in Bulaq and its outskirts was strictly prohibited. Such transgressions had been verified and summarily condemned by the decree, "which demanded acceptance, obedience and enactment, without deviation." It continues, "nothing of the varieties [of products] mentioned, not even some of them, are to be sold except through the indicated *wakayil*." The decree, directed to state and judicial officials, "obliges compliance and is conveyed by means of the indicated honourable, respected *buyuruldi*; that the indicated products are to be sold through the indicated *wakayil* and that no challenger should challenge, and no intruder should intrude upon the indicated honourable decree, dated twenty-eighth Sha'ban of [that] year, and the indicated *buyuruldi* dated the twentieth of the month . . . its contents are to be followed without exceeding its linguistic meaning or deviation from its text." A final sentence justifies the decree on the basis that it provides "benefit, and no harm to the *waqf*."[95]

The above document is perhaps an exemplar of the kind of evidence scholars employ to argue for the 'triumph' of custom and the declining authority of the Ottoman judge. However, rather than suggesting a declining Ottoman authority, the document highlights the 'exceptional' nature of the customary practice (*'amal*) tolerated in this particular case. We can only speculate why the exemption may have been granted, but we can confirm the lengths to which the decree warns officials from both the *hisba* and *shubashi*'s offices to refrain from interfering with the practice. In other words, the institutions of state appear to be disseminating the new legal hegemony rather efficiently—so efficiently, in fact, that the decree finds it necessary to repeatedly assert its consent to the practice and to warn state officials to desist from further intervention.

That said, there were other ways in which *waqf* practices could be used to promote custom, in a manner the Ottomans were unable or unwilling to control. In the case of Maliki *waqf*, A. Layish has shown how 'familial' *waqf* was used to circumvent the 'laws of succession' in Maliki *waqfiyat*.[96] Because Islamic legal theory allowed the revenue from any holdings to be bequeathed as the founder saw fit, there was little the state could do to prevent the former from circumventing the rules of sharia inheritance to bestow all, some, or none of the benefits on one or more individuals. In theory and in practice, therefore, the benefactor could disinherit his daughters, or at the other extreme, use it to exceed the portion allotted to women under the sharia.

A case from the Bab al-'Ali in the year 1055–56 (1645–46) documents the process by which the founder of an endowment disinherits all his female descendants. Before the Hanafi judge, Fatma bint Hasan 'Ala' al-Din alleged that the legal overseer for her familial *waqf*, her paternal uncle Mustafa ibn 'Ala' al-Din ibn Qasim, had dispossessed her of a *shar'i* share of her deceased father's portion of the *waqf* proceeds, over a period of four years. The defendant responded to the charge by explaining that the original founder of the *waqf* had stipulated that the proceeds should go to "his indicated children, excepting the female children of the womb and that the plaintiff was not included [among the beneficiaries] of the mentioned *waqf* on account of her female gender, and he produced in hand a copy of the *waqf* contract, written in the Salihiya and dated 13 Jamad al-'Awwal, 934/1527." The original document had been subsequently ratified in the court of the Bab al-'Ali by the Hanbali judge on 27 Rabi' al-Thani 1027 (1618). The original document, read aloud by the plaintiff, asserted that the founder endowed the property for the benefit of "his children, children's children, specifically the males to the exclusion of females." Once the contents of the original document were verified, and "the truth of the motion *(sidqat al-da'wa)* was established," the plaintiff asked the judge "to implement the honorable *shar'* in her favor. And the judge responded [to her request] and prevented the plaintiff [Fatima] from challenging the defendant on this account, because she is not one of the sons of the aforementioned and because daughters are not included *(lam yadkhulun)* in the *'amal* of the conditions of the founder."[97] Obviously, the courts were unable to reverse the clauses governing the administration of this *waqf*, even if it circumvented the 'intentions of the law' *(maqasid al-shari'a)* by disinheriting women.

Diametrically opposed to the conditions stipulated in the above *waqf* are those stipulated in another *waqf*, that of Amir Mustafa Agha, son of the former head of *Ta'ifat qali qulli* (Mamluk faction) in Egypt. Recorded in the same year as the document above (AH 618), this document occupies a page and a half in the *sijill*, recording every detail of the *waqf*'s founding, including references to numerous associated documents from 1053, the year of its founding. It was ratified by both the Hanafi chief judge and a Maliki judge, indicating that the founder belonged to the Maliki school. The conditions of the founder were that the proceeds from the *waqf* be distributed among his daughter and two wives. Future generations of male and female descendants, however, were to receive their *shar'i* share, such that "one male would receive the shares of two females."[98]

It is unclear whether Mustafa Agha had any male progeny at the time of his death. But judging by the stipulation that later generations of descendants would receive a portion of the *waqf* revenues based on the *shar'i* division of inheritance, one can assume he did not. Nonetheless, unlike the last founder, Mustafa Agha bequeathed his female descendants a share of the benefits which corresponded to their share under the Islamic laws of inheritance. The differences between the two highlight the variation that existed in practice stemming from variation in customs, but more importantly, in individual preferences.

The principle that the founder of a *waqf* has full individual autonomy in the dispensation of its proceeds is rooted in Islamic legal theory, rather than *qanun*. A comparable level of autonomy is not, however, extended to the local judiciary, which now shared its jurisdiction over *awqaf* with the Ottoman chief judge. Not one case pertaining to *waqf* could bypass his court, where he often presided alongside one or more judges from the other schools of law.[99] And while the Ottomans were unable to eliminate customs explicitly protected by legal theory, they did minimize them in marriage, divorce, public morality, and endowments.

Conclusion

As the Ottoman state attempted to regulate what were arguably the most regulated of Muslim institutions—*waqf*, marriage, and divorce—it did so with the understanding, at least for the better part of the sixteenth century, that this was a right delegated to its rulers as institutors of a perfected moral order—the *siyasat-i ilahi*. The 'rights of God' could never be changed in and of themselves, but they could be refined where informed by custom. The lowering of the evidentiary proof required for the fixed penalties, and the judicial movement to push more and more items under the discretionary authority of *ta'zir*, meant that the state was now in a position to refine the link between the rights of God and custom. Attitudes to women and public space were a good example of these new prerogatives.

Where jurisprudence generally allowed local custom to determine the threshold of modesty (such as whether to cover the face, whether to practice seclusion, and so on), it now intersected with a codified morality banishing women from public space, or conversely, guaranteeing their access to it. In both cases, custom, and the variation it fostered, were overridden. But this would not have been possible were it not for the fact that individuals found it increasingly necessary to document their legal transactions in the court, and increasingly expedient for them to assert their autonomy from the control of community and kin. The expanding autonomy of the individual, or proto-citizen, was thus a necessary catalyst to the diminished authority of the community.

As much as the Ottoman state pursued unification through the 'perfection' of moral conduct, perfection was imperfectly defined. That is, the

Conclusion

Ottoman understanding of sharia was neither static nor immutable, and continuously shifted to reflect new moral ideals. The state which oversaw the public humiliation, and sometimes torture, of 'unchaste' women in the early sixteenth century was not the same state which officiated over Hijaziya's case in the mid-seventeenth century. At the very least, it was a state with a new moral compass.

Neither the zeal, one might even say extreme conservatism, of the Ottoman chief judges in the first quarter of the sixteenth century, nor the relative liberalism they display later in the century, left much room for custom. As argued, the state and its courts remained committed to one 'ideal' law, no matter how the 'ideal' was (re)defined. This was demonstrated in the case of *waqf*, where little room for deviation, except that secured by sultanic writ, was countenanced even in the mid-seventeenth century. The only areas in which custom features prominently, albeit stealthily, are in the conditional stipulations naming the benefactors of a *waqf*, entirely the prerogative of the founder. This was one of the few areas in which the standards of a community, family, or individual consistently influenced the function of this important Islamic institution.

The argument that custom was a diminishing source of influence should not imply that the Ottoman state was opposed to custom altogether or even predisposed to a particular category of customs; rather, it favored a universal law that strove for legal standardization or, in Ottoman religious rhetoric, the 'moral perfection' of society. Custom could never be excised, given that *fiqh* had allotted it an important role, but the 'best' of customs could be universalized to establish a singular standard of 'correct conduct.' If a custom from any region conformed to the perfected ideal, it was embraced and universalized, not just as the 'best' of customs, but as the best law on which to base a single, valid jurisprudential view. Similarly, we saw an early version of judicial 'patchworking' at play in the streamlining of marriage and divorce rights.

We may now examine these issues from the perspective of the rights of humans, or *mu'amalat*, no less redacted or innovatively interpreted by the Ottoman courts.

Chapter Seven
The Rights of Humans
(Huquq al-Adamiyyin)

Introduction

If the Ottoman *namus* promoted a unified standard of Muslim moral conduct in the area of *'ibadat*, it was even more instrumental in the unification of *mu'amalat*. The relationship of *mu'amalat* to custom is well established. As the main body of laws pertaining to the 'rights of humans,' the *mu'amalat* stand in contrast to the *'ibadat*, or ritual associated with the 'rights of God' in Islamic law.[1] *Mu'amalat*, in M. Bernard's words, "preside over the relations of men among themselves"[2] by defining "juridico-human relations" to ensure that Muslim transactions conform to "juridico-moral theories."[3] In its original meaning, "*mu'amala* reflected the community's way of life at the beginning of Islam."[4] With the development of Islamic civilization, the concept evolved, became diversified, and was woven into various disciplines (notably *kalam*, *fiqh*, and *'amal*) and applied in a range of models. As a concept, however, it would never lose its original connection with the community's way of life.[5] *Mu'amalat* retain, therefore, an even more direct link to customary law than *'ibadat*. *Fiqh* forms part of the *'adat*—that is, the expression of the concept of *adab* into concrete form—by integrating *mu'amalat* into a rigorously structured body of ethics.[6]

Under the Ottomans, an extensive and popular network of courts fostered an environment in which *mu'amalat* were ever more closely scrutinized and ever further assimilated to this body of ethics. In turn, the records of the sharia court reflect the core principle at the center of these ethics—the unification of the legal process and, to a large extent, the law produced. A detailed examination of the documents will demonstrate that while references to custom are not rare, they are both qualified and limited. Thus, without implying that custom plays a minimal role in the courts, the examples culled highlight the insufficiency of the argument that custom is a prolific source of legislation in all categories of law. The sections of this chapter entitled "The Empire in the City" and "Private Mu'amala" will show that the courts clearly regarded some customs as benign, while treating others as subversive, that is, in opposition to *fiqh* or *qanun*. It is also significant that the language of the documents is highly differentiated and precisely delineated when referring to custom. Thus, the records speak in terms of the custom of a given *ta'ifa*, a particular region, locale, or even *hayy (al-jari fi al-mulk)*. It speaks of "old customs" (*'urf* or *'ada qadima*), "prevalent custom" *(al-'ada al-jariya)*, and new customs *(tajdid)*. It also speaks of fiscal practice *(mu'amala maliya)* as historic fiscal practice *(mu'amala tarikhiya)* or as fiscal practice in the Egyptian lands *(mu'amala bil diyar al-Misriya)*. Yet the language of the *sijill*s can often be misleading, as the various terms used to denote custom often indicate nonlocal practices. As shown below, when the registers use the term "old customs," they are often referring to 'old' Ottoman rather than to pre-Ottoman practices. Hence, a careful reading of the text casts doubt on the assumption that all references to custom are expressive of 'grassroots' legislative trends.

Beyond the conceptual brackets generated by variegated lexical tropes, two more conceptual bifurcations are generated by this research, between public and private *mu'amalat*. More often, custom is encountered in the latter area, the subject of "Private Mu'amala," and is invariably defined by the courts in relation to a specific community or guild in matters of taxation and metrology. In the private domain, custom is defined in relation to the individual's community, and is generally encountered in customary arbitration *(sulh)* or marriage.

Technically speaking, marriage falls under the rubric of *'ibadat*, but it also has an element that is pure *mu'amalat*, wherein the conventions regulating the relationship between two individuals, between the individual and the community, or between two communities, are outlined. An examination of these documents sheds light on the sharia court's view of the individual's linkages to, and autonomy from, the 'normative' practices of a given community. What they reveal is a consistent pattern of arbitration that seeks to relax the bonds between the individual and the community in favor of enhancing the ties between the individual and the state. *Sulh* documents, containing the terms by which a private dispute is settled, will also help us to scrutinize the means by which customs arising in private *muʿamalat* are co-opted within a defined moral-juridical paradigm and assimilated to sharia.

There are similarities, as well as differences, in the courts' view of the customs arising from public and private *muʿamalat*. While the latter regulate relations between individuals or communities, the former regulate those between the community, the individual, and state. The definition of a benign or a subversive custom is, however, generally the same in both cases. Public law, the subject of the section "Public *Muʿamalat*: The Community in the Empire," demonstrates a more pointed attempt to streamline or redact custom by assimilating community practice to *qanun*. Thus, while one encounters a good deal of tolerance for custom in the field of municipal law (where a community's normative values are allowed to define that which constitutes one person's breach of another's privacy), the majority of documents dealing with fiscal practices, particularly metrological systems, convey hostility to it. This is not to imply that such policies were absolute or that they brooked no exceptions, for the *sijill* indicates otherwise; rather, it is to argue that, in most cases, the exception proves the rule. Together, the combined evidence of the *sijill*s and historical chronicles supports the conclusion that exemptions from this general policy were granted on a conditional basis, and subject to periodic review.

Ultimately, in the system under scrutiny, communal autonomy, individual autonomy, and state dominance were delicately balanced. The often ambiguous position of custom in this model is never incoherent, however. When expedient or irrelevant from the court's perspective, custom is regarded as benign *(ʿada murdiya)* and treated with lenience by the courts. The courts appear willing, for example, to legitimate or annul benign customs at the individual's request, effectively granting the latter a wide measure of legal autonomy in accepting or rejecting certain practices associated with his/her community. They display far less willingness, however, to oblige local custom in *muʿamalat* when it threatened to undermine the territorializing agenda of the law. In such cases, the custom in question is expunged, as far as possible, from legal practice. In the final analysis, this level of engagement between the jurist and local practice is possible only when supported by two prerequisites: the need for legal documentation and an accessible court. Without the latter, it would not have been possible for jurists to penetrate private spaces and modify their boundaries. In other words, the number of citations that custom is given in the court records is indicative of the degree to which it had already been assimilated into the dominant juridical paradigm. If this claim is shown to be valid, the conclusion that community bonds were undermined by the growing bond between the individual and state is unavoidable.

As the community stands as the base of all customs, an understanding of the integrity and self-sufficiency of these social units is essential to any work which presumes to assess the role of custom in the sharia courts of Ottoman Cairo. "The Empire in the City" provides such an introduction, as well as a review of the major scholarly contributions to the study of Islamic law, urbanism, and society by broaching the debate on whether communities in this urban landscape were autonomous from, or bound to, the state and its courts.

The Empire in the City: Multiplicity and Conformity

Any study of law and society is indebted to the scholarship on the history of the Islamic city. The earliest scholars, W. Marçais,[7] his younger brother G. Marçais, J. Weulersse, and R. Tourneau, all of whom attempted to define the general characteristics of the Islamic city, have since been critiqued for viewing the Arab urban center as a parasitic entity, artificially grafted onto the countryside, a mere "gathering of individuals with conflicting interests who, each in his own sphere, acts on his own account."[8] S. Humphreys writes that they paid little heed to "Islam per se as a determining factor in urban life."[9] When Islam was considered, as by G. von Grunebaum, its relationship to urbanism was framed within an ideal but static urban typology, formulated on the basis of the 'classical city.'[10]

Further research by H. Gibb and H. Bowen, I. Lapidus, C. Cahen, and C. Geertz paved the way for more insight into the institutional and economic life of the Islamic city.[11] Cahen argued that, until the eleventh century, the Islamic city essentially retained the same features as the cities of late antiquity, while Lapidus employed a sociological approach emphasizing the study of the social groups that made up the urban populace.[12] However, O. Barkan's first studies on the tax system and demography of Anatolian towns, based on extensive Ottoman archival documents at the end of the

1930s, dispelled some of the more flagrant misconceptions of the Islamic city, as did J. Abu-Lughod's "devastating exposé" of Orientalist analysis.[13]

None of the above would have been possible, however, without the ample documentation contained within the Ottoman archives, documentation which "called into question the conception of generalized Ottoman decadence."[14] The qadi's registers (*sijill*) made clear the role of the judge in the urban administration of the city and underscored the sophisticated institutional structure needed to maintain the elaborate legal network over which he presided. Among the first to address the relationship between law and the Islamic city, R. Brunschvig demonstrated that later Maliki jurists addressed urban issues quite explicitly.[15] Giving new impetus to the study of urbanism and Islamic law, B. Johansen and others were encouraged to explore what had, until then, been considered the "silence of Islamic law on Islamic urbanism" to argue that the administration of the city was based on clear Islamic intellectual doctrines.[16] H. Gerber, R. Jennings, and U. Heyd must be credited for devoting considerable energies to identifying and quantifying these doctrines in practice through their examinations of the *sijill* and *qanunnama*s.[17] In the case of Cairo, the collective research of A. Raymond, M. Winter, S. Shaw, N. Hanna, and G. Nahal must be given special mention for their exploration of the institutional, economic, and cultural features of Cairo in the Ottoman period.[18]

While he does not address the issue of urbanism and law directly, Raymond was among the first to delineate the urban geography of Cairo and to construct a framework for the study of its communities. Ottoman administration, he concluded, was delegated on the local level, as the state came to an arrangement that allowed local structures to function autonomously, saving them the trouble of direct administration.[19] It is an indicator of the relative autonomy and self-sufficiency of the communities in their internal governance, he argues, that each community was placed under the authority of its own chiefs/shaykhs. The Jewish community of Cairo, for example, had its own closed quarter and its own judge, called a Momaraia, while seven Coptic quarters existed in and around the suburbs of Cairo.[20] Beyond religious communities, various ethnic, linguistic, and professional communities also congregated in fixed neighborhoods.[21]

Raymond argues that the self-sufficiency of ethnic groups was an important element in their strength, as "their influence depended on their national and geographic cohesion."[22] Winter confirms this cohesion, writing that even "the *riwaq*s [student apartments] were divided ethnically or regionally. Thus, there were the *riwaq*s of the Turks *(Arwam)*, Syrians, Maghribis, Upper Egyptians, natives of the Sharqiya province and so on."[23] Even the Sufi orders, he continues, "as a general rule . . . were not ethnically mixed," as there is evidence that points to separate orders for Turks and Arabs.[24] The *waqf* document for the *zawiya* (Sufi convent) of Hasan ibn Ilyas al-Rumi al-Istanbuli, for example, established in 1526 by Sulayman Pasha, governor of Egypt, stipulated that it was exclusively reserved for non-Arab residents and that "all functionaries from the shaykh down to the manual workers, had to be non-Arab."[25] The *takiya* (convent) established for the Sufi Ibrahim Gulsheni did not have a similar stipulation and yet, Winter concludes, all indications were that most residents, if not all, were Turks.[26]

Because of the physical cohesion of the communities, a degree of cultural cohesion and ethnic consciousness could be fostered.[27] Clashes, both cultural and physical, were not uncommon, and illustrate the complexity and delicacy of maintaining social harmony in a cosmopolitan city. Examples of 'culture clash' between resident Egyptians and the newly arrived 'Turks' abound. Ibn Iyas devotes a full page to an Ottoman custom that shocked and revolted the residents of Cairo. In the year of the conquest, Khayrbek called on "anyone who sees a dog to kill it and hang it above their shops," as per the customs of the new rulers.[28] The strong revulsion which this culling engendered led people to implore the *muhtasib* (market inspector), Zayni Barakat ibn Musa, to ask the governor to halt the practice. This "strange" custom, explains Ibn Iyas, originated in Istanbul, where stray dogs were culled during the *khamasin* (spring windy season) in efforts to avert plague and disease. Such episodes provided fodder for the ethnic denigration of the Ottoman Turk by Ibn Iyas, the Mamluk Turk:

> Ponder what has happened to Egypt,
> an event draped in torture.
> When the Turk cared not for spilled [human] blood,
> would they spare the blood of dogs?[29]

Another custom which provoked Khayrbek himself to intervene was the looting of Zuwayla alley, a Jewish neighborhood, by the Inshikariya troops. As it happened, this was the first sign of Sultan Salim's death, for the custom among Ottoman militias held that the looting of Jewish alleys commenced when a sultan died. A crisis was averted only when Khayrbek offered the soldiers monetary compensation in lieu of the raid.

Cultural and ethnic tensions could also end in violent conflict, as in the reign of Uways Pasha (1581–90), when a Sipahi *fitna* assumed racial and sectarian overtones. The Sipahi troops, rioting to obtain higher wages, attacked the governor's *diwan* and harassed the local populace, forcing the Arabic-speaking populace, *awlad al-'Arab*, to relinquish their white Mamluk slaves, and Jews to relinquish their concubines. Offenders, they warned, would face execution within three days.[30] The Sipahis were violently suppressed but little else is known of the social context in which the events unfolded. Nonetheless, the fact that the revolt quickly assumed 'ethnic' overtones suggests the existence of such tensions beneath the surface.

In another example of cultural tension, the anonymous Egyptian author of the Gotha manuscript, describing the guilds of Egypt in the late sixteenth century, "accuses the Ottomans of having caused the decline of the guilds and discriminating against the Arabs," conveying "the anti-Ottoman attitude prevalent among Egyptian artisans."[31] The 'Ottomans' are not, of course, a singular ethnicity, but civil and military personnel drawn from the Caucasus, the Balkans, Circassia, and Anatolia, among other regions. Their formation into an Ottoman ruling caste provoked tensions with the local populace, itself a heterogenous group. One hesitates, therefore, to call this an ethnic conflict, since it is plainly a multiethnic conglomeration of peoples on both sides of the spectrum. Nonetheless, it speaks to the cultural gulf (linguistic, ethnic, and social) between the ruling caste and the ruled *(ra'aya)*. To mediate this gulf, the state needed to remain above the ethnic fracas, and to project an image of impartiality that transcended ethnic differences through the law. One means of accomplishing this was to weaken communal bonds.

Raymond, however, argues that apart from the obvious physical and cultural cohesion of Cairo's ethnic groups into distinct communities, there was a high degree of control exercised within communities over the conduct of their inhabitants. While he says little about the courts in this regard, he does imply that arbitration and censure formed the basis of an informal legal system rooted in community customs. For that reason, *hara*s (residential quarters) were narrow and usually gated for the purposes of security. Arbitration and censure flowed from the customary laws/norms of that particular group, he concludes, as illicit behavior was "noted and acted upon by neighbors."[32]

But P. Ghazaleh has cautioned against postulating terms such as 'autonomy' or 'state control' too freely, writing that "the guilds' internal organization," for example, "further demonstrates the guilds' complex relationship with the state and society on the one hand, and the scope of their independence concerning decision-making, on the other."[33] When examining the relationship between the communities and the courts, one should heed such caution.

To assume that the communities were by and large autonomous is problematic, particularly with respect to legal matters. First, we must distinguish between *dhimmi* communities and Muslim ethnic or professional communities. The former enjoyed a degree of legal autonomy that their Muslim counterparts did not. Gated *hara*s aside, Muslim communities did not have the prerogative of establishing independent communal courts serving the interests of a particular ethnic or vocational group. Thus, while there is a measure of truth to Raymond's assertion that neighbors acted upon 'illicit conduct' within their communities, as chapter five shows, this did not preclude individuals from challenging such intervention in the sharia court.[34] In applying these insights on the nature of the Islamic city to this chapter's central discussion on *mu'amala*, we must be cognizant, therefore, of the court's role in consciously modifying community behavior in line with a dominant, juridico-moral, state paradigm.

Private *Mu'amala*: The Empire in the City
Marriage and the Moral Boundaries of Community

Among the first observations that can be made about the cultural cohesion of which Raymond spoke is that it was notable, though far from absolute, at the level of marriage. More often, people tended to marry within their ethnic or professional communities, but as a general rule, it was class, as opposed to ethnicity, which was the more insurmountable barrier. Out of thirty-eight marriage (*zawaj/nikah*) and engagement contracts (*khutuba*), twenty-six united people from the same professional or ethnic community. Another six, between *'askeris* (military men) and women of the *ra'aya* (civilian population), usually the daughters of local merchants or scholars, cut across these barriers.[35]

Assuming that many of these marriages united people of different regional backgrounds, it must be concluded that class and ethnicity, or a convergence of both, shaped these patterns. Class stratification is evident even within the *'askeri* class. For example, seven marriage contracts between *'askeri* men and the freeborn daughters of other *'askeri*s indicate high dowries. We may infer, therefore, that class played a decisive role in determining whether one married a free woman or a former slave, the assumption being that *'askeri*s of higher social class would have preferred to marry freeborn *'askeri* women. Throwing into relief the convergence of class and ethnic solidarity, the latter documents substantiate the argument that profession, in this case the military caste, and one's status within that profession, generally determined the social pool from which one drew a spouse.

The same class stratification is evident in non-*'askeri* marriages. For example, seven documents register marriages between members of subaltern groups, such as that of the local butcher to the coppersmith's daughter,[36] or the carpenter to the coffee-shop proprietor's *(qahwaji)* daughter.[37] Three document the marriages of local elites.[38]

In the final analysis, the rate at which people married within their communities indicates a high level of ethnic or linguistic solidarity, but the number of marriages across community lines suggests that this solidarity was far from absolute. One's class appears as a surer obstacle to marriage than one's ethnic or linguistic identity. Nonetheless, cultural barriers could be difficult to overcome, as evinced by the textual language of marriage contracts ratified for mixed couples. For example, the three documents in which women from Cairo marry non-Cairenes include conditional clauses which either negate the customs of the husband's community, or promote those of her own. Two stipulate that if the husband should move his wife from "Cairo and its surrounds," she is pronounced divorced through "one *talqa*."[39] Such conditions allowed women to ensure that they would not be estranged from their families and absorbed into their husband's community. Much like the conditional clause preventing husbands from exercising the right to take other wives, this condition preempted husbands from exercising absolute authority over the location of the marital domicile. Such clauses did not merely neutralize the husband's *fiqh*-based prerogatives, but also neutralized the authority of his community.

One particular contract, documenting the marriage of a Faiyumi man to the daughter of a Persian merchant, is replete with several conditional clauses negating the authority of the husband, and his community, in a number of spheres. Document no. 191 registers what is obviously an elite marriage.[40] The large dowry of 100 dinars, seventy given up front and thirty deferred until such time as "the husband's death or divorce," as well as the bride's substantial *kiswa* (clothing allowance), indicate as much. The first of several conditions stipulates that the wife will be divorced through one *talqa* when and if the husband takes a second wife, "through his own or through another's agency *(wikala)* by any means or route," or "purchases a concubine" *(ishtara 'alayha)*. The contract also prohibits the husband from moving his bride from Cairo, precluding him from contemplating a permanent return to Faiyum. It should be noted that Faiyum, an oasis barely forty miles to the south of Cairo, cannot be considered distant even by the standards of the day.

The fourth and most interesting clause, however, prohibits the husband from imposing the customs of his community on his bride. "If," the contract reads, "he should mark/create incisions *(haz)* upon her body *(jasadiha)* as ordained by the command *(bi-amr)* of his community," she retains the right to divorce him. It is unclear what is meant by *haz* in this context—incisions, tattoos, or other forms of decorative body art—but the prohibition is unambiguous, demonstrating the manner in which *fiqh*-based devices enabled the courts (and the individual) to decide, based on considerations of class, ethnicity, or even personal preference, whether to retain or annul a given custom. It also demonstrates how those same *fiqh*-based devices could be employed to expunge other *fiqh*-based rights—for example, a husband's right to move his wife from Cairo without her consent, or to impose the authority of his community upon her.

Apart from the conditions encountered in the marital contracts of 'mixed couples,' one also finds spouses fighting to preempt the given customs of their own communities. In one *mahdar*, Ahmad ibn Abi al-Husn ibn Muhammad, known as al-Adami al-Mu'azin, alleged that his wife Nur, the woman ibn Sulayman ibn Ahmad, whose father is known as al-Humusani, was refusing to move with him to an "abode of [domestic] obedience" *(ta'a)* in a "*shar'i* residence."[41] When questioned by the judge, Nur responded that she was prepared to move to a *shar'i* residence with her husband, on the condition that the marital home be located outside the *zuqaq* (alley with a single gateway) in which his family lived. Unwilling to abide the proximity of her in-laws, Nur defied her husband and willingly came to court to plead her case. As a *mahdar*, the document merely cites the complaint but does not include a judgment, making it impossible to speculate on the court's view of such complaints. Nonetheless, it does indicate the existence of a procedural system for dealing with them.

The cases above are illustrative of the legal means by which individuals could challenge customs originating in their own or their spouse's community. As far as the courts were concerned, a benign custom was mediated according to the wishes of the individual parties, who could accept or reject its judgment at their discretion. By definition, this individual prerogative weakened the absolute authority not only of the husband but, more importantly, of his community. Amicable settlements *(sulh)* are another area in which customary law and *fiqh* converge to support this claim.

Amicable Settlements *(Sulh)* and Judicial Intervention
Derived from the abstract noun from the verb *saluha* or *salah* (to be sound, righteous), *sulh* denotes the concept of reconciliation in Islamic law. The purpose of *sulh* is to end conflict through a contract of settlement, "consisting of offer *(ijab)* and acceptance *(qabul)*."[42] M. Khadduri views the process as a "form of contract *('aqd)*" which is regulated by Islamic law, "legally binding on both the individual and community levels."[43] Explaining how a divorce could be negotiated as part of an amicable settlement, however, A. Layish contradicts Khadduri's basic approach, positioning *sulh* outside the limits of the sharia by defining it as a form of customary arbitration, "that is, a settlement not involving legal proceedings."[44] Settlements such as these, he concludes, were "negotiated according to the rules of customary law," for at times it is "expressly stated that the settlement was reached out of court."[45] R.B. Serjeant shares Layish's understanding of *sulh* when assessing the latter's role in nineteenth-century Yemeni courts.[46]

If Khadduri is guilty of downplaying the importance and relevance of custom to *sulh* agreements, Serjeant and Layish can be accused of inflating it. Serjeant and Layish underestimate the assimilative powers of sharia over documents of customary arbitration, even if it took place out of court, for these, like other documents, were notarized by trained jurists and formulated in language that recorded and modified practice in line with Islamic legal theory. In other words, the preponderance of *sulh* contracts registered within the sharia court, and filed among its archival records, is not only an indication of the preponderance of customary arbitration, but a symbol of the considerable judicial authority exercised in the management of these agreements.

It is true that the terms of a *sulh* agreement could be decided out of court, either bilaterally or through the intervention of "a number of good

Muslims."⁴⁷ In the two documents below, for example, this was accomplished by the inclusion of an *iqrar* (acknowledgment). Another discrepancy between 'formal' arbitration and *sulh* arbitration is that documents for the latter do not disclose the terms of the agreement, whereas cases arbitrated in court spell them out clearly.

In the first *sulh* document I examine, a dispute between al-Sharif 'Awad ibn 'Ali ibn Husayn, a soldier from *jama'at al-qal'a al-'ulufiya* (the society of the citadel regiments), and al-Shaykh Shihab al-Din Ahmad ibn al-Shaykh Shihab al-Din Ahmad al-'Uthmani over inheritance and *waqf*, was finally mediated, after a prolonged period of "conflict and confrontation" *(niza' wa takhasum)*, by "a number of good Muslims."⁴⁸ Significantly, the document does not disclose the terms of the agreement, merely relaying that the conflict, over thirty *qurush* left over from the sale of a dagger and other items, was finally settled. By contrast, a similar case (monetary debt between two *'askeri*s, a Rumi from the Mutafarriqa corps and a Yankashari), which is arbitrated in court, discloses the full terms of the agreement while demonstrating the open place of custom as a source of arbitration.⁴⁹ The debtor, it reads, has agreed to make payments by surrendering his agency *(wikala)* over Jibayet al-Hawanit in the areas of Misr (Cairo), Bulaq, and old Cairo "as per the old custom."⁵⁰ Again, what is meant by "old custom" is opaque.

While the *sulh* document above fails to illuminate the details of the settlement, it does have an *iqrar*, interjected toward the end of the document, negating any and all potential future claims: "each has acknowledged *(aqar)*, a *shar'i* acknowledgment, that they have no rights/claims upon the other in relation to the indicated debt or for any other [such] cause." The document proceeds to list and negate the rights or claims—monetary, gold, silver, and otherwise—of each party. Significantly, the court-arbitrated settlement does not include an *iqrar*. A second *sulh* document confirms this procedure.

A settlement pertaining to homicide includes an *iqrar* obligating the two families involved to forego future claims once the obligatory blood money has been paid.⁵¹ Muhammad ibn Muslim al-Wahi al-Ballati charged Muhammad al-Hindawi with stabbing his brother Ahmad in the shoulder with an arrow "with the intention of causing his death *(qatlah)*."⁵² The injury was indeed fatal and the dying man's last words were, "None other than Muhammad al-Hindawi killed me." For his part, Hindawi admitted the slaying and agreed to compensate the surviving brother with half a million pieces of silver. The *iqrar* at the end of the contract cautions against any violation of this agreement, even warning the family of the deceased, and his descendants once they reach the age of maturity, against killing *(qatl)* Muhammad al-Hindawi. Blood feuds, a customary form of retribution, violated the tenets of Islamic law, and the *iqrar* in this document aimed to prohibit their continuation. Such cases demonstrate that endorsing customary arbitration did not mean that the courts were forsaking legal theory, but rather superimposing the guidelines of the latter upon the former.

In conclusion, whether mediating between a married couple or between two parties in conflict, the courts arbitrated, modified, and expunged custom in private *mu'amalat* in a manner which interjected *fiqh*-based guidelines into such cases and delimited community authority. By employing the conditional clause, for example, a bride could neutralize the authority of a custom arising in her husband's community. On the one hand, this demonstrated the court's willingness to loosen the woman's bonds to the spouse's community/clan, and on the other, to reinforce those between her and her own community. But it also underscores the fact that it was the link between the individual and the state *shar'i* court which made this negotiation possible. In effect, this meant that the bond between the individual and the state was nurtured and mediated at the discretion of the judiciary.

Judicial discretion was also reflected in *sulh* documents, where *iqrar*s were interjected into the textual body of a contract stemming from customary arbitration as a means of assimilating the latter to legal theory. In both cases, the laws which made it compulsory for couples to register their marriages in court, as well as the importance of documentation in cases of *sulh*, combine to suggest that, in the sphere of private *mu'amalat*, customary law was declining as a source of law independent of the sharia court. The rights of the individual were thus balanced against the customs of the community through a system of judicial intervention, a process duplicated in the area of public *mu'amalat*.

Public *Mu'amalat*: The Community in the Empire

Below we consider transactions in the areas of municipal law, taxation, metrology, and agriculture, evaluating their impact on Cairo's various communities, professional, ethnic, and residential. In all areas, a broadly defined 'custom' was upheld when, and if, it was expedient for the state, or when, and if, it served to alleviate a gross injustice arising from *qanun*. In all cases, however, references to 'old custom' should be treated with caution, as few were actually rooted in popular 'local' practice or, as often suggested in the secondary literature, representative of local capital classes and their interests.

"Old Custom" in a New State

In Ottoman Cairo, members of professional as well as ethnic communities had to negotiate a legal system in which the practices of old were 'nothing and everything.' This is demonstrated by the lexical tropes encountered in the *sijill* and the confusion they can breed. 'Old custom' (*'ada qadima*), a term frequently encountered in the records, often has a meaning quite different from that implied by the wording. The most striking examples of this are found in the areas of taxation and *iltizam* (tax-farming) documents.

I will first consider the 'old customs' which were linked to *iltizam* and used to justify the binding of the peasant (fellah) to the land. The term *multazim* denoted a tax farmer who, "from mid-16th century on," had his previously wide jurisdiction reduced to the collection of taxes and dues on behalf of the Ottoman state.[53] "Although [*multazims*] were not empowered to exact more than the amounts authorized by law from the inhabitants," writes F. Müge, "their contracts allowed them a sufficiently wide margin of profit and some exercise of authority over the peasantry."[54] Among the prerogatives of this 'authority' was a *multazim*'s right to bind the peasant to the land and, as shown below, to go so far as to pursue 'deserters' to Cairo, often decades after their alleged 'flight.' In H. Inalcik's view, this practice was upheld across the empire because the Ottoman empire suffered from a shortage of labor, "and it is probably for this reason that the peasant was bound to the soil."[55] While chronicling the practice in Anatolia, H. Inalcik does not explain how it was justified, a matter which is resolved by the *sijill*. As shown below, the practice was assimilated to *qanun* and justified on the basis that it represented "old custom." But the 'old customs' cited in such cases are not the kind normally associated with grassroots legislative trends. In the context of *iltizam* the term 'old custom' denotes old state laws employed to levy funds from that segment of the merchant classes which had recently migrated from the countryside, and to deny freedom of movement to those left behind. The 'old custom' in question was indeed ancient, probably originating in Roman imperial practice, but neither 'local' nor representative of the so-called authority of 'rising capital classes.' Indeed, the emphasis that this theory places on the growing legislative authority of the latter is brought into question by the cases below.

There are two cases which, for lack of a better term, I shall refer to as *iltizam* documents. In both, the *multazim* filed charges against persons accused of abandoning farming *(filaha)*. In the first case, a resident of Cairo, al-Shaykh Sha'ban ibn al-Shaykh Ghanim ibn al-Shaykh Najm al-Din, is identified as a merchant in the Hanafish[?] market.[56] The accused, it reads, appeared in the company of Amir Yusuf al-Jawish bil-Diwan, bearing a written document undersigned by the grand vizier. Certifying that he had resided in Cairo for fifteen years, the document was, asserted Najm al-Din, authoritative over both the *multazim* and the Amir 'Abidin of Munufiya, who "were bound by the [*wazir*'s] *nama*." Nonetheless, he complained, both had ignored the decree and persisted in demanding his relocation to the province of Munufiya to commence farming *(zira'a)*. Najm al-Din also brought forth a slew of witnesses, most of whom were merchants from his quarter, testifying that he was known to them and that he was an old resident of Cairo who had "nothing to do with farming." He also produced written fatwas, one from each of the four schools of law, stipulating that the *multazim* could not force him into farming nor fine him. We can explain the need for this extensive collection of documents and witnesses by the fact that Najm al-Din was not merely asking for a court ruling on the matter, but petitioning for a decree *(buyuruldi)* to block the *multazim* from confronting him at any point in the future. The judge, ruling in accordance with the grand vizier's orders and the opinions of the four *mufti*s, granted his request.

Notably, the defendant in the above case was a merchant of some standing who could procure a personalized document from the grand vizier while receiving the support of the Jawish al-Diwan, a representative of the latter, in court. In other words, Najm al-Din is a member of the very local capital classes said to be asserting their influence on the law produced in this period. The fact that the defendant had been absent from Munufiya for over fifteen years and that he was a prosperous merchant did little to protect him from the harassment of the province's governor or his *multazim*. Moreover, the fact that he successfully argued his case should not diminish the fact that he needed to obtain four fatwas, a written statement from the *wazir*, and the testimony of a host of witnesses to garner such immunity, even after a fifteen-year period of residency in Cairo.

It is possible that an individual's wealth may have encouraged, rather than deterred, *multazim*s, as another case, also involving a merchant from Cairo, suggests. The accuser in this case is not the *multazim*, but the shaykh of Minya, Muhammad ibn 'Ulwan, who apparently sent a soldier to apprehend Muhammad ibn al-Hajj Hinaydi. The shaykh complained that he had been mistreated and abused at the hands of Hinaydi, who had refused to abide by the "old custom in the payment of debts" *(al-'ada qadima bi-daf'i al-gharama)* for abandoning the land. For his part, Hinaydi's refusal to pay was based on the principle that he had resided in Cairo for twenty years and had never engaged in farming *(filaha)*.[57] Insisting that the accused had "*athar al-filaha*" (traces of farming) about him, the shaykh argued that the accused had been apprehended by an emissary of the *multazim*, who, by implication, recognized him. Supporting Hinaydi's claims, however, were a number of witnesses who testified that the latter had lived in Cairo for twenty years, that he had no "trace of *filaha* about him," and that they had never known him to engage in such an activity. The judge ruled in Hinaydi's favour, preventing the aforementioned from confronting or fining him.

Significantly, Shaykh 'Ulwan is not demanding that the accused be returned to farming, only that he pay a customary fine, suggesting that extortion played a part in the pursuit of peasants who became successful merchants. Thus, while the case above demonstrates that 'old customs' often allude to longstanding, pre-Ottoman state practices, the next case confirms that they could also allude to Ottoman, rather than pre-Ottoman, practices.

In 1619, an *amr* (decree) registered in the *sijill* of the Bab al-'Ali establishes the rights and obligations of the Gypsy community vis-à-vis state taxes, a ruling determined on the basis of "old prevailing custom."[58] A heading atop the text of the document reads: "A copy of the decree relevant to the community of Gypsies." After the introductory protocol, the document states that a sultanic order, delivered "into the hand of the esteemed, kind and glorious Governor . . . informs you that the community of Shashtajiya Gypsies has let us know that in the customs which prevailed of old *(al-'ada jarat fi al-qadim)*, the governor of the Hijaz collected a sum of 10 asnaf for each person." The Shashtajiya, it continues, had disclosed that the sum was eventually raised to twenty-five asnaf per person, payable once a year, and that the community had never challenged this custom. This changed when the "new governor of the Hijaz assailed them, coercing and forcing each person to pay forty nisf and dispensing receipts [for the money] with incorrect dates, causing great harm to befall them." The responding sultanic order reads, "Such as this we will not abide and we have issued a decree *(rasm)* ordering each party *(waqif)* to come forward according to the old and abiding custom *('ada al-qadima al-mustammira)*; and what was owed by virtue of custom *('ada)*, is what is owed by them to the aforementioned [*amir*], who is forbidden to oppose them, cause harm or take anything above that stipulated by '*ada* and *qanun* . . . such that none should complain to us."

Notably, the 'practices that prevailed of old,' cited above, are obviously Ottoman in origin, as they refer to that which prevailed under a previous Ottoman governor of the Hijaz. By 1619, therefore, the term 'old customs' referred, in matters of taxation, to the taxes established in accordance with *qanun* and the practice of former Ottoman, as opposed to Mamluk, governors. Whether speaking of cases of *iltizam* or taxation, therefore, we must be careful not to assume that 'old customs' are necessarily local in origin. The authority of the 'old customs' described above derive from Ottoman practice, whether issued by the office of the *multazim* or by sultanic order.

Thus far, we have considered the courts' approach to 'old custom' in relation to two communities, one rural, the other nomadic, but the custom in question in both cases is state-sponsored. In the cases dealing with professional, urban guilds, there is a marked terminological difference in the language used. Document 774 registers the appointment of a new shaykh, or guild head, to oversee *(mubasharat)* the sultanic slaughterhouse *(madhbah al-sultani)*.[59] Rather than 'old custom,' the appointment is said to have followed the protocol associated with 'known custom' *(al-'ada al-ma'rufa)*, allowing the outgoing head to appoint his successor. Unlike the 'old customs' described above, the 'known customs' described in this case refer to local, guild practices.[60] Another case, dealing with two disputants from a single guild, the camel traders, employs the phrase "what prevails in both their domains" *(al-jari fi mulkihima)* when referring to the practices of each man's community. The dispute, centering on the contested ownership of an animal, is eventually settled by reference to the practice of branding in each community. In the court's eyes, the identifiable markings on each animal determined ownership.[61]

'Old customs,' 'known customs,' and 'prevailing customs' are thus used discriminately to delineate various categories of custom, with the principle distinction centering on customs that are rooted in state practices and those that are rooted in local practices. Such examples also highlight the state's approach to 'old customs' deemed expedient, such as those assimilated to *iltizam*, and 'known/prevailing customs' deemed benign, such as those relating to certain guild practices. The neutrality of the courts to customs that contravened neither *fiqh* nor *qanun* was also apparent. A general acceptance for 'that which prevails' is made most freely, however, in the area of municipal law, although never to the exclusion of the courts' regulating influence.

Municipal Law and "What Prevails *(Jari)*" in the City

Supporting the works of Johanson and Brunschvig on Islamic law and urbanism, the documents of the Cairo *sijill* reveal the municipal sphere, with its broadly Islamic and delimited local influences, to be a heavily regulated industry. Nonetheless, while it is never referred to directly, custom does play a vital, if highly regulated, role in cases involving municipal law. But given the technical expertise required in the settlement of building disputes, the obvious need for documentation and, most importantly, judicial enforcement (often involving demolition), the courts' preeminent role in mediating such cases cannot be underestimated.

Document 785 from 1045 (1635) identifies two state officials entrusted with overseeing building policies: the *muhafiz al-mamalik al-Islamiya bil-diyar al-Misriya* (the grand vizier Ayyub Basha) and the *mi'mar bashi bi-Misr al-Mahrusa* (al-Amir Yusuf of the Mutafarriqa of the Diwan). It reveals that residents from two quarters, one predominantly Christian and the other predominantly Muslim, filed a joint complaint against the construction of a new passageway between their respective alleys.[62] The passage between al-Darb al-Wasi' and Darb al-Qabbani had exposed a Muslim women's bath located in the latter quarter. Thus, anyone entering or leaving al-Darb al-Wasi' had a clear view into the bath each time its doors were opened, exposing the women inside in various states of "nudity" (*'ariyat*). Apparently, the door to the bath did not directly open onto the bathing area, but onto the dressing hall containing the women's clothing. To ascertain the validity of the residents' complaint, the courts drew on the expert testimony of the 'expert engineers' (*ahl-khibra al-handasiya*), a local body fulfilling two functions. First they were to corroborate the complaint, and second, to provide the court with an alternate route for the passage between the quarters. In the first place, the local council of experts confirmed the veracity of the complaint and then provided a detailed plan for the construction of a new passageway, replete with surveys of the surrounding properties to be affected and the exact measurements of their distance from the suggested new passage. An agreement procured from the owners of said properties was presented, and the new passage approved. In affirmation of the "rights of the residents" *(huquq al-sukan)*, the old passage was ordered "sealed."

Custom plays an obvious role in this case. In the first place, it was the normative attitudes of the communities, rooted in the local values of Muslim and Christian residents, that motivated the complaint. Local standards of decorum defined what constituted a breach of privacy or decency. Also, the engineers called upon to ascertain the correctness of the placement of the door formulated their report on the precepts of local architectural practices. Less obvious, however, is their role as representatives of the Ottoman state. As Ottoman officials, the engineers presented their findings in the language of an Ottoman metrology, for example using the *dhira'* (cubit) outlined by Ottoman *hisba*, rather than a local measurement.[63]

In the second case, the point is made even more explicitly. A Christian man filed a complaint against his brother when the latter built a door on his side of their shared, inherited property. By his actions, the brother had exposed the women's quarters *(harim)* in the plaintiff's house.[64] Notably, the complaint is based on the claim that the construction contravened "what is practiced in the mentioned quarter *(al-jari fi mulk al-mazkur)*." Even though the brother who initiated construction had not trespassed on the other's property by opening the aperture on his side, the judge ruled against him, concluding that the latter's actions could "harm" the plaintiff. The reference to that which "is practiced in the mentioned quarter" is an explicit nod to local custom in a tight-knit urban setting. Raymond's assertion that arbitration flowed from the confines of the neighborhood or community is, therefore, lent some credence, but his assertion that the community arbitrated these disputes internally is tested by such cases. The role of the residents in raising the court's attention to such 'infractions' was important in generating legal proceedings. But ultimately, it was in the sharia court, and not the *hara*, that such cases were arbitrated and, more importantly, documented. Presumably, mundane disputes such as these could have been easily settled within the community. But ultimately, it was the growing need for documentation, and the near permanence of the guarantees it afforded, that pushed people out of community arbitration and into the courts. This is confirmed by a third document.

The construction of a *riwaq* (arcade or portico) belonging to Amir Ahmad of the Mutafarriqa was, after long delay, allowed to proceed after his neighbor, Nazirin, daughter of the deceased Shaykh Ahmad al-Hubaybi, took an oath to refrain from further interference with the project.[65] Nazirin states explicitly that she will "not prevent the builders or engineers" from undertaking the necessary demolitions. Additionally, she agrees to assume responsibility for the "prevention of harm" to her property by "blocking/ sealing" the top floor of her home. It is unclear why Nazirin, who had presumably opposed this construction project in the past, had a change of heart. We can rule out the possibility that she was summoned by the court and ordered to undertake this oath, for the case would then have included a *mahdar* of previous sessions, beginning with the initial complaint by the *amir*. More likely, therefore, Nazirin came willingly after being mollified, or sufficiently compensated out of court by the *amir*. While not a formal *sulh*, the text of the document suggests, nonetheless, that a customary agreement was reached out of court by both parties. Like a *sulh* document, however, it contains an *iqrar* deterring the woman from reversing her position. After listing a string of claims that Nazirin has renounced, the court outlines the penalties which would befall her should she default on a single item. Here the *iqrar* serves as a binding agreement, providing a measure of insurance for the *amir* that would not exist under customary arbitration.

While the similarity between the three cases is evident, the differences warrant comment. In the second case, involving two *dhimmi*s, the document refers to custom, or common practice, quite explicitly. On the other hand, the two documents involving an all-Muslim group in one case and a mixed group of Christians and Muslims in the other make no direct reference to custom. Assuming that such anomalies are not random, one may tentatively suggest that the court is exhibiting an ease in citing the customs of *dhimmi*s that is not paralleled in cases involving Muslims. This is as one might expect, given the provisions that Islamic legal theory makes for the legal autonomy of religious minorities.

Nonetheless, the court's readiness to refer to, and even dependence on, custom in the municipal sphere, even where it fails to cite it directly, is a product of the benign nature of the customs in question. Moreover, the court was utterly dependent on the complaints of residents when pursuing municipal violations that breached modesty, and was not in a position to provide a uniform code, replete with rules identifying that which constituted a breach of privacy. It was, however, in a position to stabilize, regulate, and enforce rulings in municipal disputes, rulings in which local custom, Islamic law, and Ottoman *qanun* converged to shape the urban landscape.

"The Honorable Hisba" and the Customary Economy

We may now turn our attention to those customs which may be considered 'subversive' from the perspective of a unifying state. As previously argued, the Ottoman empire, famed for its massive internal trade, could not have sustained this unified economy without recasting local fiscal practices—particularly those that affected metrology, or the system of weights and measures.

The bulk of Ottoman trade, writes Faroqhi, was internal. Istanbul, she continues, was "supplied through interregional trade, involving the shores of the Black Sea, the Aegean and even Egypt."[66] Periodizing the development of commerce, Faroqhi identifies three stages of evolution. First, the formative period, lasting until the middle of the fifteenth century, is "characterized by limited regional and local trade and concentration of international commerce in a few centres, principally Bursa."[67] The second period lasts to the end of the sixteenth century, "and its salient feature is the development of Istanbul into a giant city, by far the largest in both Europe and the Mediterranean region, providing a proportional stimulus to internal trade."[68] What facilitated this movement away from international trade and toward intraregional trade? Better yet, would such a move have been possible without the semblance of a unified metrological and legal system? A review of the evidence of the *sijill* will confirm that the Ottomans pursued this objective, seeking and succeeding in introducing a measure of fiscal unity. Before we discuss that body of evidence, however, a consideration of Ibn Iyas' reports will both contextualize and corroborate the evidence of the *sijill*.

In Ramadan 924 (1518), a public proclamation in the markets of Cairo ushered in the Ottoman coin or aqçe and Egyptian merchants were ordered to use the coins bearing the name of Salim in lieu of their Mamluk currency.[69] Ibn Iyas explains that sixteen Ottoman coins were deemed equivalent to "half a piece of silver," but that they were in fact too "light" for such a rate, effectively devaluing the local currency.⁷⁰ The losses incurred as a result of the switch caused great hardship for the merchant classes, forcing the closure of many a shop and provoking the *muhtasib* Zayni Barakat to intervene by overruling the sultanic decree. A holdover from the Mamluk era, Barakat called on merchants to treat the half piece of silver as equivalent to twenty-four of the new coins. His actions, however, provoked a visit from Ottoman officials who asked, "Has Salim Shah died that his *muʿamala* should end in Egypt?"⁷¹ Physically intimidated (beaten, according to Ibn Iyas), the venerable *muhtasib* was forced to recant. In a swift response, the merchants of Cairo called a strike.

Panic reportedly loomed among the residents of the city as merchants made good on their threats and pulled their products from the market. In an attempt to regain control, Khayrbek threatened to impale the merchants on iron stakes manufactured for this express purpose, after the *ʿid* celebrations.⁷² Fear, concludes Ibn Iyas, and fear alone, compelled the merchants to return to trading. When they did, it was at the rate of sixteen Ottoman coins for a half piece of silver. In the final analysis, the introduction of the Ottoman currency spelled a devaluation in the price of silver and gold, both of which constituted the basis for the official Muslim monetary system and which required a measure of stability to maintain economic growth. ⁷³

But the markets remained unstable, judging by the fact that two years later, in 926, the Porte saw fit to issue a decree *(marsum)* calling for a readjustment in the *muʿamala*.⁷⁴ Soon after, the governor of Egypt announced that the exchange rate for a half piece of silver would remain unchanged, but canceled the half piece of copper. When news of Salim's death arrived in 927, it was followed by the announcement that the new sultan, Sulayman, had instructed the *daftardar* (chief financial officer) to inform the governor of Egypt to initiate *islah* (reform) with respect to the *muʿamala* in gold and silver. But the governor apparently refused, declaring, "I will not change the *muʿamala* of Salim Shah, nor will I exceed what was [decreed] in his day: that the *ashrafi* gold is exchanged in the *muʿamala* for a half piece as is the custom."⁷⁵ The ensuing conflict was resolved only when the merchants were summoned to inform the governor collectively that "none of the people" would adhere to his ruling, and that they would initiate another strike.

Two days into the strike, the *muhtasib* Zayni Barakat convinced the governor to concede to the exchange of *ashrafi* gold for forty-five rather than fifty aqçes, and in cases of wholesale buying and selling, to forty-six. Shortly thereafter, the markets resumed trading. Nonetheless, the issue continued to surface in various guises, as seen in one *mahdar*, from the court of Tulun in the year 1557, where evidence of the state's attempt to curtail, if not abolish, the production of non-sultanic silver and gold standards is provided. The shaykh of a *ta'ifa* (guild) undertakes a witnessed oath to refrain from the production of gold and silver, except for that which is equivalent to the "sultanic Rumi" standard. Any violation, the document reads, will subject the offender to the discretionary punishment of the deputy governor.[76] While there may have been a limit on the production of non-sultanic standards, the evidence of the *sijill* belies the possibility of a complete ban. The *sijill*s commonly refer to local standards of gold and silver, always termed "*mu'amala bil-diyar al-Misriya.*" Generally found in marriage contracts, where the dowry is often given in gold and silver coins, the *mu'amala Misriya* is found in nineteen out of twenty-three such contracts, indicating its popularity over the Ottoman *ashrafi* gold or *dhahab jadid* found in the remainder. In effect, the persistence of non-sultanic standards allowed for the first of many devaluations to the aqçe and for the de facto creation of a separate Egyptian currency, the para. It has been argued that the para was only introduced in 1635–36.[77] But relying on the *Qanunnama* of 1524, Shaw has disproved this thesis to establish that the para was coined soon after the conquest.[78]

However, even as the Porte conceded to local *mu'amala* in terms of the standards of gold and silver (devaluing the aqçe), it was preparing to initiate another set of reforms unifying metrological systems. This is not a view endorsed by E. Ashtor, who writes:

> In the history of Oriental metrology, the spread of Islam meant no abrupt break. Whereas Charlemagne imposed in his empire a uniform system of weights and measures and introduced a much heavier pound than the Roman libra of 327.45 g, neither Muhammad nor 'Umar made such a reform; and as later rulers could not claim canonical character for their systems of weights and measures, their bewildering diversity was in the Muslim countries even greater than in mediaeval Europe, where Charlemagne's system remained as a firm basis.[79]

When the Arabs conquered the lands of the Near East, he explains, a variety of names were already used for different weights and measures, such that "the diversity of the weights and measures called by the same name was a phenomenon common to all Muslim countries."[80] Most districts had their own system of weights and measures, and "in some countries those used in the capitals were different from those of the countryside."[81] Furthermore, different weights were used for various commodities.[82]

Nonetheless, concedes Ashtor, there were rulers who attempted to establish a fixed system of weights and measures, "just as they built up an administration different from that of their predecessors." He credits the Buyid prince 'Adud al-Dawla, the Fatimids, the Il-Khan Ghazan, and the Turcoman Uzun Hassan with such ambitions, but not the Ottomans.[83] K. Salameh confirms Ashtor's general observations, writing that in the Ottoman period, weights and measures "varied from city to city and region to region."[84] Listing the various measures of weight found in the Jerusalem *sijill*, he gives the following breakdown: the Jerusalem *ratl*, the *qintar* at 100 times the *ratl* (used for weighing large quantities of seeds, rice, and flour), the *mudd* (weight used for quantities of wheat, barley, semolina, and sesame), and the *mann* (mentioned once as equivalent to 2.5 Egyptian *ratl*s). While Salameh's observations are not in dispute, his analysis and somewhat cursory conclusions may be challenged. By failing to compare the degree of variation that existed in the Ottoman Empire with its predecessor states, Salameh misses the possibility that it may have already undergone a considerable degree of redaction.

Ashtor writes that among the various weights and measures of capacity, the most common is the *ratl*.[85] In the Fatimid period, several variant *ratl*s were used. According to the sources, they included the following: the "*ratl* called *Misri* of 144 *dirham*s (444.9 gr.), used for weighing bread, meat and other articles; that of 150 *dirham*s (463 gr.), used for spices, and also cotton, called *fulfuli*, or pepper *ratl*; the *ratl layithi* of 200 *dirham*s (617.96 gr.), used for flax; and the *ratl jarwi* of 312 *dirham*s (964 gr.), used for honey, sugar, cheese and metals."[86] In the Ottoman period, however, there are no references to these varieties of *artal* (pl. of *ratl*), only to two—one the local "Egyptian *ratl*" and a more generic *ratl*. Even in Jerusalem, Salameh notes the existence of the "Jerusalem *ratl*" and the occasional reference to the "Egyptian *ratl*" but not to the numerous *artal* cited by Ashtor.

Retracing the history of Ottoman metrological policy after the conquest will clarify the argument. In 1520, a messenger arrived from Istanbul bearing a decree from Sulayman, issuing a new iron *dhira'* (the measure of the cubit of length) to be used in lieu of the Hashimi cubit heretofore used in Egypt and Syria.[87] Originally known as the Persian "king's" cubit *(dhira' al-malik)*, and known as the great Hashimi cubit *(al-dhira' al-Hashimiya)* since the caliph al-Mansur (754–75), it equaled an average of 66.5 cm.[88] It is the latter which was known in Egypt and which was replaced by the new *dhira'*, equivalent, writes Ibn Iyas, to five *qararit* (from *qirtas*, a measurement based on the size of a parchment or papyrus roll). There are two examples to support the claim that the new cubit was widely used, even if there is none indicating that its predecessor, the Hashimi cubit, disappeared altogether. One document uses the term *dhira' al-'amal* in reference to the surface of a building's hall,[89] while another simply uses the term *dhira'*.[90] It is unknown whether the former refers to the Hashimi cubit or to a variation on the new Ottoman cubit. Suffice it to say, where the word *dhira'* appears alone, it refers solely to the new Ottoman cubit.

One event that may have helped to effect the transition to Ottoman weights and measures in Cairo was the deportation of thousands of Egyptians to Istanbul. Ordered by Salim, the deportation targeted members of the elite as well as artisans, builders, and craftsmen. In their stead, people from Istanbul, also artisans, craftsmen, and builders, were brought to Egypt. Ibn Iyas refers to this policy as Salim's "custom" upon conquering a new city.[91] The rationale for this policy was twofold. For one, there was a need for the skills of the empire's best artisans in the construction of Istanbul's architectural monuments. Two, and more importantly from our perspective, such a policy ensured that artisans trained and accustomed to Ottoman standards would facilitate the switch to the new metrological system.

But the reforms did not end at the measurement of the cubit. A *qasid* had also arrived from Istanbul bearing new, standardized imperial *artal* (weights) and brass *sinaj* (weights placed as a counterpoise on the scales of a balance; sing. *sanj*).[92] When Sulayman formally abolished the Egyptian *sinaj* and *dhira'*, prohibiting their use among merchants and traders, the governor responded by "hearing and obeying." Alongside the governor, the *muhtasib* Zayni Barakat enforced the new law, forcing merchants to sign a written oath abjuring the purchase or sale of products by any weight but the "Istanbuli." Anyone who went back on their oath would face immediate hanging—without appeal—in their own shops. On the heels of this announcement, the *muhtasib*'s aides raided the markets, confiscating the old scales and weights and publicly destroying them. So successful were these tactics, concludes Ibn Iyas, that the new weights "are used to this day."[93]

Ibn Iyas' conclusions may have been premature, however, for a year later, in 1521, another decree was issued instructing the people of Cairo to abandon the weights and measures they had used since "olden times" (*qadim al-zaman*). Notably, however, the language is markedly different from that of previous decrees in that it speaks of Egyptians assimilating their practices, not to "Istanbuli weights" or "Istanbuli custom," but to the "*shar'i* standards outlined in the works of *hisba*."[94] The change in language signals an important shift in the symbolism used to bolster the state's claims, from Ottoman to Islamic.

There is no more written on the subject by Ibn Iyas, but the *sijill*s fill in important gaps. In the case considered below, the *artal* of which Ibn Iyas spoke are revealed as a source of contention between merchants and the state well into the seventeenth century. Contrary to Ibn Iyas' report, the *sijill* reveals that the Egyptian *ratl*, at 144 dirhams, continued to be used in Ottoman Egypt, although in very limited and highly contentious cases. There are, however, no documents to suggest that anything other than the 'Egyptian *ratl*' was in use, alongside the generic 'Ottoman *ratl*.' Already, therefore, there appears to have been a reduction in the sheer variety of *artal* used by comparison with previous eras. And as mentioned, the Egyptian *ratl* was no longer used indiscriminately, but appears to have been limited to certain comestible products. Even within this limited sphere, however, the *muhtasib* periodically challenged its usage.

The case of the sugar merchants, below, sheds great light, not only on the evolution of metrology systems in Ottoman Egypt, but on the latter's attempts to transform '*mu'amala* as it is' to reflect '*mu'amala* as it should be' from the perspective of a unifying state. On the face of it, the document appears to exemplify the triumph of custom. It records the victory of the sugar merchants against the chief *muhtasib* (market inspector), upholding the formers' right to use the Egyptian *ratl*—as per Egyptian custom—in lieu of the *ratl* stipulated by the 'honorable *hisba*' (Ottoman custom). As Shaw has shown, the *muhtasib*'s duties in Ottoman Egypt were "limited principally to the enforcement of standards of weights and measures, and prices in the comestible markets of Cairo."[95] A close examination of his role in this case confirms the exceptionalism and limited scope of local weights and measures in the Ottoman economy.

A *mahdar* and *hukm* from the year 1592, transcribed into the text of another document from the year 1636, allows us to follow the travails of the sugar merchants as they strive to retain an exemption from Ottoman *hisba*.⁹⁶ The original document begins by identifying the presiding judge as Shaykh al-Islam Qayd Allah Efendi, before identifying the plaintiffs before him as Governor Ahmad Pasha; "pride of the merchants" *(fakhr al-tujjar)* al-Shaykh Nur al-Din ibn al-Sharafi Yihyah, from the guild of the sugar merchants (Jama'at al-Sukkariya); and Zayni 'Abd al-Rahman al-Hakimi, Shams Muhammad ibn Shams al-Din al-Zayn, al-Nuri 'Ali al-Tuluni, 'Ali al-Halawani, al-Zayni Ibrahim, and a large number of other members of the guild from Bayn al-Qasrayn and Bab Zuwayla.

The merchants complained of the harm which had befallen them at the hands of the *qasim amin al-hisba* (officer of the treasury), when he attempted to "impose the *siyasa* upon them." Because they sold sugar, and other commodities, at the customary *ratl* of 144 dirhams, the *muhtasib* demanded they take an oath to sell at the *hisba*'s rate, equivalent to 150 dirhams. Such demands, they argued, constituted a violation of the "honorable sharia and of the old customs" *('ada qadima)*. Switching to a *ratl* of 150 dirhams, they continued, would cause great harm to befall them, as it would raise their costs of production, an unreasonable request given that the weight of the *qabban* (wholesale weight of comestible products), with which commodities were weighed in the entire empire, or "honorable sultanate," was equivalent to the Egyptian *qabban*. The *muhtasib*, they charged, had imposed his will on them, setting the measurements *(al-'iyar)* in accordance with "his whims" *(bi-ma'rifatih)*. Finally, they argued that the *muhtasib* had no jurisdiction to impose the standard weights and measurements upon them without the governor's *(hakim al-shar'i)* knowledge. This, concludes the document, was the underlying cause of this long-running dispute.

For his part, the head of the *hisba*, "*al-qasim* the aforementioned," defended his actions by claiming that in the time of the deceased *wazir* Uways Basha, an unknown official *(shakhs)* had calculated the Egyptian *ratl* at 150 dirhams. While he insisted on adhering to this precedent, the record indicates that the *qasim* could produce no witness or evidence to this effect and had nothing "in hand"—that is, produced no corroborative document to support this claim. The matter then appears to have been referred to the "eminent ulama of the four *madhahib* in the Egyptian *diyar*, may their favors persist." The indicated ulama, described as the most prominent scholars of their time, included "Mawlana al-Shaykh Nur al-Din 'Ali [?] al-Hanafi and Mawlana Nur al-Din 'Ali al-Ziyadi al-Shafi'i and Mawlana al-Shaykh 'Abd al-Rahman al-Khatib al-Zayni al-Shafi'i and Mawlana Wali al-Din al-Hanbali and Mawlana al-Shaykh Yusuf al-Damiri al-Maliki and others from among the community of scholars in Egypt. Each endorsed the following fatwa: 'What is known among scholars is that the Egyptian *ratl* is 12 *awqiya* and the *awqiya* is [equal to] 12 dirhams, and becomes 144 dirhams. That is in their custom.'" Not a single scholar dissented in this view, notes the record.

The statements above were conveyed in a *mahdar*, while the ruling was issued following an unspecified interval of time. The record states that after perusing the opinions of the scholars, the judge affirmed that the Egyptian *ratl* stands, according to prevailing ancient custom *(al-jari bih al-'ada . . . min qadim)*, at no more than 144 dirhams, and directed the "current *muhtasib*'s deputy, al-Zayni," to summon the merchants back to court. In court, the merchants said that, in their view, the "eminent current *wazir* ['Uways] had breached *(anha)* the prevailing state of affairs *(al-waqi' al-hal).*" They also demanded an official *buyuruldi* confirming the exemption and expressing an intolerance for any repeat occurrence *(ihdath)* of the muhtasib's *bida'* "as there is no license for such" *(la rukhsa fi dhalik)*, while also affirming that matters should remain constant with the "old customs" *(al-'ada qadima)*. The judge obligingly responded by ruling that legitimate *(shar'i)* weights cannot be tampered with and that the indicated customary weights must remain as they are based on the position of the sharia (as conveyed in the fatwas of the scholars) and old custom, prohibiting any intervention with the Sukkariya as "a *shar'i* prohibition." Sometime thereafter, the head of the comestible markets *(qabbaniya)*, Shaykh Muhammad, was summoned and informed that the weight of the *qabban*, and its various commodities, should correspond to the Egyptian *ratl* at 144 dirhams throughout the honorable sultanate and beyond. The transcript of the original case ends here, and is dated 20 Safar 1001 (1601).

There are two points to be made with regard to the contextual and linguistic features of the above text. First, while the *sijill* never defines what is meant by "honorable sharia," it exemplifies the manner in which such references are used to bolster various claims, either those of the imperial center when imposing state custom, or the community when it is defending local custom. In this case, custom is upheld on the pretext of "preventing the harm," upholding "old custom," and the "precedent of the sharia." But once again, the term 'old custom' refers not to pre-Ottoman practices (although in this case they are pre-Ottoman in origin), but to those local practices sanctioned by former Ottoman officials. Similarly, the phrase 'the precedent of the sharia' refers to the precedents set by former Ottoman-era jurists who sanctioned the local practice. At no time, therefore, is the pre-Ottoman practice legitimated through references to non-Ottoman sources of authority. Rather, it is only the rulings of Ottoman-era policy and law which establish both "old custom" and the "precedent of the sharia."

Second, the judge justified his ruling on the grounds that Ottoman *hisba* constituted "oppressive renewal" *(tajdid muzlim)* and negative innovation *(bid'a)*. Negating the *qanun* would in this instance 'lift the harm' in the interests of public welfare. Why such concern for the welfare of the sugar merchants? The answer is that they traded in the most vital commodity of their day. Generally speaking, the comestible market was an invaluable source of imperial revenue and economic growth. Within that market, sugar occupied a place of honor, exceeding the importance of other commodities in the late sixteenth and early seventeenth centuries, including spices.[97] The 'harm' to be lifted in this case was from society as a whole and not just one class of merchants.

In the final analysis, the case of the sugar merchants demonstrates that the exception proves the rule, the rule being standardization. The extended, drawn-out procedure, the petitioning of prominent scholars and one minister, as well as the number of sessions held, is a testament to the layers of official bureaucracy in which the exemption is wrapped. Most importantly, the exemption is subject to periodic review, a fact made obvious by the incorporation of the *hujja* document above, from 1001 (1592), into another *mahdar*, dated 1045 (1636). In that year, another legal gauntlet was thrown before the sugar merchants by the *muhtasib*.

The document from 1636 begins by introducing the guild of sugar merchants *(jama'at al-sukkariyyin)* from the districts of Bab Zuwayla and Bayn al-Qasrayn, who appeared before the chief judge to assert their right to weigh sugar according to the "old customary weights." Merchants who presented themselves in court included the head of the merchant's guild (Shah Bandar al-Tujjar), the Khawaja Muhammad al- (?), and Shaykh Ibn al-Shaykh Yusuf and the Shaykh 'Abd Allah ibn al-Hajj Muhammad, and "others from Ta'ifat al-Sukkariya." Collectively, they had come to file a complaint against the *muhtasib*, who was demanding their conformity with Ottoman standard weights. Conceding that their *ratl Misri* amounted to 144 dirhams, and did not conform to the weight of the *ratl* indicated in the honorable sultanic *hisba (al-hisba al-sharifa)*, they justified the discrepancy on the basis of "their old customs [where] their *ratl* amounted to 144, not more."

It should be clear by now that the merchants' case rested on an 'old custom' encased in, and defined by, the authoritative judicial court document *(hujja shar'iya)* dated 1001 (1592), exempting them from the standards of the *bayt al-hisba*.⁹⁸ The document, they explained, prohibited any party from confronting or challenging their practices. Moreover, it clearly stipulated that the "measures" *(i'yar)* of the sultanic *hisba* could not be imposed upon them without the knowledge of Egypt's chief judge. The *muhtasib* was not authorized to impose these measures of his own accord. The document was undersigned by the former chief judge, Mawlana Shaykh al-Islam Qayd Allah Efendi, as well as the former governor of Egypt, Ahmad Pasha. At the judge's request, a copy of the original document was faithfully transcribed into the new record.

When the judge familiarized himself with contents of the original written instrument *(madmun al-hujja)*, he found it to be in agreement with the *shari'a Muhammadiya* and with "acceptable" *(murdiya)* custom, ruling that the Sukkariya should retain, as per their customs, the Egyptian *ratl* at 144 dirhams. Moreover, he warned against any intervention in their affairs, categorically stating that they could only be made to replace their weights and measures by the chief judge, "and none other." Significantly, the ruling is justified on the grounds that the original *hujja*, as well as the testimonies of the ulama, condemn "oppressive renewal" *(tajdid muzlim)* or any action conflicting with the honorable *shar'*. A "total prohibition of such in the year 1045/1644" was thus decreed.

We cannot say how often, in the forty-four years that lapsed between the document issued in 1001/1592 and the one in 1045/1636, the merchants had to defend their practices in court. We can, however, corroborate the merchants' claim that they had used these weights prior to 1592. An *iqrar*, witnessed by the Hanbali judge in the court of Tulun, that dates from 965 (1557), thirty-six years prior to the *hujja* above, records the following: a member of the soldiery confesses to having defaulted on the payment of a debt and promises to pay it back in produce, predominantly sugar but also including other comestibles, in an amount fixed in tandem with the "Egyptian weights" *(b-il-wazn al-Masri)*.[99]

A third reference to Egyptian weights is found in a rental contract for a *waqf madrasa* in Dumyat, dated 1023 (1614). Describing the property and the instruments/tools which accrue to the renter, it lists "all twenty-four antique *('atiq)*, lead *(rusas) qintar*s, used in the Egyptian weights" and for which there is a "*shar'i* decree and [stipulating that] such [customs] prevail *(jari)* in the indicated *waqf*."[100] Although the product that is to be weighed in tandem with the Egyptian weights is never identified, it is most certainly sugar. In the first place, the tools listed (agricultural implements) indicate that it was a comestible product, and in the second, the document also places the madrasa, and its lands, near the "*khatt al-Qassabin*," or sugar-cane farmers.

Apart from the three cases culled from this sample of documents, there are no references to Egyptian weights or measures in any of the other commercial, rental, purchasing, or selling contracts. In the absence of further proof, a tentative conclusion can be offered: that only comestible products, principally sugar, were exempted from the 'honorable *hisba*' of the Ottoman state. Moreover, such variation was significantly redacted from that which existed under previous regimes.

Conclusion

Our examination of the public and private domains of *mu'amala* sheds light on the manner in which a given community's customs were legitimated or delegitimated, raising a distinction between two clusters of customary laws: those perceived as benign from the perspective of sharia and *qanun*, and those perceived as subversive from the perspective of the state's universalizing agenda. The conditional clause in marital contracts showed the court's neutrality toward certain practices. It also revealed the court's inclination to regard the individual as an entity distinct from his/her community, hence enforcing conditional marital clauses that diluted the authority of the latter. Concurrently, it also revealed a tendency to strengthen the bonds between the individual and the state and to temper the absolutism of the community as a primary unit of identification. The porous boundaries of community identity were further demonstrated by marriage contracts, which revealed that almost a third represented mixed couples hailing from diverse communities. Even marriages that united couples from the same professional community (as in *'askeri* marriages) could not be termed ethnically homogenous, and reinforced the conclusion that class, rather than ethnicity, played the determining role in one's choice of marital partner. In such an environment, the individual, particularly the bride, was in a position to challenge customs originating in her own or her spouse's community, with the help of the courts.

In its dealings with community blocs rather than individuals, the state and its courts exhibit an ambiguous, but not incoherent, approach to custom. On the face of it, the language of the documents suggests the courts were willing to accommodate 'old customs,' as in the decree concerning the taxation of the Gypsy community. On closer examination, however, it becomes evident that such terms referred to old Ottoman rather than pre-Ottoman customs. Nonetheless, references to 'old custom' could at times indicate a pre-Ottoman practice. However, as demonstrated by the cases of *iltizam*, pre-Ottoman customs did not necessarily denote models of 'grassroots legislation.' In fact, such cases problematize the assumption found within much of the secondary literature, that custom is necessarily rooted in local popular practice, or that it always signifies 'grassroots' legislative trends. Rather, the *sijill*'s validation of 'old customs' demonstrates the manner in which the courts incorporated ancient state practices into a Muslim juridico-moral paradigm.

Likewise, documents pertaining to *sulh* do not support the thesis that it represented an extrajudicial form of customary arbitration. Rather, the preponderance of *sulh*-related documents in the *sijill*s points to the triumph of the *shar'i* court as the final arbiter of custom. The registration of such cases in the Islamic court involved far more than a mere descriptive accounting of the terms of a *sulh* agreement. It included the drawing up of the agreement into a set formulary model, and its adjustment through the addition and attachment of the *iqrar*. Thus, far from merely registering these settlements, the courts transcribed the agreement in such a way as to modify the custom before assimilating it to sharia.

Except in limited areas, the courts reveal a consistent disposition to expunge rather than accommodate local custom in commercial *mu'amala*. In municipal matters, the standardization of the measurements, combined with a dependence on an expert body of local engineers, ensured the standardization of practice. Similarly, the laws governing taxation, or market weights and measures, were unified through a metrological system, or *shar'i hisba*. Thus, not only was the financial administration of Cairo centralized, but so too were the market laws governing fiscal practices *within* Cairo. To a large extent, the policy appears to have been successful, as out of tens of documents containing a bill of purchase or sale, only a few exemptions are ever made—notably for gold and silver standards in marriage dowries, and weights used on certain comestible products, such as sugar. The lengthy and complicated lobbying processes by which merchants retained such exemptions demonstrated that they were both limited and conditioned upon periodic review.

Whether in private or public *mu'amalat*, custom was an increasingly modified and redacted source of law. In relation to the new orthodoxy, it was the perceived benign or subversive nature of a given custom that determined its fate in the courts of the Ottoman Empire.

Conclusions

One often reads that Islam's crisis of modernity speaks of an acute need for a reformation akin to Christianity's. But, as the reader may have already surmised, this author would argue Islam has already had one (and many since, mediated through the predations of colonialism), and that its reformation plays no small part in its modern crisis of authority.

In the nineteenth century, a new term was coined as the empire's answer to the rising threat of separatist, nationalist movements: 'Ottomanism.' To compete with nationalism, it promised a formula of citizenship that disregarded the ethnic and, more importantly, religious identity of its populace. The term may have been new but the ideology on which it was built—namely, a covenant between the state and the individual, predicated on a parity of rights and obligations under the law—had been many centuries in the making. Ottomanism was born in the sixteenth century, when universal principles of governance had already formulated a translocal, legal orthodoxy, enhancing the autonomy of the individual even as it diminished the authority of enclave subcultures.

By the late eighteenth and nineteenth centuries, European modernity had dawned on the Ottoman Empire, overlaying its peculiar lexical brands, 'citizen,' 'nation,' 'secular,' and 'constitution,' onto the empire's political geography. The particular configuration of concepts and ideas that Chakrabarty attributed to western political modernity had come to pass. And while he had dismissed the figurative 'waiting room' to which historicism had assigned the non-Europeans of this world by proposing 'alternative modernities,' he did not posit the possibility of 'alternative early-modern' worlds. Abu-Lughod asserted the existence of such worlds in the economic sphere, but stopped short of asserting their existence in the political. Their contributions made it possible, however, for this researcher to begin investigating the possibility.

This work was as much an investigation of Islamic law as it was of Ottoman statecraft. It depicts an endogenous construction of citizenship and modern statehood in the Ottoman Empire before any later efforts to mimic European models. Without a doubt, the impact of early modern Europe's capitalist formations, with their emergent banking and corporate systems of finance, played an important role in stimulating changes in Ottoman economic and judicial life. The promotion of the document was one such example. But to assume that all transformations were generated by external European stimuli is misleading. There were, to be certain, external imperatives for enhancing the authority of documents, but there were equally propitious internal reasons for doing so. The change in the status of the document was but one reform in a series of rapid, cohesive, and well-chronicled strategic moves that consciously promoted a new social order founded on a new legal orthodoxy. A harbinger of the centralized, bureaucratic state, the new orthodoxy came replete with an implicit, rather than explicit, political covenant in which the state and the individual were repositioned in a novel configuration undermining the authority of the community. As bureaucratization devoured what had once been a private judicial guild, it rendered the law itself, in its its administration and production, a veritable state industry.

Inevitably, the argument that the Ottoman state sought to promote a new legal orthodoxy in Cairo raises several questions. What motivated this venture? How was it accomplished? What was its impact? Why is it relevant to the present? The present study has pointed to the numerous internal political, economic, and social imperatives of the early-modern venture. Social orthodoxy, I have argued, promoted cultural homogenization and minimized the risk of ethnic and sectarian differences in a vast, multi-confessional, multiethnic empire. On the economic level, it facilitated interempire trade, opening borders and enhancing the flow of commercial and migrant human traffic.

As judicial bureaucratization and legal codification accelerated, the state assumed stewardship of the 'rights of God,' personified in the early sixteenth century by Sulayman Qanuni, the self-proclaimed temporal and spiritual caliph. From the mid-sixteenth century on, however, stewardship continued to be embodied in the ruler, but only symbolically, for in practical terms the bureaucratic state, the Hanafi guild, and its state jurists had become the real stewards of the law. But whether personified in individual rulers or in a bureaucratic institution, religious and political authority had clearly been renegotiated in favor of the state.

The reach of this 'reformation' is evident in the diminished autonomy of local jurists, and of the communities they represented. The idea that judges continued to exercise absolute authority over their courts, or even their own records, and that they applied the law "as they saw fit" is simply a myth. No less mythical is the role assigned to the community and custom in shaping judicial rulings in marriage, divorce, market *hisba*, endowments, or the like, in this period. By the end of the sixteenth century, Muslims and non-Muslims alike were increasingly shunning customary arbitration outside of court. In court, they challenged customary practices through various strategies of resistance, including the conditional stipulation in the marital contract. Likewise, it was used to 'prohibit that permitted by Sunna' and Islamic law in the case of polygyny. Relieved of a traditional subordination to the ethnic, religious, or regional peculiarities of their heritage (religious and ethnic), 'subjects' moved closer to the modern notion of 'citizens.'

Islamic law functioned as a unified legal system, providing in practice what 'civil' law promises in theory. This is not to suggest that the Islamic identity of the law was somehow diluted, but to assert that it increasingly served the purposes of a civil law, in its new form as a rule-based, codified law available to any and all subjects, and temporary residents, on roughly the same terms. Civil law in the modern west is hardly different, reflecting its Christian foundations in contemporary debates on the legality of abortion, prostitution, or gay marriage. And yet, its accessibility to Christians and non-Christians alike gives it its 'civic' nature. Today in Egypt, and in the majority of the Muslim world's modern 'secular' states, Islamic law has been 'deterritorialized' in the sense that it is restricted to Muslims and cannot be applied to Coptic Christians, and simultaneously hyperterritorialized in being restricted to the nation. In other words, the modern Egyptian sharia statutes apply only to Muslims within Egypt and not to the universal umma. The added irony is that the interpretation of sharia law in the early modern era was far less rigid and far more sensitive to the distinction between sins and crimes than most of its modern counterparts.

Historically, even as the sharia continued to be the overarching Islamic framework for the law, it functioned, for both Muslims and non-Muslims, as a quasi-civil code, removed from the confines of place, ethnicity, or sect. This translocal law delegitimated many of the customs which had been assimilated into the local sharia, and reassimilated others into the Ottoman sharia through *qanun*. In practice, the changing judicial landscape yielded a more uniform set of expectations with respect to the rights and obligations one could garner in a local court—rights and obligations disembodied from the locale in which the court was found.

Because Islamic law remained a system of case laws, this covenant cannot be found in a declaratory bill of rights. Rather, it is found in the codified *qanun*s, streamlined *fiqh*, and that peculiar breed of document, the *hujja al-musattara*, which circulated in private hands and was copied in public archives. The *hujja*, a court-issued, state-backed writ of law proclaiming the holder's claim to a given right—such as a wife's right to leave the home, an order for the cessation of harassment, an enunciation of the rights of the manumitted slave, a property right, and so on—was a de facto writ of a given right. The *hujja* was thus at once a vehicle for the new orthodoxy, with its promise of greater individual autonomy, and a harbinger of demise for the authority of the community and of local custom.

I am not of course suggesting that custom and local identity ceased to have any meaning or import in the courts of Ottoman Cairo. This would be a preposterous conclusion, based on the even more absurd notion that local custom can ever be eradicated. Rather, what I have attempted to do is draw the attention of scholars and students of Middle East history to the complexity of custom, as an ontological and intellectual category that encapsulates recurrent popular practice on the one hand, and the discourse on ethics, philosophy, and law on the other. Within the latter, it assumes many forms, a term encapsulating topologies of custom (*'adat*, *'amal*, and *'urf*) and categories of custom (state, personal, universal, limited, old, and new). Within the *sijill*, custom is flagged by each of these labels, as well as reconstituted as "pleasing" (*murdiya*) or "offensive" according to Hanafi *fiqh*, *qanun*, and, increasingly, individual preference.

The examples showcased in chapters six and seven illustrate the close surveillance exercised by state officials affiliated with the office of *ihtisab* over any deviation from *qanun* in the administration of endowments, the system of weights and measures, taxation, *sulh*, and municipal law. Moreover, they highlight the problems inherent in taking references to custom in the documents as a blanket signal for, or endorsement of, local practice. A principal conclusion derived about the court's lexicon, and its categorization of customs, is that it can be misleading, for, as demonstrated by documents pertaining to the taxation of the Gypsy community and *iltizam*, references to that which is "customary" did not always reflect that which was local or even pre-Ottoman in origin.

In the second place, while they represented a victory for custom, the cases examined highlighted how anomalous such cases were, and how contingent on periodic review. Exemptions from the *qanun* were won with great difficulty and, as the travails of the sugar merchants prove, subject to continuous oversight and challenge. In all, therefore, the new orthodoxy was pragmatic in its reach, making exceptions for custom when deemed necessary, but never lax in its quest for universalization.

The territorialization of Islamic law had real implications for the local community and its degree of social solidarity. While communities remained vital to the social fabric of the city, they were also far less autonomous in managing the internal affairs of their members than at any time in Cairo's recorded history. The civil marriage law of 1521, for example, radically diminished the community's role in arbitrating marriage and divorce contracts, by transferring private law to the public domain. Marriage had become a public institution subject to judicial oversight. And increasingly over the sixteenth century, people learned new behavior, coming to court not merely to register their marriages, but to seek the court's mediation of their personal quarrels, or simply to register the quarrel in writing.

The number of marriage documents utilizing the conditional clause to abrogate customs originating in one's own community or in the community of a spouse confirms the expanded role of state institutions in mediating the relationship of the individual to her community. The myriad conditional clauses ratified and enforced by the court and its judicial bureaucracy—preventing husbands from moving their wives out of the city limits or subjecting them to the peculiar customs of their community, taking a concubine or second wife, or physically abusing them—ensured that state institutions remained the court of last resort for individuals who were unwilling to conform to the practices of their spouses, neighbors, or communities. So far as the courts were concerned, it was the multitudinous variety of customs in the empire, rather than custom per se, which constituted a source of concern, as seen in the case of the dowry.

In opposition to the Egyptian custom of dividing the dowry into 'advanced' and 'deferred' portions, a concerted effort was made to ensure that women received the *mahr al-mithl*, or full dowry, up front. Eventually, however, the practice of the Egyptians was deemed 'the best of customs,' incorporated into Hanafi *fiqh*, and enforced over and above customs in Anatolia. What is revealed is that, far from attempting to eradicate all custom, or even to impose strictly Anatolian/sultanic customs on the communities of the empire, the state judiciary sought to unify practice on the basis of a single custom. In the final analysis, the goal of the sharia court was to modify and, as far as possible, unify its overarching place in key institutions like *hisba* and marriage.

In the introduction to this book, it was argued that the state which sparked this social and political realignment also provided a template for its modern successors, yielding the bureaucratic state, public sphere, civil law, and state judiciary, which would come to characterize early-modern statecraft in the sixteenth-century Muslim Mediterranean. And while it took a rebellion against the Catholic Church and a religious reformation to accomplish the same in Europe, in the Ottoman state, where there was no church to contend with, the reforms could be engineered with less obvious rupture. Moreover, while a nascent, national ideology was part and parcel of the Protestant Reformation's bid for political sovereignty from the church, a transnational ideology remained the centerpiece of Ottoman statecraft.

In contradistinction to the smaller Protestant nation-states, the Ottoman state remained an enormous, transnational empire, its centralization motivated by very different political ends. For each state, political authority was predicated on its capacity, and willingness, to safeguard religious practice. But this principle was, and continues to be, interpreted in very different ways. For Calvin, far less than the Ottomans, the 'safeguarding of religious practice' entailed its enforcement. For later generations of Christian rulers, the answer would change. In the United States, secularism would emerge out of the principle that the state had no business with, or authority over, church doctrine. That is, the state was stripped of religious authority. In France, Germany, and England, it was exactly the opposite—religion stripped of political authority. Either way, the cleavage generated between religious and political authority in late-modern Christendom created a greater distinction between 'sins' and 'crimes' than at any point in its history. And though they continue to be confused, the bifurcation of sins and crimes remains a cornerstone of positive, secular law in the west. In Islam, the distinction between sins and crimes was made as early as the tenth century, although no less confused during long periods of its history.

But even in the Sulaymanic era, when the boundaries between temporal and spiritual authority were sorely tested, the conflation of sins and crimes (the ban on tobacco, coffee, or women appearing in public) was intermittent and short-lived. Even with the shrinking gap between temporal and spiritual authority, the tendency to sweep more and more moral offenses under the discretionary authority of the state *(ta'zir)*, and the lowering of the proof bar on sexual offenses *(zina')*, neither the Ottoman caliphate nor its state jurists could fully overcome centuries of judicial theory affirming a distinction between the 'rights of God' and the 'rights of humans,' and between sins and crimes. Nor were they inclined to do so. But the modification of this principle in Ottoman political theory inadvertently left the door on Muslim conceptions of self and moral sovereignty ajar for modern revivalists.

Not until the twentieth century, when movements inspired by Salafi, Deobandi, or Wahhabi revivalist ideology proliferated, would the distinction between sins and crimes disappear altogether. In all such ideologies, the rights of God or *'ibadat* take political precedence over the rights of humans, *mu'amalat*, which are left in any case to European codes. This is true for both the Sunni archetype of the modern Islamic state, Saudi Arabia, and its Shi'a counterpart, the Islamic Republic of Iran. The long history of these movements, and their stated aim of 'purifying' Islam by producing better Muslims, is thus founded on a principle more alien to Islamic history than 'secularism' itself. Nonetheless, it too has roots in the sixteenth-century Ottoman Empire.

While there is no denying the impact of western modernity on the cognitive, structural, and cultural development of Muslim society from the eighteenth century on, the amplification of Ottoman trends in the present is equally undeniable. Ottoman history was as much an engine of the particular configuration of elements comprising 'Muslim political modernity' as the encounter with the west was. An unwritten, much older prototype of the empire's first written constitution (1879) is found in the literature on political philosophy, in the *qanunnama*s, in the manuals of legal theory, and, most notably, in the public archive. Almost every political trend observed in the sixteenth century is amplified into the nineteenth and twentieth.

All of the empire's successor states have adopted official *madhhab*s. As mentioned in the introduction, the Egyptian legal reforms of the nineteenth century abolished the *madhhab* system in its entirety, retaining only Hanafism. The official *madhhab* for over three centuries, Hanafism had finally become the sole *madhhab*. Moreover, codification was accelerated in the area of family law through a process of judicial patchworking, or *talfiq*. *Talfiq* permitted reformers to 'patch' together a new legal code culled from the opinions of the Hanafi school and from a few non-Hanafi rulings. Moreover, the bureaucratization of religious scholars was a first step in the direction of nationalizing their institutions in the twentieth century.

But there *is* one facet of the contemporary legal scene that is patently at odds with the trajectory of Ottoman history. Custom appears to have expanded in direct proportion to the retreat of the sharia as a unified legal system. Among the more sensational, though by no means exclusive, examples of the expanding authority of custom is the phenomenon of "honor killings," as they are dubbed in the western press. While these are clearly forbidden by Islamic law, a recent article in the British newspaper *The Independent* reported that senior Muslim clerics, who are "appalled at what they know is a hidden crisis in Egypt, find their condemnation of 'honor' killing hobbled by their own sponsors. Mohamed Sayyid Tantawi, a powerful Islamic scholar who was Grand Mufti of Egypt and imam of the al-Azhar mosque and who died last March, confronted 'honor' crimes." An activist by the name of Azza Suleiman is quoted in the same article as follows:

> "We have a big problem here because the Sheikh of Al-Azhar and the Mufti, they are not respected any more . . . they are not trusted. And the reason is that the people know they have been appointed by the Hosni Mubarak government, which is corrupt. Tantawi . . . and the mufti represent the system and the people hate the system, so there is no credibility in them. And so there is a new trend. People go to their local sheikhs and tribal leaders—and many of them believe that 'honour' killings are a tradition and are not wrong."[1]

There is of course a pressing need for further research in this regard. Has the problem in fact reached the point of 'hidden crisis' and, if so, how has it happened? At least part of the answer lies in the influence of the French civil code, on which much of Egypt's modern law rests. The French code not only failed to suppress the force of custom, it encouraged it. The Egyptian civil code of 1949, for example, explicitly reverses the roles of sharia and custom. Article 1 of the code provides that "in the absence of any applicable legislation, the judge shall decide according to the custom and, failing the custom, according to the principles of Islamic Law." This stunning reversal in the order of legal precedence turned the sources of law in Muslim society on its head.

The expansion of the state at the expense of religious institutions plays a pivotal role in this modern history. Since its founding, the Egyptian nation-state has steadily devoured its religious institutions. What was left of their autonomy or credibility has long since expired, making them an ineffective bulwark against the predations of the state. The retreat of sharia and religion is met by the advance of custom which, in combination with the influence of European legal codes, is endowed with a new force and vitality.

In the Egyptian context, the authority of local custom has generated unique paradoxes with respect to the two tenets of political modernism—nationalism and citizenship. The abolition of the sharia as a unified legal system, and its replacement with a 'mixed' legal system, where Muslim family law is governed by a truncated Hanafi code and Coptic family law is determined by the sole authority of the Church, has rendered the ideal of a civil code for all citizens well-nigh impossible to achieve. In current practices, the sovereignty of custom has allowed the community to reassert its authority, effectively corralling individual members into their respective customary courts. More than at any point in Ottoman history, Coptic Christians today are subject to the dominion of the church in all aspects of family law, including inheritance rights, marriage, divorce, child custody, and all settlements arising from them. Ironically, the modern civil courts of Egypt do not try cases of family law. Moreover, Muslims are subject to codified, ossified personal status laws that hardly resemble the laws to which their ancestors once appealed.

Even under the auspices of Hanafism, the plurality of law in the Ottoman era stands in stark contrast with its truncated modern interpretation. The ease with which non-Muslim minorities accessed the sharia courts of the empire, garnering alternate rulings to those of their respective communities, also stands in stark contrast with contemporary practices. The barriers cleaving Coptic and Muslim family law into segregated legal venues leave scholars to contend with the ironic and counterintuitive conclusion that the Ottoman sharia courts were more like civil courts than their modern counterparts and possibly better custodians of citizenship. And while Islamic law posed its own limitations on the individual—it did not, for example, recognize the equality of all citizens under the law— it nonetheless provided a unified legal system accessible to all.

It is hardly surprising, therefore, to see Coptic Christians demonstrating alongside Azhari scholars in post-Mubarak Egypt —the latter for independence from the state and the former for independence from the Church. But to many, it will come as a surprise to hear that Copts are also demonstrating for right of access to the sharia courts, something that would allow them to obtain a Muslim divorce, as in the past, without converting to Islam, currently the only means available to thousands of Christians. As this work has shown, the two demands are not as unrelated as they might appear, both hinging on the balance of separation between temporal and spiritual authority, and its formula for the accommodation of the community and its customs. But more importantly, I hope, it has shown that the European Enlightenment is but one chapter in the saga of religion and state, neither the beginning nor 'end of history.'[2]

Notes

Notes to Introduction
1. Carnegie Endowment for International Peace, "An Independent Voice for Egypt's Al-Azhar?" 13 July 2011, http://www.carnegieendowment.org/sada/?fa=show&article=45052
2. Tamim Elyan, "Al-Azhar Says Grand Sheikh Should Be Elected, Not Be State Appointed," *Egypt Daily News*, 17 February 2011, http://www.thedailynewsegypt.com/religion/al-azhar-says-grand-sheikh-should-be-elected-not-state-appointed
3. For works on codification, see: U. Heyd, *Studies in Old Ottoman Criminal Law*, ed. V.L. Menage (Oxford: Clarendon Press, 1973); R. Repp, *The Mufti of Istanbul: A Study in the Development of the Ottoman Learned Hierarchy*, Oxford Oriental Institute Monographs 8 (London: Ithaca Press, 1986); and R. Repp, "*Qanun* and Shari'a in the Ottoman Context," in *Islamic Law: Social and Historical Contexts*, ed. A. al-Azmeh (London: Routledge, 1988), 125–43. For the case of Muslim India see M.R. Pirbhai, "British Indian Reform and Pre-Colonial Trends in Islamic Jurisprudence," *Journal of Asian History* 42, no. 1 (2008): 36–63. For 'governmentalization,' see M. Foucault, "Governmentality," in *The Foucault Effect: Studies in Governmentality*, ed. G. Burchell, C. Gordon, and P. Miller (Chicago, IL: Chicago University Press, 1991), 87–104.
4. Foucault, "Governmentality," 87–104.
5. "Renunciation of the faith and conversion to disbelief is admittedly the greatest of offenses, yet it is a matter between man and his Creator, and its punishment is postponed to the Day of Judgment *(al-jaza' 'alayha mu'akhkhar ila dar al-jaza')*. Punishments that are enforced in this life are those which protect the people's interests, such as just retaliation, which is designed to protect life." Shaykh al-Islam Abi Bakr Muhammad ibn Ahmed al-Sarakhsi, *Mabsut*, vol. 10 (Beirut: Dar al-Kutub al-'Ilmiya, 1993), 110.
6. K. Abou El Fadl, *Speaking in God's Name: Islamic Law, Authority and Women* (Oxford: Oneworld Press, 2001).

7   L. Peirce, *Morality Tales: Law and Gender in the Ottoman Court of Aintab* (Berkeley: University of California Press, 2003), 389.
8   Peirce, *Morality Tales*, 389.
9   Initiated by the Abbasid caliph al-Ma'mun in 833, the Mihna was both a theological and a political inquisition. Representing the state's effort to impose theological principles on the ulama in the matter of the Qur'an's status as 'created' or 'uncreated,' the consensus of scholars today is that "the point at issue during the Mihna was . . . not a particular theological doctrine, but the authority of the caliph versus those men who saw themselves, and not the caliph, as the legitimate repository and authentic transmitters of religious knowledge and tradition." J.A. Nawas, "A Re-examination of Three Current Explanations for al-Mamun's Introduction of the Mihna," *IJMES* 25, no. 4 (1994): 615.
10 The secondary sources have characterized the seventeenth century as one in which local *'urf* ('custom') asserts itself in qadi procedure alongside, if not over and above, *qanun*. H. Gerber argues that the fluidity of legal sources at the qadi's disposal resulted in 'informal' proceedings wherein local custom was often upheld in contravention of imperial orders (H. Gerber, "Shari'a, Kanun, and Custom in the Ottoman Law: The Court Records of Seventeenth-century Bursa," *International Journal of Turkish Studies* 21 (1981): 131–47). In *State, Society, and Law in Islam*, however, he devotes a chapter to the rise of qadi and sharia courts, stressing the rise of a rule-based judicial system, increasingly concerned with applying legal theory in practice (H. Gerber, *State, Society, and Law in Islam: Ottoman Law in Comparative Perspective* [Albany, NY: State University of New York Press, 1994].) A. Marcus confirms the hypothesis but delinks it from the question of the qadi's 'arbitrary' justice to argue that the courts "regularly enforced 'established custom' because it gave legislative expression to local interests" (A. Marcus, "The Middle East on the Eve of Modernity: Aleppo in the Eighteenth Century," *JESHO* 26 (1983): 104–105.) See also N. Hanna, "The Administration of Courts in Ottoman Cairo," in *The State and Its Servants: Administration in Egypt from Ottoman Times to the Present*, ed. N. Hanna (Cairo: American University in Cairo Press, 1995), 44–59.
11 N.H. Coulson, *A History of Islamic Law* (Edinburgh: University Press, 1964); W.B. Hallaq, *An Introduction to Islamic Law: Authority, Continuity and Change* (Cambridge, UK: Cambridge University Press, 2009); M.H. Kamali, *Principles of Islamic Jurisprudence* (Cambridge, UK: The Islamic Texts Society, 2000).
12 J. Wakin, *The Function of Documents* (Albany, NY: State University of New York Press, 1972), 3–4; B. Messick, *The Calligraphic State* (Berkeley, CA: University of California Press, 1993), 204.
13 D.P. Little, "The Significance of the Haram Documents for the Study of Medieval Islamic History," *Der Islam* 57 (1980): 208–209, 216–17. Also see D.P. Little, "A Fourteenth-century Jerusalem Court Record of a Divorce Hearing: A Case Study," in *Mamluks and Ottomans: Studies in Honour of Michael Winter*, ed. D.J. Wasserstein and A. Ayalon (New York: Routledge, 2006), 67–85.

14 Little, "Significance of the Haram Documents," 217.
15 The works of R. Yaron, A. Steinwenter, A. Schiller, and E. Siedl, among others, demonstrate the stability of the notarial tradition in the ancient Near East. Steinwenter has emphasized the dependence of the Coptic notarial forms on the late Byzantine ones, while E. Seidl sees more than borrowing as, he reasons, even though the documents were drawn up in Coptic, "on closer examination it becomes evident that the phrases used there were nothing but translations of those used in Greek documents." See Wakin, *The Function of Documents*, 6; R. Yaron, *Introduction to the Law of the Aramaic Papyri* (Oxford, UK: Clarendon Press, 1961); A. Steinwenter, "Die Bedeutung der Papyrologie für die koptische Urkundenlehre," *Münchener Beiträge zur Papyrusforschung und antiken Rechtsgeschichte* 19 (1934): 302–13; E. Seidl, "Law," in *The Legacy of Egypt*, ed. S.R.K. Glanville (London: Clarendon Press, 1972); A. Schiller, "Prolegomena to the Study of Coptic Law," *Archives d'Histoire du Droit Oriental* 2 (1938): 360–61; W. Seagle, *The Quest for Law* (New York: A.A. Knopf, 1941); A. Gacek, "The Ancient Sijill of Qayrawan," *Middle Eastern Library Association Notes* 46 (1989): 26–29; J. Reychmann and A. Zajaczkowski, "Diplomatics," in *EI*, CD-ROM edition.
16 Little, "Significance of the Haram Documents," 208–209.
17 For Mamluk usage, see Little, "Significance of the Haram Documents," 197. For Ottoman usage, see A. Bayinder, "The Function of the Judiciary in the Ottoman Empire," in *The Great Ottoman Turkish Civilization*, vol. 3, ed. Kemal Çiçek (Ankara: Semih Ofset, 2000), 642.
18 See D.P. Little, *A Catalogue of Islamic Documents from al-Haram aš-Šarif in Jerusalem* (Beirut: Orient-Institut der Deutschen Morgenländischen Gesellschaft, 1984); and "Significance of the Haram Documents," 189–219.
19 S.A.I. Milad, "Registres judiciaires du tribunal de la Salihiyya Nağmiyya," *AI* 12 (1974): 190–200.
20 See A. Sonbol, "Women in Shari'ah Courts: A Historical and Methodological Discussion," *Fordham International Law Journal* 27, no. 1 (2003): 225–53; Peirce, *Morality Tales*.
21 Husayn ibn Muhammad al-Damiri, *Qudat Misr fi-l-qarn al-'ashir wa awa'il al-qarn al-hadi 'ashir* (manuscript, Cairo: Dar al-Kutub).
22 L. Kopf, "al-Damiri," in *Encyclopaedia of Islam* 2, CD-ROM edition.
23 Muhammad ibn Ahmad ibn Iyas, *Bada'i' al-zuhur fi waqa'i' al-duhur*, 5 vols., ed. Muhammad Mustafa (Wiesbaden: E.J. Brill, 1975); Muhammad ibn al-Mu'ti ibn Abi al-Fath ibn Ahmad ibn 'Abd al-Mughni ibn 'Ali al-Ishaqi al-Manufi, *Akhbar al-awwal fi-man tasarraf fi Misr min arbab al-duwal* (Cairo: al-Matba'a al-'Uthmaniya, 1886); Husayn ibn Muhammad al-Damiri, *Qudat Misr fi al-qarn al-'ashir wa awa'il al-qarn al-hadi 'ashir*, MS, Dar al-Kutub, Cairo; Shaykh al-Islam Muhammad ibn al-Surur al-Bakri al-Siddiqi, *al-Nuzha al-zahiya fi dhikr wulat Misr wa-l-Qahira al-mu'izziya*, ed. 'Abd al-Razzaq 'Abd al-Razzaq 'Isa (Cairo: al-'Arabi li-l-Nashr wa-l-Tawzi', 1998); M. Winter, *Society and Religion in Early Ottoman Egypt: Studies in the Writings of 'Abd al-Wahhab al-Sha'rani* (New Brunswick, NJ: Transaction Books, 1982).

Notes to Chapter 1

1. For an introduction to the stylistic and formulary structure of the Ottoman *sijill*, see: S.A.I. Milad, "Registres judiciaires du tribunal de la Salihiyya Nağmiyya," *AI* 12 (1974): 163–253; K.J al-'Asali, *Watha'iq maqddasiya tarikhiya*, 3 vols. (Amman: Jordan University, 1983); and K. Salameh, "Aspects of the *Sijill*s of the Shari'a Court in Jerusalem," in *Ottoman Jerusalem: The Living City, 1517–1917*, ed. S. Auld and R. Hillenbrand (Jerusalem: al-Tajir World of Islam Trust, 2000). For political analysis based on the Ottoman registers, see: R.C. Jennings, "Kadi Court and Legal Procedure in Seventeenth-century Ottoman Kayseri," *SI* 48 (1978): 133–72; and "Limitations on the Judicial Powers of the Kadi in Seventeenth-century Ottoman Kayseri," *SI* 50 (1979): 151–84. For social history, see: J. Tucker, *In the House of the Law* (Berkeley, CA: University of California Press, 1998); A. Layish, "Customary *Khul'* as Reflected in the *Sijill* of the Libyan Shari'a Courts," *BOAS* 51 (1988): 428–39; and "The Sijill of the Jaffa and Nazareth Shari'a Courts as a Source for the Political and Social History of Ottoman Palestine," in *Studies on Palestine during the Ottoman Period*, ed. M. Ma'oz (Jerusalem: Magnes Press, 1975), 252–532. For an analysis of the *sijill* as a source of economic and social history, see: S. Faroqhi, "Political Activity among Ottoman Taxpayers and the Problem of Sultanic Legitimation (1500–1650)," *JESHO* 35 (1992): 1–39; and "Towns, Agriculture, and the State in Sixteenth-century Ottoman Anatolia," *JESHO* 33 (1990): 125–56. J. Reilly, *A Small Town in Syria: Ottoman Hama in the Eighteenth and Nineteenth Centuries* (Oxford: P. Lang, 2000), uses the *sijill* to provide a sociocultural, economic, and, to a more limited extent, political portrait of the city. A limited number of works, focusing on Mamluk as opposed to Ottoman documents, have deepened the discussion by elaborating on the usefulness of the documents as a source for the study of Islamic art and architecture, social history, and law. See: D.P. Little, "The Haram Documents as Sources for the Art and Architecture of the Mamluk Period," *Muqarnas* 2 (1984): 61–72; "Six Fourteenth-century Purchase Deeds for Slaves from al-Haram aš-Šarif," *Zeitschrift der Deutschen Morgenländischen Gesellschaft* 131 (1981): 297–337; and "Two Fourteenth-century Court Records from Jerusalem concerning the Disposition of Slaves by Minors," *Arabica* 29 (1982): 16–49; "The Significance of the Haram Documents for the Study of Medieval Islamic History," *Der Islam* 57 (1980): 189–219.
2. B. Shoshan, *Popular Culture in Medieval Cairo* (Cambridge, UK: Cambridge University Press, 1993), p. 67. Shoshan ignores the community, with all its disparate classes, as a possible site of cultural production.
3. See: J.C. Heesterman, "State and *Adat*," in *Two Colonial Empires*, ed. C.A. Bayly and D.H.A. Kolff (Dordrecht, the Netherlands: Nijhoff, 1986), 189–201; Z. Kling, "Images of Malay-Indonesian Identity," in *Indonesian and Malay Studies*, ed. M. Hitchcock and V.T. King (9th European Colloquium. Kuala Lumpur: Oxford University Press, 1997), 45–52.
4. One finds this view in discussions on the 'origins' and 'racial' identity of the Ottomans, the Mughals, and the Malay Sultanates, all of whom have been described as "nominal" Muslims, "shamanistic," or "Indic." See: C. Geertz,

The Religion of Java (Glencoe, IL: Free Press, 1960); R.P. Lindner, *Nomads and Ottomans in Medieval Anatolia* (Bloomington: Indiana University Press, 1983); R.C. Jennings, "Some Thoughts on the Gazi-Theses," *WZKM* 76 (1986): 151–61; M.R. Choudhury, *The Din-i Ilahi, or the Religion of Akbar* (Calcutta: Das Gupta Publishers, 1952).

5   J. Hathaway, "Egypt in the Seventeenth Century," in *The Cambridge History of Egypt*, vol. 2, ed. C.F. Petrie and M.W. Daly (Cambridge, UK: Cambridge University Press, 1998), 37–38.

6   A. Raymond, "The Ottoman Conquest and Development of the Great Arab Towns," in *Arab Cities in the Ottoman Period*, ed. A. Raymond (Ashgate, UK: Variorum, 2002), 23–24.

7   M. Winter, *Egyptian Society under Ottoman Rule* (New York: Routledge, 1992), 226.

8   See: A. Raymond, "The Role of the Communities *(tawa'if)* in the Administration of Cairo in the Ottoman Period," in *The State and Its Servants: Administration in Egypt from Ottoman Times to the Present*, ed. N. Hanna (Cairo: American University in Cairo Press, 1995), 32–43.

9   Winter, *Egyptian Society*, 227.

10 Shoshan, *Popular Culture*, 67.

11 To my knowledge the only work that directly addresses the *sijill* from the perspective of custom is H. Gerber, "Sharia, Kanun, and Custom: The Court Records of 17th-century Bursa," *International Journal of Turkish Studies* 21 (1981): 131–47.

12 The "Cambridge school" is exemplified in: H. Inalcik, "The Heyday and Decline of the Ottoman Empire," in *The Cambridge History of Islam*, ed. P.M. Holt, K.S. Lambton, and B. Lewis (Cambridge, UK: Cambridge University Press, 1971), 324, 353; and U. Heyd, "The Later Ottoman Empire in Rumelia and Anatolia," in *The Cambridge History of Islam*, 354–73. For the case of Egypt, see P.M. Holt, "The Later Ottoman Empire in Egypt and the Fertile Crescent," in *The Cambridge History of Islam*, 374–93.

13 See: H. Gerber, "Shari'a, Kanun, and Custom," where he argues that the fluidity of legal sources at the qadi's disposal resulted in 'informal' proceedings; A. Marcus, "The Middle East on the Eve of Modernity: Aleppo in the Eighteenth Century," *JESHO* 26 (1983): 104–105; and N. Hanna, "The Administration of Courts in Ottoman Cairo," in *The State and Its Servants: Administration in Egypt from Ottoman Times to the Present*, ed. N. Hanna (Cairo: American University in Cairo Press, 1995): 44–59.

14 M. Winter, "The Ottoman Occupation," in *The Cambridge History of Egypt, 641–1517*, vol. 1, ed. C.F. Petry (Cambridge, UK: Cambridge University Press, 1998), 27.

15 Hanna, "Administration," 47.

16 A. Raymond, *Cairo*, trans. W. Wood (Cambridge, MA: Harvard University Press, 2000), 189.

17 D.R. Khoury, *State and Provincial Society in the Ottoman Empire: Mosul, 1540–1834* (Cambridge, UK: Cambridge University Press, 1997), 10.

18 H. Gerber, *State, Society, and Law in Islam* (Albany, NY: State University of New York Press, 1994), 130.

19 Gerber, *State, Society, and Law*, 135.
20 Gerber, *State, Society, and Law*, 130.
21 C. Fleischer, *Bureaucrat and Intellectual in the Ottoman Empire: The Historian Mustafa Ali (1541–1600)* (Princeton, NJ: Princeton University Press, 1986), 9.
22 Gerber, *State, Society and Law*, 135.
23 See H.W. Lowry, *Studies in Defterology: Ottoman Society in the Fifteenth and Sixteenth Centuries* (Istanbul: The Isis Press, 2008).
24 R.A. Abou al-Haj, "Formation of the Modern State: The Ottoman Empire, Sixteenth to Eighteenth Centuries," *Journal of Early Modern History* 14, no. 4 (2010): 317–54; C. Kafadar, *Between Two Worlds: The Construction of the Ottoman State* (San Francisco, CA: University of California Press, 1995).
25 Abou al-Haj, "Formation of the Modern State."
26 See: L. Peirce, *Morality Tales: Law and Gender in the Ottoman Court of Aintab* (Berkeley, CA: University of California Press, 2003); and S. Buzov, "The Lawgiver and His Lawmakers: The Role of Legal Discourse in the Change of Ottoman Imperial Culture" (PhD diss., University of Chicago, 2005).
27 Buzov, "The Lawgiver," 60.
28 Peirce, *Morality Tales*, 389.
29 Peirce, *Morality Tales*, 8.
30 B.A. Ergene, *Local Court, Provincial Society, and Justice in the Ottoman Empire* (Leiden: E.J. Brill, 2003), 211.
31 Buzov, "The Lawgiver," 140–43.
32 Buzov, "The Lawgiver," 143.
33 Buzov, "The Lawgiver," 2.
34 Buzov, "The Lawgiver," 143.
35 M.B. Wilson, "The Failure of Nomenclature: The Concept of Orthodoxy in the Study of Islam," *Comparative Islamic Studies* 3, no. 2 (2007): 169.
36 M. Winter, "Ottoman Occupation," 510. Many of his views are derived from Egyptian sources, described in another of his articles, "Attitudes toward the Ottomans in Egyptian Historiography during the Ottoman Rule," *The Great Ottoman-Turkish Civilization*, vol. 3, ed. K. Çiçek (Ankara: YeniTürkiye, 2000), 290–99.
37 M. Hodgson, *The Venture of Islam*, vol. 3 (Chicago, IL: Chicago University Press, 1961), 107.
38 H. Inalcik, *The Ottoman Empire: The Classical Age, 1300–1600*, trans. Norman Itzkowitz and Colin Imber (London: Weidenfeld and Nicolson, 1973), 16.
39 P. Wittek, "De la défaite d'Ankara à la prise de Constantinople: Un demi-siècle d'histoire ottomane," *REI* 12 (1938): 8–10.
40 R.P. Lindner, *Nomads and Ottomans in Medieval Anatolia*, 153, 155.
41 R.P. Lindner, "Stimulus and Justification in Early Ottoman History," *Greek Orthodox Theological Review* 27 (1982): 216.
42 Kafadar, *Between Two Worlds*, 52.
43 Kafadar, *Between Two Worlds*, 54.
44 I. Ataseven, *The Alevi-Bektasi Legacy: Problems of Acquisition and Explanation*, ed. T. Olsson (Lund, Sweden: Nova Press, 1997), p. 102.

45 See: B. Weis, *The Spirit of Islamic Law* (Athens, GA: University of Georgia Press, 1998); and *The Islamic School of Law: Evolution, Devolution, and Progress*, ed. P. Bearman, R. Peters, and F. Vogel (Cambridge, MA: Harvard University Press, 2006).
46 M. Hoexter argues that qadis brought about change by regulating the praxis of the community and creating an "established custom." This is exemplified in the case of the Ottoman cash *awqaf*, which were accepted by courts for over a century before their existence was discussed and authorized by Ottoman muftis in the mid-sixteenth century. Also, qadis worked together with rulers to create a judicial system with predictable legal outcomes. Rulers could, and did, issue decrees that required all qadis to follow a certain legal opinion, as was frequently done by Ottoman sultans with regard to the legal opinions of their chief muftis. M. Hoexter, "Qadi, Mufti, and Ruler: Their Roles in the Development of Islamic Law," in *Law, Custom, and Statute in the Muslim World: Studies in Honor of Aharon Layish*, ed. R. Shaham, Studies in Islamic Law and Society 28 (Leiden and Boston: Brill, 2007), 67–86.
47 J. Hathaway, "Egypt in the Seventeenth Century," 35.
48 See R. Repp, "Ottoman Developments of the Qanun and Shari'a," *International Journal of Turkish Studies* 24 (1988): 33–56.
49 D. Chakrabarty, *Provincializing Europe: Postcolonial Thought and Historical Difference* (Princeton, NJ: Princeton University Press, 2000), 7.
50 Chakrabarty, *Provincializing Europe*, 7.
51 Chakrabarty, *Provincializing Europe*, 8.
52 Chakrabarty, *Provincializing Europe*, 4.
53 E. Wallerstein, *The Modern World System: Capitalist Agriculture and the Origins of the European World Economy in the Sixteenth Century* (New York: Academic Press, 1974), 1–10.
54 Wallerstein, *The Modern World System*, xxiv.
55 J.L. Abu-Lughod, *Before European Hegemony: The World System A.D. 1250–1350* (Oxford, UK: Oxford University Press, 1991).
56 Abu-Lughod, *Before European Hegemony*, 20–39.
57 Abu-Lughod, *Before European Hegemony*, 286.
58 Looking backward, Abu-Lughod sees no "inherent historical necessity" (*Before European Hegemony*, 12) that the Europeans would later achieve global hegemony, arguing that the most likely candidate to achieve hegemony was China. Had China not experienced a major economic collapse in the middle of the fifteenth century and an ensuing massive shutdown of naval exploration and trade, it would likely have become a world economic core for many centuries to come.
59 Abu-Lughod, *Before European Hegemony*, 18. Because the Mongol Empire did not entail integrated production networks, Wallerstein says it was, instead, a vast trading network. Questioning the importance of 'integrated production networks,' Abu-Lughod identifies three traits common to any world system—the invention of money and credit, mechanisms for pooling capital and sharing risk, and the accretion of merchant wealth independent of the state.

Abu-Lughod points out that all three factors were present anywhere in the system where trade was active (*Before European Hegemony*, 15–17).
60 V.P. Pecora, *Secularization and Cultural Criticism: Religion, Nation, and Modernity* (Chicago, IL: University of Chicago Press, 2006), 5.
61 S. Mahmood, "Religious Reason and Secular Affect: An Incommensurable Divide?" in *Is Critique Secular? Blasphemy, Injury, and Free Speech*, ed. T. Asad, W. Brown, J. Butler, and S. Mahmood (Berkeley, CA: Townsend Center for the Humanities, University of California Press, 2009), 87.
62 C. Geertz, "Religion as a Cultural System," in *Anthropological Approaches to the Study of Religion*, ed. M. Banton (London: Tavistock, 1966), 1–46.
63 R. Bellah, *Beyond Belief: Essays on Religion in a Post-Traditional World* (Berkeley, CA: University of California Press, 1991), 153.
64 Bellah, *Beyond Belief*, 156.
65 In the field of sociology, see: D. Karel, "Secularization: A Multi-Dimensional Concept," *Current Sociology* 29, no. 2 (1981): 1–216; and D. Martin, *A General Theory of Secularization* (Oxford, UK: Blackwell, 1978).
66 P. Laslett, *The World We Have Lost* (London: Methuen, 1971), 74.
67 Laslett, *The World We Have Lost*, 39.
68 See: O. Kane, "Izala: The Rise of Muslim Reformism in Northern Nigeria," in *Accounting for Fundamentalisms*, ed. M.E. Marty and R.S. Appleby (Chicago, IL: University of Chicago Press, 1994), 490–512; and G.H. Singleton, *Religion in the City of Angels: American Protestant Culture and Urbanization* (Ann Arbor, MI: UMI Research Press, 1979).
69 P. Berger, *The Sacred Canopy: Elements of a Sociological Theory of Religion* (New York: Doubleday Press, 1967), 127.
70 Berger, *The Sacred Canopy*, 127.
71 Blumenberg defends the idea of infinite progress as the only valid moral heuristic in a secular world of "possessive individualism" ruled by private interests and historical contingency. H. Blumenberg, *The Legitimacy of the Modern Age*, trans. R.M. Wallace (Cambridge, MA: MIT Press, 1985), 35.
72 K. Löwith, *Meaning in History* (Chicago, IL: University of Chicago Press, 1949). A post-Holocaust, Second World War, and Stalinism writer, Löwith critiques the Enlightenment idea of progress, both as scientific and moral achievement, which he associates with Voltaire, Comte, Hegel, Marx, and others. Belief in a universal 'philosophy of history,' he argues, is a mimetic expression of 'theology of history,' as history of fulfillment and salvation.
73 Pecora, *Secularization*, 62–63.
74 J.C. Monod, *La querelle de la sécularisation de Hegel à Blumenberg*, Librairie Philosophique (Paris: J. Vrin, 2002), 23, quoted and translated in Pecora, *Secularization*, 5.
75 T. Asad, "Free Speech, Blasphemy, and Secular Criticism," in *Is Critique Secular? Blasphemy, Injury, and Free Speech*, ed. T. Asad, W. Brown, J. Butler, and S. Mahmood (Berkeley: Townsend Center for the Humanities, University of California Press, 2009), 22.
76 Pecora, *Secularization*, 47. E. Said fares no better in Pecora's esteem for being too uncritically accepting of the Enlightenment narrative, "too enamored of the idiom of the heroic individual, popular sovereignty, self-determination

and too willing to characterize this process as something increasingly less significant for the study of global culture from the eighteenth century onward." Foucault, on the other hand, challenged the Enlightenment's claims to clearer thinking, distinct ideas, and better evidence replacing superstition and tradition, but "only by obscuring the question of secularization" (Pecora, *Secularization*, 28). Foucault argued that the Enlightenment was not a product of 'disenchantment' but of a sudden shift in the grammar of our thinking. The Enlightenment was able to consolidate itself, not by defining reason against revelation, but against madness (Pecora, *Secularization*, 43). Combined, this has meant that Islamic studies and, more broadly, cultural studies, anthropology, and political science, have had little room to maneuver.
77 Pecora, *Secularization*, 47–48.
78 Asad, *Free Speech*, 36.
79 By the eighth century, Islamic thought had distinguished between sins and crimes, avoiding their conflation into a single conglomerate of legal offenses. The earliest theological debates (stemming from the question of 'who is a Muslim') led to the rise of the doctrine of *irja'*, or the suspension of judgment on the question of belief. By the end of the tenth century, Islamic society had forged degrees of separation between 'spiritual' and 'temporal' authority, as things separate, although by no means unrelated. See: F. Jad'an, *al-Mihnah: Bahth fi jadaliyat al-dini wa-l-siyasi fi al-Islam* (Amman: Dar al-Shuruq li-l-Nashr wa-l-Tawzi', 1989).
80 C. Imber, *Ebu's-Su'ud: The Islamic Legal Tradition* (Stanford, CA: Stanford University Press, 1997), 90.
81 J. Calvin, *Institutes of the Christian Religion*, trans. H. Beveridge (Grand Rapids, MI: Wm B. Eerdmans, 1989), ch. 20, p. 2.
82 G.I. Williamson, *The Westminster Confession of Faith*, 2nd ed. (Phillipsburg, NJ: P & R Publishing Company, 1950), ch. 23, p. 2.
83 See: P. Brown, *The Rise of Christendom*, 2nd ed. (Oxford, UK: Blackwell Publishing, 2003); and J.R. Curran, *Pagan City and Christian Capital: Rome in the Fourth Century* (Oxford, UK: Oxford University Press, 2000).
84 See: W. Gilbert, *Renaissance and Reformation* (Lawrence, KS: Carrie, 1998), ch. 14.
85 Calvin, *Institutes*, ch. 5, p. 8.
86 Figures such as Ibn Taymiya, a favorite of revivalist Islamists, considered the enforcement of *'ibadat* a duty incumbent on ruler and community alike. But his views were not only politically marginal, but politically seditious enough to warrant imprisonment.
87 Elyse Semerdjian, *Off the Straight Path: Illicit Sex, Law, and Community in Ottoman Aleppo* (Syracuse, NY: Syracuse University Press, 2008), 37.
88 Semerdjian, *Off the Straight Path*, 37. See also: Peirce, *Morality Tales*, 132–33, 187–208; and U. Heyd, *Studies in Old Ottoman Criminal Law*, ed. V.L. Menage (Oxford, UK: Clarendon Press, 1973). Relying on the juristic works of Ibrahim al-Halabi (d. 1549), *Multaqa a-Abhur*, and Sadiq ibn Muhammad al-Saqazi (d. 1688), Ibn Nujaym, and the early opinions of Abu Yusuf (d. 798), the Ottomans used the concept of judicial doubt *(shubha)* to abandon the physical punishments.

89 Even in the west, however, this has not been a monolithic process, as the debate on abortion, prostitution, and gay marriage and the absence of debate on polygamy makes clear. In all such cases, the link between sins and crimes remains unsevered.
90 R. Peters, "What Does It Mean to Be an Official *Madhhab*?" *The School of Islamic Law: Evolution, Devolution, and Progress*, ed. P. Bearman, R. Peters, and F. Vogel (Cambridge, MA: Harvard University Law Center, 2005), 157.
91 R. Hefner and M.Q. Zaman, *Schooling Islam: The Culture and Politics of Modern Muslim Education* (Princeton, NJ: Princeton University Press, 2007), 24.
92 H. Saleh, "Egypt Rapped on Gay Persecution," *BBC News*, 1 March 2004, http://news.bbc.co.uk/2/hi/middle_east/3522457.stm
93 Over time, as M. Fadel's study of the Maliki legal school shows, the process of consensus helped coalesce competing opinions into *madhhab*s, until each *madhhab* had more or less "whittled its rulings down" into a cohesive body of authoritative rules from which to derive rulings. Fadel describes this type of compilation, the *mukhtasar*, as "codified common law." M. Fadel, "Social Logic of *Taqlid* and the Rise of the *Mukhtasar*," *Islamic Law and Society* 3 (1996): 196, and "Adjudication in the Maliki *Madhhab*: A Study of Legal Process in Medieval Islam" (PhD diss., University of Chicago, 1995), 274, 283–84.
94 F. Vogel, "Closing of the Door of *Ijtihad* and the Application of the Law," *American Journal of Islamic Social Sciences* 10, no. 3 (Fall 1993): 399.
95 S. Jackson, *Islamic Law and the State: The Constitutional Jurisprudence of Shihab al-Din al-Qarafi* (Leiden: Brill, 1996).

Notes to Chapter 2
1 See G. Libson, *Jewish and Islamic Law: A Comparative Study of Custom during the Geonic Period* (Cambridge, MA: Harvard University Press, 2003); and G. Libson, "On the Development of Custom as a Source of Law in Islamic Law," *Islamic Law and Society* 4, no. 2 (June 1997): 13–24.
2 I.R. Netton, "Siyasa," in *EI*, CD-ROM edition.
3 This is a standard division in jurisprudential theory separating laws of ritual worship from laws governing relations between men. See the section "Custom in Islamic Legal Theory" in this chapter.
4 Netton, "Siyasa."
5 See F. Gabriel, "Adab," in *EI*, CD-ROM edition.
6 K.A. Reinhart, *Before Revelation: The Boundaries of Muslim Moral Thought* (Albany, NY: State University of New York Press, 1995), 5.
7 Reinhart, *Before Revelation*, 4.
8 K. Abou El Fadl, *Speaking in God's Name: Islamic Law, Authority and Women* (Oxford, UK: Oneworld Press, 2001), 247.
9 Reinhart, *Before Revelation*, 6.
10 Reinhart, *Before Revelation*, 6–7.
11 Reinhart, *Before Revelation*, 6–7.
12 "These higher-order/lower-order values did not just refer to the five values of sharia, but also to moral imperatives." Abu El Fadl, *Speaking in God's Name*, 247.

13 Reinhart, *Before Revelation*, 8.
14 K. Masud, *Islamic Legal Philosophy: A Study of Abu Ishaq al-Shatibi's Life and Thought* (Islamabad: Islamic Research Institute, 1977), 295.
15 T. Aquinas, "Whether There Is in Us a Natural Law," *Readings in Philosophy of Law*, ed. J. Arthur and W.H. Shaw (Englewood Cliffs, NJ: Prentice-Hall, 1984), 5.
16 Aquinas, "Whether There Is in Us a Natural Law," 12.
17 Aquinas, "Whether There Is in Us a Natural Law," 13.
18 For an introduction to the four sources of law in Islam, see: J. Schacht, *The Origins of Muhammadan Jurisprudence* (Oxford: Oxford University Press, 1950); and N.H. Coulson, *A History of Islamic Law* (Edinburgh: Edinburgh University Press, 1964).
19 Libson, "On the Development of Custom," 131–55.
20 The word *'urf* and its derivative, *ma'ruf*, occur in the Qur'an. The latter, occurring more frequently, is equated with the 'good' (and its opposite the *munkar*) rather than its literal meaning, 'what is known.' The Qur'an (7:199) commands, "Hold to forgiveness, command what is right *(ma'ruf)*; but turn away from the ignorant." For a fuller discussion on Qur'anic exegesis and custom, see: Samir 'Alia, *Al-Qada' wa-l-'urf fi-l-Islam* (Beirut: al-Mu'assasa al-Jami'iya li-l-Dirasat wa-l-Nashr wa-l-Tawzi', 1986), 172.
21 Libson, "On the Development of Custom," *Islamic Law and Society* 4, no. 2 (June 1997): 139.
22 Libson, "On the Development of Custom," 142.
23 B. Hakini, "The Role of 'Urf in Shaping the Islamic City," in *Islam and Public Law*, ed. C. Mallat (Boston: Graham and Trotman, 1994), 147.
24 Libson, "On the Development of Custom," 151.
25 Masud, *Islamic Legal Philosophy*, 197.
26 R. Paret argues that *maslaha*, as a technical legal term, is not used by Shafi'i or Malik (R. Paret, "Maslaha," in *EI*, CD-ROM edition). But Masud argues that this does not mean that concepts similar to *maslaha* were not in use. For example, Ghazali said that what is meant by *maslaha* is the preservation of the intent of the law, which consists of five things: preservation of religion, of life, of reason, of descendants, and of property (Paret, "Maslaha"). There are three types of *maslaha*: 1) that which is supported by textual evidence; 2) that which is denied by textual evidence (forbidden); and 3) that for which there exists no textual evidence for or against. The latter type is known as *al-maslaha al-mursala* and is controversial. Shafi'i and Maliki jurists accepted this category if it was deemed of absolute necessity (*daruri, qat'i,* and *kulli*). As an example of how this principle works, Shatibi considers a scenario in which enemy forces use Muslims as shields. If not firing for fear of killing the Muslim hostages means the entire Muslim population is overrun, then it is *maslaha* to fire, in contravention of the principle that holds Muslims may not kill other Muslims (Paret, "Maslaha"). If it did not meet the criterion of absolute necessity, it was more akin to *istislah* or *istihsan* (judicial preference), which he considered invalid. In sum, there are two positions: 1) theological determinism—all that God commands is *maslaha*; 2) methodological determinism, which linked *maslaha* with *qiyas*, to avoid its potential for arbitrariness (Paret, "Maslaha").

27　Masud, *Islamic Legal Philosophy*, 230.
28　Masud, *Islamic Legal Philosophy*, 295.
29　Examples include *diya* (compensation paid to victims of a crime), *qasama* (compurgation), gathering on the day of 'Aruba (ancient Arabic name for Friday) for sermons, and *qirad* (loan) (Masud, *Islamic Legal Philosophy*, 295.) There is also abundant evidence that a considerable portion of family law was preserved from pre-Islamic times, including the formula for repudiation of a wife and the *nikah* marriage contract. See: Leila Ahmed, *Women and Gender in Islam* (New Haven, CT: Yale University Press, 1992), 41–45; and Schacht, *The Origins of Muhammadan Jurisprudence*.
30　Libson, *Jewish and Islamic Law*, 70.
31　Quoted in Zayn al-Din ibn Ibrahim ibn Nujaym, *al-Ashbah wa-l-naza'ir* (Beirut: Dar al-Kutub al-'Ilmiya, 1983), 93.
32　Hakini, "The Role of 'Urf," 144.
33　Libson, "On the Development of Custom," 147.
34　U. Heyd, *Studies in Old Ottoman Criminal Law*, ed. V.L. Menage (Oxford, UK: Clarendon Press, 1973), 170.
35　*'Amal* becomes defined as judicial practice based in custom, *'urf* and *'adat* as customary practice. In Andalusia "there prevailed a tendency to require judges to follow the practice of Cordova" (J. Berque, "'Amal," in *EI*, CD-ROM edition.) *'Urf* and *'ada* assume much the same meaning, 'customary practice,' and eventually came to mean *siyasa* legislation. In Persia it was known as *'urf* and in Anatolia as *qanun* (G. H. Bousquet, "'Ada," in *EI*, CD-ROM edition.)
36　Heyd, *Studies in Old Ottoman Criminal Law*, 168.
37　Heyd, *Studies in Old Ottoman Criminal Law*, 168.
38　Heyd, *Studies in Old Ottoman Criminal Law*, 169.
39　"The term 'örf ('urf), which originally meant 'common usage' and in Ottoman law often has the restricted sense of 'torture,' is used, it seems, as a synonym of kanun." Heyd, *Studies in Old Ottoman Criminal Law*, 169.
40　Heyd, *Studies in Old Ottoman Criminal Law*, 168.
41　C. Fleischer, *Bureaucrat and Intellectual in the Ottoman Empire: The Historian Mustafa Ali (1541–1600)* (Princeton, NJ: Princeton University Press, 1986), 54.
42　In general, jurists delegated all substantive criminal law to the secular authorities' discretion *(ta'zir)*. C. Imber, *Ebu's-Su'ud: The Islamic Legal Tradition* (Stanford, CA: Stanford University Press, 1997), 89.
43　Imber, *Ebu's-Su'ud*, 90.
44　In the Abbasid period, so-called secular courts (referred to as *mazalim* or *siyasa*) were established early on. See: M.H. Kamali, *Principles of Islamic Jurisprudence* (Cambridge, UK: The Islamic Texts Society, 2000), 368; and J. Nielsen, *Secular Justice in an Islamic State: Mazalim under the Bahri Mamluks* (Leiden: Nederland Historisch-Archaeologisch Instituut te Istanbul, 1985).
45　"The Turks called it Türe and the Mongols called it *Yasa*." Netton, "Siyasa," in *EI*, CD-ROM edition. Also see: D. Ayalon, "The Great Yasa of Chingiz Khan," *SI* 33 (1971): 1–15; Nielsen, *Secular Justice in an Islamic State*, 104–109; and D.O. Morgan, "The Great Yasa of Chingiz Khan and Mongol Law in the Ilkhanate," *BSOAS* 49 (1986): 163–76.

46 Ibn Taymiya objected that to argue on the basis of absolute utility (*al-maslaha al-mursala*) "is to legislate in matters of religion," as ultimately, all given *maslaha* is already found in Muslim scripture (Masud, *Islamic Legal Philosophy*, 163). But "in his analysis of the sharia definition of *maslaha*," Shatibi observed that the sharia had regularized as legal good what was considered good in the social experience (Masud, *Islamic Legal Philosophy*, 217). Sharia obligations fall under preventive and positive rules. Positive rules are *'ibadat*, *'adat*, and *mu'amalat*. Preventive rules are *jinayat* (penalties). At the other extreme, Najm al-Din al-Tufi (d. 1316) justified the use of *maslaha* to the extent of setting aside the text and argued that it prevailed over all other methods and principles (Masud, *Islamic Legal Philosophy*, 165).
47 Masud, *Islamic Legal Philosophy*, 295.
48 Masud, *Islamic Legal Philosophy*, 137.
49 *'Ibadat* protect *din*, and *'adat* protect the *nafs* and *'aql*. *Mu'amalat* also protect the *nafs* and *'aql* but through *'adat* (Masud, *Islamic Legal Philosophy*, 226).
50 To know the intent of the law, one must study *'ada* in combination with the principles inductively derived from sharia (Masud, *Islamic Legal Philosophy*, 321).
51 Masud, *Islamic Legal Philosophy*, 295.
52 Shatibi was opposed to the practices of the *fuqaha'* rather than the Sufis, including reading the *khutba* in the sultan's name and praying for him at the end of the ritual prayers. On this issue he was opposed by all the *qadi*s in Spain and North Africa as well as by political figures (Masud, *Islamic Legal Philosophy*, 105). The reason he forbade innovation in religious ritual was that "they imposed certain practices as religious obligations, whereas the right of imposing such an obligation belongs only to God" (Masud, *Islamic Legal Philosophy*, 122).
53 'Alia, *al-Qada' wa-l-'urf fi-l-Islam*, 143–44.
54 Masud, *Islamic Legal Philosophy*, 271.
55 Masud, *Islamic Legal Philosophy*, 271.
56 Some *'awa'id* are either introduced or sanctioned by sharia, hence called *al-'awa'id al-shar'iya*. Others are current in the practice of the people, hence called *al-'awa'id al-jariya*. Sharia does not oppose *al-'awa'id al-jariya*, "it shows a constant regard for them." Still others, *al-'awa'id al-mutabiddala*, are replaced by customs from elsewhere (Masud, *Islamic Legal Philosophy*, 271).
57 Masud, *Islamic Legal Philosophy*, 294.
58 Ibn Nujaym, *al-Ashbah wa-l-naza'ir*, 137.
59 Furthermore, no divorce or marriage would be ratified outside of one of the four chief judges' courts. Muhammad ibn Ahmad ibn Iyas, *Bada'i' al-zuhur fi waqa'i' al-duhur*, ed. Muhammad Mustafa, vol. 5 (Weisbaden: E.J. Brill, 1975), 417.
60 Ibn Iyas, *Bada'i' al-zuhur*, 418.
61 Ibn Iyas, *Bada'i' al-zuhur*, 427.
62 Ibn Iyas, *Bada'i' al-zuhur*, 427.
63 M. Winter, *Society and Religion in Early Ottoman Egypt: Studies in the Writings of 'Abd al-Wahhab al-Sha'rani* (New Brunswick, NJ: Transaction Books, 1982), 243. Sha'rani commends Fakhr al-Din al-Sunbati, who

abdicated his position as qadi when he learned that judges would be required to enforce *qanun*. He retired to his village, where he heard cases free of charge as a *fard kifaya* (communal religious obligation) (Winter, *Society and Religion*, 244).

64 Using the case of weights and measurements, Ibn Nujaym argues that a general ruling cannot be made on the basis of a local custom (Ibn Nujaym, *al-Ashbah*, 102.) For example, he defends the position that local Egyptian custom, in the case of the *khilliw* (down payment) for renting shops in the Egyptian market, is a right of the owner because he no longer possesses the power to evict the tenant (Ibn Nujaym, *al-Ashbah*, 103).

65 Ibn Nujaym, *al-Ashbah*, 103. For a fuller discussion, see chapter four.

66 Ibn Nujaym, *al-Ashbah*, 95.

67 According to al-Zayla'i, oaths are governed by linguistic *'urf* (local dialect), not by linguistic *haqa'iq* (literal meaning). Thus, if an oath to abstain from eating meat is given, it is custom that defines what is meant by 'meat.' If liver and stomach count as meat in a given locale, then they are included in the oath (Ibn Nujaym, *al-Ashbah*, 98).

68 Winter, *Society and Religion*, 243.

69 M. Winter, *Egyptian Society under Ottoman Rule, 1517–1798* (New York: Routledge, 1992), 11.

70 R. Repp, "*Qanun* and Shari'a in the Ottoman Context," in *Islamic Law: Social and Historical Contexts*, ed. A. al-Azmeh (London: Routledge, 1988), 128.

71 H. Inalcik, "Sulayman the Lawgiver and Ottoman Law," *Archivum Ottomanicum* 1 (1969): 112.

72 Heyd, *Studies in Old Ottoman Criminal Law*, 169.

73 Mahkamat al-Bab al-'Ali, *Sijill* 124, Doc. 68.

74 Heyd, *Studies in Old Ottoman Criminal Law*, 169.

75 Imber, *Ebu's-Su'ud*, 98. Also see M. Kunt and C. Woodhead, eds., *Sulayman the Magnificent and His Age: The Ottoman Empire in the Early Modern World* (London: Longman, 1995).

76 Imber, *Ebu's-Su'ud*, 8–20.

77 Imber, *Ebu's-Su'ud*, 104.

78 Imber, *Ebu's-Su'ud*, 104–106.

79 Imber, *Ebu's-Su'ud*, 106.

80 M. Hodgson, *The Venture of Islam*, vol. 3 (Chicago, IL: University of Chicago Press, 1961), 108, fn. 6.

81 Imber, *Ebu's-Su'ud*, 106–10.

82 These conditions include rural depopulation and urban growth, massive inflation, high taxation, swollen and inefficient central government, warfare, epidemics, and chronic food shortages. J. Hathaway, "Egypt in the Seventeenth Century," in *The Cambridge History of Egypt*, vol. 2, ed. C.F. Petrie and W.M. Daly (Cambridge, UK: Cambridge University Press, 1998), 35; and M. Zilfi, *The Politics of Piety: The Ottoman Ulema in the Postclassical Age (1600–1800)* (Minneapolis, MN: Bibliotheca Islamica, 1998), 30–31. Also see: P.M. Holt, "The Later Ottoman Empire in Egypt and the Fertile Crescent," in *The Cambridge History of Islam*, vol. 1A, ed. P.M. Holt, A.K.S. Lambton,

and B. Lewis (Cambridge, UK: Cambridge University Press, 1970), 374–93; H. Inalcik and D. Quataert, eds., *Economic and Social History of the Ottoman Empire, 1300–1914* (Cambridge, UK: Cambridge University Press, 1994), 413–14, 468–70, 572–73; D.A. Howard, "Ottoman Historiography and the Literature of 'Decline' of the Sixteenth and Seventeenth Centuries," *Journal of Asian History* 22 (1988): 52–77; H. Inalcik, *The Ottoman Empire: The Classical Age, 1300–1600*, trans. N. Itzkowitz and C. Imber (London: Weidenfeld and Nicolson, 1973); Inalcik, "Sulayman the Lawgiver and Ottoman Law," 105–38; and Heyd, *Studies in Old Ottoman Criminal Law*.

83 A. Black, *The History of Islamic Political Thought* (New York: Routledge, 2001), 216.
84 Heyd, *Studies in Old Ottoman Criminal Law*, 169–70.
85 Black, *History of Islamic Political Thought*, 216.
86 Heyd, *Studies in Old Ottoman Law*, 170.
87 M. Plessner, "Namus," in *EI*, CD-ROM edition.
88 Plessner, "Namus."
89 E.I.J. Rosenthal, *Political Thought in Medieval Islam: An Introductory Outline* (Cambridge, UK: Cambridge University Press, 1968), 145.
90 Rosenthal, *Political Thought in Medieval Islam*, 212.
91 Rosenthal, *Political Thought in Medieval Islam*, 213.
92 See A.K.S. Lambton, "Al-Dawani," in *EI*, CD-ROM ed.
93 Jalal al-Din al-Dawani, "Akhlaq-i Jalali," in *Practical Philosophy of the Muhammedan People*, trans. W.T. Thompson (London, 1839), 127–28, 322–23.
94 al-Dawani, "Akhlaq-i Jalali," 324–25, 372–79.
95 al-Dawani, "Akhlaq-i Jalali," 59–60, 345–79.
96 M. Arkoun, "Insaf," *EI* (CD-ROM edition).
97 M. Arkoun, "Insaf."
98 al-Dawani, "Akhlaq-i Jalali," 379–81.
99 Black, *History of Islamic Political Thought*, 217.
100 Black, *History of Islamic Political Thought*, 217.
101 The work in question is Lütfi Pasha, *Tevârih-i 'Al-i Osman*, ed. Ali (Istanbul, 1922). It is cited in L. Peirce, *The Imperial Harem: Women and Sovereignty in the Ottoman Empire* (New York: Oxford University Press, 1993), 161; H.A.R. Gibb, "Lutfi Pasha on the Ottoman Caliphate," *Oriens* 15 (1962): 290, 294; and Imber, "Sulayman as Caliph of the Muslims," 179–80.
102 Black, *History of Islamic Political Thought*, 217.
103 Peirce, *The Imperial Harem*, 160.
104 Peirce, *The Imperial Harem*, 161.
105 Muhyi al-Din ibn al-'Arabi, *Fusus al-hikam (The Bezels of Wisdom)*, ed. and trans. R.W.J. Austin (New York: Paulist Press, 1980), 132. For secondary writings, see: W.C. Chittick, *The Sufi Path of Knowledge: Ibn al-'Arabi's Metaphysics of Imagination* (Albany, NY: State University of New York Press, 1989); H. Corbin, *L'Imagination créatrice dans le soufisme de Ibn Arabi* (Paris: Entrelacs, 2006); and D.A. Knysh, *Ibn al-'Arabi in the Later Islamic Tradition: The Making of a Polemical Image in Islam* (Albany, NY: State University of New York Press, 1999).

106 Intoxication *(sukr)* and Sobriety *(sahw)* in Sufism, as described here, have been noted since J.S. Trimingham's seminal work, *The Sufi Orders in Islam* (Oxford: Clarendon Press, 1971).
107 See: B.G. Martin, "A Short History of Khalwati Order of Dervishes," in *Scholars, Saints, and Sufis*, ed. N.R. Keddie (Berkeley, CA: University of California Press, 1978); L. Garnett, *The Dervishes of Turkey* (London: Octagon Press, 1990); and D. Le Gall, *A Culture of Sufism: Naqshbandis in the Ottoman World, 1450–1700* (Albany, NY: State University of New York Press, 2005).
108 Nur al-Din al-Jami, *al-Durra al-fakhira (The Precious Pearl)*, trans. N. Heer (Albany: State University of New York Press, 1979), 62–63. For the political implications of a "created" Qur'an in the Mihna, see J.A. Nawas, "A Re-examination of Three Current Explanations for al-Mamun's Introduction of the Mihna," *IJMES* 26, no. 4 (1994): 615–29.
109 Hodgson, *The Venture of Islam*, vol. 3, 27–33.
110 C. Fleischer, "The Lawgiver as Messiah: The Making of the Imperial Image in the Reign of Süleyman," in *Soliman le magnifique et son temps*, ed. G. Veinstein (Paris: La Documentation française, 1992), 159–83.
111 S. Buzov, "The Lawgiver and His Lawmakers: The Role of Legal Discourse in the Change of Ottoman Imperial Culture" (PhD diss., University of Chicago, 2005), 60.
112 Much has been written on this subject, a recent and insightful account of which can be read in B.H. Auer, *Symbols of Authority in Medieval Islam: History, Religion, and Muslim Legitimacy in the Delhi Sultanate* (London: I.B.Tauris, 2012).
113 See M.S. Siddiqi, *The Bahmani Sufis* (Delhi: Idarah-i Adabiyat-i Delli, 1989).
114 When Sidi 'Ali is questioned about the legitimacy of the Ottomans' name in the *khutba*, he explains that Sulayman alone has the "right of *khutba*," attaching the distinction to his "universal" rule. Sidi 'Ali Reis, "*Mir'at al-Memalik*," in *The Sacred Books and Early Literature of the East*, vol. 4, ed. Charles F. Horne (New York: Parke, Austin, and Lipscomb, 1917), 362.
115 Sidi 'Ali Reis, "*Mir'at al-Memalik*," 345, 349. The translation is from Giancarlo Casale, *The Ottoman Age of Exploration* (New York: Oxford University Press, 2010), 121–22.
116 Casale, *The Ottoman Age of Exploration*, 123.
117 Husayn ibn Muhammad al-Damiri, *Qudat Misr fi-l-qarn al-'ashir wa awa'il al-qarn al-hadi 'ashir*, MS (Cairo: Dar al-Kutub), 232.
118 Winter, *Society and Religion*, 245.
119 J. Nielsen, "Mazalim," *Encyclopaedia of Islam*, 2nd ed., vol. 7 (Leiden: E.J. Brill, 1997), 933.
120 Ali ibn Muhammad al-Mawardi, *The Ordinances of Government: A Translation of* al-Ahkam al-sultaniyya wa al-wilayat al-diniyya, trans. Wafaa H. Wahba (Reading, UK: Garnet, 1996), 87; al-Mawardi, *al-Ahkam al-sultaniya*, ed. 'Abd al-Rahman 'Umayra (Cairo, 1994), 1:194.
121 A. Fuess, "*Zulm* by *Mazalim*? The Political Implications of the Use of *Mazalim* Jurisdiction by the Mamluk Sultans," *Mamluk Studies Review* 13, no. 1 (2009): 125.

Notes to Chapter 3

1. See H. Gerber, "Sharia, Kanun and Custom in the Ottoman Law: The Court Records of Seventeenth-century Bursa," *International Journal of Turkish Studies* 21 (1981): 131–47.
2. A. Marcus, "The Middle East on the Eve of Modernity: Aleppo in the Eighteenth Century," *JESHO* 26 (1983): 104–105.
3. N. Hanna, "The Administration of Courts in Ottoman Cairo," in *The State and Its Servants: Administration in Egypt from Ottoman Times to the Present*, ed. N. Hanna (Cairo: American University in Cairo Press, 1995), 52.
4. S. Har-El, *Struggle for Domination in the Middle East: The Ottoman–Mamluk War, 1485–91* (Leiden: E.J. Brill, 1995), 98.
5. S. Faroqhi, *Towns and Townsmen of Ottoman Anatolia: Trade, Crafts, and Food Production in an Urban Setting, 1520–1650* (New York: Cambridge University Press, 1984), 1.
6. Faroqhi, *Towns and Townsmen of Ottoman Anatolia*, 1.
7. See: J.L. Barkan and M.A. Cook, "The Price Revolution of the Sixteenth Century: A Turning Point in the Economic History of the Near East," *IJMES* 6 (1975): 3–28; L. Barkan, "La 'Méditerranée' de Fernand Braudel vue d'Istamboul," *Annales Economies, Sociétés, Civilisations* 9 (1954): 189–200; M. Zilfi, *The Politics of Piety: The Ottoman Ulema in the Postclassical Age (1600–1800)* (Minneapolis, MN: Bibliotheca Islamica, 1988); A. Raymond, "The Ottoman Conquest and Development of the Great Arab Towns," in *Arab Cities in the Ottoman Period*, ed. A. Raymond (Ashgate, UK: Variorum, 2002), 84–101; J. Hathaway, "Egypt in the Seventeenth Century," in *The Cambridge History of Egypt*, vol. 2, ed. C.F. Petry and W.M. Daly (Cambridge, UK: Cambridge University Press, 1998), 34–58; Faroqhi, *Towns and Townsmen*; N. Hanna, "The Chronicles of Ottoman Egypt: History or Entertainment?" in *The Historiography of Islamic Egypt*, ed. H. Kennedy (Leiden: E.J. Brill, 2001), and *Money, Land, and Trade: An Economic History of the Muslim Mediterranean* (Strasbourg: European Science Foundation, 2002); and H. Inalcik and D. Quataert, eds., *Economic and Social History of the Ottoman Empire, 1300–1914* (Cambridge, UK: Cambridge University Press, 1994).
8. Faroqhi, *Towns and Townsmen*, 2.
9. Raymond, "The Ottoman Conquest," 18.
10. Sauvaget, "Esquisse," 468, quoted in Raymond, "The Ottoman Conquest," 7.
11. As early as the sixteenth century, coffee appears as the new trade commodity during this period, exceeding "the volume of the spice trade which had preceded it" (Raymond, "The Ottoman Conquest," 19). First introduced in the early sixteenth century, coffee would become a vital component of economic recovery and, as shown in chapter five, of religious debate. This is but one example of how the interempire economy was also generating an interempire cultural/judicial discourse. Another example was the Hajj, which became an event of major cultural and economic import. This "brisk commercial activity . . . resulted in a spectacular growth of the economic substructures of some of the biggest Arab towns of the Empire" (Raymond, "The Ottoman Conquest," 23).

12 Raymond, "The Ottoman Conquest," 23. Raymond concludes, "We do not see any inconsistency between material development of the cities and the cultural apathy which, no doubt, characterized the Arab world at that time" (Raymond, "The Ottoman Conquest," 31). This assessment is shared by M. Winter, who characterizes the period as intellectually 'lethargic' (M. Winter, *Society and Religion in Early Ottoman Egypt: Studies in the Writings of 'Abd al-Wahhab al-Sha'rani* (London: Transaction Books, 1982), 1). One of the sources of the thesis of cultural decline originates in the disparaging comparisons made between Mamluk and Ottoman historiography. The latter is characterized as the culmination of a 'high literary' tradition, while the former is dismissed "because it is in decline." Conceding that great differences exist between the two literary traditions, Hanna has questioned the social function represented by each historical tradition to posit an innovative hypothesis. Ottoman Egyptian chronicles are written in a simplified vernacular because "a process of popularization of historical works" was underway, a direct consequence of the expanding market forces described above. An expanding consumer class and rising literacy rates, she conjectures, were generating a demand for intellectual as well as material commodities. She writes, "A wide market in fact existed outside the framework of educational institutions, in the private homes of people. This is confirmed by the court records, notably those of the courts of the *Qisma 'Askeriyya* and *Qisma 'Arabiyya*, where the property of deceased persons was divided amongst their heirs" (N. Hanna, "The Chronicles of Ottoman Egypt," 237, 241).
13 Hanna, "Administration," 47.
14 Hanna, "Administration," 49.
15 M. Winter, "The Ottoman Occupation," in *The Cambridge History of Egypt*, vol. 1, ed. C.F. Petry and W.M. Daly (Cambridge, UK: Cambridge University Press, 1998), 510.
16 Winter, "The Ottoman Occupation," 509.
17 M. Winter, "Ottoman Egypt, 1525–1609," in *The Cambridge History of Egypt*, vol. 2, ed. W.M. Daly (Cambridge, UK: Cambridge University Press, 1998), 24, 27.
18 M. Winter, "Attitudes toward the Ottomans in Egyptian Historiography during the Ottoman Rule," in *The Historiography of Islamic Egypt* (Leiden: Brill, 2001), 209.
19 Hanna, "Administration," 48.
20 Hanna, "Administration," 48.
21 Muhammad ibn Ahmad ibn Iyas, *Bada'i' al-zuhur fi waqa'i' al-duhur*, ed. Muhammad Mustafa, vol. 5 (Wiesbaden: E.J. Brill, 1975), 184, 187.
22 Husayn ibn Muhammad al-Damiri, *Qudat Misr fi-l-qarn al-'ashir wa awa'il al-qarn al-hadi 'ashir*, MS (Cairo: Dar al-Kutub), 18.
23 al-Damiri, *Qudat Misr*, 93.
24 This occurred under the auspices of Governor Muhammad Pasha. See: Shaykh al-Islam Muhammad ibn al-Surur al-Bakri al-Siddiqi, *al-Nuzha al-zahiya fi dhikr wulat Misr wa-l-Qahira wa-l-mu'izziya*, ed. 'Abd al-Razzaq 'Abd al-Razzaq 'Isa (Cairo: al-'Arabi li-l-Nashr wa-l-Tawzi', 1998), 181.

25 H. Gerber, *State, Society, and Law in Islam* (Albany, NY: State University of New York Press, 1994), 130.
26 Gerber, *State, Society, and Law*, 135.
27 Gerber, *State, Society, and Law*, 130.
28 Writing in the 1950s, Hodgson set forth the paradigm that "it was only in the nuclear provinces of [Anatolia and Rumelia] that the distinctive Ottoman institutions were fully developed." In these areas, "not only were diverse heritages effectively integrated; this integration was embodied in numerous interdependent institutions locally established and hallowed by custom." M. Hodgson, *The Venture of Islam*, vol. 3 (Chicago, IL: University of Chicago Press, 1961), 106.
29 Winter, "Ottoman Egypt, 1525–1609," 11, 13.
30 Winter, "The Ottoman Occupation," 507.
31 P. M. Holt, *Egypt and the Fertile Crescent* (Ithaca, NY: Cornell University Press, 1966), 73, 85, 90–92.
32 Hathaway, "Egypt in the Seventeenth Century," 42.
33 D. Ayalon, "Studies in al-Jabarti: I. Notes on the Transformation of Mamluk Society in Egypt under the Ottomans," in *Studies on the Mamluks of Egypt* (London: Variorum Reprints, 1977), 152.
34 Ayalon, "Studies in al-Jabarti," 152. Also see D. Ayalon, "Studies on the Structure of the Mamluk Army," *BSOAS* 15, no. 1 (1953): 203–28.
35 Gerber, *State, Society and Law*, 20, 21.
36 C. Imber, *Ebu's-Su'ud: The Islamic Legal Tradition* (Stanford, CA: Stanford University Press, 1997), 45.
37 Imber, *Ebu's-Su'ud*, 58. Also see: R. Repp, "Ottoman Developments of the Qanun and the Shari'a," *International Journal of Turkish Studies* 24 (1988): 33–56, and "Qanun and Shari'a in the Ottoman Context," in *Islamic Law: Social and Historical Contexts*, ed. A. al-Azmeh (London: Routledge, 1988), 125–43. Building on Barkan's thesis, Repp argues that this occurred when the cooption of the ulama into the state system rendered them willing to work "with the secular government for the common good" (Repp, "Qanun," 131).
38 Imber, *Ebu's-Su'ud*, 104.
39 Massive inflation, due to an influx of Spanish-American silver, led to a debasement of the aqçe (Ottoman silver currency) and delayed the payment of troop salaries. (See Hathaway, "Egypt in the Seventeenth Century," 34–69.) In Anatolia itself, writes Zilfi, "debilitating warfare, rural depopulation, urban pressure, epidemics, inflation, capricious execution, a swollen and erratically paid central government, high taxation and chronic food shortages" were the order of the day. The empire's course of continuous territorial expansion (from the mid-fifteenth century through to the late sixteenth century) had ground to a halt (Zilfi, *The Politics of Piety*, 30–31). See also: P.M. Holt, "The Later Ottoman Empire in Egypt and the Fertile Crescent," in *The Cambridge History of Islam*, vol. 1A, ed. P.M. Holt, A.K.S. Lambton, and B. Lewis (Cambridge, UK: Cambridge University Press, 1970), 374–93; Faroqhi, *Town and Townsmen of Ottoman Anatolia*, 1–8; Inalcik and Quataert, *Economic and Social History of the Ottoman Empire*, part

2, 413–14, 468–70, 572–73; and D.A. Howard, "Ottoman Historiography and the Literature of 'Decline' of the Sixteenth and Seventeenth Centuries," *Journal of Asian History* 22 (1988): 52–77.

40 Hathaway, "Egypt in the Seventeenth Century," 35. Also see: L. Barkan, *Kanunlar* (Istanbul: Burhaneddin Matbaası, 1943), 350–54; H. Inalcik, *The Ottoman Empire: The Classical Age, 1300–1600*, trans. N. Itzkowitz and C. Imber (London: Weidenfeld and Nicolson, 1973) and "Sulayman the Lawgiver and Ottoman Law," *Archivium Ottomanicum* 1 (1969): 105–38; and U. Heyd, *Studies in Old Ottoman Criminal Law*, ed. V.L. Menage (Oxford, UK: Clarendon Press, 1973).

41 Imber, *Ebu's-Su'ud*, 104.

42 C. Fleischer, "The Lawgiver as Messiah: The Making of the Imperial Image in the Reign of Süleyman," in *Soliman le magnifique et son temps*, ed. G. Veinstein (Paris: La Documentation française, 1992), 159.

43 S. Buzov, "The Lawgiver and His Lawmakers: The Role of Legal Discourse in the Change of Ottoman Imperial Culture" (PhD diss., University of Chicago, 2005), 60.

44 Buzov, "The Lawgiver," 140–43.

45 Buzov, "The Lawgiver," 143.

46 Buzov, "The Lawgiver," 2.

47 Winter, "Ottoman Egypt, 1525–1609," 6.

48 R.A. Abou al-Haj, "Aspects of the Legitimation of Ottoman Rule as Reflected in the Preambles to Two Early Liva Kanunnameler," *Turcica* 21–22 (1991): 373. Suggesting that Islam was but one of three sources of political inspiration, C. Kafadar writes that Ottoman sultans used three titles interchangeably—'khan,' 'caliph,' and 'emperor.' See: C. Kafadar, *Between Two Worlds: The Construction of the Ottoman State* (San Francisco, CA: University of California Press, 1995).

49 Imber, *Ebu's-Su'ud*, 47.

50 Buzov, *The Lawgiver*, 143.

51 D. Behrens-Abouseif, *Egypt's Adjustment to Ottoman Rule: Institutions, Waqfs, and Architecture in Cairo—16th and 17th Centuries* (Leiden: E.J. Brill, 1994), 70.

52 D. Sourdel, "Khalifa," in *EI*, CD-ROM edition.

53 The tripartite schism which developed after the first *fitna* in 650–51 between Mu'awiya and 'Ali was the first incident to shake the classical legal assumption that a universal caliphate existed and held dominion over a unified state. The second was the Abbasid revolution of 750, which one might argue was the culmination of the *fitna* of 650. The Abbasid state's claim to universal sovereignty was challenged by the birth of the Umayyad state in Spain in 756. By the ninth century, the Tahirid dynasty (822–73) had established its political dominion over the Iranian highlands and northeast lands. In Egypt, the Tulunids (868–905) ruled autonomously, while in the Maghrib the Shi'a Idrisids (788–974) ruled from Fez and the Aghlabids (801–909) ruled from Qayrawan. Hodgson, *The Venture of Islam*, vol. 1, 489.

54 Har-El, *Struggle for Domination*, 11.

55 Har-El, *Struggle for Domination*, 10.

56 Har-El, *Struggle for Domination*, 10–11.

57 K. Jindan, "The Islamic Theory of Government according to Ibn Taymiyya" (PhD dissertation, Georgetown University, 1979), 40–47.
58 The vehicle for the transmission of legal knowledge, from its inception in theory to its assimilation in practice, is the legal response, or fatwa. The fatwa is a figurative bridge between the law and society, the road by which theoretical constructs find application in juristic practice. See: M.K. Masud, B. Messick, and D. Powers, eds., *Islamic Legal Interpretation: Muftis and Their Fatwas* (Cambridge, UK: Harvard University Press, 1996). That *ifta'* was an instrument of state policy is attested to in one of several criticisms made of Bayezid I's grand vizier by "Ašikpašazade," who complains of "those who came and made the fetva an instrument of trickery and did away with piety" (R. Repp, *The Mufti of Istanbul: A Study in the Development of the Ottoman Learned Hierarchy* (London: Ithaca Press, 1986), 114).
59 Har-El, *Struggle for Domination*, 11.
60 Har-El, *Struggle for Domination*, 11.
61 Repp, *The Mufti of Istanbul*, 114.
62 Sultan Orhan is reported to have asked Taj al-Din Kurdi for a fatwa on the legality of breaking an agreement over booty made with one of his commanders (Repp, *The Mufti of Istanbul*, 112).
63 The Ottomans claimed to be the rightful heirs to the Seljuk dynasty and invented a genealogy which traced their ancestry to Noah and to Oghuz Khan, "the legendary ancestor of the western Turkish peoples" (Imber, *Ebu's-Su'ud*, 73). Between 1512 and 1520, Salim fought the Safavids as declared 'heretics' (Imber, *Ebu's-Su'ud*, 74).
64 Mustafa 'Ali, "Künhü al-Ahbar," in *Pure Water for Thirsty Muslims: A Study of Mustafa Ali of Gallipoli's* Künhü al-Ahbar, trans. and ed. Jan Schmidt (Leiden: Het Oosters Instituut, 1991), 230.
65 Har-El, *Struggle for Domination*, 3.
66 A crisis of legitimation was fueled during and after the battle of Ankara in 1402 when Sultan Bayezid's troops deserted on the battlefield. His critics levied severe accusations against him (P. Wittek, "De la défaite d'Ankara à la prise de Constantinople," *REI* (1938): 8–10). So long as the Ottoman state had limited itself to the jihad in *dar al-harb*, Egyptian ulama, with the consent of the Mamluk sultans, routinely issued Ottoman sultans fatwas authorizing their jihad. In the late fifteenth century, however, alarmed by the Ottoman state's expansion into Muslim territories, Egyptian scholars refused to issue further fatwas. When Mehmed annexed the Muslim Turcoman principality of Isfendiyar (Kastamonu) in 1461, relations between the two Sunni giants became openly hostile (Har-El, *Struggle for Domination*, 79).
67 Repp, *The Mufti of Istanbul*, 214.
68 'Ali, "Künhü al-Ahbar," 313.
69 Repp, *The Mufti of Istanbul*, 215.
70 Repp, *The Mufti of Istanbul*, 112.
71 Har-El, *Struggle for Domination*, 206.
72 Har-El, *Struggle for Domination*, 206.
73 C. Imber, *Studies in Ottoman History and Law* (Istanbul: Isis University Press, 1996), 122.

74 Al-Ghuri was unpopular in Egypt, making Salim's task of vilifying the Mamluk regime somewhat easy. "In Ghuri's state, we witnessed strange things and bore more than we had the capacity to bear. And enough transpired in our [last] year from lack of security and highway robbery" (Ibn Iyas, *Bada'i' al-zuhur*, 14).

75 Mamluks dressed in Ottoman military garb were accused of imperiling the Ottoman army's reputation by robbing traveling merchants and harassing the general populace (Ibn Iyas, *Bada'i' al-zuhur*, 213).

76 Winter, "The Ottoman Occupation," 511–12.

77 The *amir*s were forbidden from having servants walk, or ride behind them on a mule, when they rode horseback through the streets. Instead the servant was to walk in front of his Mamluk master "according to Ottoman custom" (Winter, "The Ottoman Occupation," 512). The shock which Ibn Iyas expresses at the easy informality with which Ottoman soldiers carried themselves suggests to Winter that Ottoman military *adab* was a marked departure from Mamluk *adab*. "Egyptians were displeased by the apparently egalitarian spirit in the Ottoman army" (Winter, "The Ottoman Occupation," 505). Ayalon writes that it would have been inconceivable in the Mamluk army for a Mamluk to ride mounted from his patron's house alone, to marry, to enter business, and so on. However, in the Ottoman period, Mamluks married, acquired houses and servants of their own, rode horses, and had the temerity to smoke on their rides in the main streets. Other trends that hint at a breakdown in the rigid hierarchy of the army include a Mamluk riding to his patron's house on hearing that a notable had died, to ask for the widow's hand. Patrons seemingly accommodated such requests, and would accompany the Mamluk "to the house of the deceased even before the funeral" (Ayalon, "Studies in al-Jabarti," 160–61).

78 Ibn Iyas, *Bada'i' al-zuhur*, 208.

79 While this may have been the case for Mamluk and Ottoman soldiery, it was less true for recruits (*wafida*) from among the *awlad al-'Arab*, who were brought into the seven corps (*ojaqat*) of the Ottoman garrison in high numbers toward the end of the century. Bucking the trend, members of the *ojaq*s tried to prevent *awlad al-'Arab* from entering the army and from wearing "Rumi" clothing, even resorting to murder (Ayalon, "Studies in al-Jabarti," 318).

80 Ibn Iyas, *Bada'i' al-zuhur*, 226.

81 Ibn Iyas, *Bada'i' al-zuhur*, 285.

82 Winter, "The Ottoman Occupation," 506.

83 Ibn Iyas, *Bada'i' al-zuhur*, 245.

84 Ibn Iyas, *Bada'i' al-zuhur*, 276.

85 Ibn Iyas, *Bada'i' al-zuhur*, 280.

86 Behrens-Abouseif, *Egypt's Adjustment*, 50. Also see: Celalzade Mustafa Çelebi, "Tabaqat al-Mamalik wa-darajat al-Masalik," in *Geschichte Sultan Sulayman Kanunis, von 1520 bis 1557* (Wiesbaden: E.J. Brill, 1981), 140. He writes that to be ruler of Egypt is "a gift from God."

87 Abou al-Haj, "Aspects of the Legitimation," 379.

88 *Qanunnama Misr*, trans. and ed. M.A. Fu'ad (Cairo: Anglo-Egyptian Bookshop, 1986), 3–4.

89 Originally meaning 'bachelor,' the term was eventually applied to a wide variety of troops that resided in the citadel. Their members were called *mushah* and were rivals of the *inshikariya* (sometimes written as *yanjiriya* or *yankijriya* in the *sijill*s); another faction stationed at the citadel were known as the *awjaq al-sultaniya* because they represented sultanic authority. The *'azban*'s duties included protecting the citadels in and outside of Cairo and protecting the pasha. Because they resided in the citadel, asserts al-Bakri, they were able to control and influence *siyasa* in Cairo (al-Bakri, *al-Nuzha al-zahiya*, 25–26).
90 *Qanunnama Misr*, 5.
91 Chroniclers, writes 'Isa, often refer to them as Yanjiriya or Yankijriya (al-Bakri, *al-Nuzha al-zahiya*, 25). This militia came to Egypt with Salim and took residence in the citadel. It became known as the *awjaq al-sultaniya* because they represented sultanic authority. Eventually, members of this group took control of *dar darb al-nuqud* (the mint) (al-Bakri, *al-Nuzha al-zahiya*, 26).
92 Ibn Iyas, *Bada'i' al-zuhur*, 452. The *rusum* in question are the court fees introduced by the Ottomans.
93 *Qanunnama Misr*, 5.
94 Buzov, *The Lawgiver*, 58.
95 U. Heyd, "Kânûn and Sharî'a in Old Ottoman Criminal Justice," *Proceedings of the Israel Academy of Sciences and Humanities* 3, no. 1 (1969): 1, 2–3.
96 H. Inalcik, "Kanunname," in *EI*, CD-ROM edition.
97 Behrens-Abouseif, *Egypt's Adjustment*, 35–45.
98 *Qanunnama Misr*, 30, 32, 33.
99 Imber, *Ebu's-Su'ud*, 44.
100 Heyd, *Studies in Old Ottoman Criminal Law*, 169.
101 *Qanunnama Misr*, 34.
102 Ibn Iyas, *Bada'i' al-zuhur*, 243.
103 Ibn Iyas, *Bada'i' al-zuhur*, 243.
104 Ibn Iyas, *Bada'i' al-zuhur*, 340.
105 al-Damiri, *Qudat Misr*, 221.
106 Sayyidi Jalabi (Çelebi), "the greatest of Sultan Sulayman's qadis and their most senior," was announced as the first "*qadi 'asker*" (Ibn Iyas, *Bada'i' al-zuhur*, 453–54). The *qadi 'askar* was the top legal authority in Cairo. Appointed from Istanbul, his tenure was recorded in the *sijill*s (al-Bakri, *al-Nuzha al-zahiya*, 36).
107 Ibn Iyas, *Bada'i' al-zuhur*, 282.
108 Ibn Iyas, *Bada'i' al-zuhur*, 418–20.
109 Ibn Iyas, *Bada'i' al-zuhur*, 55.
110 Ibn Iyas, *Bada'i' al-zuhur*, 184.
111 Ibn Iyas, *Bada'i' al-zuhur*, 184.
112 Ibn Iyas, *Bada'i' al-zuhur*, 187.
113 Ibn Iyas, *Bada'i' al-zuhur*, 418.
114 al-Damiri, *Qudat Misr*, 8–9.
115 al-Damiri, *Qudat Misr*, 8–9.
116 al-Damiri, *Qudat Misr*, 24.

117 al-Damiri, *Qudat Misr*, 102.
118 al-Damiri, *Qudat Misr*, 103.
119 al-Damiri, *Qudat Misr*, 117.
120 Most significantly, on his departure from Egypt, Rawa Zada sought out a copy of the last section of Ibn Nujaym's *Sharh al-Kanz* and publicly asked God's forgiveness for the sins committed by 'Abd al-Wahhab. Ibn Nujaym's work, considered a definitive sixteenth-century Hanafi text, attempted to grant custom a formal place in Islamic legal theory. It is not surprising, therefore, that Rawa Zada was praised as a scholar who upheld "public welfare and custom" *(al-masalih wa-l-ma'ruf)* (al-Damiri, *Qudat Misr*, 117).
121 al-Damiri, *Qudat Misr*, 117.
122 al-Damiri, *Qudat Misr*, 24–25, 100–101.
123 See Fleischer, *The Lawgiver as Messiah*, 159–83.
124 Fleischer, *The Lawgiver as Messiah*, 192.
125 The definition and understanding of *ijtihad mutlaq* changes from the classical period to the middle period. By this time, it is generally understood as the right of scholars to engage in independent reasoning within the boundaries of the schools' methodology and hermeneutics. For a fuller discussion on the early construction and evolution of *ijtihad*, see: W.B. Hallaq, "Was the Gate of Ijtihad Closed?" *Journal of Middle East Studies* 16, no. 1 (1984): 3–41; and B. Weiss, "Interpretation in Islamic Law: The Theory of Ijtihad," in *Islamic Law and Legal Theory*, ed. I. Edge (Aldershot: Dartmouth, 1996), 237–86.
126 al-Damiri, *Qudat Misr*, 194.
127 Winter, *Society and Religion*, 244.
128 Winter, *Society and Religion*, 244.
129 Until the end of the century, the matter continued to rankle locals, judging by Sha'rani's warning, "pay willingly the money due to the *qanun* and the *qassam*. If one does not give of his free will, he will give in spite of himself. He is wise who knows his time" (M. Winter, *Egyptian Society under Ottoman Rule, 1517–1798* (New York: Routledge, 1992), 243).
130 al-Damiri, *Qudat Misr*, 232.
131 al-Damiri, *Qudat Misr*, 222.
132 Winter, *Society and Religion*, 222.
133 Each time a judge incurs the death penalty in al-Damiri's work, it arrives on the same day that the culprit dies of either natural causes or "fever." This is an obvious literary device indicating that the sentences had more symbolic than actual significance, as no judge was ever actually executed.
134 al-Damiri, *Qudat Misr*, 222.
135 al-Damiri, *Qudat Misr*, 17. Again, when it came to the consumption of intoxicants, judicial opinion varied. See: Ibn Taymiya, *al-Siyasa al-shar'iya* (Cairo: Dar al-Kutub al-'Arabiya, 1966), 120; and al-Mawardi, *al-Ahkam al-sultaniya*, ed. 'Abd al-Rahman 'Umayra (Cairo, 1994).
136 al-Damiri, *Qudat Misr*, 105–10.
137 al-Damiri, *Qudat Misr*, 105–10.
138 For example, the *tulba*, an illegal tax imposed on farmers.
139 Qaraçli-Zada also allocated portions for the poor and *ashab al-a'zar* (the needy) (al-Damiri, *Qudat Misr*, 62).

140 Imber, *Ebu's-Su'ud*, 7.
141 G. al-Nahal, *The Judicial Administration of Ottoman Egypt in the Seventeenth Century* (Minneapolis, MN: Bibliotheca Islamica, 1979), 9–11.
142 al-Damiri, *Qudat Misr*, 66.
143 al-Damiri, *Qudat Misr*, 68.
144 al-Damiri, *Qudat Misr*, 67.
145 al-Damiri, *Qudat Misr*, 67.
146 al-Damiri, *Qudat Misr*, 69.
147 al-Damiri, *Qudat Misr*, 237.
148 al-Damiri, *Qudat Misr*, 249.
149 al-Damiri, *Qudat Misr*, 252–56.
150 al-Damiri, *Qudat Misr*, 260.
151 al-Damiri, *Qudat Misr*, 86.
152 al-Damiri, *Qudat Misr*, 83.
153 al-Damiri, *Qudat Misr*, 149.
154 al-Damiri, *Qudat Misr*, 152.
155 al-Damiri, *Qudat Misr*, 169.
156 al-Damiri, *Qudat Misr*, 118.
157 al-Damiri, *Qudat Misr*, 185.
158 See N. Hanna, "The Administration;" Gerber, *State, Society, and Law*; and A. Cohen, *A World Within: Jewish Life as Reflected in Muslim Court Documents from the* Sijill *of Jerusalem* (Philadelphia, PA: Center for Judaic Studies, University of Pennsylvania, 1994).

Notes to Chapter 4
1 A. Manna', "The *Sijill* as a Source for the Study of Palestine during the Ottoman Period, with Special Reference to the French Invasion," in *Palestine in the Late Ottoman Period: Political and Economic Transformation*, ed. D. Kushner (Jerusalem: Yad Izhak Ben-Zevi, 1986), 351–53.
2 See D.P. Little, "The Significance of the Haram Documents for the Study of Medieval Islamic History," *Der Islam* 57 (1980): 189–219; J. Wakin, *The Function of Documents* (Albany, NY: State University of New York Press, 1972); De Blois, "Sidjill," in *EI*, CD-ROM edition; S. Faroqhi, "Sidjill," in *EI*, CD-ROM edition; J. Mandaville, "The Ottoman Court Records of Syria and Jordan," *Journal of the American Oriental Society* 86 (1996): 311–19; R.Y. Ebeid and J.L. Young, *Some Arabic Documents of the Ottoman Period* (Leiden: E.J. Brill, 1976), 1–2.
3 A. Sonbol, "Women in Shari'ah Courts: A Historical and Methodological Discussion," *Fordham International Law Journal* 27, no. 1 (2003): 238; and I.A. Grohmann, *Awraq al-bardi al-'arabiya bi Dar al-Kutub al-Misriya* (Cairo: Matba'at Dar al-Kutub al-Misriya, 1934), for examples of Islamic marriage contracts from third- to fifth-century Egyptian courts.
4 "The rules of court registration took place within the 'es-Surut' and 'al-Mahadir ve's-sicillat' parts of the Islamic law books" (A. Bayinder, "The Function of the Judiciary in the Ottoman Empire," in *The Great Ottoman Turkish Civilization*, vol. 3, ed. K. Çiçek (Ankara: Semih Ofset, 2000), 642).
5 Little, "The Significance of the Haram Documents," 189.

6 See M.G.S. Hodgson and L. Gardet, "Hudjdja," in *EI*, CD-ROM edition.
7 Bayinder, "The Function of the Judiciary," 642.
8 Wakin, *The Function of Documents*, 46–47.
9 A *hujja* can be both "proof and the presentation of proof." The term is Qur'anic in origin, and is applied to any argument attempting to prove what is false as well as what is true: "Men should have no Hudjdja against God" (IV, 165). As a 'proof,' *hujja* is closely associated with *dalil*, and in the sense of 'argument' it is associated with *burhan*. But where *dalil* serves as the 'guide' to certainty, *hujja* "suggests the conclusive argument that leaves an opponent without a reply." And where *burhan* is evidence of an irrefutable proof, *hujja* "retains the idea of a contrary argument. 'Dialectical proof' would perhaps be the translation that best renders the primary meaning of hujja." It also assumes a technical meaning in the science of Hadith and becomes one of the initiatory degrees of Isma'ili gnosis. For the *mutakallimun* and the *falasifa* (in treatises on logic or methodology), "it remains, according to the authors' inclinations, somewhat imprecise" (L. Gardet, "Hudjdja," in *EI*, CD-ROM edition).
10 Wakin, *The Function of Documents*, 46.
11 Mahkamat al-Bab al-'Ali, Sijill 96, Doc. 96.
12 All examples of 'old' documents at my disposal originated in Cairo, and most often contained the judgment of a former chief judge. Often they were *'ilam*s. (See al-Bab al-'Ali, Sijill no. 66, Doc. 7.)
13 al-Bab al-'Ali, Sijill 124, Doc. 822.
14 Shaykh al-Islam Muhammad ibn al-Surur al-Bakri al-Siddiqi, *al-Nuzha al-zahiya fi dhikr wulat Misr wa-l-Qahira al-mu'izziya*, ed. 'Abd al-Razzaq 'Abd al-Razzaq 'Isa (Cairo: al-'Arabi li-l-Nashr wa-l-Tawzi', 1998), 50.
15 al-Bab al-'Ali, Sijill 96, Doc. 72.
16 Bab al-'Ali, Sijill 96, Doc. 96.
17 al-Mahkamat al-Qisma al-'Askeriya, Sijill 5, Doc. 3.
18 al-Qisma al-'Askeriya, Sijill 5, Doc. 39.
19 al-Bab al-'Ali, Sijill 96, Doc. 2833.
20 "A capable copyist (nasikh) might advance to being a munshi (Suli 118). Ibn al-Sayrafi 142 mentions copying as an important occupation, and also mentions a fair-copyist (mubayyid). Copies are marked with nusikha or nusikhat, and, like originals, could be attested by sahh. The copies were archived, and it may well be that some collected works of the insha' literature were compiled from collections of drafts or books of copies." M. Hamidullah has collected "269 texts attributed to the period before 652." See W. Björkman, "Diplomatic," in *EI*, CD-ROM edition.
21 B. Messick, *The Calligraphic State* (Berkeley: University of California Press, 1993), 211.
22 Messick, *The Caaligraphic State*, 204.
23 F. Rosenthal, "Of Making Books There Is No End," in *The Book in the Islamic World: The Written Word and Communication in the Middle East*, ed. G.N. Atiyeh (Albany: State University of New York Press, 1995), 36. Within the specialized domain of evidence, the unique authority of the spoken word represented certainty, the very embodiment of 'presence' of

the testifying human witness. Quintessentially, witnesses (*shuhud*, sing. *shahid*) are defined as "those present" *(al-hudur)*, a quality that has two dimensions. The first is 'presence' at the word or deed borne witness to, and the second is 'presence' at the moment of litigation before a judge. In stark contrast to the written document, Messick writes:

> Witnesses "carry" testimony, ideally embodying (memorizing) the evidence involved securely within themselves from the moment of its original apprehension to the moment of its communication to the court. (Messick, *The Calligraphic State*, 210)

The centrality of memory is reflected in the juristic literature on the conduct of judges *(adab al-qadi)*. An oft-asked question in these manuals is, can judges appeal exclusively to their written records if they are unable to recollect the documents from memory? Prominent among those who argued that a judge's "written records provide grounds for further litigation" in the absence of memory are the Hanafi jurists Ibn Abi Layla and Abu Yusuf, who overruled the opinion of their founding father to attain this judgment. Not so the thirteenth-century Shafi'i Nawawi, who admonished judges who ratified documents issued from their own court and bearing their seals, before they had recalled it to memory.

24 Wakin, *The Function of Documents*, vii, 5.
25 Wakin, *The Function of Documents*, 4.
26 Messick, *The Calligraphic State*, 210.
27 Wakin, *The Function of Documents*, p. 4.
28 Turan makes the added claim that "in a civil case against Turks, tributaries, or other subjects of the Grand Signior, the merchants and subjects of the King can not be summoned, molested, or tried unless the said Turks, tributaries, and subjects of the Grand Signior produce a writing from the hand of the opponent, or a 'heudjet' from the kadi. The main purpose of these requirements was to lessen the kadi's reliance on Muslim witnesses and focus his attention less on matters of probity, religious observance, faith, and national origin than on the written agreement. With a document, witnesses could still be heard if its validity was questioned. But the burden of proof would fall on the challenger of the document, so the possibility of escaping a contractual obligation, or of fabricating a liability, would diminish" (Wakin, *The Function of Documents*, 27).
29 Wakin, *The Function of Documents*, 11. What is more, this perspective ignores the equally contested role of documents in the history of western law. In eighteenth-century England, Gilbert's Law of Evidence was cited in support of the argument that a written deposition ought not to be admitted because "we cannot cross-examine" the declarant. See *Birchal & Brook v. Kelly*, 16 Ryder N.B. 77, 86 (1756). But Roman law was as suspicious of the written document as Islamic law. E. Rabel traced the Statute of Frauds to a French model; see E. Rabel, "The Statute of Frauds and Comparative Legal History," *Law Quarterly Review* 174 (1947): 63. J. Beardsley also points to the influence of French procedure on the European tradition of

preferring written proof. "French civil procedure is marked by a strong preference for written proof and by the tendency of French judges to avoid factual determinations that must be based on evidence which is complex or otherwise difficult to evaluate" (J. Beardsley, "Proof of Fact in French Civil Procedure," *American Journal of Comparative Law* 459 (1986): 34).

30 Wakin, *The Function of Documents*, 10.
31 Wakin, *The Function of Documents*, 12–13. She also notes that the Hanbalis produced no *shurut* works that are known of, and were averse to *hiyal* altogether.
32 Wakin, *The Function of Documents*, 9.
33 See A.M. Geunther, "Hanafi *Fiqh* in Mughal India: The Fatawa-i 'Alamgiri," in *India's Islamic Traditions, 711–1750*, ed. R.M. Eaton (New Delhi: Oxford University Press, 2003), 214–15.
34 *Fatawa 'Alamgiri*, ed. 'Abd al-Latif Hasan 'Abd al-Rahman, vol. 6 (Karachi, n.d.), 193–293.
35 *Fatawa 'Alamgiri*, 200.
36 See R.P. Dozy, *Supplément aux dictionnaires arabes*, 3rd ed. (Leiden: E.J. Brill, 1967).
37 al-Bab al-'Ali, *Sijill* 66, Doc. 13.
38 al-Bab al-'Ali, *Sijill* 66, Docs. 184, 185.
39 al-Bab al-'Ali, *Sijill* 66, Doc. 207.
40 J. Derrida, *Archive Fever: A Freudian Impression* (Chicago: University of Chicago Press, 1996).
41 As part of the effort to guard the document against forgery, Salameh notes that "no blank spaces are left on the pages, whether between the documents or in the margins. Each double page is filled up completely with writing over all four sides." If a space is left, the word *battal* appears so as to prevent forgery. In the selection at my disposal, the word *battal* is used stylistically (K. Salameh, "Aspects of the *Sijill*s of the Shari'a Court in Jerusalem," in *Ottoman Jerusalem: The Living City, 1517–1917*, ed. S. Auld and R. Hillenbrand (Jerusalem: al-Tajir World of Islam Trust, 2000), 107).
42 W. Björkman, "Diplomatic." Also see J. Barthold, *Arkhivnie Kursi*, vol. 1 (St. Petersburg: n.p., 1920).
43 Björkman, "Diplomatic."
44 Little, *A Catalogue of Islamic Documents from al-Haram aš-Šarif in Jerusalem* (Beirut: Orient-Institut der Deutschen Morgenländischen Gesellschaft, 1984), 1.
45 Occasionally, a copy of the original *sijill* would be made for the new judge while the retired judge retained the original *sijill* in his private collection. In the early centuries of Islam, this *sijill* consisted of loose sheets of paper carried in the judge's 'kerchief.' Muhammad ibn Masruq, an Egyptian judge from 793 to 800, is believed to have been the first to use a *qimatr* (type of bookcase for the document). See W.B. Hallaq, "The Qadi's Diwan *(Sijill)* before the Ottomans," *BSOAS* 61, no. 3 (1998): 418, 433.
46 A. Sonbol, "Women in Shari'ah Courts," 240.
47 N. Hanna, "The Administration of Courts in Ottoman Cairo," in *The State and Its Servants: Administration in Egypt from Ottoman Times to the Present*, ed. N. Hanna (Cairo: American University in Cairo Press, 1995), 46.

48 Muhammad ibn Ahmad ibn Iyas, *Bada'i' al-zuhur fi waqa'i' al-duhur*, ed. Muhammad Mustafa, vol. 5 (Weisbaden: E.J. Brill, 1975), 418.
49 Sonbol, "Women in Shari'ah Courts," 239.
50 Sonbol, "Women in Shari'ah Courts," 239.
51 Sonbol, "Women in Shari'ah Courts," 239. Speaking of the storage facilities in which these unified *sijill*s would have been kept, Milad argues that incomplete *sijill*s (such as those from the Salihiya Najmiya) were retained within the actual court, that is, in its main hall *(qa'a)* or within its residential quarters, presumably in the judge's personal quarters. Finished *sijill*s, on the other hand, were collated in a special "depot" reserved for all complete judicial registers from Cairo's various courts. Basing her case on three isolated *(mufrada)* documents found within the archives of the Ministry of Waqf, Milad argues that this 'unified archive' was stored within the court of the Bab al-'Ali, located within the walls of the Cairo citadel. One of those documents contains the following line: "Ceci est une copie provenant du registre de la Sublime Porte, se trouvant conservé au dépôt des registres complets à Misr ["This is a copy issued from the register of the Sublime Porte, found preserved at the comprehensive register depository in Egypt"]" (S.A.I. Milad, "Registres judiciaires du tribunal de la Salihiyya Naǝmiyya," *AI* 12 (1974): 166).
52 al-Bakri, *al-Nuzha al-zahiya*, 52.
53 Little, "The Significance of the Haram Documents," 210.
54 al-Bab al-'Ali, Sijill 66, Docs. 5, 193, 196, 213.
55 al-Bab al-'Ali, Sijill 96, Docs. 15, 72, 73 74, 75, 76, 77; Mahkamat Tulun, Sijill 165, Docs. 164, 165, 4, 5, 6, 7, 8, 9, 10.
56 See: Wakin, *The Function of Documents*, 6; R. Yaron, *Introduction to the Law of the Aramaic Papyri* (Oxford, UK: Clarendon Press, 1961); A. Steinwenter, "Die Bedeutung der Papyrologie für die koptische Urkundenlehre," *Münchener Beiträge zur Papyrusforschung und antiken Rechtsgeschichte* 19 (1934): 302–13; E. Seidl, "Law," in *The Legacy of Egypt*, ed. S.R.K Glanville (London: Clarendon Press, 1972); A. Schiller, "Prolegomena to the Study of Coptic Law," *Archives d'Histoire du Droit Oriental* 2 (1938): 360–61; W. Seagle, *The Quest for Law* (New York: A.A. Knopf, 1941); and A. Gacek, "The Ancient Sijill of Qayrawan," *Middle Eastern Library Association Notes* 46 (1989): 26–29. In pre-Islamic Arabia too, Wakin, Tyan, and J. David-Weill confirm that the written document was known and served the bustling commercial activity and financial operations of the Meccans. Wakin has argued that "the use of legal documents is an institution in the Near East that has an unbroken tradition since cuneiform times" (Wakin, *The Function of Documents*, 5). Also see E. Tyan, *Le notariat et le régime de la preuve par écrit dans la pratique du droit musulman* (Harissa, Lebanon: Imprimerie Saint Paul, 1959). Based on David-Weill's research, Wakin writes, "title deeds inscribed on wood or stone on private houses, buildings of pious foundations and other structures are nothing less than legal documents too, drawn up in the same legally valid form as a contract" (Wakin, *The Function of Documents*, 5, fn. 2). Later Arabic formularies are an independent genre of literature of which three types may be identified: "1) collections of models similar to the formularies of the West, 2) treatises on stylistics and rules

concerning the drawing up of the documents, similar to the Western artes or summaedictaminis, 3) a mixture of both, that is to say, formularies with theoretical commentary, or theoretical treatises with examples from practice, similar to the ones found in the West from the 12th century onwards" (J. Reychmann and A. Zajaczkowski, "Diplomatics," in *EI*, CD-ROM edition).

57 Grohmann attempted to classify Arabic documents "with and without legal content, public and private documents, cancellarial and non-cancellarial documents, mandates, diplomas, evidential and business documents, etc." Arab scholars like al-Qalqashandi "likewise classified their documents clearly" (I.A. Grohmann, *Awraq al-bardi al-'arabiya bi Dar al-Kutub al-Misriya* (Cairo: Matba'at Dar al-Kutub al-Misriya, 1934)). The following are general terms encountered: *kitab, wathiqa, sakk, sanad, hujja, sijill, zahir*. In the earlier periods, documents of state were simply known as *kutub*, although a distinction was made between *kutub al-'amma* or *mutlaqat*, and *kutub khassa*, soon thereafter. These were further subdivided according to content and subject. "Their inclusion under the heading of 'state documents' gives this a very wide meaning. Consequently, the exchange of letters concerning matters of state was called *mukatabat* by the Abbasids, and the chancellery the *diwan al-mukatabat*. This was also usual in Egypt, under the Fatimids, Ayyubids, and Mamluks. For specifically legal documents of state, *yarligh* indicated a pass for foreign ambassadors, while *itlaqat* was the term used in reference to the orders issued by former rulers." For a complete list and description of Arabic documents see Steinwenter, "Die Bedeutung der Papyrologie."

58 De Blois, "Sidjill."
59 De Blois, "Sidjill."
60 De Blois, "Sidjill."
61 D.P. Little, "Sidjill," in *EI*, CD-ROM edition.
62 Little, "Sidjill."
63 Little, "Sidjill." Also see Wakin, *The Function of Documents*, 11. She bases this assessment on Tyan, *Judicial Organization*, 181, n. 7. In the analysis of each, *sijill* was "used to mean the text of a judgment and by extension the register of judicial decisions and even any official register" (Little, "Sidjill").
64 *Fatawa 'Alamgiri*, 199, 201.
65 Little, "Sidjill."
66 Faroqhi, "Sidjill." Like their Mamluk counterparts, the judges' register included deeds *('uqud)* of purchase and lease, bills of sale, marriage and divorce; testamentary bequests (*wasiya*s); written legal depositions made before legal witnesses (*ishhad*s); written, witnessed, and binding legal acknowledgments (*iqrar*s) (all reported in Little, "The Significance of the Haram Documents," 208–209). Estate inventories; decrees (*marsum* in Mamluk usage, but in Ottoman usage one also encounters the terms *berat, amr*, and *buyuruldi*); petitions (*qisas* in Mamluk usage, and *ma'rud/ma'ruz* in Ottoman registers) are reported in Bayinder, "The Function of the Judiciary," 642. There are also vouchers; receipts *(qabd)*; reports *(mutala'at)*; death inventories (the format of which is called *daftar* in Ottoman records); the solicitation of a legal opinion and the reply (*istifta'* and *futya*); and

finally, court records containing a summary of the case and the decision of the judge. See Little, *A Catalogue of Islamic Documents* and "The Significance of the Haram Documents."
67 Salameh, "Aspects of the Sijills," 110.
68 Milad, "Registres judiciaires," 190–200.
69 Bayinder, "The Function of the Judiciary," 642.
70 Little, "The Significance of the Haram Documents," 212.
71 Faroqhi, "Sidjill."
72 Faroqhi, "Sidjill." The "qassam came from Istanbul to impose a tax on bequests." The latter collected a 20 percent inheritance tax. See M. Winter, "The Ottoman Conquest of Egypt," in *The Cambridge History of Egypt*, vol. 2, ed. C.F. Petrie and M.W. Daly (Cambridge, UK: Cambridge University Press, 1998), 510.
73 Little, "The Significance of the Haram Documents," 205.
74 Faroqhi, "Sidjill."
75 D.P. Little and A.U. Turgay, "Documents from the Ottoman Period in the Khalidi Library in Jerusalem," *Die Welt des Islam* 20 (1980): 48.
76 Salameh, "Aspects of the Sijills," 108.
77 al-Bab al-'Ali, Sijill 124, 1.
78 Faroqhi, "Sidjill."
79 Bayinder, "The Function of the Judiciary," 642.
80 Little, "The Significance of the Haram Documents," 203.
81 Little, "The Significance of the Haram Documents," 209.
82 al-Bab al-'Ali, *Sijill*s 124, 96, and 66 contain a total of eighteen *ishhad*s; from the court of Ibn Tulun, Sijill 165, there are two; from the Qisma al-'Askeriya, Sijill 5, there are eight; from the Qisma al-'Arabiya, Sijill 5, there are five.
83 Salameh, "Aspects of the Sijills," 108; Qisma al-'Askeriya, Sijill 5, Docs. 6, 7, 8, 9, 10.
84 Salameh, "Aspects of the Sijills," 108.
85 Salameh, "Aspects of the Sijills," 110.
86 For a complete and systematic overview of the documents comprising the *sijill* of the court of the Salihiya al-Najmiya, see the appendix to Milad's article, which enumerates the types of documents as well as the opening and closing statements of each: Milad, "Registres judiciaires," 190–200.
87 al-Qisma al-'Askeriya, Sijill 5, Docs. 6, 7, 8, 9, 10, 44, 45.
88 The same formula is contained within the documents from the Najmiya al-Salihiya (Milad, "Registres judiciaires," 209).
89 al-Bab al-'Ali, Sijill 66, Doc. 181.
90 al-Bab al-'Ali, Sijill 124, 1.
91 R. Vesely, "Die Hauptprobleme der Diplomatik arabischer Privaturkurden aus dem spätmittelalterlichen Ägypten," *Archiv Orientali* 40 (1972): 333–34.
92 Vesely, "Die Hauptprobleme der Diplomatik," 332.
93 al-Bab al-'Ali, Sijill 96, Doc. 5.
94 Vesely, "Die Hauptprobleme der Diplomatik," 322.
95 Former judges were often recruited by incoming judges and served as notaries for the courts from which they had been discharged. Moreover, there were families who were distinguished as notary or professional

witness families, indicating the high status of such occupations (Vesely, "Die Hauptprobleme der Diplomatik," 321).
96 Vesely, "Die Hauptprobleme der Diplomatik," 322.
97 Wakin, *The Function of Documents*, 7.
98 R.C. Jennings, "Limitations on the Judicial Powers of the Kadi in Seventeenth-century Ottoman Kayseri," *SI* 50 (1979): 161.
99 S. Faroqhi, "Political Activity among Ottoman Taxpayers and the Problem of Sultanic Legitimation (1500–1650)," *JESHO* 35 (1992): 13.
100 G. al-Nahal, *The Judicial Administration of Ottoman Egypt in the Seventeenth Century* (Minneapolis, MN: Bibliotheca Islamica, 1979), 22.
101 C.F. Petry, *The Civilian Elite of Cairo in the Later Middle Ages* (Princeton, NJ: Princeton University Press, 1981), 225.
102 Vesely, "Die Hauptprobleme der Diplomatik."
103 Ibn Iyas, *Bada'i' al-zuhur*, 469.
104 Vesely, "Die Hauptprobleme der Diplomatik," 324.
105 al-Bakri, *al-Nuzha al-zahiya*, 48.
106 Vesely, "Die Hauptprobleme der Diplomatik," 324.
107 al-Nahal, *The Judicial Administration*, 10. This view is rejected by Hallaq, who argues that the "function of the scribe must here be differentiated from that of the notary . . . who did not sit in the qadi's court and whose function was a private not public one, which the katib's was" (Hallaq, "The Qadi's Diwan," 423). The *'udul* were seated in a semicircle behind each of the chief judges in the court of the Bab al-'Ali (al-Nahal, *The Judicial Administration*, 16).
108 al-Bab al-'Ali, Sijill 124, Doc. 821.
109 G. Khan, ed., *Arabic Legal and Administrative Documents in the Cambridge Genizah Collection*, Cambridge University Library Genizah Series 10 (Cambridge, UK: Cambridge University Press, 1993), 8.
110 Wakin, *The Function of Documents*, 69.
111 al-Bab al-'Ali, Sijill 124, Doc. 96.

Notes to Chapter 5
1 J. Derrida, *Archive Fever: A Freudian Impression* (Chicago, IL: University of Chicago Press, 1996), 1. The meaning of 'archive' comes from the Greek word 'arkheion,' the house of the archons, magistrates.
2 V.H. Askan and D. Goffman, eds., *The Early Modern Ottomans* (Cambridge, UK: Cambridge University Press, 2007), 2–3.
3 N. Qattan, "Inside the Ottoman Courthouse: Territorial Law at the Intersection of State and Religion," in *The Early Modern Ottomans*, edited by V.H. Askan and D. Goffman (Cambridge, UK: Cambridge University Press, 2007), 201.
4 A. Fattal, *Le status légal des non-musulmans en pays d'Islam* (Beirut: Imprimerie Catholique, 1958), 357–58.
5 Qattan, "Inside the Ottoman Courthouse," 209.
6 Qattan, "Inside the Ottoman Courthouse," 211.
7 J. Derrida, *Resistances of Psychoanalysis* (Stanford, CA: Stanford University Press, 1998), 15.
8 Derrida, *Resistances of Psychoanalysis*, 7.

9   Derrida, *Archive Fever*, 2.
10 N. Qattan, "Discriminating Texts: Orthographic Marking and Social Differentiation in the Court Records of Ottoman Damascus," in *Arabic Sociolinguistics: Issues and Perspectives*, ed. Yasir Suleiman (Richmond: Curzon Press, 1994), 65.
11 Qattan, "Inside the Ottoman Courthouse," 210.
12 Mahkamat Tulun, Sijill 165, Doc. 1303; Mahkamat al-Bab al-'Ali, Sijill 66, Docs. 45, 47; Sijill 96, Doc. 1023; Mahkamat al-Qisma al-'Askeriya, Sijill 5, Docs. 6, 8.
13 al-Bab al-'Ali, Sijill 134, Docs. 6, 27, 66, 93; Sijill 66, Docs. 2, 12, 218, 219, 238; Sijill 96, Doc. 2820.
14 al-Bab al-'Ali, Sijill 66, Doc. 961. *Khawaja* was a term used to refer to Persian merchants in these centuries.
15 al-Qisma al-'Askeriya, Sijill 5, Docs. 7, 23, 24, 29, 31; al-Bab al-'Ali, Sijill 66, Docs. 958, 954. In the latter case, the freeborn daughter of a freed Circassian *'askeri* marries a freed member of the Muttafariqa militia.
16 al-Bab al-'Ali, Sijill 96, Doc. 2823. al-Qisma al-'Askeriya, Sijill 5, Docs. 9, 10, 11, 14, 18, 19, 22.
17 "Their military service was only nominally required," writes Holt, "[but] their financial contributions bought them the protection of their corps" (P.M. Holt, "Misr," in *EI*, CD-ROM edition).
18 While this may have been the case for Mamluk and Ottoman soldiery, it was less true for recruits *(wafida)* from among the *awlad al-'Arab*, who were brought into the seven corps *(ojaqat)* of the Ottoman garrison in high numbers toward the end of the century. Bucking the trend, members of the *ojaq*s tried to prevent *awlad al-'Arab* from entering the army and from wearing "Rumi" clothing, even resorting to murder. D. Ayalon, *Studies in the Mamluks of Egypt (1250–1517)* (Collected Studies Series. London: Variorum Reprints, 1977), 318.
19 al-Bab al-'Ali, Sijill 66, Doc. 32.
20 al-Bab al-'Ali, Sijill 66, Doc. 191.
21 Tulun, Sijill 165, Doc. 962.
22 al-Qisma al-'Askeriya, Sijill 5, Docs. 7, 23, 24, 29, 31; al-Bab al-'Ali, Sijill 66, Docs. 958, 954.
23 al-Bab al-'Ali, Sijill 96, Doc. 2823; al-Qisma al-'Askeriya, Sijill 5, Docs. 9, 10, 11, 14, 18, 19, 22.
24 D. Ayalon, "Mamluk," in *EI*, CD-ROM edition.
25 Ayalon, "Mamluk."
26 al-Bab al-'Ali, Sijill 124, Doc. 10.
27 B. Braud and B. Lewis, *Christians and Jews in the Ottoman Empire: The Functioning of a Plural Society* (New York: Holmes & Meier, 1982).
28 A. Cohen, *Jewish Life under Islam: Jerusalem in the Sixteenth Century* (Cambridge, MA: Harvard University Press, 1984), 8.
29 Cohen, *Jewish Life under Islam*, 119.
30 A. Shmuelevitz, *The Jews of the Ottoman Empire in the Late Fifteenth and the Sixteenth Centuries: Administrative, Economic, Legal, and Social Relations as Reflected in the Responsa* (Leiden: E.J. Brill, 1984), vii.

31 In its first constitutional era, the Ottoman Empire brought in a constitutional monarchy based on the promulgation of the Kanun-ı Esasi (Foundational Law), authored by members of the Young Ottomans. This era lasted from 23 November 1876 until 13 February 1878, and ended unceremoniously with the suspension of the Ottoman parliament by Abdülhamid II.
32 Shmuelevitz provides extensive evidence for a ban against bringing cases to the *mahkama* (sharia court) in the Jewish community (Shmuelevitz, *The Jews of the Ottoman Empire*, 68–73).
33 Cohen, *Jewish Life under Islam*, 121.
34 Cohen, *Jewish Life under Islam*, 119.
35 al-Bab al-'Ali, Sijill 124, Doc. 101.
36 al-Bab al-'Ali, Sijill 124, Doc. 771.
37 al-Bab al-'Ali, Sijill 124, Doc. 104.
38 al-Bab al-'Ali, Sijill 124, Doc. 830.
39 al-Bab al-'Ali, Sijill 124, Doc. 743.
40 al-Bab al-'Ali, Sijill 124, Doc. 784.

Notes to Chapter 6
1 Shaykh al-Islam Muhammad ibn al-Surur al-Bakri al-Siddiqi, *al-Nuzha al-zahiya fi dhikr wulat Misr wa-l-Qahira al-mu'izziya*, ed. 'Abd al-Razzaq 'Abd al-Razzaq 'Isa (Cairo: al-'Arabi li-l-Nashr wa-l-Tawzi', 1998), 265. The poem is addressed to the critics of Birkat al-Ratli, a settlement around a lake that Maqrizi described as a den of iniquity. Al-Bakri writes that boats used to ply these waters laden with passengers, and that scandalous incidents took place as men and "disreputable" women intermingled, alcohol flowed freely, and drunkenness was displayed (al-Bakri, *al-Nuzha al-zahiya*, 261). When Ibn Hajar al-'Asqalani resided in the *birka*, he was appalled at these occurrences and worked to stop them in the year AH 796/CE 1393 (al-Bakri, *al-Nuzha al-zahiya*, 262). Al-Mansuri's poem is a rejoinder to such efforts.
2 For example, the practice of deferring the dowry, once vigorously opposed by legists as an Egyptian custom, was eventually incorporated and modulated by later generations of jurists. By the Ottoman period, the custom was so well established that Abu al-Su'ud abolished the *kabin*, an Anatolian marriage gift, in favor of the deferred and immediate portions of the dower, as per the custom of the Egyptians. See "Civil Marriage," below.
3 Imber, *Ebu's-Su'ud*, 89–90.
4 Imber, *Ebu's-Su'ud*, 90.
5 Imber, *Ebu's-Su'ud*, 94.
6 Imber, *Ebu's-Su'ud*, 94.
7 L. Peirce, *Morality Tales: Law and Gender in the Ottoman Court of Aintab* (Berkeley, CA: University of California Press, 2003), 364.
8 Muhammad ibn Ahmad ibn Iyas, *Bada'i' al-zuhur fi waqa'i' al-duhur*, ed. Muhammad Mustafa (Wiesbaden: E.J. Brill, 1975), 273.
9 Ibn Iyas, *Bada'i' al-zuhur*, 254–55.
10 A wealthy Persian *('ajami)* merchant from the east, accused by Khayrbek of being a spy for Shah Isma'il al-Sufi, is wrongly executed, according to Ibn

Iyas, who accuses the governor of coveting the man's vast wealth (Ibn Iyas, *Bada'i' al-zuhur*, 263.)
11 Ibn Iyas, *Bada'i' al-zuhur*, 358–59.
12 Ibn Iyas, *Bada'i' al-zuhur*, 414, 274.
13 Ibn Iyas, *Bada'i' al-zuhur*, 244.
14 Ibn Taymiya, *Al-siyasa al-shar'iya* (Cairo: Dar al-Kutub al-'Arabiya, 1966), 112–14.
15 al-Mawardi, *al-Ahkam al-sultaniya* (London: Ta-Ha Publishers, 1996), 245–47.
16 Often referred to as secular courts, the *mazalim* were a longstanding Muslim institution. Representing state justice *(siyasa)*, the *mazalim* functioned as parallel courts to the sharia courts. See M.I. Khalil, "Wali al-Mazalim or the Muslim Ombudsman," *Journal of Islamic and Comparative Law* 6 (1976): 1–9.
17 Ibn Iyas, *Bada'i' al-zuhur*, 338.
18 Husayn ibn Muhammad al-Damiri, *Qudat Misr fi-l-qarn al-'ashir wa awa'il al-qarn al-hadi 'ashir* (Cairo: Dar al-Kutub), 17.
19 M. Winter, *Egyptian Society under Ottoman Rule, 1517–1798* (New York: Routledge, 1992), 231.
20 Muhammad ibn al-Mu'ti al-Ishaqi al-Manufi, *Akhbar al-awwal fi-man tasarraf fi Misr min arbab al-duwal* (Cairo: al-Matba'a al-'Uthmaniya, 1886), 156.
21 They also arrested al-Mahalawi's slave, who swore his master had freed him before his death. He was released only after the governor ordered his ear cut off. Ibn Iyas considers this an injustice against al-Mahalawi, who "did not deserve such a fate" (Ibn Iyas, *Bada'i' al-zuhur*, 313).
22 Damiri, *Qudat Misr fi-l-qarn al-'ashir*, 17.
23 Winter, *Egyptian Society*, 231.
24 M. Winter, *Society and Religion in Early Ottoman Egypt: Studies in the Writings of 'Abd al-Wahhab al-Sha'rani* (London: Transaction Books, 1982), 190.
25 Winter, *Society and Religion*, 190.
26 Winter, *Society and Religion*, 190–91.
27 Winter, *Society and Religion*, 191.
28 Mahkamat al-Bab al-'Ali, Sijill 96, Doc. 107.
29 al-Bab al-'Ali, Sijill 124, Doc. 765.
30 al-Bab al-'Ali, Sijill 124, Docs. 51, 74.
31 Ibn Taymiya, *al-Siyasa*, 120.
32 al-Mawardi, *al-Ahkam*, 248.
33 Ibn Iyas, *Bada'i' al-zuhur*, 211–12.
34 Ibn Iyas, *Bada'i' al-zuhur*, 290.
35 Ibn Iyas, *Bada'i' al-zuhur*, 332.
36 Ibn Iyas, *Bada'i' al-zuhur*, 461–62.
37 Ibn Iyas, *Bada'i' al-zuhur*, 461–62.
38 Ibn Iyas, *Bada'i' al-zuhur*, 467.
39 Ibn Iyas, *Bada'i' al-zuhur*, 469.
40 Mustafa 'Ali, *Mustafa 'Ali's Description of Cairo of 1599*, trans. and ed. A. Tietze (Vienna: E.J. Brill, 1975), 102.
41 Winter, *Egyptian Society*, 238.
42 Winter, *Society and Religion*, 292–93.

43 al-Bab al-'Ali, Sijill 124, Doc. 65.
44 S.A.I. Milad, "Registres judiciaires du tribunal de la Salihiyya Nağmiyya," *AI* 12 (1974): 235.
45 Imber, *Ebu's-Su'ud*, 165; G.H. Bousquet and J. Prins, "Ada," in *EI*, CD-ROM edition.
46 See J. Schacht, "Nikah," in *EI*, CD-ROM edition.
47 Furthermore, no divorce or marriage would be ratified outside of one of the four chief judges' courts (Ibn Iyas, *Bada'i' al-zuhur*, 417).
48 Ibn Iyas, *Bada'i' al-zuhur*, 418.
49 Ibn Iyas, *Bada'i' al-zuhur*, 418.
50 A. Sonbol, "Women in Shari'ah Courts: A Historical and Methodological Discussion," *Fordham International Law Journal* 27, no. 1 (2003): 239.
51 T. J. Wengert, *Harvesting Martin Luther's Reflections on Theology, Ethics, and the Church* (Grand Rapids, MI: W.B. Eerdmans Publishing, 2004), 175.
52 R.B. Outhwaite, *Clandestine Marriage in England* (Rio Grande, OH: Hambledon Press, 1995), 3, 140.
53 Mahkamat al-Qisma 'Askeriya, Sijill no. 5, Doc. 27.
54 Ibn Iyas, *Bada'i' al-zuhur*, 461.
55 Mahkamat Tulun, Sijill 165, Doc. 1310.
56 Tulun, Sijill 165, Doc. 1303.
57 A. Sonbol, "A History of Marriage Contracts in Egypt," in *Case Studies in Islamic Family Law*, ed. A. Quraishi and F.E. Vogel (Cambridge, MA: Harvard University Press, 2008), 87.
58 al-Qisma al-'Askeriya, Sijill 5, Docs. 6, 8, 23; al-Bab al-'Ali, Sijill 96, Doc. 1023; Sijill 66, Doc. 32, 34.
59 K. Salameh, "Aspects of the *Sijill*s of the Shari'a Court in Jerusalem," in *Ottoman Jerusalem: The Living City, 1517–1917*, ed. S. Auld and R. Hillenbrand (Jerusalem: al-Tajir World of Islam Trust, 2000), 136.
60 See Ibn Qudamah, *al-Mughni*, vol. 7 (Cairo: al-Matba'a al-Shaf'iya, 1962), 71; Ibn Abi Shaybah, *al-Musannaf*, vol. 4 (Karachi: Idrat al-Qur'an wa-l-'Ulum al-Islamiya, 1987), 200; 'Abd al-Razzaq, *al-Musannaf*, vol. 6, 2nd ed. (Beirut: al-Maktab al-Islami, 1983), 227–31; Hussain ibn Mas'u al-Baghwi, *Sharh al-Sunna*, vol. 9 (Beirut: al-Maktab al-Islami, 1983), 55.
61 Abdel-Rahim Omran, *Family Planning in the Legacy of Islam* (London: Routledge, 2012), 21–22; Abu Muhammed ibn Hazm, *al-Muhalla*, vol. 8 (Beirut: Dar al-Kutub al-'Ilmiya, 1998), 412–20.
62 N.B.E. Baillie, *A Digest of Mohummudan Law*, vol. 1, 2nd ed. (Lahore: Premier Book House, 1965), 76. Early Hanafi legalists such as al-Sarakhsi (d. 1090) and al-Kasani (d. 1189) imposed many restrictions on contractual freedom in general. Their theories were reflected in the contents of the Ottoman *Majalla*.
63 K. Kaser, *Patriarchy after Patriarchy: Gender Relations in Turkey and in the Balkans, 1500–2000* (Munster: LIT Verlag, 2008), 34.
64 Kaser, *Patriarchy after Patriarchy*, 34.
65 Elite marriage in al-Bab al-'Ali, Sijill 96, Doc 1023; subaltern marriage in Sijill 124, Doc. 27.
66 Y. Rapport, "Matrimonial Gifts in Early Islamic Egypt," *Islamic Law and Society* 7, no. 1 (Feb. 2000): 30. Rapport finds no difference between marriage contracts

signed by Copts or Muslims on the matter of the deferred *sadaq* in the ninth century. But the practice, he concludes, must have been prevalent in the eighth century, judging from Malik ibn al-Nas' explicit references to the practice.

67 Rapport, "Matrimonial Gifts," 1.
68 Rapport, "Matrimonial Gifts," 6.
69 This practice is referred to neither in the Qur'an nor in the Sunna of the Prophet (Rapport, "Matrimonial Gifts," 9).
70 Rapport, "Matrimonial Gifts," 9.
71 The Qayrawani jurist al-Qabisi (d. 1012) says that in his time it was common to pay the deferred *sadaq* on death or divorce. The twelfth-century Maghribi scholar Abu Ishaq al-Gharnati (d. 1183) instructed notaries to set a fixed and definite date by which the *sadaq* would be payable. Two caliphal edicts were issued by Hisham 'Abd al-Malik ibn 'Abd al-Malik to the chief judge of Egypt instructing, "if a wife claims her deferred *sadaq* [*al-mu'akhar*] from her husband, she should receive it under a specific condition," that is, if he takes another wife or if he moves her from her locale (Rapport, "Matrimonial Gifts," 11).
72 Rapport, "Matrimonial Gifts," 13.
73 In Sunni jurisprudence it was transformed from an obligatory payment to a recommended payment (Rapport, "Matrimonial Gifts," 21).
74 Imber, *Ebu's-Su'ud*, 175.
75 "The wife's claim to the full *mahr* or the full *mahr al-mithl* arises only when the marriage has been consummated; if the marriage is dissolved by the man prior to then, the wife can only claim half the *mahr* or a present *(mut'a)* fixed arbitrarily by the man; these regulations go back to *sura* II, 237–8 (cf. XXIII, 48)" (A. Layish and R. Shaham, "Mahr," in *EI*, CD-ROM edition).
76 Imber, *Ebu's-Su'ud*, 183.
77 Imber, *Ebu's-Su'ud*, 177.
78 al-Qisma al-'Askeriya, Sijill 5, Docs. 6, 7, 8, 9, 10.
79 al-Bab al-'Ali, Sijill 124, Doc. 10.
80 al-Bab al-'Ali, Sijill 124, Doc. 827.
81 Imber, *Ebu's-Su'ud*, 187.
82 Imber, *Ebu's-Su'ud*, 187.
83 al-Qisma al-'Askeriya, Sijill 5, Doc. 3.
84 al-Qisma al-'Askeriya, Sijill 5, Doc. 3.
85 al-Bab al-'Ali, Sijill 124, Docs. 47, 58, 118.
86 al-Bab al-'Ali, Sijill 124, Doc. 12.
87 al-Bab al-'Ali, Sijill 124, Docs. 47, 58.
88 al-Bab al-'Ali, Sijill 124, Doc. 12.
89 al-Bab al-'Ali, Sijill 124, Doc. 12.
90 al-Damiri, *Qudat Misr*, 47.
91 They descended on the province of Sharqiya, he writes, and interfered with every facet of agricultural production, collecting from the local populace more than 100,000 dinars (Ibn Iyas, *Bada'i' al-zuhur*, 263).
92 Ibn Iyas, *Bada'i' al-zuhur*, 453–54; N. Hanna, "The Administration of Courts in Ottoman Cairo," in *The State and Its Servants: Administration in Egypt from Ottoman Times to the Present*, ed. N. Hanna (Cairo: American University in Cairo Press, 1995), 46.

93 Ibn Iyas, *Bada'i' al-zuhur*, 281–82.
94 These include *halum* (cheese), ox cheese, licorice root, oil, ghee, honey, leather products, Upper Egyptian birds, vegetables, dates, cotton, bulgur, *shi'riya* (type of thin wheat noodle), fruit, Faiyumi apples, and a gamut of other products (Ibn Iyas, *Bada'i' al-zuhur*, 281–82).
95 al-Bab al-'Ali, Sijill 124, Doc. 33.
96 A. Layish, "The Maliki Family *Waqf* According to Wills and *Waqfiyyat*," *BSOAS* 46, no. 1 (1983): 9–10.
97 al-Bab al-'Ali, Sijill 124, Doc. 5.
98 al-Bab al-'Ali, Sijill 124, Doc. 12.
99 In cases of large *awqaf*, it is not uncommon to see judges from all the schools of law presiding.

Notes to Chapter 7
1 According to M. Bernard, *mu'amalat* brings us into the fields of *kalam fiqh* and, more precisely, *'amal*. In *fiqh*, it deals with problems of conduct, as opposed to *kalam*, which is the branch that deals with dogmatic theology. In its strict and first sense *mu'amalat* refers to transactions of credit granted by a donor to a beneficiary (M. Bernard, "Mu'amala," in *EI*, CD-ROM edition).
2 Bernard, "Mu'amala." Also see H. Laoust, *Essai sur les doctrines sociales et politiques d'Ibn Taimiyya* (Cairo: Institut français d'archéologie orientale, 1939).
3 Bernard, "Mu'amala." Also see R. Brunschvig, *Études d'Islamologie* (Paris: Maisonneuve et Larose, 1976).
4 Bernard, "Mu'alama."
5 In the formative period, the term *mu'amala* included contracts of cultivation (*mizara'a*) as well as a "body of rental transactions governing employer–employee relations." Al-Jahiz (d. 869) gave the concept "a psycho-social significance" and "a cultural coloring." With him, the word designated the broad "behavior dictated by a body of moral rules." In the *Ihya'* of al-Ghazali (d. 1111), the study of *mu'amalat* is contained in that of *fiqh*. The rights and obligations of created beings form the basis for the "customs (*al-'adat*) that can be looked at from two viewpoints: (a) exchanges, such as buying, selling, association, giving, lending, debt, (b) contracts, such as marriage, divorce, emancipation, slavery, rights of succession, etc." (Bernard, "Mu'amala"). See also L. Gardet, *Introduction à la théologie musulmane* (Paris: J. Vrin, 1948), 119.
6 Ibn Khaldun stressed the sociological aspect of the question, insisting on the fact that this problematic is dependent on reasoning. To him, the science of *mu'amalat* represented a branch (*far'*) of *'ilm al-hisab*, which forms part of rational, positive (*'aqliya tabi'iya*) knowledge as opposed to traditional, scriptural (*'aqliya wad'iya*) knowledge. These two types of knowledge are diversified and refined in proportion to the development of civilizations. In this sense, Ibn Khaldun opens the door to innovation (Bernard, "Mu'amala").
7 See W. Marcais, "L'islamisme et la vie urbaine," *Comptes-rendus de l'Académie des Inscriptions et Belles-Lettres* (1928): 86–100.

8   In his *Alepp*, Sauvaget concluded that "the Muslim era . . . is unaccompanied by any positive contribution. . . . the only thing we can credit it with is the dislocation of the urban centre . . . the work of Islam is essentially negative." J. Sauvaget, *Essai sur le développement d'une grande ville syrienne, des origines au milieu du XIX siècle* (Paris: Geuthner, 1941), quoted in A. Raymond, "Islamic City, Arab City: Orientalist Myths and Recent Views," *Arab Cities in the Ottoman Period*, Variorum Collected Studies Series (Ashgate: Variorum, 2002), 54.

9   They also argued that there was a specifically urban population existing parasitically, and in isolation from the countryside. Weulersse used the phrase "encysted like a creation imposed on the countryside it dominates and exploits" (quoted in R.S. Humphreys, *Islamic History: A Framework for Inquiry*, rev. ed. (Princeton, NJ: Princeton University Press, 1991), 229). Also see A. Raymond, "Islamic City, Arab City," 3.

10 G. von Grunebaum, "The Structure of the Muslim Town," in *Islam: Studies in the Nature of a Cultural Tradition* (Menasha, WI: American Anthropological Society, 1955): 141–58.

11 See: H.A.R. Gibb and H. Bowen, *Islamic Society and the West*, 2 vols. (London: Oxford University Press, 1957); I. Lapidus, *Muslim Cities in the Later Middle Ages* (Cambridge, UK: Cambridge University Press, 1984); C. Cahen, "L'histoire économique et sociale de l'Orient musulman médiéval," *SI* 2 (1955): 93–115; and O. Grabar, "The Architecture of the Middle Eastern City from Past to Present," in *The Art and Architecture of Islam, 650–1250*, ed. E. Richard and O. Grabar (New York: Pelican History of Art, 1987): 26–46.

12 Humphreys, *Islamic History*, 230.

13 See Raymond, "Islamic City, Arab City," 7–8. He writes that "a variety of things account for this phenomenon: historical reasons (artificial settling by foreign masters), a . . . variation on the often repeated theme of the incapacity of the Arabs to govern themselves and their submitting to 'foreign' dynasties."

14 Raymond, "Islamic City, Arab City," 8.

15 R. Brunschvig, "Urbanisme médiéval et droit musulman," *REI* 15 (1947): 127–55.

16 Raymond, "Islamic City, Arab City," 8.

17 U. Heyd, *Studies in Old Ottoman Criminal Law*, ed. V.L. Menage (Oxford, UK: Clarendon Press, 1973); R.C. Jennings, "Kadi Court and Legal Procedure in Seventeenth-century Ottoman Kayseri," *SI* 48 (1978): 133–72, and "Limitations on the Judicial Powers of the Kadi in Seventeenth-century Ottoman Kayseri," *SI* 50 (1979): 151–84; H. Gerber, "Sharia, Kanun, and Custom: The Court Records of Seventeenth-century Bursa," *International Journal of Turkish Studies* 21 (1981): 131–47, and *State, Society, and Law in Islam: Ottoman Law in Comparative Perspective* (Albany, NY: State University of New York Press, 1994).

18 N. Hanna, "The Administration of Courts in Ottoman Cairo," in *The State and Its Servants: Administration in Egypt from Ottoman Times to the Present*, ed. N. Hanna (Cairo: American University in Cairo Press, 1995), 44–59; G. al-Nahal, *The Judicial Administration of Ottoman Egypt in the Seventeenth Century* (Minneapolis, MN: Bibliotheca Islamica, 1979).

19 This policy, he argues, "could only strengthen these communities and give them free reign in order to carry out their activities, under the watchful eye of the Ottoman political and judicial authorities" (A. Raymond, "The Role of the Communities *(Tawa'if)* in the Administration of Cairo in the Ottoman Period," in *The State and Its Servants: Administration in Egypt from Ottoman Times to the Present*, ed. N. Hanna (Cairo: American University in Cairo Press, 1995), 36).
20 Raymond, "The Role of the Communities," 36.
21 The various ethnicities, religious groups, and residential and trade guilds that formed the subject of the law were physically divided into "geographical communities gathering inhabitants of a given quarter together." The Turks were known to reside in the Khan al-Khalili district, where they established a merchant community trading in tobacco for the most part, but later also coffee. Cairo's large Maghribi community established itself in trade on the pilgrimage route and was clustered into neighborhoods around al-Ghuriya and al-Fahhamin and around the mosque of Ibn Tulun. The Syrian community, which was smaller than the others and traded in fabric, coffee, and soap, lived around Khan al-Hamzawi and in the Jamaliya quarter. Finally, the Europeans lived along the Khalij banks (M. Winter, *Egyptian Society under Ottoman Rule, 1517–1798* (New York: Routledge, 1992), 228).
22 "Obvious linguistic and cultural reasons," he argues, facilitated the assimilation of Syrians and North Africans into the local population, rendering their communities "less visible in the geography of the city." Not so the Turks, who "because of the linguistic difference, stood out very noticeably" (Raymond, "The Role of the Communities," 240). Winter concurs, writing that as far the Maghribis went, "family groups such as the Shadhilis, the Wafa'is or the Sha'ranis, lost their Maghribi traditions and became wholly Egyptianized. More recent newcomers, however, retained their Maghribi clothes, dialect and custom" (Winter, *Egyptian Society*, 160).
23 Winter, *Egyptian Society*, 119.
24 Winter, *Egyptian Society*, 156.
25 Winter, *Egyptian Society*, 156.
26 This is corroborated by Evliya Celebi's description, written 150 years after its founding (Winter, *Egyptian Society*, 157).
27 As far as the Sufi guilds went, Winter writes: "If there was friction between Turkish and Arab Sufis in Ottoman Egypt, the sources do not mention it. Yet it is significant that the most serious incident between Turkish-speaking and Arabic-speaking Muslims in Ottoman Egypt started as an attack on Sufism" (Winter, *Egyptian Society*, 157). Followers of the Turkish fundamentalist writer Birgili Mehmet (d. 1573), the preacher known as al-Wa'iz al-Rumi, rioted in October 1711 when he put out a list of "blameworthy innovations" and incited his all-Turkish audience to denounce and remove them from Cairo. Winter interprets this as, in part, a confrontation between 'pre-Wahhabites' and 'neo-Hanbalites' but also between Egyptians and Turks (Winter, *Egyptian Society*, 159).

28 Muhammad ibn Ahmad ibn Iyas, *Bada'i' al-zuhur fi waqa'i' al-duhur*, ed. Muhammad Mustafa, vol. 5 (Weisbaden: E.J. Brill, 1975), 246.
29 Ibn Iyas, *Bada'i' al-zuhur*, 248–49, 366.
30 Shaykh al-Islam Muhammad ibn al-Surur al-Bakri al-Siddiqi, *al-Nuzha al-zahiya fi dhikr wulat Misr wa-l-Qahira al-mu'izziya*, ed. 'Abd al-Razzaq 'Abd al-Razzaq 'Isa (Cairo: al-'Arabi li-l-Nashr wa-l-Tawzi', 1998), 163–65. This chronicler (1589–1676) writes that their demands were met when they kidnapped 'Uways Pasha's son. No one, not the chief judge, the pasha, the *daftardar*, or other *akabir*, could dissuade them from disobeying the sultan. The Sipahis were eventually subdued by the next governor, Ahmad Hafiz al-Khadim, who reigned for five years (al-Bakri, *al-Nuzha*, 163–65).
31 G. Baer, *Egyptian Guilds in Modern Times* (Jerusalem: Israel Oriental Society, 1964), 14. He also describes a seventeenth-century struggle between guild shaykhs and the governor over the control of the guilds.
32 Raymond, "The Role of the Communities," 243.
33 P. Ghazaleh, "The Guilds: Between Tradition and Modernity," in *The State and Its Servants*, ed. N. Hanna (Cairo: American University in Cairo Press, 1995), 65.
34 Hijaziya's case amply demonstrated this in chapter six (Mahkamat al-Bab al-'Ali, Sijill 124, Doc. 65).
35 Mahkamat Tulun, Sijill 165, Doc. 1303; al-Bab al-'Ali, Sijill 66, Docs. 45, 47; Sijill 96, Doc. 1023; Mahkamat al-Qisma al-'Askeriya, Sijill 5, Docs. 6, 8.
36 al-Bab al-'Ali, Sijill 134, Doc. 6.
37 al-Bab al-'Ali, Sijill 134, Docs. 27, 93; Sijill 66, Docs. 12, 218, 219, 238.
38 al-Bab al-'Ali, Sijill 96, Doc. 2820; Sijill 134, Doc. 93; Sijill 66, Doc. 2.
39 Tulun, Sijill 165, Doc. 1303; al-Bab al-'Ali, Sijill 66, Docs. 2, 191.
40 al-Bab al-'Ali, Sijill 66, Doc. 191.
41 S.A.I. Milad, "Registres judiciaires du tribunal de la Salihiyya Nağmiyya," *AI* 12 (1974): 235–36.
42 M. Khadduri, "Sulh," in *EI*, CD-ROM edition.
43 Khadduri, "Sulh." "The objects of the *sulh* are essentially the same as those in contracts of sale, consisting of material and non-material objects, and are subject to the same limits and prohibitions as other Islamic legal contracts."
44 A. Layish, "Sharia and Custom in the Cyrenaican Family," *The Seventh Stanford–Berkeley Law and Colonialism Symposium: Muslim Family Law and Colonialism in Africa*, Stanford University, 11–12 May 2001, 174. Nonetheless, he does concede that in other areas, a complex relationship between shari'a and custom may be "divided into two main categories: one in which custom reigns almost absolutely, outside the control of the *shari'a*, with slight concessions in deference to the venue where the cases are heard, and one prominently displaying the impact of the *shari'a*, which yields assimilative power over the custom" (Layish, "Sharia and Custom in the Cyrenaican Family," 172).
45 Layish, "Sharia and Custom in the Cyrenaican Family," 172.
46 See R.B. Serjeant, *Custom and Shari'ah Law in Arabian Society* (Brookfield, VT: Variorum, 1991); and *Studies in Arabian History and Civilisation* (London: Variorum, 1981).

47 al-Bab al-'Ali, Sijill 124, Doc. 780.
48 al-Bab al-'Ali, Sijill 124, Doc. 763.
49 Tulun, Sijill 165, Doc. 1306.
50 Tulun, Sijill 165, Doc. 1306. Here, the term 'old custom' is ambiguous at best. It does not tell us whether it is Mamluk or Ottoman *'askeri* practice and underscores the problems inherent in viewing all references to custom as denoting 'local' practice.
51 Milad, "Registres judiciaires," 242–43.
52 Milad, "Registres judiciaires," 242.
53 F. Müge Göçek, "Multazim," in *EI*, CD-ROM edition.
54 Müge Göçek, "Multazim."
55 H. Inalcik, "Filaha," in *EI*, CD-ROM edition.
56 al-Bab al-'Ali, Sijill 124, Doc. 743.
57 al-Bab al-'Ali, Sijill 124, Doc. 784.
58 al-Bab al-'Ali, Sijill 96, Doc. 2826.
59 al-Bab al-'Ali, Sijill 96, Doc. 774.
60 While such an example supports Raymond's general argument that local institutions functioned autonomously, we must be aware that this was not always the case. As mentioned by the authors of the Gotha manuscript, guild members often complained harshly at what they perceived to be Ottoman interference in their internal management. In the case of the butchers' guild, we may, at least, confirm that appointments followed the customs of the guild in that year. No doubt, the level of intervention was determined by many factors, such as the vitality of the industry in question to the state economy.
61 al-Bab al-'Ali, Sijill 96, Doc. 817.
62 al-Bab al-'Ali, Sijill 124, Doc. 785.
63 For more on Ottoman metrology, see "'The Honorable *Hisba*' and the Customary Economy," below.
64 al-Bab al-'Ali, Sijill 124, Doc. 114.
65 al-Bab al-'Ali, Sijill 124, Doc. 59.
66 A third period begins with the political and economic crisis of the 1580s, when northern European merchants enter the Mediterranean in force. Their demands change patterns in the spice and silk trades and have an impact on production in certain regions, such as Syria or the Aegean seaboard. After the crisis of the late sixteenth and early seventeenth centuries, there is some recovery, but it is soon interrupted by the Habsburg–Ottoman war of 1683–99. Until 1477–78, when the first Ottoman gold coin was minted, roughly corresponding in weight and fineness to the Venetian ducat, the Ottoman mints turned out silver coins only, the aqçe. Before the devaluation brought about by Mehmed the Conqueror, it weighed 1.01 gram, and .83 gram thereafter. Throughout most of the sixteenth century, the aqçe stood at 0.73 gram; a new wave of devaluation occurred at the end of the sixteenth century, at a time when imports of silver from the New World had also resulted in a price rise. The latter was viewed as a major calamity, affecting not only trade, but also the legitimacy of the state. In spite of several currency reforms, in the course of the seventeenth and eighteenth centuries the aqçe was devalued to such an extent that it disappeared from the market

and only survived as a money of account (S. Faroqhi, "Othmanli: II. Social and Economic History," in *EI*, CD-ROM edition).
67 Faroqhi, "Othmanli."
68 Faroqhi, "Othmanli."
69 Ibn Iyas, *Bada'i al-zuhur'*, 214.
70 Ibn Iyas, *Bada'i' al-zuhur*, 214. Meaning "small white," it was the name given in Turkish to the Ottoman silver coin habitually referred to by European writers as the *aspre* or *asper*, from the Greek *aspron*. The term was already in use under the Saljukids of Iraq during the twelfth century and was applied to the first Ottoman coin to be struck, under Orhan in 1327. During the fourteenth and fifteenth centuries the Ottoman coin was usually called simply 'Uthmani, but from the reign of Salim I onward, it came to be known simply as the aqçe (Ibn Iyas, *Bada'i' al-zuhur*, 214).
71 Ibn Iyas, *Bada'i' al-zuhur*, 214.
72 Ibn Iyas, *Bada'i' al-zuhur*, 244, 358–59.
73 A.S. Ehrenkreutz, "Dhahab," in *EI*, CD-ROM edition. This was secured by the exploitation of gold mines located in the Muslim empire and the importation of bullion from adjacent countries. Although medieval sources refer to many mining areas (see D.M. Dunlop, "Sources of Gold and Silver in Islam according to al-Hamdani (Tenth Century A.D.)," *SI* 8 (1957): 29–49), the region of Wadi al-Allaqi was particularly famous for intensive mining activities, and Ghana for the excellent quality of its ore. War expenditures connected with the operations of the Crusaders, a gradual reestablishment of European hegemony in the Mediterranean balance of trade, and a later absorption of West Sudanese gold by the Portuguese led to a drastic draining of Near Eastern gold reserves (M. Lombard, "Les bases monétaires d'une suprématie économique: L'or musulman du VIIe au XIe siècle," *Annales Économies, Sociétés, Civilisations* 2 (1947): 142–60). See also F. Braudel, "Monnaies et civilisations: De l'or du Soudan à l'argent d'Amérique," *Annales Économies, Sociétés, Civilisations* 1 (1946): 9–22.
74 Ibn Iyas, *Bada'i' al-zuhur*, 354.
75 Ibn Iyas, *Bada'i' al-zuhur*, 354.
76 Tulun, Sijill 165, Doc. 17.
77 See Gibb and Bowen, *Islamic Society and the West*, vol. 1, part 2.
78 S. Shaw, *The Financial and Administrative Organization and Development of Ottoman Egypt, 1517–1798* (Princeton, NJ: Princeton University Press, 1962), xxii. He writes that "it was a direct descendant of the silver mu'ayyidi used in the Mamluk Empire in Egypt since Sultan Mu'ayyad and first minted 818/1415–16."
79 E. Ashtor, "Mawazin," in *EI*, CD-ROM edition.
80 The *mudd*, a measure of capacity, was equivalent to about 1.05 liters in Iraq, 3.673 liters in Syria, and 2.5 liters in Egypt (Ashtor, "Mawazin").
81 This is what the Arabic geographers tell about Jibal and its capital Rayy, about Khuzistan, and about Aleppo and its province. In many provinces meat was weighed by a *ratl* different from that of other articles. In all provinces of Upper Egypt there was a *ratl* for meat and bread and another for other commodities (Ashtor, "Mawazin").

82 In many countries there were particular *ratl*s for pepper, silk, and so on. For grain, there was one measure of capacity used in all Arab countries; liquids had other measures. The sources show, however, that in the course of time there was a trend in several countries to use weights for liquids, and to replace weights (and measures of capacity) by bigger ones. Despite the mutual influence between the metrological systems of the Near Eastern countries, there remained through the Middle Ages (and also later) a marked difference between the Persian and Arab countries, although there was some overlap. From Roman–Byzantine rule over the Near East, "a two-sided structure of the metrological systems of all the Muslim countries" emerged—sexagesimal and decimal—also a feature of the metrological system of the Greco-Roman world. The survival of the metrological systems of antiquity, argues Ashtor, overshadows "the almost insignificant influence of the weights and measures of Arabia upon the newly-conquered countries" (Ashtor, "Mawazin").
83 Ashtor, "Mawazin."
84 K. Salameh, "Aspects of the *Sijill*s of the Shari'a Court in Jerusalem," in *Ottoman Jerusalem the Living City, 1517–1917*, ed. S. Auld and R. Hillenbrand (Jerusalem: al-Tajir World of Islam Trust, 2000), 114.
85 Originating in the Aramaic from Greek, "the (100 *ratl*s) is obviously the Latin *centenarius*; and the *qafiz* is the Persian name of a measure of capacity" (Ashtor, "Mawazin").
86 Ashtor, "Mawazin."
87 Ibn Iyas, *Bada'i' al-zuhur*, 414.
88 Hinz, "Dhira'."
89 al-Bab al-'Ali, Sijill 124, Doc. 785. This appears to be the architectural cubit measuring 79.8 cm. (Hinz, "Dhira'").
90 al-Bab al-'Ali, Sijill 124, Doc. 742.
91 Ibn Iyas, *Bada'i' al-zuhur*, 188. Ibn Iyas considers this the greatest atrocity committed by Salim against Egypt, writing that there were women and children among the exiles who were forced into "mixing/consorting with nations other than their own" (Ibn Iyas, *Bada'i' al-zuhur*, 229).
92 Weights of balance (in full *sanajat al-mizan* [sing. *sanja*]) also applied to balances, steelyards, and the weights of a clock. There are two recognized plural forms, *sinajat* and *sinaj* (in modern Egyptian Arabic *sinag*, plural of *singa*) (J. Walker and D.R. Hill, "Sanadjat," in *EI*, CD-ROM edition).
93 Ibn Iyas, *Bada'i' al-zuhur*, 415.
94 Ibn Iyas, *Bada'i' al-zuhur*, 444.
95 Shaw, *The Financial and Administrative Organization*, p. 118.
96 al-Bab al-'Ali, Sijill 124, Doc. 68.
97 See: Shaw, *The Financial and Administrative Organization*, chapter one.
98 A term used to denote two ideas: (1) the duty of every Muslim to "promote good and forbid evil;" and (2) the function of a person entrusted with the application of this rule in the supervision of moral behavior and more particularly of the markets. The person entrusted with the *hisba*, meaning 'calculation' or 'sufficiency,' was called the *muhtasib*. See: C. Cahen and M. Talbi, "Hisba," in *EI*, CD-ROM edition; and R. Mantran, "Hisba: II. Ottoman Empire," in *EI*, CD-ROM edition.

99 Tulun, Sijill 165, Doc. 1305.
100 al-Bab al-'Ali, Sijill 96, Doc. 2822.

Notes to Conclusions
1. Robert Fisk, "The Lie behind Mass 'Suicides' of Egypt's Young Women," *The Independent*, 9 September 2010, http://www.independent.co.uk/voices/commentators/fisk/robert-fisk-the-lie-behind-mass-suicides-of-egypts-young-women-2074229.html
2. F. Fukuyama, *The End of History and the Last Man* (New York: Avon Books, 2006).

Abbreviations

AI	*Annales Islamologiques*
BSOAS	*Bulletin of the School of Oriental and African Studies*
EI	*Encyclopedia of Islam*
IJMES	*International Journal of Middle Eastern Studies*
JESHO	*Journal of the Economic and Social History of the Orient*
REI	*Revue des études islamiques*
SI	*Studia Islamica*
WZKM	*Wiener Zeitschrift für die Kunde des Morgenlandes*

Bibliography

Court Records
Mahkamat al-Bab al-'Ali (Islamic Court of the Bab al-'Ali). Sijill 96: 10–22, 445–46, 1023–24H; Sijill 66: 1–5, 51–65, 1005–1006H; Sijill 124: 1–20, 160–78, 405–408, 1055–56H.
Mahkamat al-Qisma al-'Arabiya (Islamic Court of Civilian/Arab Affairs). Sijill 5: 1–2, 442–52, 985H.
Mahkamat al-Qisma al-'Askeriya (Court of Military Affairs). Sijill 5: 1–15, 275–85, 970H.
Mahkamat Tulun (Tulun Islamic Court). Sijill 165: 1–5, 284–87, 965–66H.

Primary Sources
'Abd al-Razzaq. *Al-Musannaf*. Vol. 6. 2nd ed. Beirut: al-Maktab al-Islami, 1983.
Abdelrahman, Abdel Rahim. *The Documents of the Egyptian Courts Related to the Maghariba and Their Importance in Studying the Economic, Social, Cultural History of the Arab World*. Vols. 1–2. Cairo: Publications du Centre et recherches ottomanes, morisque, de documentation et d'information, 1992.
'Ali, Mustafa. "Künhü al-Ahbar." In *Pure Water for Thirsty Muslims: A Study of Mustafa Ali of Gallipoli's* Künhü al-Ahbar, translated and edited by Jan Schmidt. Leiden: Het Oosters Instituut, 1991.
———. *Mustafa Ali's Description of Cairo of 1599*. Translated and edited by A. Tietze. Vienna: E.J. Brill, 1975.
al-Baghwi, Hussain ibn Mas'u. *Sharh al-Sunna*. Vol. 9. Beirut: al-Maktab al-Islami, 1983.
al-Bakri al-Siddiqi, Shaykh al-Islam Muhammad ibn al-Surur. *al-Nuzha al-zahiya fi dhikr wulat Misr wa-l-Qahira al-mu'izziya*. Edited by 'Abd al-Razzaq 'Abd al-Razzaq 'Isa. Cairo: al-'Arabi li-l-Nashr wa-l-Tawzi', 1998.
Celalzade Mustafa Çelebi. "Tabaqat al-Mamalik wa-darajat al-Masalik." *Geschichte Sultan Sulayman Kanunis, von 1520 bis 1557*. Edited by Petra Kappert. Wiesbaden: E.J. Brill, 1981.

al-Damiri, Husayn ibn Muhammad. *Qudat Misr fi-l-qarn al-'ashir wa awa'il al-qarn al-hadi 'ashir.* Manuscript. Cairo: Dar al-Kutub.
al-Damurdashi, Ahmad. *al-Damurdashi's Chronicle of Egypt: al-Durra al-musana fi waqi' al-kinana.* Translated and edited by Daniel Crecilius and 'Abd al-Wahhab Bakr. Leiden: E.J. Brill, 1991.
Fatawa 'Alamgiri. Edited by 'Abd al-Latif Hasan 'Abd al-Rahman. Vol. 6. Karachi: n.d.
Ibn Abi Shaybah. *al-Musannaf.* Vol. 4. Karachi: Idrat al-Qur'an wa-l-'Uloom al-Islamiya, 1987.
Ibn Hazm, Abu Muhammed. *al-Muhalla.* Vol. 8. Beirut: Dar al-Kutub al-'Ilmiya, 1998.
Ibn Iyas, Muhammad ibn Ahmad. *Bada'i' al-zuhur fi waqa'i' al-duhur.* 5 Vols. Edited by Muhammad Mustafa. Wiesbaden: E.J. Brill, 1975.
Ibn Nujaym, Zayn al-Din Ibrahim. *al-Ashbah wa-l-naza'ir.* Beirut: Dar al-Kutub al-'Ilmiya, 1983.
———. *Rasa'il Ibn Nujaym.* Beirut: Dar al-Kutub al-'Ilmiya, 1980.
Ibn Qudamah. *al-Mughni.* Vol. 7. Cairo: al-Matba'a al-Shaf'iya, 1962.
Ibn Taymiya. *al-Siyasa al-shar'iya.* Cairo: Dar al-Kutub al-'Arabiya, 1966.
al-Manufi, Muhammad ibn al-Mu'ti ibn Abi al-Fath ibn Ahmad ibn 'Abd al-Mughni ibn 'Ali al-Ishaqi. *Akhbar al-awwal fi-man tasarraf fi Misr min arbab al-duwal.* Cairo: al-Matba'a al-'Uthmaniya, 1886.
al-Mawardi, *al-Ahkam al-sultaniya.* London: Ta-Ha Publishers, 1996.
Qanunnama Misr. Translated and edited by M.A. Fu'ad. Cairo: Anglo-Egyptian Bookshop, 1986.
al-Saffarini, Muhammad ibn Ahmad. *al-Tahqiq fi butlan al-talfiq.* Edited by 'Abd al-'Aziz ibn Ibrahim al-Dukhayl. Riyadh: Dar al-Sumay'i li-l-Nashr wa-l-Tawzi', 1998.
al-Turkmani, Idris ibn Baydakin. *Kitab al-lum'a fi-l-hawadith wa-l-bid'a.* 2 vols. Edited by Subhi Labib. Cairo: Qism Dirasat al-Islamiya bil-Ma'had al-Almani li-l-'Athar, 1986.

Secondary Sources

Abou al-Haj, R.A. "Aspects of the Legitimation of Ottoman Rule as Reflected in the Preambles to Two Early Liva Kannunameler." *Turcica* 21–22 (1991): 371–83.
———. "Formation of the Modern State: The Ottoman Empire, Sixteenth to Eighteenth Centuries." *Journal of Early Modern History* 14, no. 4 (2010): 317–54.
Abou El Fadl, K. *Speaking in God's Name: Islamic Law, Authority and Women.* Oxford, UK: Oneworld Press, 2001.
Abu-Lughod, J.L. *Before European Hegemony: The World System* A.D. *1250–1350.* Oxford, UK: Oxford University Press, 1991.
Abu Talib, A.H. *'Urubat Misr: bayn al-tarikh wa-l-siyasa.* Cairo: Markaz al-Mahrusa li-l-Buhuth wa-l-Tadrib wa-l-Nashr, 1996.
Agmon, I. "Muslim Women in Court according to the *Sijill* of Late Ottoman Jaffa and Haifa: Some Methodological Notes." In *Women, the Family, and Divorce Laws in Islamic History,* edited by A. Azhary Sonbol, 126–41. Syracuse, NY: Syracuse University Press, 1996.
Ahmed, Leila. *Women and Gender in Islam.* New Haven, CT: Yale University Press, 1992.

'Alia, S. *al-Qada' wa-l-'urf fi-l-Islam*. Beirut: al-Mu'assasa al-Jami'iya li-l-Dirasat wa-l-Nashr wa-l-Tawzi', 1986.

Anderson, B. *Imagined Communities*. New York: Verso, 1991.

Ansari, Z.I. "Islamic Juristic Terminology before al-Shafi'i." *Arabica* 19, no. 3 (1972): 288–94.

Aquinas, T. "Whether There Is in Us a Natural Law." In *Readings in Philosophy of Law*, edited by J. Arthur and W.H. Shaw, 4–14. Englewood Cliffs, NJ: Prentice-Hall, 1984.

Arkoun, M. "Insaf." In *EI*, CD-ROM edition.

Asad, T. "Free Speech, Blasphemy, and Secular Criticism." In *Is Critique Secular? Blasphemy, Injury, and Free Speech*, edited by T. Asad, W. Brown, J. Butler, and S. Mahmood, 20–63. Berkeley, CA: Townsend Center for the Humanities, University of California Press, 2009.

———. "Medieval Heresies: An Anthropological View." *Social History* 11 (1986): 354–62.

al-'Asali, K.J. *Watha'iq maqdasiya tarikhiya*. 3 vols. Amman: Jordan University, 1983.

Ashtor, E. "Mawazin." In *EI*, CD-ROM edition.

Askan, V.H., and D. Goffman, eds. *The Early Modern Ottomans*. Cambridge, UK: Cambridge University Press, 2007.

Ataseven, I. *The Alevi-Bektasi Legacy: Problems of Acquisition and Explanation*. Edited by T. Olsson. Lund, Sweden: Nova Press, 1997.

Auchterlonie, P. *Arabic Biographical Dictionaries: A Summary Guide and Bibliography*. Durham, UK: Middle East Libraries Committee, 1987.

Auer, B.H. *Symbols of Authority in Medieval Islam: History, Religion, and Muslim Legitimacy in the Delhi Sultanate*. London: I.B. Tauris, 2012.

Ayalon, D. "Aspects of the Mamluk Phenomenon: Ayyubids, Kurds, and Turks." *Der Islam* 43, no. 2 (1976): 1–32.

———. "The Great Yasa of Chingiz Khan." *SI* 33 (1971): 1–15.

———. "Mamluk." In *EI*, *CD-ROM edition*.

———. *Studies in the Mamluks of Egypt (1250–1517)*. Collected Studies Series. London: Variorum Reprints, 1977.

———. "Studies on the Structure of the Mamluk Army." *BSOAS* 15, no. 1 (1953): 203–28.

Baer, G. *Egyptian Guilds in Modern Times*. Jerusalem: Israel Oriental Society, 1964.

———. "Popular Revolt in Ottoman Cairo." *Islam* 54 (1977): 213–42.

———. "The *Waqf* as a Prop for the Social System (16th–20th Centuries)." *Islamic Law and Society* 4, no. 3 (1997): 264–97.

Baillie, N.B.E. *A Digest of Mohummudan Law*, vol. 1. 2nd ed. Lahore: Premier Book House, 1965.

Barkan, J.L., and M.A. Cook. "The Price Revolution of the Sixteenth Century: A Turning Point in the Economic History of the Near East." *IJMES* 6 (1975): 3–28.

Barkan, L. *Kanunlar*. Istanbul: Burhaneddin Matbaa, 1943.

———. "La 'Méditerranée' de Fernand Braudel vue d'Istamboul." *Annales Economies, Sociétés, Civilisations* 9 (1954): 189–200.

Barnes, J.R. *An Introduction to Religious Foundations in the Ottoman Empire*. Leiden: E.J. Brill, 1986.

Barthold, J. *Arkhivnie Kursi*. Vol. 1. St. Petersburg: n.p., 1920.
Bayinder, A. "The Function of the Judiciary in the Ottoman Empire." In *The Great Ottoman Turkish Civilization*, vol. 3, edited by K. Çiçek, 630–51. Ankara: Semih Ofset, 2000.
Beardsley, J. "Proof of Fact in French Civil Procedure." *American Journal of Comparative Law* 34, no. 3 (1986): 459–86.
Behrens-Abouseif, D. *Egypt's Adjustment to Ottoman Rule: Institutions, Waqfs, and Architecture in Cairo—16th and 17th Centuries*. Leiden: E.J. Brill, 1994.
Bellah, R. *Beyond Belief: Essays on Religion in a Post-Traditional World*. Berkeley, CA: University of California Press, 1991.
Berger, P. *The Sacred Canopy: Elements of a Sociological Theory of Religion*. New York: Doubleday Press, 1967.
Berkey, J. *The Transmission of Knowledge in Medieval Cairo*. Princeton, NJ: Princeton University Press, 1992.
Bernard, M. "Mu'amala." In *EI*, CD-ROM edition.
Berque, J. "'Amal." In *EI*, CD-ROM edition.
Björkman, W. "Diplomatics." In *EI*, CD-ROM edition.
Black, A. *The History of Islamic Political Thought*. New York: Routledge, 2001.
Blumenberg, H. *The Legitimacy of the Modern Age*. Translated by R.M. Wallace. Cambridge, MA: MIT Press, 1985.
Bousquet, G.H. "Ada." In *EI*, CD-ROM edition.
Bousquet, G.H., and J. Prins. "Ada." In *EI*, CD-ROM edition.
Braud, B., and B. Lewis. *Christians and Jews in the Ottoman Empire: The Functioning of a Plural Society*. New York: Holmes & Meier, 1982.
Braudel, F. "Monnaies et civilisations: De l'or du Soudan à l'argent d'Amérique." *Annales Économies, Sociétés, Civilisations* 1 (1946): 9–22.
Bravmann, M.M. *The Spiritual Background of Early Islam: Studies in Ancient Arab Concepts*. Leiden: E.J. Brill, 1972.
Brockopp, J.E. "Early Islamic Jurisprudence in Egypt: Two Scholars and Their *Mukhtasar*." *International Journal of Middle East Studies* 30 (1998): 167–82.
Brown, C. "A Revisionist Approach to Religious Change." In *Religion and Modernization: Sociologists and Historians Debate the Secularization Thesis*, edited by S. Bruce, 31–58. Oxford, UK: Clarendon Press, 1992.
Brown, P. *The Rise of Christendom*. 2nd ed. Oxford, UK: Blackwell Publishing, 2003.
Brunschvig, R. *Études d'Islamologie*. Paris: Maisonneuve et Larose, 1976.
———. "Urbanisme médiéval et droit musulman." *REI* 15 (1947): 127–55.
Burton, J. *The Sources of Islamic Law: Islamic Theories of Abrogation*. Edinburgh: University of Edinburgh, 1990.
Buzov, S. "The Lawgiver and His Lawmakers: The Role of Legal Discourse in the Change of Ottoman Imperial Culture." PhD diss., University of Chicago, 2005.
Cahen, C. "L'histoire économique et sociale de l'Orient musulman médiéval." *SI* 2 (1955): 93–115.
Cahen, C., and M. Talbi. "Hisba." In *EI*, CD-ROM edition.
Calder, N. *Studies in Early Muslim Jurisprudence*. Oxford: Oxford University Press, 1993.
Calvin, J. *Institutes of the Christian Religion*. Translated by H. Beveridge. Grand Rapids, MI: Wm. B. Eerdmans, 1989.

Carnegie Endowment for International Peace. "An Independent Voice for Egypt's Al-Azhar?" 13 July 2011, http://www.carnegieendowment.org/sada/?fa=show&article=45052.

Casale, Giancarlo. *The Ottoman Age of Exploration*. New York: Oxford University Press, 2010.

Chakrabarty, D. *Provincializing Europe: Postcolonial Thought and Historical Difference*. Princeton, NJ: Princeton University Press, 2000.

Charnay, I. "Pluralism normatif et ambiguïté dans la *fiqh*." In *L'ambivalence dans la culture arabe*, edited by J. Berque and J.P. Charnay, 382–96. Paris: Paris Edition Anthropos, 1967.

Chartier, R. "Culture as Appropriation: Popular Cultural Uses in Early Modern France." In *Understanding Popular Culture: Europe from the Middle Ages to the Nineteenth Century*, edited by S.L. Kaplan, 229–53. Berlin: Mouton, 1984.

Chatterjee, P. *The Nation and Its Fragments*. Princeton, NJ: Princeton University Press, 1993.

Chittick, W.C. *The Sufi Path of Knowledge: Ibn al-'Arabi's Metaphysics of Imagination*. Albany, NY: State University of New York Press, 1989.

Choudhury, M.R. *The Din-i Ilahi, or the Religion of Akbar*. Calcutta: Das Gupta Publishers, 1952.

Cohen, A. *Jewish Life under Islam: Jerusalem in the Sixteenth Century*. Cambridge, MA: Harvard University Press, 1984.

———. "Sixteenth-Century Egypt and Palestine: The Jewish Connection as Reflected in the *Sijill* of Jerusalem." In *Egypt and Palestine: A Millennium of Association*, edited by A. Cohen, 232–40. Jerusalem: Ben-Zvi Institute for the Study of Jewish Communities in the East, 1984.

———. *A World Within: Jewish Life as Reflected in Muslim Court Documents from the* Sijill *of Jerusalem*. Philadelphia, PA: Center for Judaic Studies, University of Pennsylvania, 1994.

Corbin, H. *L'Imagination créatrice dans le soufisme de Ibn Arabi*. Paris: Entrelacs, 2006.

Coulson, N.H. *A History of Islamic Law*. Edinburgh: Edinburgh University Press, 1964.

———. "Muslim Custom and Case Law." In *Islamic Law and Legal Theory*, edited by I. Edge, 259–70. Aldershot, UK: Dartmouth, 1996.

Curran, J.R. *Pagan City and Christian Capital: Rome in the Fourth Century*. Oxford, UK: Oxford University Press, 2000.

al-Dawani, Jalal al-Din. "Akhlaq-i Jalali." In *Practical Philosophy of the Muhammedan People*, translated by W.T. Thompson. London: 1839.

De Blois, F.C. "Sidjill." In *EI*, CD-ROM edition.

Denny, F. *Introduction to Islam*. 3rd ed. Upper Saddle River, NJ: Prentice Hall, 2006.

Derrida, J. *Archive Fever: A Freudian Impression*. Chicago, IL: University of Chicago Press, 1996.

———. *Resistances of Psychoanalysis*. Stanford, CA: Stanford University Press, 1998.

Donner, F. *The Early Islamic Conquests*. Princeton, NJ: Princeton University Press, 1981.

Doumani, B.B. "The Islamic Court Records of Palestine." *Birzeit Research Review* 2 (1985): 3–29.

———. "Palestinian Islamic Court Records: A Source for Socio-economic History." *MESA Bulletin* 19 (1985): 155–72.
Dozy, R.P. *Supplément aux dictionnaires arabes*. 3rd ed. Leiden: E.J. Brill, 1967.
Dunlop, D.M. "Sources of Gold and Silver in Islam according to al-Hamdani (Tenth Century A.D.)" *SI* 8 (1957): 29–49.
Ebeid, R.Y., and J.L. Young. *Some Arabic Documents of the Ottoman Period*. Leiden: E.J. Brill, 1976.
Ehrenkreutz, A.S. "Dhahab." In *EI*, CD-ROM edition.
EI (*Encyclopedia of Islam*), CD-ROM edition. Edited by P.J. Bearman, T. Blanquis, C.E. Bosworth, E. van Donzel, and W.P. Heinrichs. 2nd ed. 12 vols. Leiden: E.J. Brill, 1960–2005.
Elyan, Tamim. "Al-Azhar Says Grand Sheikh Should Be Elected, Not Be State Appointed." *Egypt Daily News*, 17 February 2011, http://www.thedailynewsegypt.com/religion/al-azhar-says-grand-sheikh-should-be-elected-not-state-appointed-dp2.html
Ergene, B.A. *Local Court, Provincial Society, and Justice in the Ottoman Empire*. Leiden: E.J. Brill, 2003.
Escovitz, J.H. *The Office of Qadi al-Qudat in Cairo under the Bahri Mamluks*. Berlin: Klaus Schwarz Verlag, 1983.
Fadel, M. "Adjudication in the Maliki *Madhhab*: A Study of Legal Process in Medieval Islam." PhD diss., University of Chicago, 1995.
———. "Social Logic of *Taqlid* and the Rise of the *Mukhtasar*." *Islamic Law and Society* 3 (1996): 193–233.
Faroqhi, S. *Approaching Ottoman History: An Introduction to the Sources*. Cambridge, UK: Cambridge University Press, 1999.
———. "Civilian Society and Political Power in the Ottoman Empire: A Report on Research in Collective Biography (1480–1830)." *IJMES* 17 (1985): 109–17.
———. "Othmanli: II. Social and Economic History." In *EI*, CD-ROM edition.
———. "Political Activity among Ottoman Taxpayers and the Problem of Sultanic Legitimation (1500–1650)." *JESHO* 35 (1992): 1–39.
———. "Sidjill." In *EI*, CD-ROM edition.
———. "Towns, Agriculture, and the State in Sixteenth-century Ottoman Anatolia." *JESHO* 33 (1990): 125–56.
———. *Towns and Townsmen of Ottoman Anatolia: Trade, Crafts, and Food Production in an Urban Setting, 1520–1650*. New York: Cambridge University Press, 1984.
Fattal, A. *Le statut légal des non-musulmans en pays d'Islam*. Beirut: Imprimerie Catholique, 1958.
Fay, M.A. "Women and *Waqf*: Towards a Reconsideration of Women's Place in the Mamluk Household." *IJMES* 29, no. 1 (1997): 33–51.
al-Fikyaki, A.H. "The Shu'ubiyya in Arab Nationalism." In *Political and Social Thought in the Contemporary Middle East*, edited by A.K. Khater, 166–70. New York: Houghton Mifflin, 2004.
Findley, C. *Bureaucratic Reform in the Ottoman Empire: The Sublime Porte 1789–1922*. Princeton, NJ: Princeton University Press, 1980.
Fisk, R. "The Lie behind Mass 'Suicides' of Egypt's Young Women." *The Independent*, 9 September 2010, http://www.independent.co.uk/voices/

commentators/fisk/robert-fisk-the-lie-behind-mass-suicides-of-egypts-young-women-2074229.html

Fleischer, C. *Bureaucrat and Intellectual in the Ottoman Empire: The Historian Mustafa Ali (1541–1600)*. Princeton, NJ: Princeton University Press, 1986.

———. "The Lawgiver as Messiah: The Making of the Imperial Image in the Reign of Süleyman." In *Soliman le magnifique et son temps*, edited by G. Veinstein, 159–83. Paris: La Documentation française, 1992.

Foucault, M. "Governmentality." In *The Foucault Effect: Studies in Governmentality*, edited by G. Burchell, C. Gordon, and P. Miller, 87–104. Chicago, IL: University of Chicago Press, 1991.

Frank, F.M. *Al-Ghazali and the Ash'arite School*. Durham, NC: Duke University Press, 1994.

Fuess, A. "*Zulm* by *Mazalim*? The Political Implications of the Use of *Mazalim* Jurisdiction by the Mamluk Sultans." *Mamluk Studies Review* 13, no. 1 (2009): 121–47.

Fukuyama, F. *The End of History and the Last Man*. New York: Avon Books, 2006.

Gabriel, F. "Adab." In *EI*, CD-ROM edition.

Gacek, A. "The Ancient Sijill of Qayrawan." *Middle Eastern Library Association Notes* 46 (1989): 26–29.

Gardet, L. "Hudjdja." In *EI*, CD-ROM edition.

———. *Introduction à la théologie musulmane*. Paris: J. Vrin, 1948.

Garnett, L. *The Dervishes of Turkey*. London: Octagon Press, 1990.

Geertz, C. "Religion as a Cultural System." In *Anthropological Approaches to the Study of Religion*, edited by M. Banton, 1–46. London: Tavistock, 1966.

———. *The Religion of Java*. Glencoe, IL: Free Press, 1960.

Gellner, E. *Thought and Change*. London: Weidenfeld and Nicholson, 1964.

Gerber, H. "Sharia, Kanun, and Custom in the Ottoman Law: The Court Records of Seventeenth-century Bursa." *International Journal of Turkish Studies* 21 (1981): 131–47.

———. *State, Society, and Law in Islam: Ottoman Law in Comparative Perspective*. Albany, NY: State University of New York Press, 1994.

Geunther, A.M. "Hanafi *Fiqh* in Mughal India: The *Fatawa-i 'Alamgiri*." In *India's Islamic Traditions, 711–1750*, edited by R.M. Eaton, 209–33. New Delhi: Oxford University Press, 2003.

Ghazaleh, P. "The Guilds: Between Tradition and Modernity." In *The State and Its Servants*, edited by N. Hanna, 60–74. Cairo: American University in Cairo Press, 1995.

Gibb, H.A.R. "Lutfi Pasha on the Ottoman Caliphate." *Oriens* 15 (1962): 287–95.

Gibb, H.A.R., and H. Bowen. *Islamic Society and the West*. 2 vols. London: Oxford University Press, 1957.

Gilbert, J. "Institutionalization of Muslim Scholarship and Professionalization of the 'Ulama in Medieval Damascus." *SI* 52 (1980): 105–34.

Gilbert, W. *Renaissance and Reformation*. Lawrence, KS: Carrie, 1998.

Glendon, M.A., et. al. *Comparative Legal Traditions*. 2nd ed. New York: West Publishing, 1999.

Glenn, H.P. *Legal Traditions of the World*. Oxford: Oxford University Press, 2000.

Goldziher, I. *Introduction to Islamic Theology and Law*. Translated by R. Hamori. Princeton, NJ: Princeton University Press, 1981.

Gorman, A. *Historians, State, and Politics in Twentieth-century Egypt: Contesting the Nation*. New York: Routledge, 2002.

Grabar, O. "The Architecture of the Middle Eastern City from Past to Present." In *The Art and Architecture of Islam, 650–1250*, edited by E. Richard and O. Grabar, 26–46. New York: Pelican History of Art, 1987.

Graham, W. *Divine Word and Prophetic Word in Early Islam*. The Hague: Mouton, 1977.

Grohmann, I.A. *Awraq al-bardi al-'arabiya bi Dar al-Kutub al-Misriya*. Cairo: Matba'at Dar al-Kutub al-Misriya, 1934.

Gronke, M. *Arabische und persische Privaturkunden des 12. und 13. Jahrhunderts aus Ardabil (Aserbaidschan)*. Berlin: Karl Schwartz, 1982.

Guha, R., and G. Spivak, eds. *A Subaltern Studies Reader, 1986–1995*. Minneapolis, MN: University of Minnesota Press, 1998.

Guraya, M.Y. "Judicial Institutions in Pre-Islamic Arabia." *Islamic Studies* 18 (1979): 323–49.

Hakini, B. "The Role of 'Urf in Shaping the Islamic City." In *Islam and Public Law*, edited by Chibli Mallat, 141–55. London: Graham and Trotman, 1993.

Hallaq, W.B. *An Introduction to Islamic Law: Authority, Continuity and Change*. Cambridge, UK: Cambridge University Press, 2009.

———. "The Qadi's Diwan *(Sijill)* before the Ottomans." *BSOAS* 61, no. 3 (1998): 415–36.

———. "Was the Gate of Ijtihad Closed?" *Journal of Middle East Studies* 16, no. 1 (1984): 3–41.

Hammuda, M. *al-Madkhal ila dirasat al-watha'iq al-'Arabiya*. Cairo: Dar al-Thaqafa, 1980.

al-Hanna, M. *Misr li-kull al-Misriyyin*. Cairo: Markaz Ibn Khaldun li-l-Dirasat al-Ijtima'iya, 1993.

Hanna, N. "The Administration of Courts in Ottoman Cairo." In *The State and Its Servants: Administration in Egypt from Ottoman Times to the Present*, edited by N. Hanna, 44–59. Cairo: American University in Cairo Press, 1995.

———. "The Chronicles of Ottoman Egypt: History or Entertainment?" In *The Historiography of Islamic Egypt*, edited by H. Kennedy, 237–50. Leiden: E.J. Brill, 2001.

———. "Culture in Ottoman Egypt." In *The Cambridge History of Egypt*, edited by W.M. Daly, 87–112. Cambridge, UK: Cambridge University Press, 1998.

———. *Making Big Money in 1600: The Life and Times of Isma'il Abu Taqiyya, Egyptian Merchant*. Syracuse, NY: Syracuse University Press, 1998.

———. *Money, Land, and Trade: An Economic History of the Muslim Mediterranean*. Strasbourg: European Science Foundation, 2002.

Har-El, S. *Struggle for Domination in the Middle East: The Ottoman–Mamluk War, 1485–91*. Leiden: E.J. Brill, 1995.

Hathaway, J. "Egypt in the Seventeenth Century." In *The Cambridge History of Egypt*, vol. 2, edited by C.F. Petrie and W.M. Daly, 34–58. Cambridge, UK: Cambridge University Press, 1998.

———. *The Politics of Households in Ottoman Egypt*. Cambridge, UK: Cambridge University Press, 1997.
Heesterman, J.C. "State and *Adat*." In *Two Colonial Empires*, edited by C.A. Bayly and D.H.A. Kolff, 189–201. Dordrecht, the Netherlands: Nijhoff, 1986.
Hefner, R., and M.Q. Zaman. *Schooling Islam: The Culture and Politics of Modern Muslim Education*. Princeton, NJ: Princeton University Press, 2007.
Heyd, U. "Kânûn and Sharî'a in Old Ottoman Criminal Justice." *Proceedings of the Israel Academy of Sciences and Humanities* 3, no. 1 (1969): 1–18.
———. "The Later Ottoman Empire in Rumelia and Anatolia." In *The Cambridge History of Islam*, vol. 2B, edited by P.M. Holt, K.S. Lambton, and B. Lewis, 295–323. Cambridge, UK: Cambridge University Press, 1971.
———. "The Ottoman *'Ulama'* and Westernization in the Time of Salim III and Mahmud II." In *Studies in Islamic History*, edited by U. Heyd, 29–59. London: Taurus, 1996.
———. *Studies in Old Ottoman Criminal Law*, edited by V.L. Menage. Oxford, UK: Clarendon Press, 1973.
Hinz, W. "Dhira'." In *EI*, CD-ROM edition.
Hodgson, M. *The Venture of Islam*. 3 vols. Chicago, IL: University of Chicago Press, 1961.
Hodgson, M.G.S., and L. Gardet. "Hudjdja." In *EI*, CD-ROM edition.
Hoexter, M. "Qadi, Mufti, and Ruler: Their Roles in the Development of Islamic Law." In *Law, Custom, and Statute in the Muslim World: Studies in Honor of Aharon Layish*, edited by R. Shaham, 67–86. Studies in Islamic Law and Society 28. Leiden and Boston: Brill, 2007.
Holt, P.M. *Egypt and the Fertile Crescent*. Ithaca, NY: Cornell University Press, 1966.
———. "The Later Ottoman Empire in Egypt and the Fertile Crescent." In *The Cambridge History of Islam*, edited by P.M. Holt, A.K.S. Lambton, and B. Lewis, 374–93. Cambridge, UK: Cambridge University Press, 1970.
———. "Misr." in *EI*, CD-ROM edition.
Homma, H. "Some Aspects of the Ottoman *Fetva*." *BSOAS* 32 (1969): 35–36.
Hopwood, D. *Egypt: Politics and Society, 1945–1984*. Boston: Unwin Hymen, 1985.
Howard, D.A. "Ottoman Historiography and the Literature of 'Decline' of the Sixteenth and Seventeenth Centuries." *Journal of Asian History* 22 (1988): 52–77.
Humphreys, R.S. *Islamic History: A Framework for Inquiry*. Rev. ed. Princeton, NJ: Princeton University Press, 1991.
Hussayn, T. *The Future of Culture in Egypt*. Washington, DC: Washington Council of Learned Societies, 1954.
Ibn al-'Arabi, Muhyi al-Din. *Fusus al-hikam (The Bezels of Wisdom)*, edited and translated by R.W.J. Austin. New York: Paulist Press, 1980.
Ibrahim, S. *Judhur al-salbiya al-sha'biya fi Misr*. Cairo: Dar al-Bustani li-l-Nashr wa-l-Tawzi', 2000.
Imber, C. *Ebu's-Su'ud: The Islamic Legal Tradition*. Stanford, CA: Stanford University Press, 1997.
———. *Studies in Ottoman History and Law*. Istanbul: Isis University Press, 1996.

———. "Sulayman as Caliph of the Muslims." In *Soliman le Magnifique et son temps*, edited by G. Veinstein, 179–84. Paris: La Documentation française, 1992.

Inalcik, H. "Filaha." In *EI*, CD-ROM edition.

———. "The Heyday and Decline of the Ottoman Empire." In *The Cambridge History of Islam*, edited by P.M. Holt, K.S. Lambton, and B. Lewis, 295–323. Cambridge, UK: Cambridge University Press, 1971.

———. "Kanunname." In *EI*, CD-ROM edition.

———. *The Ottoman Empire: The Classical Age, 1300–1600*. Translated by N. Itzkowitz and C. Imber. London: Weidenfeld and Nicolson, 1973.

———. "Sulayman the Lawgiver and Ottoman Law." *Archivium Ottomanicum* 1 (1969): 105–38.

Inalcik, H., and D. Quataert, eds. *Economic and Social History of the Ottoman Empire, 1300–1914*. Cambridge, UK: Cambridge University Press, 1994.

Jackson, S. *Islamic Law and the State: The Constitutional Jurisprudence of Shihab al-Din al-Qarafi*. Leiden: Brill, 1996.

Jad'an, F. *al-Mihnah: Bahth fi jadaliyat al-dini wa-l-siyasi fi al-Islam*. Amman: Dar al-Shuruq li-l-Nashr wa-l-Tawzi', 1989.

al-Jami, Nur al-Din. *al-Durra al-Fakhira (The Precious Pearl)*. Translated by N. Heer. Albany, NY: State University of New York Press, 1979.

Jennings, R.C. "Kadi Court and Legal Procedure in Seventeenth-century Ottoman Kayseri." *SI* 48 (1978): 133–72.

———. "Limitations on the Judicial Powers of the Kadi in Seventeenth-century Ottoman Kayseri." *SI* 50 (1979): 151–84.

———. "Some Thoughts on the Gazi-Theses." *WZKM* 76 (1986): 151–61.

Jindan, K. "The Islamic Theory of Government according to Ibn Taymiyya." PhD diss., Georgetown University, 1979.

Johansen, B. "Legal Literature and the Problem of Change: The Case of the Land Rent." In *Islam and Public Law*, edited by C. Mallat, 29–47. London: Unwin and Unwin, 1993.

Joseph, S. *Family, Body, Sexuality and Health*. Encyclopedia of Women and Islamic Cultures 3. Leiden and Boston: Brill, 2003–2007.

al-Jundi, D. "The Foundations and Objectives of Arab Nationalism." In *Political and Social Thought in the Contemporary Middle East*, edited by K.H. Karpat. New York: Praeger, 1982.

Juynboll, G.H. *Muslim Tradition: Studies in Chronology, Provenance, and Authorship of Early Hadith*. Cambridge, UK: Cambridge University Press, 1983.

Kafadar, C. *Between Two Worlds: The Construction of the Ottoman State*. San Francisco, CA: University of California Press, 1995.

Kamali, M.H. *Principles of Islamic Jurisprudence*. Cambridge, UK: The Islamic Texts Society, 2000.

Kane, O. "Izala: The Rise of Muslim Reformism in Northern Nigeria." In *Accounting for Fundamentalisms*, edited by M.E. Marty and R.S. Appleby, 490–512. Chicago, IL: University of Chicago Press, 1994.

Karel, D. "Secularization: A Multi-Dimensional Concept." *Current Sociology* 29, no. 2 (1981): 1–216.

Karpat, K. *The Ottoman State and Its Place in World History*. Leiden: E.J. Brill, 1974.

Kaser, K. *Patriarchy after Patriarchy: Gender Relations in Turkey and in the Balkans, 1500–2000*. Munster, Germany: LIT Verlag, 2008.
Keddie, N., ed. *Scholars, Saints, and Sufis: Muslim Religious Institutions in the Middle East since 1500*. Berkeley, CA: University of California Press, 1972.
Khadduri, M. *The Islamic Conception of Justice*. Baltimore, MD: Johns Hopkins University Press, 1984.
———. "Sulh." In *EI*, CD-ROM edition.
Khalidi, T. *Arab Historical Thought in the Classical Period*. Cambridge, UK: Cambridge University Press, 1994.
Khalil, M.I. "Wali al-Mazalim or the Muslim Ombudsman." *Journal of Islamic and Comparative Law* 6 (1976): 1–9.
Khan, G., ed. *Arabic Legal and Administrative Documents in the Cambridge Genizah Collection*. Cambridge University Library Genizah Series 10. Cambridge, UK: Cambridge University Press, 1993.
Khoury, D.R. *State and Provincial Society in the Ottoman Empire: Mosul, 1540–1834*. Cambridge, UK: Cambridge University Press, 1997.
Kindi. *Wulat*. Beirut: n.p., 1908.
Kister, M.J. *Studies in Jahiliyya and Early Islam*. London: Variorum, 1980.
Kling, Z. "Images of Malay-Indonesian Identity." In *Indonesian and Malay Studies*, edited by M. Hitchcock and V.T. King, 45–52. Ninth European Colloquium. Kuala Lumpur: Oxford University Press, 1997.
Knysh, D.A. *Ibn 'Arabi in the Later Islamic Tradition: The Making of a Polemical Image in Islam*. Albany, NY: State University of New York Press, 1999.
———. "Orthodoxy and Heresy in Medieval Islam: An Essay and Reassessment." *The Muslim World* 83 (January 1993): 48–67.
Kopf, L. "al-Damiri." In *EI 2*, CD-ROM edition.
Köprülü, F.M. *Islam in Anatolia after the Turkish Invasion*. Salt Lake City, UT: University of Utah Press, 1993.
———. *The Origins of the Ottoman Empire*. Albany, NY: State University of New York Press, 1992.
Kraemer, Joel. "Heresy versus the State in Medieval Islam." In *Studies in Judaica, Karaitica, and Islamica Presented to Leon Nemoy on His Eightieth Birthday*, edited by S.R. Brunswick, 167–80. Ramat Gan, Israel: Bar Ilan University Press, 1982.
Kunt, M., and C. Woodhead, eds. *Sulayman the Magnificent and His Age: The Ottoman Empire in the Early Modern World*. London: Longman, 1995.
Lambton, A.K.S. "Al-Dawani." In *EI*, CD-ROM edition.
Laoust, H. *Essai sur les doctrines sociales et politiques d'Ibn Taimiyya*. Cairo: Institut français d'archéologie orientale, 1939.
Lapidus, I. *A History of Islamic Societies*. Cambridge, UK: Cambridge University Press, 1988.
———. *Muslim Cities in the Later Middle Ages*. Cambridge, UK: Cambridge University Press, 1984.
Laslett, P. *The World We Have Lost*. London: Methuen, 1971.
Lawrence, R. *The Anthropology of Justice: Law as Culture in Islamic Society*. Cambridge, UK: Cambridge University Press, 1989.
Layish, A. "Customary *Khul'* as Reflected in the *Sijill* of the Libyan Shari'a Courts." *BSOAS* 51 (1988): 428–39.

———. "The Maliki Family *Waqf* According to Wills and *Waqfiyyat*." *BSOAS* 46, no. 1 (1983): 1–32.

———. "Sharia and Custom in the Cyrenaican Family." *The Seventh Stanford–Berkeley Law and Colonialism Symposium: Muslim Family Law and Colonialism in Africa*. Stanford University, 11–12 May 2001.

———. "The *Sijill* of the Jaffa and Nazareth Shariʿa Courts as a Source for the Political and Social History of Ottoman Palestine." In *Studies on Palestine during the Ottoman Period*, edited by M. Maʿoz, 252–332. Jerusalem: Magnes Press, 1975.

Layish, A., and R. Shaham. "Mahr." In *EI*, CD-ROM edition.

Leeder, S.H. *Modern Sons of the Pharaohs: A Study of the Manners and Customs of the Copts of Egypt*. London: Hodder and Stoughton, 1918.

Le Gall, D. *A Culture of Sufism: Naqshbandis in the Ottoman World, 1450–1700*. Albany, NY: State University of New York Press, 2005.

Leiser, G. "The Madrasa and the Islamization of the Middle East: The Case of Egypt." *Journal of the American Research Center in Egypt* 20 (1985): 29–47.

Libson, G. *Jewish and Islamic Law: A Comparative Study of Custom during the Geonic Period*. Cambridge, MA: Harvard University Press, 2003.

———. "On the Development of Custom as a Source of Law in Islamic Law." *Islamic Law and Society* 4, no. 2 (June 1997): 131–55.

Lindner, R.P. *Nomads and Ottomans in Medieval Anatolia*. Bloomington, IN: Indiana University Press, 1983.

———. "Stimulus and Justification in Early Ottoman History." *Greek Orthodox Theological Review* 27 (1982): 207–24.

Little, D.P. *A Catalogue of Islamic Documents from al-Haram aš-Šarīf in Jerusalem*. Beirut: Orient-Institut der Deutschen Morgenländischen Gesellschaft, 1984.

———. "A Fourteenth-century Jerusalem Court Record of a Divorce Hearing: A Case Study." In *Mamluks and Ottomans: Studies in Honour of Michael Winter*, edited by D.J. Wasserstein and A. Ayalon, 67–85. New York: Routledge, 2006.

———. "The Haram Documents as Sources for the Art and Architecture of the Mamluk Period." *Muqarnas* 2 (1984): 61–72.

———. "Haram Documents Related to the Jews of Late Fourteenth-century Jerusalem." *Journal of Semitic Studies* 30 (1985): 227–64.

———. *An Introduction to Islamic Historiography*. Montreal: McGill–Queens University Press, 1970.

———. "Relations between Jerusalem and Egypt during the Mamluk Period according to Literary and Documentary Sources." In *Egypt and Palestine: A Millennium of Association*, edited by A. Cohen and G. Baer, 73–93. Jerusalem: Ben-Zvi Institute, 1984.

———. "Sidjill." In *EI*, CD-ROM edition.

———. "The Significance of the Haram Documents for the Study of Medieval Islamic History." *Der Islam* 57 (1980): 189–219.

———. "Six Fourteenth-century Purchase Deeds for Slaves from al-Haram aš-Šarīf." *Zeitschrift der Deutschen Morgenländischen Gesellschaft* 131 (1981): 297–337.

———. "Two Fourteenth-century Court Records from Jerusalem concerning the Disposition of Slaves by Minors." *Arabica* 29 (1982): 16–49.

Little, D.P., and A.U. Turgay. "Documents from the Ottoman Period in the Khalidi Library in Jerusalem." *Die Welt des Islam* 20 (1980): 44–72.
Lombard, M. "Les bases monétaires d'une suprématie économique: L'or musulman du VIIe au XIe siècle." *Annales Économies, Sociétés, Civilisations* 2 (1947): 142–60.
Löwith, K. *Meaning in History*. Chicago, IL: University of Chicago Press, 1949.
Lowry, H.W. *Studies in Defterology: Ottoman Society in the Fifteenth and Sixteenth Centuries*. Istanbul: The Isis Press, 2008.
Mahmood, S. "Religious Reason and Secular Affect: An Incommensurable Divide?" In *Is Critique Secular? Blasphemy, Injury, and Free Speech*, edited by T. Asad, W. Brown, J. Butler, and S. Mahmood. Berkeley, CA: Townsend Center for the Humanities, University of California Press, 2009.
Makdisi, G. *The Rise of Colleges: Institutions and Learning in Islam and the West*. Edinburgh: Edinburgh University Press, 1981.
Mandaville, J. "The Ottoman Court Records of Syria and Jordan." *Journal of the American Oriental Society* 86 (1996): 311–19.
Manna', A. "The *Sijill* as a Source for the Study of Palestine during the Ottoman Period, with Special Reference to the French Invasion." In *Palestine in the Late Ottoman Period*, edited by D. Kushner, 351–62. Jerusalem: Yad Izhak Ben-Zevi, 1986.
Mannheim, K. *Ideology and Utopia*. Translated by L. Wirth and E. Shils. San Diego: Harcourt Brace Jovanovich, 1985.
Mantran, R. "Ča'ush." In *EI*, CD-ROM edition.
———. "Hisba: II. Ottoman Empire." In *EI*, CD-ROM edition.
Marçais, W. "L'islamisme et la vie urbaine." *Comptes-rendus de l'Académie des Inscriptions et Belles-Lettres* (1928): 86–100.
Marcus, A. "The Middle East on the Eve of Modernity: Aleppo in the Eighteenth Century." *JESHO* 26 (1983): 104–105.
Martin, B.G. "A Short History of Khalwati Order of Dervishes." In *Scholars, Saints, and Sufis*, edited by N.R. Keddie. Berkeley, CA: University of California Press, 1978.
Martin, D. *A General Theory of Secularization*. Oxford, UK: Blackwell, 1978.
Masud, K. *Islamic Legal Philosophy: A Study of Abu Ishaq al-Shatibi's Life and Thought*. Islamabad: Islamic Research Institute, 1977.
Masud, M.K., B. Messick, and D. Powers, eds. *Islamic Legal Interpretation: Muftis and Their Fatwas*. Cambridge, MA: Harvard University Press, 1996.
al-Mawardi, Ali ibn Muhammad. *The Ordinances of Government: A Translation of* al-Ahkam al-sultaniyya wa al-wilayat al-diniyya. Translated by Wafaa H. Wahba. Reading, UK: Garnet, 1996.
Memon, M.U. *Ibn Taymiyya's Struggle against Popular Religion*. The Hague: Mouton, 1976.
Messick, B. *The Calligraphic State*. Berkeley, CA: University of California Press, 1993.
Milad, S.A.I. "Registres judiciaires du tribunal de la Salihiyya Nağmiyya." *AI* 12 (1974): 163–253.
Morgan, D.O. "The Great Yasa of Chingiz Khan and Mongol Law in the Ilkhanate." *BSOAS* 49 (1986): 163–76.

Müge Göçek, F. "Multazim." In *EI*, CD-ROM edition.
al-Nahal, G. *The Judicial Administration of Ottoman Egypt in the Seventeenth Century*. Minneapolis, MN: Bibliotheca Islamica, 1979.
Naqqash, S.K. *Misr li-l-Misriyyin*. Alexandria: Matba'at Jaridat al-Mahrusa, 1998.
Nawas, J.A. "A Re-examination of Three Current Explanations for al-Mamun's Introduction of the Mihna." *IJMES* 26, no. 4 (1994): 615–29.
Netton, I.R. "Siyasa." In *EI*, CD-ROM edition.
Nielsen, J. "Mazalim." *Encyclopedia of Islam*. 2nd ed. Vol. 7: 933. Leiden: E.J. Brill, 2005.
———. *Secular Justice in an Islamic State: Mazalim under the Bahri Mamluks*. Leiden: Nederland Historisch-Archaeologisch Instituut te Istanbul, 1985.
Noth, A. *The Early Arabic Historical Tradition*. Translated by M. Bonner. Princeton, NJ: Princeton University Press, 1994.
Omran, Abdel-Rahim. *Family Planning in the Legacy of Islam*. London: Routledge, 2012.
Othman, M.Z. "Institution of *Waqf*." *Islamic Culture* 58 (1984): 55–62.
Outhwaite, R.B. *Clandestine Marriage in England, 1500–1850*. Rio Grande, OH: Hambledon Press, 1995.
Paret, R. "Maslaha." In *EI*, CD-ROM edition.
Pecora, V.P. *Secularization and Cultural Criticism: Religion, Nation, and Modernity*. Chicago, IL: University of Chicago Press, 2006.
Peirce, L. *The Imperial Harem: Women and Sovereignty in the Ottoman Empire*. New York: Oxford University Press, 1993.
———. *Morality Tales: Law and Gender in the Ottoman Court of Aintab*. Berkeley, CA: University of California Press, 2003.
Peters, R. "What Does It Mean to Be an Official *Madhhab?*" *The School of Islamic Law: Evolution, Devolution, and Progress*, edited by P. Bearman, R. Peters, and F. Vogel, 147–58. Cambridge, MA: Harvard University Law Center, 2005.
Petry, C.F. *The Civilian Elite of Cairo in the Later Middle Ages*. Princeton, NJ: Princeton University Press, 1981.
———. *Protectors or Praetorians?* Albany, NY: State University of New York Press, 1994.
Pirbhai, M.R. "British Indian Reform and Pre-Colonial Trends in Islamic Jurisprudence." *Journal of Asian History* 42, no. 1 (2008): 36–63.
Plessner, M. "Namus." In *EI*, CD-ROM edition.
Qattan, N. "Discriminating Texts: Orthographic Marking and Social Differentiation in the Court Records of Ottoman Damascus." In *Arabic Sociolinguistics: Issues and Perspectives*, edited by Yasir Suleiman, 57–77. Richmond, UK: Curzon Press, 1994.
———. "Inside the Ottoman Courthouse: Territorial Law at the Intersection of State and Religion." In *The Early Modern Ottomans*, edited by V.H. Askan and D. Goffman, 201–12. Cambridge, UK: Cambridge University Press, 2007.
———. "Textual Differentiation in the Damascus *Sijill*: Religious Discrimination or Politics of Gender?" In *Women, the Family, and Divorce Laws in Islamic History*, edited by A. Azhary Sonbol, 191–201. Syracuse, NY: Syracuse University Press, 1996.

Rabel, E. "The Statute of Frauds and Comparative Legal History." *Law Quarterly Review* 174 (1947): 178–82.
Rabie, H. *The Financial System of Egypt, AH 564–741/AD 1169–1341*. London: Oxford University Press, 1972.
Rafeq, A.K. "The Law Court Registers of Damascus with Special Reference to Craft Corporations during the First Half of the Eighteenth Century." In *Les Arabes par leurs archives, XVIe–XXe siècles*, edited by J. Berque and D. Chevalier, 219–26. Paris: Centre National de la Recherche Scientifique, 1976.
Rahman, F. "*Sunnah* and Hadith." *Islamic Studies* 1 (1962): 33ff.
Rahman, H.M. "The Role of Islamic Customs in the Islamic Laws of Succession." *Islamic and Comparative Law Quarterly* 7 (1987): 217–39.
Rapport, Y. "Matrimonial Gifts in Early Islamic Egypt." *Islamic Law and Society* 7, no. 1 (February 2000): 1–30.
al-Rawandi, M. *Rahat al-Sudur*. Edited by M. Iqbal. London: Luzac, 1921.
Raymond, A. *Cairo*. Translated by W. Wood. Cambridge, MA: Harvard University Press, 2000.
———. "Les documents du Mahkama comme source pour l'histoire économique et sociale de l'Egypte au XVIIIe siècle." In *Les Arabes par leurs archives, XVIe–XXe siècle*, edited by J. Berque and D. Chevalier, 125–39. Paris: Centre National de la Recherche Scientifique, 1976.
———. "Islamic City, Arab City: Orientalist Myths and Recent Views." *Arab Cities in the Ottoman Period*. Variorum Collected Studies Series. Ashgate, UK: Variorum, 2002.
———. "The Ottoman Conquest and Development of the Great Arab Towns." In *Arab Cities in the Ottoman Period*, edited by A. Raymond, 84–101. Ashgate, UK: Variorum, 2002.
———. "The Role of the Communities *(Tawa'if)* in the Administration of Cairo in the Ottoman Period." In *The State and Its Servants: Administration in Egypt from Ottoman Times to the Present*, edited by N. Hanna, 32–43. Cairo: American University in Cairo Press, 1995.
Reilly, J. *A Small Town in Syria: Ottoman Hama in the Eighteenth and Nineteenth Centuries*. Oxford, UK: P. Lang, 2000.
Reinhart, K.A. *Before Revelation: The Boundaries of Muslim Moral Thought*. Albany, NY: State University of New York Press, 1995.
———. "Transcendence and Social Practise: Muftis and Qadis as Religious Interpreters." *AI* 27 (1993): 5–28.
Repp. R. "The Altered Nature and Role of the *Ulama*." In *Studies in Eighteenth-century Islamic History*, edited by T. Naff and R. Owen, 277–87. Carbondale, IL: Southern Illinois University Press, 1977.
———. *The Mufti of Istanbul: A Study in the Development of the Ottoman Learned Hierarchy*. Oxford Oriental Institute Monographs 8. London: Ithaca Press, 1986.
———. "Ottoman Developments of the *Qanun* and Shari'a." *International Journal of Turkish Studies* 24 (1988): 33–56.
———. "*Qanun* and Shari'a in the Ottoman Context." In *Islamic Law: Social and Historical Contexts*, edited by A. al-Azmeh, 124–45. London: Routledge, 1988.

Reychmann J., and A. Zajaczkowski. "Diplomatics." In *EI*, CD-ROM edition.
Rosenthal, E.I.J. *Political Thought in Medieval Islam: An Introductory Outline.* Cambridge, UK: Cambridge University Press, 1968.
Rosenthal, F. *A History of Muslim Historiography.* Leiden: E.J. Brill, 1968.
———. "Of Making Books There Is No End." In *The Book in the Islamic World: The Written Word and Communication in the Middle East,* edited by G.N. Atiyeh, 39–43. Albany, NY: State University of New York Press, 1995.
Salama, M. *Ma hiya al-nahda?* Cairo: Salama Musa li-l-Nashr wa-l-Tawziʻ, 1961.
Salameh, K. "Aspects of the *Sijill*s of the Shariʻa Court in Jerusalem." In *Ottoman Jerusalem the Living City, 1517–1917,* edited by S. Auld and R. Hillenbrand. Jerusalem: al-Tajir World of Islam Trust, 2000.
Saleh, H. "Egypt Rapped on Gay Persecution." *BBC News*, 1 March 2004. http://news.bbc.co.uk/2/hi/middle_east/3522457.stm
al-Sarakhsi, Shaykh al-Islam Abi Bakr Muhammad ibn Ahmed. *Mabsut.* Vol. 10. Beirut: Dar al-Kutub al-ʻIlmiya, 1993.
Sauvaget, J. *Essai sur le développement d'une grande ville syrienne, des origines au milieu du XIX siècle.* Paris: Geuthner, 1941.
Schacht, J. "Foreign Elements in Ancient Islamic Law." *Journal of Comparative Law* 3–4 (1950): 9–16.
———. "Nikah." In *EI*, CD-ROM edition.
———. *The Origins of Muhammadan Jurisprudence.* Oxford: Oxford University Press, 1950.
Schiller, A. "Prolegomena to the Study of Coptic Law." *Archives d'Histoire du Droit Oriental* 2 (1938): 360–61.
Schinder, J. "Career Line Formation in the Ottoman Bureaucracy, 1648–1750." *JESHO* 16 (1973): 217–37.
Seagle, W. *The Quest for Law.* New York: A.A. Knopf, 1941.
Seidl, E. "Law and the Legal System in Ancient Egypt." In *The Legacy of Egypt,* edited by S.R.K. Glanville, 198–217. London: Clarendon Press, 1972.
Semerdjian, E. *Off the Straight Path: Illicit Sex, Law, and Community in Ottoman Aleppo.* Gender, Culture, and Politics in the Middle East. Syracuse, NY: Syracuse University Press, 2008.
Serjeant, R.B. *Customary and Shariʻah Law in Arabian Society.* Brookfield, VT: Variorum, 1991.
———. *Studies in Arabian History and Civilization.* London: Variorum, 1981.
Shaham, R. "Customary Islamic Law and Statutory Legislation." *Islamic Law and Society* 2ii (1995): 258–81.
Shahid, I. "The Authenticity of Pre-Islamic Poetry: The Linguistic Dimension." *al-Abhath* 44 (1996): 3–29.
———. "*Sunna*, Quran, and *Urf.*" *Law and the Islamic World* (1995): 3–48.
Shaw, S. *The Financial and Administrative Organization and Development of Ottoman Egypt, 1517–1798.* Princeton, NJ: Princeton University Press, 1962.
Shmuelevitz, A. *The Jews of the Ottoman Empire in the Late Fifteenth and the Sixteenth Centuries: Administrative, Economic, Legal, and Social Relations as Reflected in the Responsa.* Leiden: E.J. Brill, 1984.
Shoshan, B. *Popular Culture in Medieval Cairo.* Cambridge, UK: Cambridge University Press, 1993.

Siddiqi, M.S. *The Bahmani Sufis*. Delhi: Idarah-i Adabiyat-i Delli, 1989.
Sidi 'Ali Reis. "*Mir'at al-Memalik*." In *The Sacred Books and Early Literature of the East*, vol. 4, edited by Charles F. Horne. New York: Parke, Austin, and Lipscomb, 1917.
Singleton, G.H. *Religion in the City of Angels: American Protestant Culture and Urbanization*. Ann Arbor, MI: UMI Research Press, 1979.
Smith, W.C. *Islam in Modern History*. New York: Penguin, 1968.
Sonbol, A. "A History of Marriage Contracts in Egypt." In *Case Studies in Islamic Family Law*, edited by A. Quraishi and F.E. Vogel, 87–122, 225–53. Cambridge, MA: Harvard University Press, 2008.
———. "Women in Shari'ah Courts: A Historical and Methodological Discussion." *Fordham International Law Journal* 27, no. 1 (2003): 225–53.
Sourdel, D. "Khalifa." In *EI*, CD-ROM edition.
Steinwenter, A. "Die Bedeutung der Papyrologie für die koptische Urkundenlehre." *Münchener Beiträge zur Papyrusforschung und antiken Rechtsgeschichte* 19 (1934): 302–13.
Stephens, R. *Nasser: A Political Biography*. Middlesex, UK: Penguin Books, 1971.
Stillman, N.A. "*Waqf* and the Ideology of Charity in Medieval Islam." In *Studies in Honour of Clifford Edmund Bosworth*, edited by I. Netton, 357–72. Leiden: E.J. Brill, 2000.
Stowasser, K. "Manners and Customs at the Mamluk Court." *Muqarnas* 2 (1984): 13–20.
Strauss, E. "L'inquisition dans l'état mamlouke." *Revista degli Studi Orientali* 25 (1950): 16–17.
Trimingham, J.S. *The Sufi Orders in Islam*. Oxford, UK: Clarendon Press, 1971.
Tucker, J. *In the House of the Law: Gender and Islamic Law in Ottoman Syria and Palestine*. Berkeley, CA: University of California Press, 1998.
Tyan, E. "Judicial Organization." In *Law in the Middle East*, edited by M. Khadduri and H.J. Liebesny. Washington, DC: Middle East Institute, 1955.
———. *Le notariat et le régime de la preuve par écrit dans la pratique du droit musulman*. Harissa, Lebanon: Imprimerie Saint Paul, 1959.
Udovitch, A.L. "Islamic Law and the Social Context of Exchange in the Medieval Islamic Middle East." *History and Anthropology* 1 (1985): 445–65.
———. "Theory and Practice of Islamic Law: Some Evidence from the Geniza." *SI* 32 (1970): 289–303.
Vesely, R. "Die Hauptprobleme der Diplomatik arabischer Privaturkunden aus dem spätmittelalterlichen Ägypten." *Archiv Orientali* 40 (1972): 312–43.
Vikor, K. *Sufi and Scholar on the Desert Edge: Muhammad b. 'Ali al-Sanusi and His Brotherhood*. London: Hurst and Co., 1995.
Vogel, F. "Closing of the Door of *Ijtihad* and the Application of the Law." *American Journal of Islamic Social Sciences* 10, no. 3 (Fall 1993).
Von Grunebaum, G. "The Structure of the Muslim Town." In *Islam: Studies in the Nature and Growth of a Cultural Tradition*, 141–58. Menasha, WI: American Anthropological Society, 1955.
Wakin, J. *The Function of Documents*. Albany, NY: State University of New York Press, 1972.
Walker, J., and D.R. Hill. "Sanadjat." In *EI*, CD-ROM edition.

Wallerstein, E. *The Modern World System: Capitalist Agriculture and the Origins of the European World Economy in the Sixteenth Century*. New York: Academic Press, 1974.
Watt, W.M. *The Formative Period of Islamic Thought*. Edinburgh: Edinburgh University Press, 1973.
Weis, B. *The Islamic School of Law: Evolution, Devolution, and Progress*, edited by P. Bearman, R. Peters, and F. Vogel. Cambridge, MA: Harvard University Press, 2006.
———. *The Spirit of Islamic Law*. Athens, GA: University of Georgia Press, 1998.
Weiss, B. "Interpretation in Islamic Law: The Theory of Ijtihad." In *Islamic Law and Legal Theory*, edited by I. Edge, 237–86. Aldershot, UK: Dartmouth, 1996.
Wengert, T.J. *Harvesting Martin Luther's Reflections on Theology, Ethics, and the Church*. Grand Rapids, MI: W.B. Eedrmans Publishing, 2004.
Wheeler, B. *Applying the Canon in Islam: Authorization and Maintenance of Interpretive Reasoning in Hanafi Scholarship*. Albany, NY: State University of New York Press, 1996.
Williamson, G.I. *The Westminster Confession of Faith*. 2nd ed. Phillipsburg, NJ: P & R Publishing Company, 1950.
Wilson, M.B. "The Failure of Nomenclature: The Concept of Orthodoxy in the Study of Islam." *Comparative Islamic Studies* 3, no. 2 (2007): 169–94.
Winter, M. "Attitudes toward the Ottomans in Egyptian Historiography during the Ottoman Rule." In *The Great Ottoman-Turkish Civilization*, vol. 3, edited by K. Çiçek, 290–99. Ankara: YeniTürkiye, 2000.
———. *Egyptian Society under Ottoman Rule, 1517–1798*. New York: Routledge, 1992.
———. "The Ottoman Conquest of Egypt." In *The Cambridge History of Egypt*, vol. 2, edited by C.F. Petrie and M.W. Daly, 1–33. Cambridge, UK: Cambridge University Press, 1998.
———. "The Ottoman Occupation." In *The Cambridge History of Egypt, 641–1517*, vol. 1, edited by C.F. Petry, 490–516. Cambridge, UK: Cambridge University Press, 1998.
———. *Society and Religion in Early Ottoman Egypt: Studies in the Writings of 'Abd al-Wahhab al-Sha'rani*. London: Transaction Books, 1982.
———. "Turks, Arabs, and Mamluks in the Army of Ottoman Egypt." *WZKM* 72 (1982): 100–22.
Wittek, P. "De la défaite d'Ankara à la prise de Constantinople." *REI* 12 (1938): 1–34.
Yaron, R. *Introduction to the Law of the Aramaic Papyri*. Oxford, UK: Clarendon Press, 1961.
Ziadeh, F. "*Urf* and Law in Islam." *The World of Islam* (1959): 60–67.
Ziaydeh, K. *Arkiyulujiya al-mustalah al-watha'iqi*. Tripoli: al-Jam'iya al-Lubnaniya, 1986.
———. *al-Sura al-taqlidiya li-l-mujtama' al-madini: qira'a manhajiya fi sijillat mahkamat Tarabulus al-shar'iya fi-l-qarn al-sabi' 'ashar wa-bidayat al-qarn al-thamin 'ashar*. Tripoli: al-Jam'iya al-Lubnaniya, 1983.
Zilfi, M. "The Kadizadelis: Discordant Revivalism in Seventeenth-century Istanbul." *Journal of Near Eastern Studies* 45, no. 4 (1986): 251–69.
———. *The Politics of Piety: The Ottoman Ulema in the Postclassical Age (1600–1800)*. Minneapolis, MN: Bibliotheca Islamica, 1988.

Index

Abbasid 6, 38–39, 41, 47, 56–57, 62, 64, 70, 80, 82, 111
Abu al-Suʿud (Ebu el-Suʿud) 23, 56–59, 62, 78, 97, 148, 155, 165, 167–68
ʿada/adat 45, 48–49, 51–55, 64, 93, 143, 214
Ahali 85–86, 94, 150, 153
Aleppo 20, 69, 88, 106
ʿamal 49, 51, 87, 99, 172–73, 177, 201, 214
ʿaqid 52, 156
ʿasker(i) 86, 106, 130–32, 158, 167, 185, 188, 208
al-Azhar 1–2, 39, 52, 96, 147, 156, 170, 218

Bab al-ʿAli 13, 92, 106–107, 110, 113, 117, 122, 147, 167, 169, 173, 192
Bab Zuwayla 149, 203, 205–206
Bahmanid Sultanate 62
Balkans 21, 81, 130, 132, 183
Bayyina 136

Cairo 7, 10–13, 16, 18–20, 26–27, 39–40, 53–54, 62, 69–70, 72–74, 79, 83, 85, 87–93, 95–97, 99–100, 106–107, 112–22, 128–30, 132, 135, 137, 144–46, 148–54, 161, 163, 165, 167–68, 170, 180–94, 197–98, 201–202, 209, 212, 214–15

caliph 6, 23, 55–57, 59–60, 62–64, 66–67, 76, 79, 80, 82, 115
caliphate 41, 55–57, 59–61, 63, 77, 80, 82, 86, 101, 217
Calvin, John 35, 36–38, 157, 216
Christians 18–19, 146, 196, 213, 219–20
citizenship 8, 28, 31, 40, 126, 134, 137, 139, 211–13, 219–20. *See also* proto-citizen
civil government 33, 35–37
civil marriage 128–29, 142–43, 155–58, 215
coffee 5, 95, 144, 147–48, 185, 217. *See also* qahwaji
Constantinople (Istanbul) 4, 6, 22, 107–108, 120, 145
constitution 26, 134, 211; Constitution of 1879 217
custom 131, 134–35, 138, 142–43, 148, 150–51, 153–54, 158–60

al-Damari 10, 14–15, 63, 74, 91–101, 144–46, 169–70, 204
Damascus 6, 16, 20, 26, 54, 72, 87, 88
Darar 99, 162, 168
al-Dawwani 58–62, 66
Derrida, Jacques 30, 111, 125, 129
dhikr 107, 146, 151

dhimmi 60, 95, 102, 127–28, 139, 146, 184, 196
divorce 11, 13–14, 30, 52, 90, 94, 104–105, 115–16, 127, 134–37, 142, 148, 155–56, 160–69, 174–75, 185–87, 213, 215, 219–20
diwan 57, 87, 97–98, 110, 113, 116, 156, 183, 191, 194

faskh 106, 166, 168–69
Fatawa 'Alamgiriya 110, 115, 122, 162
fatwa 3, 13, 26–27, 38, 56, 81–82, 95, 100, 108, 147, 153, 191–92, 204; *futya* 13, 119; *istifta'* 13, 119
fiqh 2, 5, 7, 11–12, 23–24, 26, 41, 45–46, 48–49, 53, 58–60, 63, 66, 78, 81, 90, 101, 110, 148, 150, 153, 159, 164, 165, 169, 175, 177, 178, 185–87, 189, 194, 214, 216

Geneva 35–36
al-Ghuri 79, 82, 86, 170
guilds 73, 122, 183–84, 193

Hadith 7, 35, 41, 47, 52, 93, 109, 156
Hanafi 12, 23, 26, 38–39, 47–48, 54, 59, 77, 79, 87–100, 106, 109–10, 113, 117, 119, 122, 127, 143–44, 150, 152, 161–62, 165, 167, 172–73, 191, 204, 213–14, 216, 218–19
Hanbali 80, 89, 93, 97–98, 161–62, 167–69, 173, 204, 206
hisba 171–72, 195, 197, 202, 207, 209, 213; Bayt al-Hisba 206; Bayt al-Mal 53, 170
hudud 30, 50, 142–43, 145
hujja 11, 14, 16, 103, 105–11, 120, 126–27, 133–35, 137–38, 152, 154–55, 167, 205, 206, 214
Humayun (Mughal emperor) 63
huquq al-adamiyyin 5, 11, 35, 141
huquq Allah 5, 11, 34–35, 141

'ibadat 9, 34, 42–43, 48, 51–52, 54, 143, 177–78, 217

Ibn Arabi, Muhyi al-Din 60, 96
Ibn Iyas 14, 15, 52, 74, 79, 83–84, 89–92, 95, 99, 101, 112, 145–46, 149–51, 156, 159, 170–71, 182, 197, 198, 201, 202
Ibn Nujaym 9–10, 42–43, 49, 50, 53, 80, 147, 161
ijma' 7, 41, 47, 147
ijtihad 71, 93–95, 101
iltizam 14, 138, 190–91, 193–94, 208, 215. See also *multazim*
Inshikariya 131, 146, 182
iqrar 13–14, 110, 116, 188–89, 196, 206, 208
Istanbul *see* Constantinople
istihsan 42, 45–49, 59, 169

Jews 19, 134–36, 146, 149, 163, 181, 183
jihad 3, 25, 70, 79–83, 86

katib 122
khawaja 110, 130, 132, 205
Khayrbek 52, 75, 83, 85, 156, 182–83, 198
khutuba 130, 159, 184
kiswa 133, 159, 166, 186

Laqani, Maliki Shaykh Sham al-Din 53, 93–95

madhhab 8, 13, 16, 20, 26, 35, 38–39, 71, 73, 88–89, 93–94, 99, 100–101, 113–14, 157, 162, 166, 204, 218
madrasa 56, 95, 98, 112, 207
Maghribi community 19, 54, 182
mahdar 115, 153, 186, 196, 199, 203–205
mahkama 13, 16, 103, 114
mahr 143, 163; *mahr al-mithl* 165, 216
majlis: *majlis al-hukm* 111, 113–14; *shar'i majlis* 107, 112
Maliki 15, 47–48, 52, 89, 93, 100, 122, 161, 164, 170, 172–73, 181, 204
Mamluk 5–6, 13–15, 18, 21, 43, 50, 70–72, 75–76, 78–79, 82–86, 89, 104–105, 111–16, 118–20, 131–33,

151, 157, 169–70, 173, 182–83, 193, 194, 197–98
maslaha 42, 45–46, 48–51, 99–100, 169
mass culture 3, 16, 27, 28, 125
al-Mawardi 145, 147, 165
mazalim 50, 64–65, 145–46
Mejelle 109, 110, 122
Mihna 6, 78
modernity 2–4, 9–10, 27–28, 30–31, 33, 37, 39–40, 61, 211, 217
mu'amalat 9, 35, 38, 42–43, 48, 51–54, 67, 175, 177–79, 189, 209, 217
mufti 4, 26, 38
Mughal 59, 63, 66, 76–77, 82, 96–97, 104, 110, 119, 191, 218
muhtasib 182, 198, 201–205
multazim 110, 138, 190–93. *See also iltizam*
muqaddim 52, 113, 152–53
Mutafarriqa 131–32, 188, 194, 196

namus (nomos) 42, 55, 58–59, 62–64, 66–67, 94, 177
nikah 130, 161, 168, 184

Protestantism 35–36, 126, 158
Protestant Reformation 32, 157, 216
proto-citizen 126, 128, 133, 134, 139, 142, 174. *See also* citizenship

qadi 20, 39, 48, 50, 52, 54, 69, 73, 88–89, 94, 96–101, 109, 113, 114, 117, 127, 135, 156, 181; qadi *'asker* 97, 112, 113, 150–51, 159
qadi al-qudah/chief qadi 15, 39, 73, 88, 107
qahwaji 137, 147, 185. *See also* coffee
qanun 5–7, 9–11, 13, 16, 19, 20, 22–24, 26–27, 37, 40, 42–43, 49–50, 52–55, 57–58, 63–64, 67, 71, 76–78, 85–87, 90, 94–96, 99–101, 117, 129, 142, 143, 148–51, 153, 156, 159–60, 168, 171, 174, 178–79, 190, 193–94, 197, 199, 205, 207, 214–15
qanunnama 37, 50, 55, 77–78, 85–87, 146, 181, 199, 218

qasim 145, 203
Qaytbay 82, 84, 86–87
Qisma al-'Askeriya 13, 106, 167
qiyas 7, 41, 47, 59
Qur'an 3, 7, 35, 37, 41, 47, 54, 61, 62, 79, 84, 108, 114, 143, 164
Quraysh 56–57, 59, 61–62, 66–67

rasm 90, 94
ratl 200, 206
Rumi 131, 145, 188, 199
al-Rumi, 'Abd al-Wahhab ibn Ibrahim 74, 91, 96–98

Salim, Sultan 25, 37, 56, 79, 82, 86–88, 123–24, 145, 169, 170, 182, 197–98, 201
Sarakhsi, Abu Bakr Muhammad ibn Ahmed 47–48, 50
secularism 2–4, 9, 16, 27–28, 30–40, 43, 50, 64, 139, 157–58, 211, 216–17
Shafi'i 38, 57, 60, 99, 100–102, 105, 173, 176
shahid 52, 73, 89, 91, 118, 121–22, 156
sharia 2–5, 7–8, 10, 12, 20, 23–27, 34, 37–38, 39–41, 45–46, 48, 50–51, 54–60, 62–65, 69, 71, 76–78, 80, 85, 91, 101–102, 124, 126–27, 134, 136–37, 139, 142, 145–46, 148, 150, 153, 171–72, 178–80, 184, 187, 189, 195, 203, 204–205, 207, 208, 213–14, 216, 218–20
al-Shatibi 42, 45, 48–49, 51–53
sijill 7–14, 16–17, 22, 54, 69–71, 103–106, 108–22, 127–34, 142–43, 147, 151, 154, 159–60, 163, 165–69, 171, 173, 178–79, 181, 190, 192, 194, 197, 199–200, 202, 204, 208, 214
siyasa 2, 10, 42–43, 46, 49–51, 53, 55, 57–59, 63–64, 66, 94, 142, 144–46, 149, 203; *hukkam al-siyasa* 74, 96, 99, 171; *siyasat-i ilahi* 58–59, 62, 67; *siyasat-i sultani* 58
sukkariya 130, 203–204, 206
Sulayman, Sultan Qanuni 6, 22–24, 37, 53, 56, 59, 61–63, 66, 76–78, 83, 85–86, 88, 93, 97, 99, 182, 198, 201, 213, 217

sulh 124, 178, 187–89, 208, 215
Sunna 52–54, 58, 76, 85, 143, 156, 161, 213
al-Suyuti 42
Syrians 10, 18–19, 24, 128, 130, 143, 164, 182

al-Tahawi 106, 109, 111
tajdid 4, 10, 27, 54–55, 69–71, 73, 79, 83, 87, 101, 178, 205–206
tawriq 110
ta'zir 217
theocracy 31, 37–38
Turks 5, 18–19, 22–23, 42, 64, 75, 82, 85, 105, 116, 128, 130, 151, 157, 163, 182
Tursun Beg 57–58

'urf 47–50, 53, 55, 58, 69, 87, 121, 131, 158, 165, 178, 214; *ahl al-ma'ruf* 99; *ahl al-'urf/ahl al-khibra* 121, 194

wakil 73, 89, 106, 118, 123, 137, 163
waqf 11, 14, 91, 95, 105, 106, 110, 147, 169-75, 182, 188, 207
wazir 60, 63, 191–92, 203, 204
Weber, Max 31–32, 112
wikala 123, 135, 137, 165, 186, 188
witnesses, *see shahid*

zawaj 130–31, 158, 184
zina 37–38, 44, 217
zulm 54, 81–82; *zalim* 145